RAINFOREST
SHAMANS

RAINFOREST SHAMANS

Essays on the Tukano Indians
of the Northwest Amazon

GERARDO REICHEL-DOLMATOFF

Themis Books

Published in 1997
by Themis Books, an imprint of
Green Books Ltd, Foxhole, Dartington,
Totnes, Devon, TQ9 6EB, UK,
in association with the COAMA Programme,
Colombia and The Gaia Foundation, London

This publication was funded by the Commission of the European Union
(DGI B Tropical Forest Unit) within the framework of the COAMA Programme.

All photographs were taken by Gerardo Reichel-Dolmatoff in the Northwest
Amazon, Pira-paraná river region, Colombia, with the exception
of that on page 2, which was taken by Alicia de Reichel-Dolmatoff;
those on pages 18, 39, 66, 94, 185 and 228 which were taken
by Fernando Urbina; and those on pages 40, 41, 106, 173 and 248
which were taken by Diego Samper.

Type and make-up by Chris Fayers, Soldon, Devon
Line illustrations by Efraín Sánchez
Printed by Biddles Ltd, Guildford, Surrey

The paper used in this book is made from wood from managed plantations,
where replanting exceeds the trees harvested. These are in North America, coastal
areas of Brazil (eucalyptus plantations, harvested every seven years), Portugal and
Spain. The paper is acid-free and elemental chlorine-free.

A catalogue record for this book
is available from the British Library

ISBN 0 9527302 4 3

CONTENTS

INTRODUCTION   1

I   COSMOLOGY AS ECOLOGICAL ANALYSIS:
A VIEW FROM THE RAINFOREST   7

II   DESANA ANIMAL CATEGORIES, FOOD RESTRICTIONS,
AND THE CONCEPT OF COLOUR ENERGIES   23

III   TAPIR AVOIDANCE IN THE COLOMBIAN NORTHWEST AMAZON   77

IV   A HUNTER'S TALE FROM THE COLOMBIAN NORTHWEST AMAZON   111

V   SOME SOURCE MATERIAL ON DESANA SHAMANISTIC INITIATION   121

VI   DESANA SHAMANS' ROCK CRYSTALS
AND THE HEXAGONAL UNIVERSE   149

VII   DESANA CURING SPELLS:
AN ANALYSIS OF SOME SHAMANISTIC METAPHORS   163

VIII   BRAIN AND MIND IN DESANA SHAMANISM   213

IX   DRUG-INDUCED OPTICAL SENSATIONS
AND THEIR RELATIONSHIP TO APPLIED ART
AMONG SOME COLOMBIAN INDIANS   243

X   ASTRONOMICAL MODELS OF SOCIAL BEHAVIOUR
AMONG SOME INDIANS OF COLOMBIA   261

XI   BIOLOGICAL AND SOCIAL ASPECTS OF THE
YURUPARI COMPLEX OF THE COLOMBIAN VAUPÉS TERRITORY   277

BIBLIOGRAPHY   314

INDEX   321

SOURCES OF ESSAYS

I   COSMOLOGY AS ECOLOGICAL ANALYSIS:
        A VIEW FROM THE RAINFOREST
        Huxley Memorial Lecture, 1975, at the Royal Anthropological
        Institute, London. First Published in *Man* (N.S.) II (3) pp307-318.
        Reproduced by kind permission of the Royal Anthropological
        Institute.

II   DESANA ANIMAL CATEGORIES, FOOD RESTRICTIONS,
        AND THE CONCEPT OF COLOUR ENERGIES
        First published in *Journal of Latin American Lore*,
        4:2, 1978, pp243-291 © Copyright University of California,
        Los Angeles. Reproduced by kind permission of UCLA, the sole
        Licensor.

III   TAPIR AVOIDANCE IN THE COLOMBIAN NORTHWEST AMAZON
        First published in *Animal Myths and Metaphors in South America* edited
        by Gary Urton, University of Utah Press. Reproduced here by
        kind permission of Gary Urton of Colgate University.

IV   A HUNTER'S TALE FROM THE COLOMBIAN NORTHWEST AMAZON
        First published in *Journal of Latin American Lore*,
        12:1, 1986, pp65-74 © Copyright University of California,
        Los Angeles. Reproduced by kind permission of UCLA, the sole
        Licensor.

V   SOME SOURCE MATERIAL ON DESANA SHAMANISTIC INITIATION
        First published in *Antropológica*, Caracas, No. 51, 1979, pp26-61 and
        reproduced by kind permission of the Editor, Werner Wilbert, Ph.D.,
        Fundación La Salle de Ciencias Naturales, Caracas.

VI   DESANA SHAMANS' ROCK CRYSTALS
        AND THE HEXAGONAL UNIVERSE
        First published in *Journal of Latin American Lore*,
        5:1, 1979, pp117-128 © Copyright University of California,
        Los Angeles. Reproduced by kind permission of UCLA, the sole
        Licensor.

VII   DESANA CURING SPELLS:
AN ANALYSIS OF SOME SHAMANISTIC METAPHORS
First published in *Journal of Latin American Lore*,
2:2, 1976, pp157-220 © Copyright University of California,
Los Angeles. Reproduced by kind permission of UCLA, the sole
Licensor.

VIII BRAIN AND MIND IN DESANA SHAMANISM
First published in *Journal of Latin American Lore*,
7:1, 1981, pp73-98 © Copyright University of California,
Los Angeles. Reproduced by kind permission of UCLA, the sole
Licensor.

IX   DRUG-INDUCED OPTICAL SENSATIONS
AND THEIR RELATIONSHIP TO APPLIED ART
AMONG SOME COLOMBIAN INDIANS
First published in *Art in Society*, published by Gerald Duckworth
and Co. Ltd., London, 1978, pp289-304 and reproduced by kind
permission.

X   ASTRONOMICAL MODELS OF SOCIAL BEHAVIOUR
AMONG SOME INDIANS OF COLOMBIA
First published in *Ethnoastronomy and Archaeastronomy in the
American Tropics*, Annals of the New York Academy of Sciences, Vol.
385, ed. Anthony F. Aveni and Gary Urton © Copyright New York
Academy of Sciences and reproduced by kind permission.

XI   BIOLOGICAL AND SOCIAL ASPECTS OF THE
YURUPARI COMPLEX OF THE COLOMBIAN VAUPÉS TERRITORY
First published in *Journal of Latin American Lore*,
15:1, 1989, pp95-136 © Copyright University of California,
Los Angeles. Reproduced by kind permission of UCLA, the sole
Licensor.

INTRODUCTION

The vast rain forests of the Colombian Northwest Amazon have always been a refuge area for native tribes[1] belonging to different linguistic families and distinct cultural traditions. The central part of this area, the so-called Vaupés territory, is at present inhabited mainly by Indians belonging to the Eastern Tukanoan Linguistic Family, represented by some twenty tribes or, rather, phratries, named descent groups each of which speaks its own language and constitutes a separate exogamous unit.

Some of the better known phratries are the Desana, the Barasana, the Bará, the Tukano proper, and the Tatuyo, names that became known to European ethnologists, linguists, and museologists early this century, mainly through Theodor Koch-Grünberg's classic travel account: *Zwei Jahre unter den Indianern: Reisen in Nordwest Brasilien 1903/1905*. The title of this book already expresses the somewhat marginal character of the Vaupés territory; Koch-Grünberg had been led to believe that he was travelling in Brazil; but even today, with clearly defined political frontiers, Colombian sovereignty is only weakly represented in this immense expanse of forests and rivers.

The mighty Rio Negro has been for centuries an important contact route between the upper Orinoco and the Amazon Basin, but its affluent the Vaupés River, coming down from the Andean foothills in the West, was much less frequented by travellers. While the Rio Negro had but a few formidable rapids, in the Vaupés, the Apaporis, and their affluents there were hundreds of dangerous falls and rapids. In a country where almost all transportation and communication is by river these accidents of nature constitute serious obstacles to navigation, a fact which undoubtedly has contributed to make of this territory a refuge area, a back country. While travel and culture contact continued and increased along the Rio Negro, the Colombian Vaupés, lying to the West of it, remained isolated. Any people, migrating for any reason, travelling upriver toward the West, could find a measure of safety once they had gone beyond a stretch of dangerous rapids.

This relative isolation of cultural developments in the Colombian Vaupés is an important fact. In the first place, the majority of the Indians do not inhabit the so-called *varzea*, the Amazonian lowlands which are periodically exposed to flooding, but occupy what is called *terra firme*, a region where only occasionally some riverbanks might be inundated, and that only for a short time. In the second place, it must be kept in mind that some aspects of Tukanoan culture, as found along the Rio Negro and the Brazilian side of the Vaupés River, are likely

Desana and Pira-Tapuya Indians with G. Reichel-Dolmatoff, near Mitú

to be different from those of the Colombian side where acculturational influences and pressures are much less pronounced and of a quite different nature.

Agents of change, however, have been multiplying in the Colombian Vaupés. By the end of the first half of this century Catholic missionaries operating from the newly (1936) founded district capital of Mitú assured public opinion that the aboriginal tribes had been evangelised and were rapidly being integrated into Colombian national society. It was difficult in those years to obtain accurate information on ethnological matters and some anthropologists began to wonder about the real situation. Occasional reports by botanists, rubber gatherers, and government agents suggested that in some regions of the Vaupés territory aboriginal life continued much as in Koch-Grünberg's time. The unobtrusive presence of Irving Goldman, an American ethnologist who in 1939-40 studied the Cubeo, a Tukanoised Arawakan tribe of the Vaupés, had gone almost unnoticed, and since his monograph was published only in 1963, at mid-century the Tukanoan Indians and their immediate neighbours were hardly ever mentioned in anthropological circles in the country's capital.

INTRODUCTION

In 1952 I had the opportunity to make a short field survey on a government mission to the Vaupés. What I saw convinced me that, although acculturation was advancing, there still was time to gather much valuable information on many little-known aspects of Tukanoan culture. When a year later, in 1953, a young Colombian anthropologist, Marcos Fulop, who had been studying at Columbia University in New York, joined the Colombian Institute of Anthropology where I was working and I was asked to draw up a plan for his field research, I suggested the Tukano of the Papurí River, a major affluent of the Vaupés. Fulop worked there between 1953 and 1954, and concentrated on mythology and social organisation. Eventually, encouraged by Professor Robert von Heine-Geldern, whose Vienna-based *Bulletin of the International Committee on Urgent Anthropological and Ethnological Research* had reached me, I wrote an appeal to the international community of ethnologists, to study the Indians of the Vaupés. This initiative proved to be highly successful; British, French, and Northamerican anthropologists arrived and by the middle of the sixties a period of intensive ethnological research was inaugurated. At present, the Tukanoan Indians of the Colombian Vaupés are probably among the best-known native societies of the upper Amazon rainforest. I myself had turned my attention to Tukanoan shamanism, the use of hallucinogenic substances, and had begun a programme of tape-recording shamanistic oral traditions in their aboriginal languages.

The urgency of my appeal had not been exaggerated. In a matter of only a few years the Indians' situation underwent profound changes. The international drug taffic, guerrilla banditry, and local gold rushes combined into an atmosphere saturated with the worst elements 'civilisation' could offer to the Indians who, in many cases, became the tools and victims of violence, greed, and utter corruption. It is saddening to think that some of the books anthropologists wrote and still write on the Indians of the Vaupés, are by now memorials of things past. Only in a few remote corners do traditional ways of life still continue.

* * * * *

Many books which contain the results of field work carried out among the Tukanoan Indians during the sixties and seventies are still in print and readily available at libraries.[2] There exist, however, many research articles treating specific topics, which were published in professional journals that are not always easy to locate. In view of the present interest in Amazonian Indian societies I have gathered in the present book a number of my articles, most of which appeared in North America, but may be of interest to a wider English-speaking public in Europe. Although these articles refer to particular aspects of Tukanoan culture as represented by the Desana, they all contain short outlines of the wider geographical and social context. In this manner, the reader will soon grasp the overall picture and be able to relate the specific topic to the broader scene.

The first article in this volume is the author's Huxley Memorial Lecture delivered in 1970 at the Royal Anthropological Institute. This lecture will introduce the reader into the Tukanoan concepts of energy flow and human adaptive strategies in terms of native ecological understandings. The second article expands this theme and presents a lengthy analysis of discrete cosmic energies conceived as colours, odours, sounds, flavours, textures, temperatures and so forth, together with their relationships with animal categories and, through them, with food restrictions. The problems related to the balancing of these 'energies' are not confined to the sphere of esoteric shamanistic beliefs and practices, but are faced by the individual in everyday life and are, therefore, of fundamental importance to personal and social behavioural norms. These two articles, then, set the stage: the rainforest and its wildlife, and the forces which, according to the Indians, govern the environment.

The third article is concerned with an ethnohistorical problem. It seems that the Tukanoans were newcomers to the Vaupés territory, and questions of tribal origins and contacts loom large in oral tradition. Their migration myths speak of successive groups of people – mostly men – travelling up the Rio Negro where, at a certain major rapids, they first made contact with 'other people'. These autochthonous inhabitants are referred to in oral tradition as 'Tapir People'. Most probably Arawak-speaking Indians who were sedentary horticulturalists, lived in huge longhouses, and practised local endogamy. The central theme of many myths and tales refers to these contacts in terms of a search for women, at first by forceful abduction and subsequently by increasingly formalised exchange patterns leading to virilocal exogamy. Tapir, the 'owner' of women and demanding father-in-law plays an ambivalent role in these traditions, and the Tapir image continues to occupy Tukanoan thought patterns. The next article, the fourth in this volume, is based upon a tape-recording in which a young Tukano hunter speaks of this double aspect of Tapir: an ancestral presence and a game animal.

The next group of articles consists of four studies of Tukanoan shamanism. Article five is based on tape-recordings in which shamans speak of their initiatory experiences. The statements are accompanied by detailed notes and commentaries which, together with the original recordings, constitute a valuable first-hand document. The next article – number six – describes the principal power tool of Tukanoan shamans, the hexagonal rock crystal which provides the model for many aspects of the shamanistic worldview, and is thought to contain the essence of life-giving energies. The seventh article contains an analysis of ten shamanic curing spells presented in their original form. This is an important document in which Tukanoan concepts of illness and its cure are commented on in detail.

The eighth article attempts to describe shamanistic concepts of human brain structure and functions, a field native practitioners are much interested in. This interest is related to the topic of the ninth article, which is the use of native hallucinogenic substances. Narcotic drugs, most of them of plant origin, play an important role in Tukanoan religious experiences. Altered states of consciousness and their ritual representations are thought to offer dimensions of the imaginary in which personal and social conflicts or desires can be brought into focus, to be solved or otherwise fulfilled. The Tukanoan idea that the hallucinatory sphere is the origin of all art forms is of interest in view of the relationship between drug-induced luminous sensations and decorative patterns executed in body paint and other arts and crafts.

The tenth article refers to the ways in which two Colombian tribes, the Kogi of the Sierra Nevada of Santa Marta and the Desana of the Northwest Amazon, observe cyclic time, and see in the tropical night sky a blueprint of terrestrial events. These observations are related to concepts of space and to the relationships that seem to exist between certain heavenly bodies, as interpreted by the Indians.

The eleventh and last article is concerned with a major myth complex of Amazonian Indians, and with its Tukanoan versions. The central theme is that of *yuruparí*, a patriarchal foundation myth. The article explores the relationship between palm symbolism and social organisation, together with the origins of the complex male initiation rituals of the Tukanoan Indians.

Notes

1.   The term tribe is used in this book in a restricted sense, referring to an exogamous patrilineal descent unit the male members of which speak the same language. These tribes, however, do not occupy a distinct territory; neither do they have a chief or any other form of authority on the tribal level.

2.   See bibliography of Gerardo Reichel-Dolmatoff on the Tukano Indians of the Vaupés territory at the end of this book.

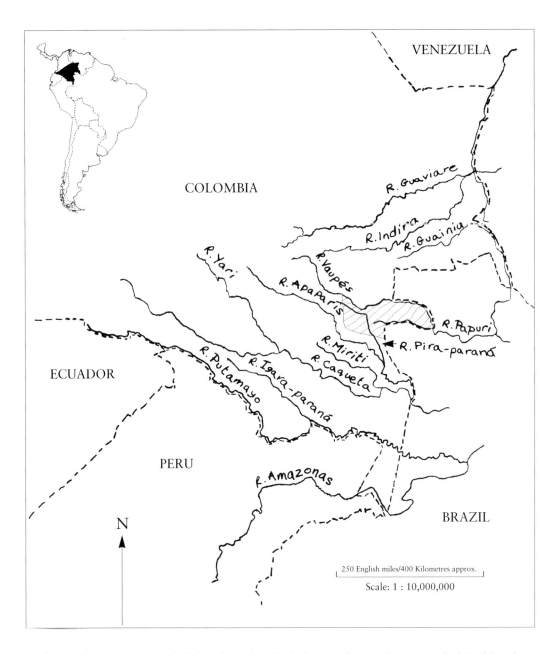

The south-east corner of Colombia; the shaded part shows the area inhabited by the Tukanos

I

COSMOLOGY AS ECOLOGICAL ANALYSIS: A VIEW FROM THE RAINFOREST

[1]Among the Tukano Indians of the Colombian Northwest Amazon, carrying capacity is defined mainly in terms of the conservation of protein resources such as game, fish and certain wild fruits. In order to maintain an equilibrium and to avoid frequent relocation of settlements, the Indians have developed a set of highly adaptive behavioural rules which control population growth, the exploitation of the natural environment, and interpersonal aggression. The belief that the spirits of game animals cause illness restricts overhunting and, similarly, a large body of beliefs that regulate sex and food habits try to adjust the birth-rate and to counterbalance socially disruptive behaviour. Shamanism thus becomes a powerful force in the control and management of natural resources, and hallucinatory visions induced by native narcotic drugs become an important tool of shamanistic power. In many aspects Tukano concepts of cosmology represent a blueprint for ecological adaptation and the Indians' acute awareness of the need for adaptive norms can be compared with modern systems analysis.

I

Until relatively recent times the cultural image of the Indian tribes of tropical America has been that of a group of rather primitive and hostile peoples whose contribution to human thought had been negligible and whose level of social

[1] I am deeply conscious of the great honour of having been asked to give the 1975 Huxley Memorial Lecture. I am most grateful to the British Council and to the Royal Anthropological Institute, especially the Esperanza Fund, for their generous assistance. I also wish to express my sincere personal gratitude to Donald Lathrap, Martin Moynihan, Olga Linares de Moynihan and J. Wilbert, for having been kind enough to read a draft of this lecture; their suggestions have proved to be very stimulating and helpful.

complexity had remained far below that of most aboriginal societies of the Old World. In fact, only the higher civilisations of America – the ancient Mexicans, Mayas and Peruvians – were occasionally credited with having created fairly elaborate social, political and religious institutions, but even in their case seldom has there been explicit discussion of native philosophical systems or something approaching an integrated world-view. Sometimes one was almost led to believe that the tropical forest Indians were fossil societies; societies which, in a sense, were incomplete; which had not evolved and had nothing to teach us. They were 'out of the mainstream', some people said, and those of us who made these societies the subject of their studies, struggled against the stigma of working somewhat 'out of the mainstream'.

In the more recent past, however, this image has undergone a notable change. Ethnological research among the surviving tribes of the tropical rainforest has begun to reach a depth and breadth of inquiry that were formerly unthought of, and these newly gained insights are beginning to shed an entirely new light upon the intellectual achievements of the aboriginal peoples of the Amazon Basin, the Orinoco Plains and many other regions of the American Tropics, a vast area covering more than six million square kilometres. It seems that the old stereotypes are disappearing at last; and instead we are presented with a new image: the Indian, not only as a highly pragmatic thinker and an individual with a sound sense of reality, but also the Indian as an abstract philosopher, a builder of intricate cosmic models, and a planner of sweeping moral designs. Also at the same period, in view of current interest in natural resources, many scientists and technologists who have turned their attention to the tropical rainforest areas of the world, have become concerned with the many problems of ecological adaptation which traditional societies have had to solve in these environments. In the case of the Amazon Basin it takes a healthy and energetic society to cope with the rigorous climatic conditions and with the management of easily depleted natural resources, a society that would develop not only a set of highly adaptive behavioural rules for survival – framed within effective institutional bodies – but, more important still, a society with a coherent belief system, with a foundation of strongly motivating values which would make endurable the problems of man's existence in an unpredictable world.

In this lecture it is my purpose to describe and examine some aspects of adaptive behaviour as I have been able to observe it in the course of my contacts with several Indian groups in the Colombian lowlands. I should add here that by 'adaptive' I mean anything that increases the probability of survival of the individual or the group. In the following I shall mainly refer to the Tukano Indians of the Northwest Amazon, especially the Desana (Eastern Tukano), and my chief concern will be to trace some connections that exist between the cosmological concepts of these Indians, and the realities of adaptation to a given physical environment. In doing so I shall try to demonstrate that aboriginal cosmologies and myth structures, together with the ritual behaviour derived from them, represent in all respects a set of ecological principles and that these formulate a system of social and economic rules that have a highly adaptive value in the continuous endeavour to maintain a viable equilibrium between the resources of the environment and the demands of society.

II

The Tukano Indians occupy a large area in the central portion of the Northwest Amazon. Although most of the country is flat and densely forested, a transitional terrain of hilly uplands lies on the western fringe, while towards the north the forest is sometimes broken by stretches of grassy, tree-strewn savanna country. Although this rainforest area has often been described as a rather homogeneous region, many environmental differences exist which have considerable bearing upon the range and success of human adaptive responses. Game animals, amphibians and reptiles, edible fruits, nuts and insects, and suitable horticultural lands are not evenly distributed and considerable resource fluctuation can be said to exist within and among subregions.

The Tukano are bound to their rainforest habitat by a number of circumstances. In the first place, according to myth and tradition, the land inhabited by them at present was originally peopled by their forefathers in ancient, heroic times, and was handed on to their descendants as a solemn investiture in a perpetual trust. These tribal ancestors whose names and deeds are remembered in myths and genealogical recitals had given proper designations to the rivers and the hills, the rocks and the rapids and to all other notable natural features. This, then, continues to be their country, the homeland of the ancients. It is of interest to observe here that, although the Tukano habitat can, to a large degree, be described as a truly 'natural environment', they themselves perceive it as a man-made environment, transformed and structured in the past not so much by any exploitative activities of their ancestors, but by having been imbued by them with symbolic meaning. There is, then, a time-perspective to their understanding of the environment.

In the second place, Tukano territory is surrounded by lands occupied by other people, be they tribal Indians or be they Colombian or Brazilian settlers. The Tukano, then, must of necessity exist within the limitations of their given environment and must make the best of it. They have to rely utterly upon their local resources and upon their own traditional skills for exploiting them.

The traditional settlement pattern consists of widely scattered large and well-built communal houses, occupied by extended families whose members derive much of their basic food supply from cultivating manioc gardens. However, seasonal hunting, fishing and gathering play an important part in their economic and social life. Tukano society is divided into more than twenty named exogamic groups; descent is patrilineal and residence is patrilocal, with cross-cousin marriage said to be preferred. Marriage between these different units implies a rigidly structured relationship which is expressed in many forms of reciprocity and exchange. Most of these activities, both social and economic, are closely connected with ceremonies directed by the shaman who also officiates at the rituals of the life cycle and is active as a healer of illness. Warfare is not institutionalised.

Here is a brief summary of how the Tukano imagine the origin and structure of the universe and the elementary forces that animate it. The creator was the Sun Father, an anthropomorphic god who designed a three-layered cosmos consisting of a flat earth, a celestial vault, and a place of bliss situated under the earth. He then peopled the land and created animals and plants giving to each species a set of rules according to which they were to live and multiply. However, the Sun-Father created only a limited number of animals and plants, placing both categories under the constant care of specific spirit-beings who were to guard and protect them against eventual abuses. What is more, he assigned to his creation only a restricted, roughly circular, stretch of land, limited on all sides by permanent landmarks. In other words, the creation of the Tukano universe was not conceived as an all-embracing or expanding system, but was a limited, well-defined proposition with finite and restricted resources. Nor was it accomplished as a single act limited in time: it still continues uninterruptedly because, ever since its initiation, the Sun-Father exercises a fertilising action upon it. It is the energy of the sun, imagined by the Tukano in terms of seminal light and heat, that causes plants to grow and fruit to ripen, that makes mankind and animals reproduce, and that is thought to be creative not only in a germinal, biological sense, but also in the sense of spiritual illumination and the attainment of esoteric wisdom. The essence of this force is imagined as a masculine power that fertilises a feminine element that is this world. In Tukano thought, the biosphere has both male and female aspects, but seen in its totality it has primarily a feminine character over which the sun exercises his power.

The seminal energy of the sun is thought to constitute a huge circuit in which the entire cosmos participates. This circuit is imagined as having a limited quantity of procreative energy that flows continuously between man and animal, between society and nature. Since the quantity of energy is restricted, man may remove what he needs only under certain conditions and must convert his quantum of 'borrowed' energy into an essence that can be reincorporated into the circuit. For example, when an animal is killed or when a crop is harvested the energy of the local fauna and flora are thought to be diminished; however, as soon as the game or fruit are converted into nourishment, the energy is conserved, now on the level of society, because the consumers of the food have now acquired a reproductive life force that previously belonged to an animal or plant.

III

The striking point about these ideas is that this bears a remarkable resemblance to modern systems analysis. In terms of ecological theory, the Tukano thus conceive the world as a system in which the amount of energy output is directly related to the amount of input the system receives. According to the Tukano, the system handles these inputs in two ways: sexual energy which has been repressed in the individual, returns directly to the capital of total energy in which the biotic components of the system participate; mere health and well-being, resulting from controlled food consumption, represent an input which energises also the abiotic components of the system, for example, the movements of the stars or meteorological phenomena. The individual should never cause a disturbance in this general equilibrium, that is, he should never use energy without restoring it as soon as possible. The entire system is largely derived from the model of sexual physiology. The Tukano concept of solar energy includes a large number of things to which a seminal symbolism is attributed because of their colour, shape, texture or other characteristics; while a number of other things are associated with a female concept of fecundity and gestation. The associations of images and symbols are interpreted by the Tukano on various levels of abstraction and eventually dissociate themselves farther and farther from natural and physiological facts until, at a higher cognitive level, they come to constitute a systems theory of balanced, finite energy flow.

This cosmological model of a system which constantly requires rebalancing in the form of inputs of energy retrieved by individual effort, constitutes a religious proposition which is intimately connected with the social and economic organisation of the group. In this way, the general balance of energy flow becomes a religious objective in which native ecological concepts play a dominant organisational role. To understand the structure and functioning of the ecosystem becomes therefore a vital task to the Tukano. It follows that the Indian's ethnobiological knowledge of the natural environment is not casual and is not something he assimilates through gradually increasing familiarity and repeated sense experience; it is a structured, disciplined knowledge which is based upon a long tradition of enquiry and which is acquired of necessity as part of his intellectual equipment for biological and cultural survival.

Among the Indians there is usually little interest in new knowledge that might be used for exploiting the environment more effectively and there is little concern for maximising short-term gains for obtaining more food or raw-materials than are actually needed. But there is always a great deal of interest in accumulating more factual knowledge about biological reality and, above all, about what the physical world requires from man. This knowledge, the Indians believe, is essential for survival because man must bring himself into conformity with nature if he wants to exist as part of nature's unity, and must fit his demands to nature's availabilities.

Animal behaviour is of greatest interest to the Indians because it often constitutes a model for what is *possible* in terms of successful adaptation. On the one hand, the Indians have a detailed knowledge of such aspects as seasonal variation and microdistributions of the animal and plant species of their habitat. They have a good understanding of ecological communities, of the behaviour of social insects, of bird flocks, the organisation of fish schools, the patterns of fish runs, and other forms of collective behaviour. Such phenomena as parasitism, symbiosis, commensalism and other relationships between co-occurring species have been well observed by them and are pointed out as possible models of adaptation. On the other hand, myths and tales abound with accounts of visits to the animal world, of people turning into animals in order to learn more about their habits, or of animals teaching men how to make use of certain resources. Shamanistic wisdom often contains detailed descriptions of such contacts and exchanges, and many shamans claim to have acquired part of their specific knowledge from animals which revealed to them some unexpected food resource, a cure for an illness, or a practical procedure in solving some everyday problem. Some of this wisdom may then be considered esoteric and secret, remaining the private property of a shaman, but often enough this specialised knowledge of animal behaviour becomes part of prescribed patterns of human action and interaction because of its obvious adaptive value. Moreover, mythology emphatically tells of animal species which have become extinct or which were punished or degraded for *not* obeying certain prescribed rules of adaptive significance. Thus gluttony, improvidence, aggressiveness and all forms of overindulgence are punished by the superior forces, to serve as examples not only to the animal community, but also to human society. Animals, then, are metaphors for survival. By analysing animal behaviour the Indians try to discover an order in the physical world, a world-order to which *human* activities can then be adjusted.

In Tukano culture, the individual person is conscious that he forms part of a complex network of interactions which include not only society but the entire universe. Within this context of an essential interrelatedness of all things, a person has to fulfil many functions that go far beyond his or her social roles and that are extrasocietal extensions of a set of adaptive norms. These rules or norms, then, guide a person's relationships not only with other people – past or present, kin or ally – but also with animals, plants, as a matter of fact with all biotic and non-biotic components of the environment. The rules the individual has to follow refer, above all, to cooperative behaviour aimed at the conservation of ecological balance as the ultimately desirable quality. Thus the relationship between man and his environment is being formulated not only on a cognitive level, but clearly it also constitutes an affective personal relationship in which individual animals and plants are treated with respect and caution.

The Tukano are quite aware of the fact that, in order to maintain a stable balance of input and output, a number of regulatory mechanisms have to be instituted and, what is more, have to be fully respected by all members of the society. These social controls of necessity possess marked adaptive implications and must be enforced primarily in those aspects of existence which, to a large degree, determine survival. I shall mention here: population growth, the exploitation of the physical environment, and aggression in interpersonal relations. It is quite clear to the Tukano that, in order to ensure individual and collective survival and well-being, adaptive rules have to be established to adjust the birth-rate, the harvest-rate, and to counter-balance all socially disruptive behaviour.

IV

I shall first turn to the problem of population growth and regulations. Two mechanisms are used by the Indians to control the birth-rate: oral contraceptives and sexual continence. Tukano women use herbal concoctions which, in varying concentrations, cause temporary sterility, and by this means they manage to space their offspring over several years in such a way that when a woman has her second child the first is already sufficiently independent not to be a bother. The number of children is kept low and couples with many children are criticised quite openly as socially irresponsible.

The second mechanism is abstention. Sexual abstinence and sexual repression are practised on many occasions and are among the most important prerequisites for many ritual activities. It is important to point out here that, in Tukano thought, food and sex are closely related and are symbolically equivalent. This idea of relationship between caloric and sexual appetite is expressed in many ways; on a metaphorical level sexual intercourse and eating are equated, and in ritual exchange certain foodstuffs come to represent the exchange of women. Since strict exogamic rules constitute the main organising principle in Tukano society, the consumption or avoidance of certain foods are geared to the concept of exogamy in such a way that dietary restrictions come to stand for sexual restrictions. The selective use of certain foods may thus be said to be subject to the laws of *exophagy*, which determine the permissibility of certain foods under diverse circumstances. There are 'male' and 'female' foods and food preparations, and these rules refer not only to animal-derived foods, but also to vegetable foods.

These aspects are best illustrated by the ideas that guide the activities of the hunter. All game animals are subject to the Master of Animals, a dwarf-like spirit-being with marked phallic attributes. This supernatural gamekeeper jealously guards his flock consisting of deer, tapir, peccary, agouti, paca, monkeys and all other animal species that are a common food resource of the Indians. The Master of Animals is directly their protector and procreator and they all live inside steep rocky hills or in deep pools in the river, both dwelling-places being maintained as large store-houses teeming with game and fish. In order to obtain the supernatural Master's permission to kill a game animal, the prospective hunter must undergo a rigorous preparation which consists of sexual continence, food restrictions, and purification rites ensuring the cleansing of the body by bathing and emetics. For some days before going on a hunting excursion, the man should refrain from all sexual relations and, what is more, he should not have had any dreams with an erotic content. Moreover, it is necessary that none of the women who live in his household is menstruating. Another mechanism that restricts overhunting is this: according to cosmological myths all game animals are associated with certain constellations, as defined by the Tukano. However, a species can only be hunted *after* its constellation has risen over the horizon, and it is said that the animals cry and weep with fear when they realise that their time is approaching. It may be mentioned here also that the hunt itself is more than a mere food quest: it is imagined as a courtship in which the prey has to be seduced to submit to the hunter.

Whenever game is scarce, the shaman must visit the Master of Animals in a narcotic trance and try to obtain from him the release of some of his charges. He will not ask for individual animals but rather for herds or for a good hunting season and in return he promises to send to the Master's abode the souls of persons who, at their death, must return to this great store-house to replenish the energy of those animals the supernatural gamekeeper gives to the hunters. The Master of Animals and his numerous personifications are thus conceived as administrators of usufruct rights; since game resources are limited, restrictive rights to their use are instituted by these spirit-beings, and it falls to the shaman to become the mediator.

From the examples I have mentioned it is obvious that the combination of all these prerequisites represents in itself a body of highly adaptive rules which notably restrict the activities of any hunter or fisherman. A person cannot go hunting or fishing simply any time he needs food, but only after having undergone a more or less anxiety-charged period of preparation, the purpose of which is to avoid over-hunting. Illness or misfortune in hunting are almost always attributed to neglect of any of the numerous rules a hunter has to observe.

Food restrictions are not only observed in connection with economic activities, but are a standard practice on most ritual occasions and in many other everyday circumstances. For example, a man whose wife is expecting a child should eat neither tapir, peccary nor monkey meat because this might affect the good health of his yet unborn offspring. A man whose hunting or fishing gear has become polluted from being casually touched by a woman, must observe a liquid diet for several days. When fish run to spawn, those present in one's stretch of the river should not be eaten, nor are birds' eggs ever collected for food, and the flesh of some reptiles is avoided during their breeding season. All these interdictions are verbalised by the Indians in terms of dangers to the consumer's health. Especially strict prohibitions keep people from eating normally while engaged in the acquisition of esoteric knowledge and, similarly, all rituals of the individual life cycle involve temporary dietary restrictions. In summary, during pregnancy, childbirth and menstruation; during mourning periods, or while gathering medicinal herbs; during the couvade or while engaged upon the preparation of poisons, narcotics or love potions, people carefully control their food intake and, as a general rule, refrain from eating the meat of game animals.

Similar prohibitions restrict the gathering of wild fruits and nuts, of honey and of edible insects. Even the extraction of raw-materials used in technological manufactures is controlled by ritual restrictions. The gathering of thatch for a roof, of clay for pottery making, or of scarce woods or fibres for a number of specific end products, are subject to permits which have to be obtained from the spirit-owners of the respective resources.

This complex of dietary and sexual restrictions is closely related to the control of aggressive attitudes. The principal mechanism which checks socially disruptive behaviour is the organisation into exogamic groups which are linked by alliances and stand in a relationship of reciprocal exchange. Besides exchanging women, these complementary units will give and receive foods, raw-materials or manufactured goods, and on these periodic occasions which constitute highly formalised rituals, the dances, songs and ceremonial dialogues emphasise over and over again the paired linkages that unite Tukano society.

It appears from the foregoing that the Tuakno definition of what constitutes carrying capacity, refers mainly to a certain balance of protein-rich food resources such as game, fish and wild fruits. Environmental degradation is interpreted *not* in terms of soil exhaustion, but in terms of the eventual depletion of game and of increased walking time. Because of the relative scarcity of protein resources, restrictive rights to their use have to be established in order to avoid frequent relocation of settlements. Propitious conditions for horticultural activities are perhaps not plentiful, but land for productive garden plots *is* available. However, the nutrient content of practically all vegetable foods of the rainforest is very low and carrying capacity is therefore determined by the existence of protein resources, and population size and density are functions thereof.

The three aspects I have mentioned – population growth, the exploitation of the physical environment and the control of aggression – can be reduced to one single problem, that is, the maintenance of a balanced ecosystem. The Indians know that their daily existence depends upon the proper functioning of these adaptive interactions. The question arises, how can a people be made to follow these prescriptions and regulations which impose such severe restrictions upon their social behaviour and their biological needs?

V

The mechanisms which, in the native groups I am concerned with here, enforce the rules are closely related to the aboriginal theory of disease. To begin with, the specific bodily or mental conditions which, according to the Tukano, constitute illness and which manifest themselves through a large number of signs and symptoms, are always thought to be caused by an agent external to the body. The possible pathogenic agencies fall into three categories (1) the revenge of game animals; (2) the ill-will of other people, and (3) the malevolence of supernatural beings such as the Master of Animals or other spirit-beings.

This malevolence of people and animals is not an arbitrary force that blindly strikes its unsuspecting victim. On the contrary, illness is always interpreted as a quite natural consequence of a person's breach or neglect of cultural norms. Apart from its being socially and emotionally disturbing, illness is, in the Tukano view, nothing but a reaction to the ecologically inadequate behaviour of the patient, to his maladaptive performance. It is the patient who causes the disease, by making himself vulnerable to it. The diagnosis the shaman establishes has, therefore, two different aspects: one refers to the patient's complaints, to the symptoms he has developed; the other aspect refers to the question *why* the person became a victim of the disease. And here we can recognise another important aspect of the shaman's function, an aspect that is closely related to the problem of ecological adaptation.

In shamanistic practice, illness is taken to be the consequence of a person's upsetting a certain aspect of the ecological balance. Overhunting is a common cause and so are harvesting activities in which some relatively scarce natural resource has been wasted. The delicate balance existing within the natural environment, between nature and society, and within society itself, constitutes a series of systems in which any disturbance, however slight, is bound to affect the whole. For example, meddling with certain women who should be avoided is the same kind of affront as eating certain fish that should not be eaten; while killing too many animals of a certain species must always be avoided. These are offences the consequence of which is likely to be an illness. In the diagnostic process, which is often accompanied by divinatory practices, the shaman is interested in the patient's illness not so much as a function of biology, but rather as a symptom of a disorder in the energy flow. His main concern is about the relationship between society and the supernatural Masters of game, fish and wild fruits, on whom depend success in harvesting and who command many pathogenic agents. To the shaman it is therefore of the essence to diagnose correctly the causes of the illness, to identify the exact quality of the inadequate relationship (be it adultery, overhunting, or any other over-indulgence or waste), and then to redress the balance by communicating with the spirits and by establishing reconciliatory contacts with the game animals. To mention just one example of how a diagnosis is established: a man who has killed too many animals of a certain species, will appear in the shaman's dream or trance states in the shape of that animal and the image will be accompanied by a certain luminosity, a certain degree of light. It is quite remarkable that differences in high or low light intensity are recognised to be very important in the flow of solar energy, as understood by the Tukano, and that shamans will mention in their spells and incantations up to seven shades of 'yellow light' that energise the biosphere.

In summarising this aspect I want to emphasise that the shaman as a healer of illness does not so much interfere on the individual level, but operates on the level of those supra-individual structures that have been disturbed by the person. To be effective, he has to apply his treatment to the disturbed part of the ecosystem. It might be said then that a Tukano shaman does not have individual patients; his task is to cure a social malfunctioning. The diseased organism of the patient is secondary in importance and will be treated eventually, both empirically and ritually, but what really counts is the re-establishment of the rules that will avoid overhunting, the depletion of certain plant resources, and unchecked population increase. The shaman becomes thus a truly powerful force in the control and management of resources.

The shaman then interferes quite directly with hunting, fishing, gathering and most other harvesting activities. For example, a shaman will personally control the quantity and concentration of fish-poison to be used on a certain stretch of river; he will determine the number of animals to be killed when a herd of peccary is reported, and he will decide on a suitable harvesting strategy for the gathering of wild fruits. He will determine *which* fish have to be thrown back into the water after a haul has been made, and occasionally he even might completely prohibit the killing of certain animals in a restricted area of the forest. He will also control such technological activities as the construction of a communal house, the manufacture of a canoe, or the opening of a trail. All these activities obviously affect the natural environment since trees have to be felled and many plants have to be destroyed or used in the process, and the shaman's role as a protector of game and plant-life explains why animals and plants figure so prominently as his spirit-helpers. All this, I should like to point out here, is not speculation; the Indians are quite explicit in these matters and explain that the spirit-owners of nature must not be angered and that it is the shaman's task to reconcile them.

The very large denotative vocabulary of a shaman expresses his great concern with establishing the complete inventory of the ecosystem. In order to be able to administer this great store-house, he has to know, name and categorise all its contents. This knowledge eventually provides him with the criteria for ecological planning and this, of course, is problem-solving by anticipation. The fact that many daily activities such as hunting, fishing, gathering, the clearing of a new field or the curing of a disease are subject to divinatory practices in order to locate the most propitious spot or time, or to find the most effective procedure in coping with this or that predicament, gives the shaman ample opportunity to protect wild-life by random scheduling of hunting excursions whenever he thinks that a certain species is endangered, or to channel any other exploitative activity in directions he believes to be best. I know of several cases where shamans initiated limited migratory movements by asking people to abandon their homes in order to avoid an approaching epidemic or the presence of evil spirits, both calamities being revealed in divinatory trance. The true reason, however, seems to have been the advanced depletion of protein resources. In view of the observation of a number of related cases, it seems not unlikely that shamanistic divinatory practices operate with models and that, in this manner, many adaptive changes are being introduced by shamans.

One might ask here: how far is a shaman actually conscious of his role as an ecological broker? Does he always act quite rationally and with an adequate understanding of ecological principles?

There exist, of course, differences. Some shamans, notably the younger and less experienced ones, tend to verbalise their conceptions in quite simplistic terms by saying that overhunting and overharvesting are bound to annoy both the spirits and the game animals, and that illness will be the punishment. They will readily point out changes in prey abundance and will attribute the biotic impoverishment of certain restricted areas to the action of vengeful spirits. Others however will not make use of these mystical interpretations but will blame greed and ignorance for the depletion of protein resources. They will attribute some (if not all) diseases to nutritional deficiencies and will state quite plainly that protein resources are scarce and have to be protected.

To be sure, the fact that most economic activities are accompanied by rituals does not mean that the shaman simply asks the supernatural forces for abundance, for plenty, for a maximum amount of what the environment can produce, but rather that occasions are being provided for stock-taking, for weighing costs and benefits, and for the eventual re-distribution of resources. At these moments the shaman's book-keeping shows the general system inputs and outputs. In point of fact, most shamanistic activities such as curing rituals, rain-making, the periodic reaffirmation of alliances or food exchange between exogamic groups might be viewed as rituals concerned with resource management and ecological balance. This fact has sometimes been obscured by a tendency to describe native shamans in terms of mere witchdoctors or religious fanatics.

VI

The Tukano and many other Colombian tribes believe that the entire universe is steadily deteriorating. Thus it is thought that formerly people were healthier, stronger and more intelligent than they are at present; that animals and fruits were larger and that they were more abundant than now. The Indians will point out stretches of forest, rivers or lagoons saying that in former times animal life was plentiful there. It is true that, at present, this feeling of impending doom is partly justified; in many parts the world of the rainforest Indians *is* on the wane. But the Indian's sense of entropy, of the tendency toward disorder and chaos, does not seem to be a consequence of his present plight, but rather represents an existential anxiety that forms part of native cosmology and philosophy, and that is based upon the close and daily observation of the biological cycles of growth and decline. The important point is that this idea of increasing disorder is always followed by the institutionalised resolution to *re-create* the world and to re-establish its order and purpose as stated in cosmological tradition. This continuous cycle of ritual creation, destruction and re-creation can be found in many tropical forest societies and is indeed an important mechanism of cultural and biological survival.

In the course of these ceremonial occasions, when the universe and all its components are being renewed, one goal becomes of central importance: the reaffirmation of links with past and future generations, together with the expression of concern about the future well-being of society. The emphasis of the ritual is upon unifying the social group, upon continuity, upon the close bonds of identity that unite society with the past and make it the foundation of the future. It seems that this sense of union provides deeply motivating values and strong incentives for ecological responsibility. The lengthy genealogical recitals and the ritual dialogues have a powerful cohesive function, and in many of these rituals animal and plant-spirits are thought to participate, expressing by their presence their interrelatedness and interdependency. It must be pointed out here that the ritual re-creation of the universe is generally accompanied by the collective use of narcotics of plant origin. During these drug-induced trance states, or other forms of dissociate phenomena, the participants establish contact with the mythical past, in fact, they see themselves return to the time of divine Creation and thus take part in it. It is clear that, here again, the officiating shaman can adaptively orient the interpretations of the visions people project upon the vivid background of their hallucinations.

During most or all of these rituals which can be said to be essentially concerned with ecological balance, the recital of myths and genealogies is of great importance. These myths explain man's nature and trace man's destiny from birth and infancy through maturity to decline and death; from the sin of incest to chaos and near-destruction, and hence to a new order and the establishment of law. These myths and tales, I should like to emphasise here, are not mere 'literature'; they represent a truly remarkable effort at intellectual interpretation, at providing a cognitive matrix for life. They are a guide for survival because they establish rules of conduct, not only for ritual occasions but for everyday life; a fact which sometimes goes unnoticed as long as one has not discovered the metaphorical code in which the myths are transmitted.

The cosmological myths which express the Tukano world-view do not describe Man's Place in Nature in terms of dominion, of mastery over a subordinate environment, nor do they in any way express the notion of what some of us might call a sense of 'harmony with nature'. Nature, in their view, is not a physical entity apart from man and, therefore, he cannot confront it or oppose it or harmonise with it as a separate entity. Occasionally man can unbalance it by his personal malfunctioning as a component, but he never stands apart from it. Man is taken to be a part of a set of supra-individual systems which – be they biological or cultural – transcend our individual lives and within which survival and the maintenance of a certain quality of life are possible only if all other life forms too are allowed to evolve according to their specific needs, as stated in cosmological myths and traditions.

In closing, I should like to note the following. Until quite recently ethnologists and archaeologists have attempted to explain cultural evolution and change in terms of linear cause-and-effect models and this approach is still used by most specialists in these fields. Gregory Bateson was the first ethnographer to sense the need for a systems theory model to account for his ethnographical data, although his now classic monograph on New Guinea was written long before the formal aspects of systems theory had been developed.

Archaeologists have been particularly prone to dependence on cause-and-effect explanations and models constructed on the principles of linear causality, and these trends have been emphasised in the intellectual movement called 'New Archaeology'. It is only recently that Flannery has noted that two very different kinds of explanatory models are used by the 'New Archaeology'. One of these schools is explicit in its adherence to linear causality. Flannery has applied the term 'law-and-order' archaeology to this school. The other less popular trend has been an application of systems theory to account for cultural change, attributing its dynamics to very slow deviations which originate in a part of the system and then develop into major modifications. It seems that this approach is far more likely to produce significant models than is 'law-and-order' archaeology.

It is striking then that in the last decade ethnographers and archaeologists are coming to accept as the only kind of explanatory model which can be used to handle ecological relationships the kind of overall systems model which was adopted by 'primitive' Indians a very long time ago.

Toucan

II

DESANA ANIMAL CATEGORIES: FOOD RESTRICTIONS, AND THE CONCEPT OF COLOUR ENERGIES

The Desana have developed an elaborate system of food categories based upon a number of diagnostic classificatory criteria that refer both to animal and plant resources. The criteria involve a set of sensorially perceptible qualities such as colour, odour, and taste, but furthermore combine with them many symbolic associations which are culture-specific, and in this manner the classificatory systems gain an organizational importance that goes far beyond the spheres of mere food procurement and consumption. This essay concerns some aspects of the formulation and uses of these systems.

It would seem that the description of classificatory systems as such is of limited value unless it is accompanied by cultural interpretations. It is therefore my principal objective to put these systems into the context of ethnographic reality, and to offer a large body of accurate factual information on how the Indians explain their ecological situation, in the light of their own organizational ideas.

It is certain that this is only a small part of the Desana sociocultural system, and I must refer the interested reader to previous publications in which I have presented some materials on symbolism, narcotic drugs, and the relationship between shamanism and ecological adaptation (Reichel-Dolmatoff 1971, 1975, 1976a, 1976b, 1978a). I introduce the present topic with a page from Desana mythology.

> In the beginning of time, the Sun Father, an invisible principle of energy, chose a spot on the equatorial line where his staff would stand upright without casting a shadow. Drops of semen fell from it into a whirlpool on earth; soon the first human beings emerged and eventually embarked in huge canoes shaped like anacondas which now took them upriver. Inside these canoes people sat according to tribe and rank, chiefs toward the head-section, behind them singers, warriors in the centre, then shamans, and Makú servants toward the

tail. At certain spots along the river people disembarked and settled. With the help of divine beings and wise shamans they acquired their institutions, their esoteric knowledge, their sustenance, technological processes, and other traits. In the depths of the forests and on the riverbanks they encountered other beings that had been there before them, but they were not quite human. There were fish in the rivers, and in the forests were game and fruits, and there were soils for planting manioc. The Sun Father ordered that every tribe in a group of three should choose a certain way of living, either by hunting, fishing, or horticulture. And so the Desana chose to be hunters, the Pira-Tapuya decided to be fishermen, and the Tukano took to horticulture. To all creatures on earth the Sun Father allotted a certain amount of vital energy that was now to flow through plants, animals, and men, always emerging from the sun and always returning to him. To regulate this flow the Sun Father instituted on this earth the Master of Animals, who was to be the mediator between man and his environment; among men, the Sun Father instituted the shamans to act as mediators between their people and the Master of Animals. As a means of communication between the visible and the invisible world, shamans were given narcotic plants and a rock crystal. And this was how the tribes settled the Vaupés territory, within a space delimited by six outstretched anacondas, joined at six great waterfalls.

The tribes referred to in this brief summary of a voluminous body of myths, tales, and traditions are designated in the literature as Eastern Tukano, and constitute some twenty exogamic units, each with its own language (Sorensen 1967), and each one divided into up to twenty ranked and named sibs. Descent is patrilineal, residence virilocal, and cross-cousin marriage is said to be preferential. Traditionally three of these exogamic units exchange women and, theoretically at least, occupy adjoining territories. The Desana, Pira-Tapuya, and Tukano proper constitute such a tripartite assembly, and, although their present social and territorial reality has undergone many changes, the traditional scheme continues to form the firm foundation of their world-view.[1]

The purpose here is to examine some aspects of the premises expressed in Desana tradition with reference to man-animal relationships, and to Desana theories of energy and transformation. In other words, the Sun Father's aims and demands are examined in terms of the relationship between the shamanistic world-view and ecological adjustment in this part of the Northwest Amazon.[2]

Animal Classification

I first refer to the different physical environments in which game animals, fish, and certain important plant resources are located and list the species that, according to the Indians, are characteristic of each region.[3] This list is an abbreviated inventory which contains only those species that are of major importance in the food quest.

The Desana and their neighbours[4] distinguish six principal ecological environments within their wider habitat: deep forest, open forest, forest swamps, secondary growth, riverbanks, and lakes.

1. Forest, *nëngë*, sometimes designated as *nëngë boa*, the last word referring to an observable diversity of different kinds of biota.[5] This is primary rainforest of tall, straight trees, unflooded and of relatively sparse undergrowth. Because of its dense canopy, little sunlight filters through into the lower parts. According to the Indians this environment includes *nëngë buru*, 'forest hills',[6] that is, occasional steep rock formations which are the remnants of the Guiana Shield, and are sometimes topped by flat plateaus: they are surrounded by *nëngë* and undergrowth, but their elevated upper regions represent *tara boa* forest, an ecological type described in more detail below. The *nëngë* forests cover by far the largest extension of the entire Indian territory. Most game animals, birds, insects, and reptiles are said to be of 'black' coloration, thought of as an inherently dangerous quality that is quite independent of their actual coloration. I later return to this aspect. The animals and fruits shown in table 1 are said to be characteristic.

TABLE 1
PRINCIPAL GAME ANIMALS AND FRUITS IN THE FOREST

COMMON NAME	TAXONOMIC NAME	DESANA NAME
Tapir	*Tapirus terrestris*	*vehkë*
White-lipped peccary	*Tajassu peccari*	*yehsé*
Collared peccary	*Tajassu tajacu*	*yehsé bura*
Brocket deer, dark	*Mazama* sp.	*nyamá uyige*
Howler monkey	*Alouatta seniculus*	*urá*
Woolly monkey	*Lagothrix lagotricha* sp.	*poré turu*
Spider monkey	*Ateles belzeputh*	*mahsá gahki*
Cacajao monkey	*Ichacha chucuto*	*seégë*
Night monkey	*Aotus* sp.	*ahëáme*
Squirrel	*Sciurus* sp.	*mihsóka*
Bush dog	*Speothos venaticus*	*diayë*
Giant anteater	*Myrmecophaga tridactyla*	*bugú*
Sloth	*Bradypus Infuscatus*	*kerá*
Sloth	*Choloepus didactylus*	*kerá*
Jaguar, all Felidae	*Panthera onça*	*yee*

Trumpeter bird	*Psophia crepitans*	*moaborébu*
Toucan, black	*Rhamphastos culminatus*	*nahsí o tucanus*
Curassow	*Nothocrax urumutum*	*nuhpí*
Tortoise	*Geochelone denticulata*	*peyú buru*
Ant	*Eciton* sp.	*mengá*
Rubber tree	*Hevea pauciflora*	*vahsú*
Rubber tree	*Hevea* sp.	*vahsá*
Rubber tree	*Hevea* sp.	*vahsúpe*
Leguminosae	*Dahlbergia* sp.	*sëmé*
Ukuki (LG)	*Pouteria ucuqui* Schultes	*poé*
Cashew nut	*Anacardium occidentale*	*sorá*
Guamo	*Inga* sp.	*mëré*
Star apple, caimo	*Chrysophyllum vulgare*	*kuré*
Seje palm	*Jessenia bataua*	*nyumu-nyu*
Guarana (LG)	*Paullinia cupana*	*guame kuiro*

It should be added here that, among inedible but otherwise important animals, the *nëngë* environment is the preferred habitat of the cock of the rock, *ëhte-teöro* (*Rupicola rupicola*), the oropendola, *umú* (Icteridae), the long-tailed lizard called *vai-mahsë yee* (*Plica plica* L.), and a spiny-tailed lizard called *kumú yee* (*Urocentron werneri*).

TABLE 2
PRINCIPAL GAME ANIMALS AND FRUITS OF OPEN FOREST

COMMON NAME	TAXONMIC NAME	DESANA NAME
Brocket deer	*Mazama* sp.	*nyamá uyige*
Agouti	*Dasyprocta fuliginosa*	*buí*
Titi monkey	*Callicebus torquatus*	*waú*
Squirrel	*Sciurus* sp.	*mihsóka*
Pigmy squirrel	*Microsciurus* sp. o *sciurillus gujanensis*	*dëtë*
Coati	*Nasua nasua*	*mihpí*
Tayra	*Tayra barbara senilis*	*vahsó-hi*
Pigmy anteater	*Cyclopes didactylus*	*kerá mihpi*
Bucconidae	*Monassa morpheus peruana*	*piakurúro*
Hummingbird	Trochilidae	*mimi*
Toucan	*Rhamphastus culminatus* o *tucanus*	*nahsí*
Woodpecker	Picidae	*koré*
Pigeon, dove	Columbidae	*buhá*
Uasai palm	*Euterpe precatoria*	*mihi*
Rubber tree	*Hevea pauciflora*	*vahsú*
Rubber tree	*Hevea* sp.	*mahá vahsú*
Indeterminate	Indeterminado	*purí*

2. Low open forest, *tara boa*; the soil of this *caatinga* forest environment is often sandy, and the canopy allows sunlight to filter to the ground; high scrub is present. The environment is said to be inhabited mainly by 'brownish' animals. The principal game animals and wild-growing fruit are listed in table 2.

3. Swamp forest, *tará*; this is low swampy forest, partly covered by sheets of water, but too shallow for navigation. Most of the vegetation consists of palm trees; it is said to be an environment for 'red' animals, who are intrinsically 'evil'.

The following inedible animals are frequently found in this environment: anaconda, *dia oréro* (*Eunectes murinus gigas*), turkey vulture, *goro-pora* (*Cathartes urubutinga*), and many small frogs, *oéro*. This is also the environment of the caraná (LG) palms, called *muhí*, the leaves of which are used for thatch.

4. Secondary growth, *viado*; this environment consists mainly of abandoned clearings in the forest, old overgrown fields or former house sites. It is the habitat of a highly valued fauna of minor game animals and is rich in fruits. The fauna is said to be of a 'brownish' colour, and the environment as a whole is considered to be very attractive. Table 4 includes the more characteristic species.

TABLE 3
PRINCIPAL GAME ANIMALS AND FRUITS OF SWAMP FOREST

COMMON NAME	TAXONOMIC NAME	DESANA NAME
Tapir	*Tapirus terrestris*	*vehke*
Jaguar	*Panthera onça*	*yee*
Capybara	*Hidrochoerus capivara*	*dia vehkë*
Paca	*Coelogynis paca*	*semé*
Agouti	*Dasyprocta fuliginosa*	*buí*
Kinkajou	*Potus flavus*	*ukuamë*
Curassow	*Nothocrax urumutum*	*nuhpí*
Anhinga darter	*Anhinga anhinga*	*dehkó nahsí*
Ibis	*Ibis* sp.	*koro*
Yabiru stork	*Jabiru mycteria*	*oóbegë*
Turtle	*Phrynops rufipes*	*peyu diagé*
Frog	Several species	*omá*
Moharra fish	*Cichlasoma* spp.	*nari*
Piranha	*Serrasalmus* sp.	*unyú*
Electric eel	*Electrophorus electricus*	*buihegé*
Very small fish	Indeterminate	*imika*
Fish	Indeterminate	*megusibá*
Fish	Indeterminate	*dihkia*
Fish	Indeterminate	*sai*
South American caiman	*Caiman sclerops*	*diake*
Miriti palm	*Mauritia flexuosa*	*neé*
Palm	*Mauritia* sp.?	*gohá*

An Indian setting a trap with sticks and strings

South American caiman

Swallow-tailed kite (*pingusea*)

Tame guan in Tatuyo longhouse. Pira-paraná river

The following inedible animals are characteristic: opossum, *oá* (*Didelphis marsupialis* sp.), oropendola, *umú* (*Icteridae*), little bluebird, *ërimiri* (*Thraupis virens mediana*), harpy eagle, *gaa* (*Harpya harpia*), swallow-tailed kite, *pingusea* (*Elanoides forficatus*).

5. Riverine environment, *dia vehk*a, literally, 'adjoining the river'. This is the environment of riverbanks and the shores of river lakes that are connected with the larger streams. It can be further subdivided into the banks of the large rivers, *vëári-ya*, and the margins of small creeks, *maëri*. The fauna is said to be 'of all colours'. Many animals of the forest environment, *nëngë*, visit this region.

The flora of the riverine environment is a combination of *nenge, tara bóa, tará*, and *viado*. For a listing of fishes see table 9.

6. Lakes, *dihtáru*; this environment is constituted by large navigable river lakes and their swampy shores. The fauna is said to vary in 'colour'.

On the shores of these lakes grow many palm trees,[7] and also guamo, *mëré* trees (*Inga* sp.). Anacondas are said to be frequent in this environment.

TABLE 4
PRINCIPAL GAME ANIMALS AND FRUITS IN SECONDARY GROWTH

COMMON NAME	TAXONOMIC NAME	DESANA NAME
Collared peccary	*Tajassu tajacu*	*yehsé bura*
Brocket deer, brown	*Mazama* sp.	*nyamá uyige*
Capuchin monkey	*Cebus albifrons*	*mëré gahki*
Titi monkey	*Callicebus torquatus*	*waú*
Agouti	*Dasyprocta fuliginosa*	*buí*
Cavi	*Myoprocta* sp.	*bohsó*
Squirrel	*Sciurus* sp.	*mihsóka*
Pigmy squirrel	*Microsciurus* sp.	
	o *sciurillus gujanensis*	*dëtë*
Coati	*Nasua nasua*	*mihpí*
Tayra	*Tayra barbara senilis*	*vahsó-hi*
Giant anteater	*Myrmecophaga tridactyla*	*bugú*
Giant armadillo	*Priodontes maximus*	*mahsá pamu*
Armadillo	*Dasypus novemcinctus*	*pamu*
Guan	*Penelope jackuaco*	*kara-mahánge*
Toucan	*Rhamphastus vitellinus culminatus*	*guruyá nahsí*
Toucan	*Ramphastus tucanus cuvieri* Wagler	*nahsi*
Chachalaca	*Ortalis guttata guttata*	*vagaró*
Pheasant	*Odontophorus guianensis buckleyi*	*angá yërëge*
Tinamou	*Tinamidae* F.	*angá borége*
Tinamou	*Crypturellus* sp.	*boóru*
Tinamou	*Crypturellus cf.variegatus*	*nyairó*

Jessenia palm	*Oenocarpus bataua*	*nyumú*
Babassú palm	*Orbygnia* sp.	*engá*
Peach palm	o pejibaye *Bactris gasipaes*	*ëri*
Uvilla	*Pourouma cecropiaefolia*	*igí*
Soursap	*Annona muricata* L.	*mikú*
Umari (LG)	*Poraqueiba sericea*	*mee*
Guamo	*Inga* sp.	*mërë*
Avocado	*Persea americana*	*unyú*
Vivapichuna (LG)	Indeterminate	*toá*
'Deer leaf'	*Phytolacca rivenoides*	*nyama-pu*

TABLE 5
PRINCIPAL GAME ANIMALS AND FRUITS OF RIVERINE ENVIRONMENT

COMMON NAME	TAXONOMIC NAME	DESANA NAME
Tapir	*Tapirus terrestris*	*vehke*
White-lipped peccary	*Tajassu peccari*	*yehsé*
Collared peccary	*Tajassu tajacu*	*yehsé bura*
Brocket deer	*Mazama* sp.	*nyamá uyige*
Howler monkey	*Alouatta seniculus*	*urá*
Capuchin monkey	*Cebus albifrons*	*mërë gahki*
Titi monkey	*Callicebus torquatus*	*waú*
Paca	*Coelogynis paca*	*semé*
Agouti	*Dasyprocta fuliginosa*	*buí*
Jaguar	*Panthera onça*	*yee*
South American caiman	*Caiman sclerops*	*diake*
Curassow	*Nothocrax urumutum*	*nuhpí*
Guan	*Penelope jackuaco*	*kara-mahánge*
Toucan	*Rhamphastos culminatus*	

TABLE 6
PRINCIPAL GAME ANIMALS AND FRUITS OF LAKE ENVIRONMENT

COMMON NAME	TAXONOMIC NAME	DESANA NAME
Guacamayo	*Ara* sp.	*moha*
Loro	*Amazonia* sp.	*goí*
Paloma	Columbidae	*buhá*
Mojarra	*Cichlasoma* spp.	*nari*
Piraña	*Serrasalmus* sp.	*unyú*
Raya	*Potamotrygon* sp.	*anyá*
Tortuga	*Phrynops rufipes*	*peyu diagé*
Rana	Several species	*omá*

Another environment that is occasionally mentioned by the Indians is that of windfalls, *mirúnye poé*, lit. 'wind-field'. Windfalls are often located near river-

Forest gap near the Pira-paraná river

banks and are known to attract otters, anacondas, and caimans; pacas too will visit these spots. Because of the fallen trees, uprooted trunks, and entangled undergrowth, however, these places are not often visited by hunters.

The foregoing faunal and floral distribution by ecological regions, well known to every Desana man or woman, presents certain interesting details. In the first place, the deep forest regions, *nëngë*, are shown to contain large game animals, several of which are gregarious, social species, such as white-lipped peccaries, monkeys, trumpeter birds, and social insects, a fact which is often pointed out by the Indians. The 'black' colour ascribed to many forest animals refers, in part at least, to the protective coloration of certain species, but to a large degree it refers to certain abstract qualities demanding precautions. Obviously, these are profitable hunting grounds, but the forest is a sombre place and these regions are lonely and dark. In the second place, the swamplands, *tara*, occupy the other extreme of the ecological scale as conceived by the Indians. This is open, semi-aquatic country, sunlit, and often loud with the voices of waterfowl and parrakeets. Instead of the tall, vine-covered forest trees, we here find large stands of palms of many different species. There are relatively few mammals, but many edible reptiles, plenty of fish, and, of course, the very important *mirití* palm. Most animals are said to be 'red', that is, they demand caution, and the swamp environment is thought to be somewhat endangered by the invisible presence of the *boráro* (or 'curupira'), one of the manifestations of the supernatural Master of Animals. The open forest, *tara boa*, and, above all, the areas of secondary growth, *viado*, and of riverine environments, *dia vehke*, are thought to be the best hunting and fishing grounds. These regions are inhabited by rather solitary animals, by many rodents, and, in general, by game that is easy to attract or to stalk. The fauna as a whole is said to be of a 'brownish' colour, indicating its essential inoffensiveness. The lake environment, *dihtáru*, constitutes an occasional fishing ground, visits to which are usually combined with fishing in adjacent river environments.

The differential concentration of food resources in these eco-niches constitutes, in the minds of the Desana, the basic background against which all social behaviour is acted out, always with full awareness of the specific variation of the surrounding landscape and its seasonal changes.

The Desana and their neighbours classify the fauna and flora of their habitat in several different ways, using various sets of criteria, according to the specific objective of the categories to be established. A few preliminary clarifications must be made here referring to certain general definitions. The need to classify, to organize categories, is strongly felt by all Desana, and every person masters a number of categories that, in one way or another, are related to daily subsistence and experience. The true specialists, however, in classificatory systems are the shamans who, because of their practical and esoteric activities, must handle enormous masses of data. To bring order into the visible and invisible universe, as conceived by the Desana, and to make all tangible and unseen phenomena amenable to manipulation and control are tasks all shamans must cope with, and the methods and aims of classificatory systems are often a matter of discussion by shamans and elders. It is of some significance to mention here that the average person in Desana society is likely to pattern his classificatory concepts according to a dualistic scheme, a polarity of good and evil, male and female, dark and light, and so forth; but shamans will point out that between these apparent extremes exists a detailed scale of values, a long chain of nuances that have to be taken into account in evaluating specific situations, together with the interconnectedness of all phenomena.

The concept of classification is expressed in Desana by the verb *beyéri*, meaning 'to select, to choose'; *beyéro* is the art of selection, and *beyéra* is the result, that is, a class, a category. One might use, for example, these expressions:

vai-mëra beyéri	to classify game animals
mahsá beyéri	to classify people
nomé beyéri	to classify women
bári beyéri	to classify food

In trying to further elucidate the classificatory process, it is important to add that *beyéri* means, essentially, 'to select for ripeness' and is related to *bëgëari*, 'to ripen', a term that can be applied to fruits, animals, and people.

The two basic categories of all living beings are *mahsá*, 'people', and *vai-mëra*, 'animals'. The plural form, *mahsá*, corresponds to the singular *mahsë*, meaning 'man, person', related to the verb *mahsarí*, 'to be born', with the alternative meaning of 'to be cured'. To know, to have cognisance, is *mahsíri* and man is a 'knowing' creature who was not only born into this world, but was 'cured', that is, transformed, by his birth. Animals are not transformed when they are born. The designation *vai-mëra* is composed of two words: *va'i*, the common word for fish, and *mëra*, a term that, according to context and intention, can mean 'beings, creatures, animals, beasts, vermin' and, in a despective or mythological sense, 'oldsters', the ancient ones. The term *vai*, or *va'i*, is related to *bari*, 'to eat'; fish is man's basic food in the river system of the Vaupés, and so are *vai-mëra*, the beasts of the forest. Animals, then, can be classified into *vai-mëra bará*, 'edible animals', *vai-mëra nyéra*, 'bad', that is, inedible animals, and *vai-mëra ehóra*, 'fed animals' or pets, a term including domestic animals such as dogs and chickens.

Another simple classification refers to 'day-belonging animals', *vai-niëra ëmë mahára*, 'night-belonging animals', *vai-mëra nyamí mahára*, and 'twilight-belonging animals', *vai-mëra boyóro mahára*. Table 7 shows a classification of animals by basic locomotory behaviour.

TABLE 7
CLASSIFICATION OF ANIMALS BY LOCOMOTORY BEHAVIOUR

DESANA NAME	LOCOMOTORY BEHAVIOUR	EXAMPLES
vai-mëra paará	'beasts that walk' quadrupedally	Mainly mammals; also tortoises
vai-mëra mërirá	'beasts that climb'	Squirrels, sloths, coatis, tayras
vai-mëra hurirá	'beasts that jump'	All monkeys
vai-mëra vërá	'beasts that fly'	All birds
vai-mëra baará	'beasts that swim'	Fish, frogs, armoured beasts (Crustacea, fish)
vai-mëra payara	'beasts that float'	Otters, ducks
vai-mëra tarará	'beasts that drag themselves'	Snakes, caimans, lizards, toads
vai-mëra gobéri sanyára	'beasts that live underground'	Armadillos, worms
vai-mëra toréri sanyóra	'beasts that live in holes above the ground'	Bats, anacondas, bushmasters
vai-mëra yebári mahára	'earth-belonging beasts'	Ants, snails
yukhëri mahára	'tree-belonging beasts' (not recognised as part of *vai-mëra*)	Termites, wasps, honey-bees, cicadas, spiders

The fundamental preoccupation of Desana daily existence concerns the *edibility* of the available food resources. Palatability, digestibility, or other similar aspects have little or nothing to do with this quality which mainly depends upon the presence, absence, or intensity of certain harmful aspects thought to be inherent in many foodstuffs, and which have to be recognised, neutralised, and transformed. Desana classificatory systems thus constitute devices by which one can ascertain the specific quality of edibility, in accordance with the specific quality of receptiveness of the consumer. The systems establish rules of compatibility, of what may be eaten, how, when, and by whom, and these prescriptions and restrictions form the foundation of an all-important network of behavioural rules. Before discussing the ethnographic details which underlie and explain these rules and their functions, some of these classificatory outlines, as conceived by the Desana, are presented.

To begin with, game and fish are classified by odour. Table 8 shows the odour classification of game animals, *vai-mëra*, together with some others that are not eaten but which, for other reasons, occupy an important position, for example, in myth; they are marked with an asterisk.

The classification of fish is also based upon odour and, also, on their supposedly inherent qualities of 'warm' and 'cold'. As in the case of game, every species of fish is thought to appear under three colours: black, red, and brown. Although these colours can be recognised perceptually, their true significance lies on a symbolic level. Table 9 shows the classification of the more common species. The hours of catch are approximate, the points of reference being sunrise, sunset, and the meridian position of the sun.

TABLE 8
ANIMAL CLASSIFICATION (COMMON NAME) ACCORDING TO ODOUR

ODOUR

GOOD	BAD	BAD	NONE
*Jaguar, all Felidae	Tapir	*Harpy eagle	*Parakeet
Brocket deer, red	White-lipped peccary	*Turkey vulture	*Lizard
Titi monkey	Collared peccary	Ashinga darter	River crab
Capybara	Brocket deer, black	Woodpecker	Crawfish
Paca	*Bush dog	Swallow-tailed kite	Caterpillar, small
Agouti	Giant anteater	Caiman	
Cavi	Giant armadillo	Turtle	
Squirrel	Howler monkey	*Anaconda	
Pigmy squirrel	Woolly monkey	*Boa constrictor	
Duck	Spider monkey	*Bushmaster	
Oropendola	Sloth	Frog, edible	
Trumpeter	Squirrel, large	*Amphisbaena	
Ant (*tara boa*)	Coati	Black tree worm	
Tayra	Opossum	Ant (*nëngë*)	
*Pigmy anteater	Curassow	*Kinkajou	
Armadillo			
Guan			
Pigeon, dove			
Tinamou			
Macaw			
Toucan			
Cock of the rock			

* Not eaten

From these classifications it has become clear that the Desana choose different frames of reference when grouping animals into categories. Desana classificatory thought is not so much concerned with morphological characteristics as it is with meanings and relationships that can be attached to an animal's habitat, colour, odour, and behaviour. This, of course, does not in any way mean that there is no interest in 'zoological' aspects; on the contrary, the Indians are keenly aware of the organisation of animal communities, of interspecific behaviour, of breeding and feeding habits, and even of phenomena as complex as symbiotic and parasitic relationships and the behaviour of the social insects. But all these aspects have little or nothing to do with the criteria on which these classifications are

TABLE 9

CLASSIFICATION OF FISH BY ODOR, TEMPERATURE, AND TIME OF CATCH

COMMON NAME	TAXONOMIC NAME	DESANA NAME	TEMPERATURE	TIME OF CATCH
Araçú	Leporinus copelandi	boréka	warm	black/red: 9 pm-3 am; brown: 6 pm-9 pm; 3 am-6 am
Piranha	Serrasalmus sp.	umyú	warm	black/red: 9 pm-3 am; brown: 6 pm-9 pm; 3 am-6 am
Tucunaré	Chichla ocellaris	buú	cold	black/red: 6 am-9 am; 3 pm-6 pm; brown: 9 am-3 pm
Pacú	Doras dorsalis	ubú	cold	black/red: 6 am-9 am; 3 pm-6 pm; brown: 9 am-3 pm
Mojarra	Cichlasoma spp.	uari	warm	black/red: 6 am-9 pm; 3 pm-6 pm; brown: 9 pm-3 pm
Cascudo	?	yaká	warm	black/red: 6 am-9 pm; 3 pm-6 pm; brown: 9 pm-3 pm
'Pez espada'	Boulengerella maculata	pasika	warm	black/red: 6 am-9 pm; 3 pm-6 pm; brown: 9 am-3 pm
'Sardine'	Triportheus spp.	seápaga	warm	black/red: 6 am-9 am; 3 pm-6 pm; brown: 9 am-3 pm
Yacundá	Crenichichla sexatilis	mëhá	cold	black/red: 6 am-9 pm; 3 pm-6 pm; brown: 9 am-3 pm
Surubim	Platystoma sp.	kavíria	cold	black/red: 9 pm-3 am; 6 am-6 pm; brown: 6 pm-9 pm; 3 am-6 am
Payala	?	yuandoáro	cold	black/red: 9 pm-3 am; brown: 6 pm-9 pm
Pirahiba	Brachyplatystoma sp.	vaipë doragë	cold	black/red: 9 pm-3 am; brown: 6 pm-9 pm; 3 am-6 am
Guavina	?	pavá	cold	black/red: 9 pm-3 am; brown: 6 pm-9 pm; 3 am-6 am
Tarira	Erythrinus tarieira	doé	cold	black/red: 9 pm-3 am; brown: 6 pm-9 pm; 3 am-6 am
Electric eel	Electrophorus electricus	saa	cold	black/red: 9 pm-3 am; brown: 6 pm-9 pm; 3 am-6 am
Stingray	Potamotrygon sp.	anyá	old	black/red: 9 pm-3 am; brown: 6 pm-9 pm; 3 am-6 am
Cuyucuyú	?	nyakú teámë	cold	black/red: 9 pm-3 am; brown: 6 pm-9 pm; 3 am-6 am
'Pez espada'	?	soo	cold	black/red: 9 pm-3 am; brown: 6 pm-9 pm; 3 am-6 am
Cachama	?	saí	warm	black/red: 9 pm-3 am; brown: 6 pm-9 pm; 3 am-6 am
Nyandiá	Platystonia sp.	poorá	warm	black/red: 9 pm-3 am; brown: 6 pm-9 pm; 3 am-6 am
Indeterminate	?	dihkipáru	warm	black/red: 9 pm-3 am; brown: 6 pm-9 pm; 3 am-6 am
Indeterminate	?	mengasibá	warm	black/red: 9 pm-3 am; brown: 6 pm-9 pm; 3 am-6 am
Indeterminate	?	ehtaboro vai	warm	black/red: 9 pm-3 am; brown: 6 pm-9 pm; 3 am-6 am
Indeterminate	?	ahkiro	warm	6 pm-9 pm only
Indeterminate	?	megatogëru	warm	all day and night
Indeterminate	?	urú	warm	6 pm-9pm only

based. In Desana classification, a characteristic odour, a pair of sharp claws, or the occurrence of a red spot on some body part might cut across orders and families and link together animals of quite different species into categories that are significant to the Desana, but meaningless to the outsider. For this reason, the Indians are not concerned with whether a bat is a bird, or whether freshwater dolphins are fish or mammals. They simply are not interested in phylogenetic relationships, nor in setting generic limits, nor in taxonomy as such. Quite obviously, to the Desana mind, animal classifications are not devices to bring order into the animal world, but to programme and control man-animal relationships or, in a wider sense, to programme the interaction between society and the natural environment.

Food classification, restrictions, and prescriptions constitute a voluminous and very complex body of lore that regulates food procurement and consumption in culturally approved ways. Since this sanction refers not only to individual well-being, but to the welfare of society, food lore is of signal importance to ecological and ethnological studies. It is, after all, the lore of survival. With this preliminary idea in mind I now turn to an interrelated range of Desana concepts in which men and animals are shown to share in an elaborate set of relationships.

Energy

The Desana universe is conceived as a circuit formed by six straight lines which enclose a hexagonal space and thereby connect six *turi*, an expression that can be glossed as 'systems' or 'dimensions' (fig. 1). At two opposite points are the sun and the moon, occupying *ëmé abé turi*, 'day-sun-system' (or *ëmékori mahsë turi*, 'day-revolving-male person-system'), and *nyamí abé turi*, 'night-sun-system' (or *nyamírí mahsó turi*, 'night-revolving-female person–system'). These two are the actual, visible sun and moon; the invisible personifications of the sun, *abé pagë*, or Sun Father, and the moon, *abé tingó*, or Sun Sister, are imagined as existing outside the hexagonal space, under the abstract form of 'light' and 'darkness'.

Sun and moon are the principal sources of energy, *bogá* (plural, *bogári*). The sun contains and emits heat, *ahsiri*, and light, *gohséri*, that give origin to one part of the colour spectrum, consisting of three colour 'energies': (1) *boré gohsé siriro*, 'white-brilliant-reflection', (2) *bo're gohsé siriro*, 'yellow-brilliant-reflection', and (3) *diabírí gohsé siriro*, 'red strong-brilliant-reflection'. These energies are already in existence in the Sun Father, under these designations, but, once transferred to the visible sun, the word *ahsí*, 'hot', is added after each colour designation.

While the sun's 'whiteness' is conceived as a generalised, live-giving force that pervades the entire universe, 'yellowness' is said to represent male seminal, generative power; 'redness' stands for female, uterine fecundity. The sun's heat fur-

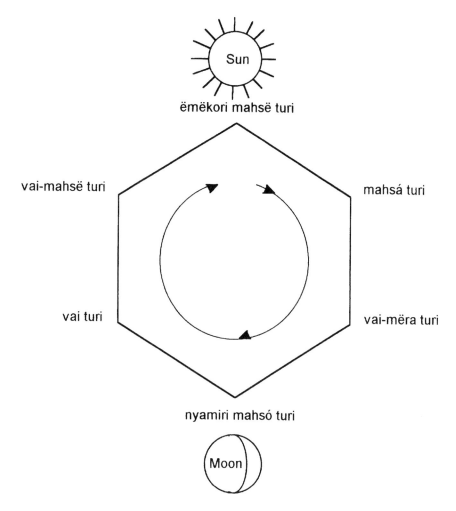

FIGURE 1. Outline of the Desana concept of the energy circuit between six *turi* or 'systems'

thermore gives rise to three additional 'energies': (1) *waro pore surí*, 'good odour', (2) *kunyu poréra*, 'warm temperature', and (3) *ëserira*, 'good flavour'.

The moon contains a complementary set of 'energies' which are, first of all, *nyiró*, 'blackness', and *gëhsári*, 'coldness', both associated with death. These negative energies originate another triad of colour energies: (1) *yahsá gohseró*, 'greenish-pale', (2) *bo're gohseró* 'yellow-pale', and (3) *diabiri nyiró*, 'red strengthened [with] black'. The greenish aspect of the moon is associated with the initial, unripe stage of plant growth, called *saveri*; the yellowish aspect with ripeness, *bogë*; and the violet stage, with rottenness, *boáro*. All men and women contain an equal amount of colour energies which are transmitted by the semen of their fathers and the blood of their mothers. At death, the colours return to

Barasana woman with body paint. Ohkoya creek

Taibano hunter and his son with ritual facial paint, before going hunting

their original source, the sun, and become once more part of the 'brilliance', *gohséri*.

In order to explain the fundamental importance this colour symbolism has on human affairs, I must refer here in some detail to Desana colour classification. In common, everyday practice the Desana refer to four colours: *boréro*, 'white', *bo'ré*, 'yellow', *diáro*, 'red', and *nyíro*, 'black'. It is obvious that the first two words have the same stem, *bo*, and that the last two words also are derived from a common root, in this case, *di* or *ni*. There are then only two named colour concepts: 'whiteness' and 'blackness'. The use the Desana make of colour concepts is extremely complex, however, and pervades every aspect of life. Indeed, colour categories and their significance are of paramount importance to an understanding of Desana culture. Colour classification is energy classification, and energy is conceived in terms of biological processes.

The term *boréro*, 'white', is used almost exclusively in the abstract sense of whiteness. It is said to emanate from the Sun Father and to lend tangible things their clear, light appearance. But it does not only illuminate by its brilliance; in this sense it is not really a colour but a luminous quality with certain moral connotations. The stem *bo* is found in the verb *boréri*, 'to whiten', in *boyóri*, 'to illuminate', in *boyo*, 'dawn', and also appears in the word *bogá*, a term that can be glossed as potential energy. Whiteness stands for the principle of life, of health and well-being. It seems that, contrary to other colour terms, no derivative forms are based on it; one might hear the expression *waro boréro*, 'good white', but otherwise the word stands for itself and is, in all essence, a qualifying concept, a colour quality that lends intensity to other colours.

The word *bo'ré*, 'yellow',[8] does not carry this abstract meaning. It is applied to a wide range of yellow hues, all associated with masculine generative power. Most importantly, *bo ré* means 'bundle', 'encapsulated germ or sprout', and is often used in shamanic language to describe procreation. The Desana see an evolutionary sequence in this: first was whiteness which gave origin to yellowness; yellowness emanates from the visible sun. Redness, *diáro*, complements yellowness in that it stands for female fecundity. There are as many hues of red as there are of yellow. The word is related to *dií*, 'blood', *díi*, 'flesh', and, most significantly, to *dia*, 'river, lake'. As we have seen already, the generative origins of mankind, as conceived by the Desana, are located in primordial waters from which the rivers, like pulsating veins, rose to irrigate the land. The word for black, *'nyíro'*, is the same as that for evil, *nyéro*, and again, as in the case of whiteness, blackness stands alone as an individual qualifier of other colours. The expression *boréro gohseró*, 'white-bright', refers to *bogá*, the invisible cosmic energy. Its impact produces a visible yellow potency and this, in turn, flows into red potential. This sequence is called *tulári*, a moving force that communicates the white power to the male principle and, through it, to the female one.

It is clear from this discussion that the problem of colour combinations, that is, of balancing good and evil, male and female, looms large in Desana thought. In shamanic language, many derivative terms are used to express the different hues and their respective significance. The basic colours, yellow and red, are modified by several additional concepts, first of all by *gohséri*, 'brightness', and, more rarely, by *naitáro*, 'dullness'. Next to these we find some others: the term *yahsáro*, a word that refers to plant growth and sprouting leaves, conveys the idea of greenness and of developing life in the womb. It is most often used in conjunction with white or yellow, to express greenish hues that signify that stage of organic development. On the other hand, the concept of *bahsí* modifies colours by introducing a range of yellowish tints. The term can be glossed as 'combination, relation', meaning articulating two components by weakening their inherent intensities.

These colour hues are expressed in ordinary shamanic language in this way:

Jaguar

Desana Term	Colour Hue	Gloss
boyó borëgë	whiteness-white	a luminous white colour
boréri-da	white-dull	especially moonlight
boréri bahsí	white-articulated	a yellowish white
bo'ré-da	yellow-dull	moonlight
bo'ré-diabiríro	yellow-strengthened with red-articulated	consists of *bo ré* and *diari bahsí*, a yellowish hue with a pale pink tint
bo'ré diabirínye	yellow-strengthened with red	a pale, transparent pink
boyó bo ré diabirígë	white-yellow-strengthened with red	a very pale yellow
bo'ré gohseró	yellow-bright	for example, sunrays
bo'ré yahsáro	yellow-greenish	
yahsári-da	greenish-blue	an aspect of moonlight
bo'ré yahsá diabiríro	yellow-greenish-strengthened with red	a yellow hue with a green tint
bo'ré bahsí	yellow-articulated	a reddish yellow
boyó diágë	whiteness-male red	a reddish aura of persons or objects
boyó diabirígë	whiteness-strengthened with male red	a whitish aura of persons or objects
waro turáro diáro	good-strong-red	a deep red colour
waro diabiríro	good-strengthened with red	a dull light red
dia diabiríro	red-strengthened with red	a combination of dark red with light red, that is, *dia* plus *diabíri bahsi*; the colour is conceived as a light red centre surrounded by dark red radiations; the opposite of *diabíri gohseró* (see below)
diabiri nyiró	red-strengthened with black	a very dark, almost black, colour
dia gohseró	red-bright	explained as 'similar to a sunset over the river'
diabiri gohseró	red-strengthened with red-bright	a combination of light red, with luminous yellowish reflections. The colour is conceived as a dark centre, with light red-yellowish radiations of a transparent nature; the opposite of *dia diabiriro* (see above)
diari bahsí	red-articulated	a strong orange colour
diari-da	reddish-dull	a certain aspect of the moon
diabiríri bahsí	black-strengthened with red	a transparent dark-brown colour
daberó nyiró	a little-black	an olive-grey colour

Speaking of *yahsári*, as applied to a pale green, I repeat that this is not a colour term; the stem is *gah*, *goh*, 'to germinate, to sprout', related to *gohséri*, 'to

Young jaguar

shine'. The term is used in shamanic language when referring to the colour of young coca leaves, as in:

ahpí yahsáro	coca-sprouting
ahpí yahsá deyóro	coca-green sprout-visible
ahpí yahsá diábiriro	coca-green sprout-strengthened with red
ahpí yahsá gohseró	coca-green sprout-bright

Shamanic colour concepts and use are thus very complex. Shamans will refer in their spells and incantations to a detailed, spectral continuum and will mention many minor hues. Shamanic colour designations are often based on comparisons; animals, fruits, and other objects in nature are called upon to describe colours, and the basic colours are combined and recombined in endless associations and modifications, with an abundance of verbal forms that refer to the widest possible range of hues.

I must return once more to certain aspects of Desana cosmology. The Desana divide the universe into two basic components: first is *deyóri turi*, the 'visible' or 'transparent' world which comprises all of nature and what we can perceive in it with our senses as a material dimension of colours, temperature, movements, olfactory or acoustic sensations, or taste and texture. In this world, people are engaged in the pursuit of food, *deyo bari*, and food is sensorially perceived. The other dimension is *deyóbiri turi*, the 'invisible' world. It contains a different set of meanings, not hidden, but only different in their relevance to men. To be visible is *deyóri*, and *kuíru deyóri* is the capacity of the human eye to perceive form, colour, or movement. But *kuíru boyóri* means to recognise the unseen qualities of things; it conceptualises and interprets. The verb *boyóri* means 'to shed light upon something', and the word for dawn, *boyóro*, is derived from it. It can be employed in the physical sense of 'lighting up', in the sense of 'seeing clearly', or in the sense of the English expression 'it dawned upon me'. Desana shamans say that, in order to be able to live in the visible world, one must look at it through insights gained in the invisible world. Not all people are able to do this, and only 'knowledgeable people', *mahsá deyokë iía*, can recognise, translate, and transform the meanings of *deyóbero*, the invisible, and can thus spiritually nourish themselves. All foodstuffs consumed in this tangible world must be evaluated and handled according to their unseen qualities. In summary, *deyóro*, the perceptible, and *deyóbero*, the unseen, might be translated as 'material' and 'spiritual', respectively.

Let me continue now with the different 'energy' currents mentioned above. Between the visible sun and moon are located four 'systems'. The first is *vai-mahsë turi*, 'animal-person system', the realm of the Master of Animals. *Vai-mahsë* is, first of all, associated with the fertility of nature, of game, fish, and wild-growing fruits. For this very reason his celestial trajectory is the Milky Way, called *vai-mahsë maá*, his 'trail' which, originally, is the Sun Father's stream of semen but, in other images, is a celestial representation of the life-bearing anaconda of the Creation Myth. On this earth, it is the rainbow that represents *vai-mahsë*'s ejaculation. In his humanoid form he is imagined as a red dwarf, in all essence a phallic being, in charge of the propagation of the animal world. He is first and foremost a gamekeeper who protects his wards, and who constantly has to admonish the hunters and fishermen not to exceed themselves in the pursuit of their prey. *Vai-mahsë* will appear to people in many disguises and, since he is said to be a very strict administrator of all game resources, his appearance in times of scarcity is feared because, to the hunter, it might be an indictment of having exceeded himself. But in times of abundance, or shortly before fish begin their seasonal run to the spawning grounds, or before fruit are beginning to ripen, his fleeting appearance is taken to be a propitious omen.

To the Master of Animals, the entire earth is an enormous horizontal spider web, *bëhpë suriro*, also hexagonal in shape, the cartwheel structure of which

Cock of the rock

symbolizes the network of prescribed pathways on which men and beasts must move without ever straying off them. The Desana say that, just as a man might crush such an orb web he encounters on his forest trail, so *vai-mahsë* dominates the animal world. It is said to be a fragile world, easily upset and disturbed, and this is why the Master of Animals is said to exercise so unremitting a control over it. He himself might appear to be hunter in spider form[9] and spider, *bëhpë*, is identified with thunder, *buhpú*. *Vai-mahsë* often wanders over the Milky Way and from this vantage point he watches the doings of men and beasts. He then descends to the 'white cloud level', *boréri bogá*, below which lies *dehkó bogá*, 'rain-energy', the dark rain clouds, and hence, in the form of lightning, he will project himself to the ground. Assuming the functions of a fertilizing rain god, he is imagined as hurling his thunderbolts of white quartz splinters or, rather, he turns himself into a bolt that suddenly strikes a hill, a tree, or even a house. People say: *vai-mahsë mohó yuriáya*, '*vai-mahsë*-weapon his-let fall'; or they might say: *yee mohó yuriáya*, the word *yee* standing for either jaguar or shaman. In fact, the Master of Animals is both; in jaguar form he dominates all other animals, and among his creatures he is the wise shaman, the protector, the mediator between the hunter and his prey. He also might manifest himself in a great storm, or as a cock of the rock displaying his bright yellow plumage, or as a lizard,[10] a fish, or a cacique bird. Sometimes, again, he might manifest himself in the strong smell of certain lichens and mosses after a rain shower, which grow on the jungle floor in some parts of the forest, in the smell of youthfulness, *mamári*, as the Desana call it, alluding to its erotic connotations and its similarity to the scent of small bundles of aromatic herbs, *bará*, that young men wear at dances. But *vai-mahsë* is also identified with the *boráro*, the forest monster, known under the name of *curupira* by many Amazonian Indians. In summary, *vai-mahsë* is conceived as an immediate force of nature, and as such he is sometimes designated as *tulári bogá*, 'force-energy'.

I shall anticipate here some observations on *vai-mëra turi*, 'game-animal-system', Nature, the domain of *vai-mahsë*, understood here as the physical environment inhabited by animals and plants is thought to contain in all its manifestations, the *same* interrelated set of energies, *bogári*. First, all animals and plants, both as taxonomic categories and as individual specimens, are said to contain the same series of chromatic energies that are derived from the visible sun and moon, respectively. The exact proportional distribution is of importance and, in the case of game and fish, is described thus: a large component of blackness, occupying about half of the entire colour set, is accompanied by a lesser amount of redness (female growth potential), and a still lesser amount of pale, weak yellowness (male generative potential). The second set of 'energies', also present in all animals, consists of the inherent qualities of odours, which are musky, estrous, or floral; of temperatures such as 'warm' and 'cold'; and flavours such as 'sweet' and 'bitter'. The entire scheme can also be applied to all wild-growing and cultivated foods.

Whereas, in the Desana system of thought, men participate in the original solar energy, with which they share an equal amount of all colour energies, animal life is said to be entirely dependent upon men. This idea is expressed in several ways. In the first place, the Master of Animals is imagined as a mighty hunter walking over the Milky Way from east to west, returning from the chase. On his back he carries his prey, a game animal symbolized by a certain constellation that has just risen over the horizon. Throughout the year, *vai-mahsë* will thus be carrying game, fish, and fruits over his celestial trail, for all to see. As soon as a certain animal species becomes aware that *its* constellation is rising, it knows that its breeding season is near, and that its specific food such as fruits, berries, leaves, or roots will soon be available, thanks to the Master of Animals. Since the Master is the mediator between animals and men, a relationship of dependence is being established. Human energy is transmitted through the circuit and, at the death of a person, returns to its solar source. But animals, for reasons explained later, do not participate in this human circuit; theirs is the circuit in which man, by consuming animals, transmits their energy and transforms it into their life-force which is restricted to this world. Animals will weep at the death of a person, because a potential carrier, a link in their energy circuit, has disappeared. Animal energy depends to a large degree upon the spells and incantations shamans pronounce in their favour. In this way, animals are thought to depend on shamanic fertility rituals, and on the distribution of resources practised by the Maser of Animals who, in their midst is a representative of the hunters. I return to this point again.

Vai-turi, 'fish-system', also designated as *dehkó turi*, 'water-system', includes all rivers, creeks, lakes and swamps of the Desana, Pira-Tapuya, and Tukano habitat, together with all species of fish. This dimension is imagined to be divided into three superimposed layers according to relative depth; the deepest layer is said to be inhabited mainly by 'black' and 'cold' fish, the middle layer by 'red' and 'cold' fish, while the upper layer is inhabited by 'brownish' fish, of a 'warm' condition (see table 9). This division into various ranges of depth is emphasised in the case of deep pools that lie at the foot of many rapids, and at the bottom of which *vai-mahsë*, in his manifestation as Master of Fish, has his abodes.

I have spoken already of *vai-mëra turi*, 'game-animal-system'; to the same system belongs *yuhkëri turi*, 'tree system', including *ohtéri turi*, 'cultivation-system', which stand directly under the influence of lunar 'energies'. They include all vegetation, especially fruit-bearing trees and cultivated plants, together with some medicinal, aromatic, and technologically important raw materials. Every tree or plant is conceived as divided into three horizontally superimposed layers, the respective fruits of which are said to be greenish at the bottom, yellowish-red in the middle, and brownish on the top layer. This triple stratification is also applied to the underground section of tuber-bearing plants. For example, it is

Creek at the headwaters of the Pira-paraná river

A view of Ohkoya creek, Barasana territory. Pira-paraná

said that the deepest manioc tubers are thick and of a yellowish colour, those of middle depth are said to be somewhat elongated and reddish, while the upper-most tubers are notably elongated and of a brownish colour. The vertical division of plants is taken into account in connection with culinary, medical, or narcotic preparations.

I turn now to another aspect of energy. Desana shamans, as a matter of fact most shamans of the Eastern Tukano, use transparent rock crystals as power objects. Such a quartz crystal, sometimes up to fifteen centimetres in length, is called *ëhta bohóru*, meaning 'stone-condensed'. While the suffix *-ru* indicates a masculine essence, the word *boho* is derived from *bohóri*, 'to dry up, to become condensed, to become concentrated'. The word *ëhta*, for stone, contains the stem *ëh*; *ëhëri* means 'to turn, to receive or emit great heat' and, in a wider sense, 'to transform'. A rock crystal is said to be condensed heat, and heat is *ahsíri*, related to the stem *ëh*, and also to *ah*, *ahp*, which, as I have mentioned elsewhere (Reichel-Dolmatoff 1971:151), is related to the concept of transformation. Indeed, according to the Desana, a crystal is a result of transformation and, at the same time, it is an instrument for transforming. A shaman's rock crystal thus represents many different, but interrelated, concepts. First of all, on an abstract level, it contains the 'whiteness' of the sun, not of the visible sun but of the Sun Father, the creator of the universe. In this context the crystal is referred to as *abé yeéru*, 'sun-penis', and is said to consist of crystallized semen. It thus contains a powerful creative force. But in other contexts the crystal becomes a clitoris and is referred to as *igo yanyée*, 'her-thing'. A crystal, then, is a hermaphroditic element of creation and transformation and can be used for many different ends. It is also closely connected with the jaguar and, as I have pointed out before, the word for jaguar and for shaman is the same, *yee*, and is derived from *yeéri*, 'to copulate'. A crystal can be referred to as *yeea vii*, 'house-of the shaman', or 'house-of the jaguar'. It is also called *dehkó siriro*, 'water-stone', and is said to consist of solidified water.

I begin by explaining a few empirical observations on which shamans base their beliefs in the crystal's powers. If one should watch a large crystal, with the light falling upon it from behind one's back or from the side, perhaps from the sun or, better still, from a torch or an open fire, one soon will catch a glimpse of vivid reflections. When slowly turning the stone in one's hands, one will perceive in the depths of the crystal, near its base where there are specks and clouds, a glimmer of lights, and suddenly a rainbow pattern will appear. With some practice one can learn to control these reflections and then, depending upon the light source and the angle at which the stone is being held, one can repeat these luminous effects in a certain order. It is a fact, then, that the primary colours of the prismatic spectrum to which Desana shamans constantly refer are originally being observed in the glow inside the stone; shamans confirm these reflections as the original energies of creation. Similar observations of colour spectra, changing hues, or luminous sensations of fleeting spots are made with regard to rainbows (*vai-mahsë*'s semen), to rainbow patterns seen on the screen of a waterfall, or in the spray of droplets from a paddle stroke, a jumping fish, or a stone thrown into the water, in droplets caught in a spider web, or in the beads of dew in the early morning. Other comparable visual impressions are derived from shooting stars, or from sparks flying from a fire, in darkness. All these visual experiences are, of course, strongly brought into focus by frequent hallucinatory trances during which these colours appear in all their dazzling hues and, what is more, they now come into view in a sacred context, as explained by the shamans who are present at these collective rituals.

The crystal as a whole is said to be enveloped in, and saturated with, the 'white light'; in fact, the crystal *is* the white light and thus contains an abstract, invisible potential, '*bogá*', which, in turn, is activated by *tulári bogá*, 'force-energy' or, shall we say, kinetic energy. The colour spectrum, together with its white and black components, is thought to be present in all of nature, and since nature's components are interdependent, their reproductive forces have to be controlled; yellow and red must be balanced and must be geared to the demands each part of nature makes upon the other. Men depend on animals and plant resources for their survival, but since these resources are limited (their yellow-ness being 'weak'), men must control their birthrate and must abstain from over-hunting, overfishing, and all other excesses in the exploitation of nature. Should people disregard these restrictive rules, they will be punished by illness; the Master of Animals will use his wards to bring illness to men, women, and children, in retaliation for the persecution of game, fish, and other resources (Reichel-Dolmatoff 1976a).

Under normal circumstances colour energies are thought to be balanced and to maintain a certain fixed relationship, but as soon as resources are being mis-used, the equilibrium of colours present in a person is expected to change and to produce effects that are harmful to health. A certain colour might increase or weaken another; yellow maleness might overwhelm red femaleness, or vice versa. The state of a person's energies can be ascertained by a shaman, by slowly passing the crystal over the patient's body and watching the subtle changes in reflection. This process is called *yee uhúri*, lit. 'shaman-absorb', but here mean-ing 'to detect'; moreover, the verb *uhúri* is closely related to *ëhëri*, 'to transform'; in fact, the shaman transforms his patient. Once the nature of these chromatic changes has been established, the shaman's task consists of applying the inex-haustible energies contained in his crystal to restore the lost balance. This entails a process of mixing, blending, diminishing, and strengthening of colours; of introducing certain hues; of dimming a brilliance here, or of brightening a dull-ness there; all this is done in lengthy spells and incantations, with both shaman and patient often being in a narcotic trance. The fundamental idea underlying these procedures consists of the belief that curing practices are equivalent to the rebirth of the patient who has to be recreated *ab ovo*, that is, from an embryonic state. The Desana words for 'to be born' and 'to be cured' are the same, as I have mentioned above. I shall return to this theme; here I only want to underline the importance of colour symbolism in reestablishing a patient's health impaired by an abuse of natural resources.

In the hands of the shaman, the crystal constitutes a microcosm. In one sense it is a powerful tool that can be used to create life, to restore it, or even to destroy it; in another sense it is a model of the universe, or of a particular part of it. The shaman can either look into it and search for clues about its latent energies, or the doings of other shamans, or he can place himself inside the crystal and then look out upon an otherwise invisible world. Since the crystal is also the model of a longhouse, the shaman can spot in it any dwelling he wants to watch. There he can see other shamans at work and can observe all activities that go on in any place he chooses to see inside his crystal.

The Desana believe that all game animals dwell inside certain rocky hill formations deep in the forest, which are womblike places where spirit-animals, imagined in human form, live and reproduce, being periodically released by the Master of Animals to fall prey to the hunters. Fish are thought to dwell in the same manner at the bottom of deep dark pools in rivers or lakes. In the shaman's mind the crystal can turn into one of these abodes, and so he can watch the animals, recognise their kinds, count their numbers, and, in this manner, keep stock of food resources. Both 'hill houses', called *ëhtëgë vii*, and 'water houses', or *dia vii*, are imagined exactly like geodes, that is, approximately globular bodies in a limestone matrix, the hollow interior of which is coated with a drusy crust of innumerable minute, inward-projecting crystals. To the Desana these formations have an organic, uterine significance, attested to by the growing chalcedonic layers that surround the nodular stone. The interior lining of a multitude of scintillating multicoloured crystals conveys to the Indians an image of powerful life-creating forces. Both game and fish are imagined to live in these gleaming cavities. Again, a comparison with hallucinatory visions comes to mind and is readily elaborated by the Desana.

Most important is the shaman's perspective from inside the crystal. The hexagonal prism, standing vertically, provides the shaman with six perspectives which cover a tripartite horizon. The Desana traditionally intermarry exogamously with the Pira-Tapuya and the Tukano, and each pair of adjoining crystal-faces looks out upon one of the three exogamic units, one face on its men and another face on its women (fig. 2). By placing himself inside the crystal, the shaman can watch his own and the two neighbouring exogamic groups, each in an arc of 120 degrees. He will also see all food resources, however hidden; he will see the different manifestations of the Master of Animals, he will see their women, and he will even hear their shrill laughter through the striated prism faces, as if through a wall of plaited palm leaves. This, too, is a vantage point

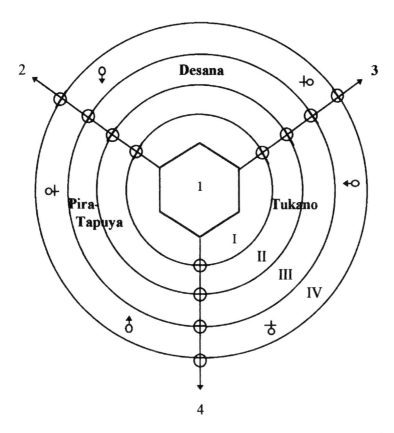

Figure 2 A shaman's perspective from inside his rock crystal (1); (2-4) tabu divisions between territories: (I-IV), ranked sibs; at the crossings are hills or pools

from which to keep stock of resources. Should he observe a scarcity of a certain species of animals or fruits in his own sector, he immediately will know that this must be blamed upon the shamans of a neighbouring exogamic unit and, being in a triadic position, he will summon the shamans of the third unit and enlist their help to restore the balance and provide the necessary energies to replenish the respective resources while, at the same time, willfully diminishing those of the other group. It all becomes a matter of balance, of watching and blending colours, of the strategy of resource management.

Although the dividing lines between adjoining exogamic groups are at present largely imaginary, the Desana insist that in the past each group occupied a circumscribed territory formed by a wedge-shaped sector. In the centre was the mythical spot of tribal origins, a deep whirlpool at a rapids, whence the First People emerged. Since each exogamic unit is composed of a number of ranked sibs organised by their order of emergence, the members of the first-ranking sib are said to have formed with their longhouses an inner circle, those of the second-ranking sib, an adjoining outer circle, and so on, until the territorial division was both tripartite and of concentric hexagons. Marriage rules demand that couples form unions between sibs of equal rank and so, ideally, the three divisory lines separating the exogamic units were crossed only at the ritual gatherings between two groups that exchanged women, who then went to join their husband's longhouse units. These imaginary but, in the past, perhaps, quite real meeting places on these divisory lines are therefore important points of articulation. The three divisory radii consist of alignments of certain hills, pools, or lakes, that is, of supernatural abodes where game and fish are supposed to dwell under the care of the Master of Animals. In other words, the very same spots where social continuity is being guaranteed by the exchange of women are also the spots whence emerge the food resources that guarantee individual survival.[11]

The tripartite layout of the tribal territories constitutes the domain of the Master of Animals. In order to produce and store the necessary vital energies, he must first of all provide a large quantity of fruits; these fruits fall into two categories: those with a seminal connotation and a yellow essence, and those with a red, female connotation and that are consumed in a liquid, cooked form. To offer an example of how these fruits are ennumerated in a shamanic spell, a few of them, together with their specific fertility associations, are listed here:

yatutú pogá boréri	peanut-starch-yellow	peanuts symbolise testes
semé pogá boréri	*Dalilbergia* sp.-starch-yellow	semen-coloured
vahsú pogá boréri	*Hevea* sp.-starch-yellow	its tripartite fruit is compared to testes and a penis: the gelatinous flesh and the latex of the tree are compared with semen
mëmë pogá boréri	*Poraqueiba sericea*-starch-yellow	a fruit with a mucilaginous 'female' connotation

It is clear that the *pogá*, 'starch' essence, of these fruits is equivalent to the wider *bogá* energy. The same is true of the 'essence' derived from 'red' liquid fruit preparations, of which I quote a few examples:

meré nyohká diari	*Inga* sp.-broth-red
nëë nyohká diari	*Pouteria ucuqui* Schultes-broth-red
nyumú nyohká diari	*Oenocarpus bataua* broth-red
ëngá nyohká diari	*Orbignya* sp.-broth-red[12]

The Master of Animals prepares these foods and beverages inside the 'hill houses' and 'water houses', a process that eventually leads to an abundance of wild-growing fruits. This season of the year is introduced by *vai-mahsë*'s observation of the appearance of animal constellations on the horizon. The next step involves *vai-mahsë*'s preparing a network of sweet-scented trails that lead from the hills and pools to the spots where the particular fruits are ripening. These trails are called *deyóbiri bara maári*, 'invisible-food-trails', and can be seen only by the animals and their Master. To them they appear just like man's *deyó bari maári*, the 'visible-food-trails' that leads from the longhouses to the fields and to the hunting or fishing ground. Attracted by the scent, the animals now emerge from their abodes and go to feed on the ripe fruits. The 'yellow' and 'red' energies they thus acquire manifest themselves almost immediately in their estral comportment; they not only couple within each species, but they 'offer themselves' to the hunter and fisherman: they display a comportment called *vai-mëra gumetarári*, 'game-making love'. The animals are 'ripe' and solicit men to 'eat' them.

According to the Desana, the abundant food resources that exist during these months lead to increased sexual energies in humans, giving origin to socially very disrupting tendencies that have to be controlled and channeled into culturally sanctioned expressions. Individual and social survival depends upon food and procreation; both objectives – food and women – have to be transformed before they become 'edible', because only in this manner can people maintain the traditions and values that distinguish them from the beasts of the jungle. The diverse processes by which these and other transformations can be accomplished and exemplified have long become part, not only of shamanic practice, but also, of everyday life.

The entire process of chromatic energy flow, as conceived by the Desana, is being closely watched by shamans who, through their crystals, hallucinatory trances, and, of course, sound empirical observation, observe the increase or depletion of animals, the growth of fruits, the distribution of feeding grounds, spawning beds, the estrous comportment of the different species, and the change of seasons. The swirling colour patterns of narcotic trance are interpreted by them as manifestations of fertility, of uterine gestation, and of the 'processing' of and giving birth to edible foods and marriageable females. Since among the Desana all initiated males consume narcotic drugs, mainly *Banisteriopsis* potions, administered during collective rituals in which shamans are ready to 'explain' a sequence of visions, a consensus is thus being established with reference to the chain of energies provided by the Master of Animals. An extraordinary complex body of spells and incantations is used by shamans to describe, orient, blend, and balance the different strands of energy and, at the same time, to extol the harmfulness of overhunting and overharvesting any given food resource.

Odour

The Desana are extremely conscious of odours, and categories of odour are important criteria in the classification of animals, fruits, people, and processed foods. Odour in general is called *sëriri* and is said to be the consequence of heat, *ahsíri*, the heat of the visible sun being meant. Two overall categories are distinguished: *waro sërigë*, 'good-odour', and *nyéro sërígë*, 'bad-odour'. Good odours are the smells of flowers, *pore suri*, from *poréri*, 'to flower', and *sëríri*, 'odour'. Bad odours are mainly body odours; in the case of animals they refer to musk glands, estrous odours, or the peculiar odours of fish and insects; in the case of humans, most bad odours are associated with menstrual blood.

The concept of odour is not limited to a purely sensorial experience, but includes what we might call an 'air', or an ill-defined sensation of attraction, repulsion, or fear. The Desana state this quite clearly when they say that odours are perceived not only by the nose, but that they constitute an element of communication which somehow involves the whole body. Such abstract odours are expressed, for example, by saying *mahsá sëriró*, 'people-odour', or *nomé sëriró*, 'women-odour'; this refers to *deyóri*, to an unseen presence. Or one might say, upon entering a certain territory: *mahsá vihígë yimí*, 'people-smelling-it is', even if there is no evidence at all of any human activity. To say *nomé vihígë yimí* refers to a man who is looking for adventures, and the word *vihígë* is derived from *vihíri*, 'to contaminate', to 'pollute', and is used in describing the incompatibility of partners because of conflicting marriage rules, or the inedibility of foods because of their particular state. When saying *nomé siriri*, 'woman-smell', however, one refers to a 'transparent, grid-like' quality called *siriro*, which allows smells to be perceived by the olfactory organs. Thus, *mahsá siriri*, 'people-smell', refers to body odours in general; *omá siríri* is the peculiar odour a person 'carries', *omári*, and exudes.

Shamans will often refer to odours when pronouncing spells during increase rituals; the following expressions are an example:

nomé pore suri	women-good-odour
*vai-mëra pore suri*game	animals-good-odour
vai pore suri	fish-good-odour
nëngë pore suri	forest-good-odour
goró pore suri	open space-good-odour
yeéa pore suri	shamans-good-odour
vai-mahsë pore suri	Master of Animals-good-odour

In their spells they will recite long lists of animals to which important odours are attributed, such as:

vehkë sëriri tapir-odour
nyamá sëriri deer-odour
gahkí sëriri monkey-odour
bugú sëriri anteater-odour

Some human body odours are said to be attractive. The expression *máma sëriri* is derived from *mamári*, 'to make oneself young' by the use of aromatic herbs, body paint, and other adornments. But this is exceptional; what really counts are bad odours and it is said that they are common to humans and animals. The most offensive odour is that of menstrual blood: the smell of human blood, raw meat, or fish being cleaned is said to be *omá sëriri* and loathsome. Another very repulsive smell is *poa sëriri*, the smell of singeing an animal, of burning hair or feathers. Flatulence, *nyaha puri*, is thought to be far less offensive. It is the particular odour of menstruation that is mentioned by all in very emotional terms and that figures prominently in shamanic spells and ritual prescriptions. It is *piá sëriri*, a stale smell, the smell of tainted meat, of spoiled fruit, or of overcooked food. Some fruits are said to smell of musk, such as *vahsú* and *vahsúpë* (*Hevea* sp.), but others such as *umarí* (*Poraqueiba sericea*), *poé* (*Pouteria ucuquí* Schultes), *sëmé* (*Dahlbergia* sp.), *purí*, *niá-dëhka*, and others, when overripe, are said to acquire the odour of menstrual blood.

The Desana say *dií omá sëriri*, 'blood-carries-odour' to refer to certain animals and certain women. The animals in question are mainly those of the deep forest, *nëngë*, environment: tapir, deer, peccary, monkey, anteater, sloth, and the forest ants; they all are said to have the odour of menstrual blood. To worker bees the same odour is attributed. Women are said to have the same feral estrous smell, especially Desana and Tukano women, while Pira-Tapuya women are rather said to smell of fish. Pira-Tapuya men say that Desana women smell of *puíkaro*, referring to the particular odour of the carrying strap of bark they use on their baskets; or they will say that they smell of *mengá* ants, a forest species with a very strong, pungent odour. In both cases reference is made to estral odours. Desana women are also said to have the same odour as certain large (20cms.) worms called *bahpáru* that live in paraphytic plants on forest trees and are collected and smoked in bundles by Tukano men who then exchange them on ritual occasions, receiving in turn smoked game from the Desana. Desana women are directly referred to as *bahpára sërira nomé*, 'worm-odour-women', and it is interesting to observe that the name of these worms, *bahpáru*, relates to vahpára, 'opponents', referring to the members of the opposed exogamic unit. As a general rule, women of the speaker's group have a pleasant odour, except when menstruating, while those of other exogamic units are said to be foul-smelling.

These odours are said to pollute, *vihsíri*, and a menstruating woman is exposed to *being* polluted by animals. Menstruation means that she has passed from her normal, human state to an abnormal one that links her to the beasts of the forest, and in this lies a great danger, *gea-bëari*, to all men, to herself, her off-spring, and also to the game animals. Her state affects the very essence of nature's fertility and introduces a serious conflict into all man-animal relation-ships. Snakes and other poisonous animals will harm her family; forest spirits will frighten her; the hunters of her family unit will be unsuccessful. Fish will suf-fer should she go to the river, and all plants and minor game animals will be seri-ously affected if she should go to the fields.

The Desana say that because of feral estrous odours, women will attract game from far away, and hunters might profit from this. Menstruating women often claim to have erotic dreams involving 'red' male animals, and in these cases a man might take his wife along on a hunting excursion to serve as bait, because the animals will approach without fear.

A man who prepares himself ritually for a hunt does so in accordance with the animals he intends to pursue. If he is after game of the 'brownish' category, he will consume a boiled diet and will absorb crude liquid pepper through his nostrils, in order to eliminate his body odours, so the game will not catch his scent. But should he intend to hunt the large 'black' game, he will eat smoked meat and plenty of smoked pepper, in order to acquire the estrous smell that will attract the forest animals. A fisherman will follow the same rule; when about to fish for *aracú*, 'red' catfish, *pavá, soó, pogabú*, and other 'cold' fish, he will eat a diet of smoked fish and smoked pepper to make himself attractive.

When a woman is menstruating, she places herself outside all cultural norms. People will say to her: *vai-bëgë ariri mëëa vereri pebigë*, 'animal-wild-are-you-words [norms] hearing not'. She then is exposed to attacks by *vai-mahsë*, and the Indians explain that the Master of Animals himself does not respect any exogamic rules and that he simply turns into an aggressive male. He and his 'black' and 'red' animals might pollute the woman and, in this way, do harm to her and to her kin. While sex relations between men and women are controlled by strict cultural rules, those existing between *vai-mahsë* and his animals – including menstruating women – are utterly uncontrolled and, therefore, of a dangerously dissociating nature. Should such a woman die, her animal essence would enter one of the 'hill houses' where the game animals dwell.

Children should never be near women in parturition, nor should they be allowed to see the butchering of game. They should not be exposed to the odours of singeing or smoking game or fish, nor to the odour of roasting, especially when the old people roast and eat liver, which is their privilege. All this would be extremely harmful because of the polluting smell of blood.

Flavour

Flavour is an important attribute of human beings; it is of a certain importance in fruits, but of no importance in animals. In food preparations, however, it is an essential quality.

Flavour is *ësiri*, and the principal categories are *mukúro*, 'bitterness', *ëmisiri*, 'sweetness', *piarí*, 'acidity', *uhúri*, 'astringency', and *puriri*, 'spice'. With reference to people, only 'bitterness' and 'sweetness' are distinguished, and these are believed to be inherent qualities of a person. If one should use an expression like *ëmisiri bogá*, 'sweetness-energy', an abstract quality of compatibility between people is meant, and not a sensorial fact.

The nature of flavours is described in the following manner: the white primordial brilliance of the invisible sun gave origin to heat, heat turned into colour, colour and heat combined into odour and so gave origin to flavour. This is an abstract *bogá* circuit that always returns to the sun. The actual, transformational circuit of flavour has the following stages: life is heat, and heat gives origin to yellow maleness and red femaleness. Their combination, or impregnation, has the flavour of white peanuts, that is, a fruit that is compared to testes. The next phase is the odour of gestation and ripeness: the foetus now acquires its particular flavour, according to its parentage. The last phase is birth, which is the end result of flavour combinations; the child now has his or her characteristic flavour which will be carried throughout life and passed on to another generation.

Flavours are part of the exogamic system; compatible marriage partners are those who have opposite flavours. To a sweet-flavoured Pira-Tapuya or Tukano woman, Desana semen, *dehkó mukúri bogá*, is bitter, and, therefore, acceptable, but a 'sweet' Desana woman cannot marry an equally 'sweet', *dehkó imísiri bogá*, Desana man; the same is true in reverse.

Transformation

The *edible* and the *marriageable* are both the result of cultural processing, and the Desana concept of transformation links cooking and gestation into a closely related pair. Desana theories of conception and fetal development are discussed first.

The choice of the colours yellow and red is based upon the belief that the human embryo is the product of semen, *ëma momé*, lit. 'male-honey', becoming mixed with female blood proceeding from the liver, *dií diari ohokaríri*, lit. 'blood-red-vital'. The entire concept of colour energies revolves around this idea which, in turn, is based upon the certainty that female blood *must* be a basic component of life, since menstruation, which is 'putrid' blood, stops as soon as conception has taken place. Every coitus is believed to fertilize the woman's blood which, eventually, develops in one of two directions: the birth of a child, or menstruation. In the first case, the process is believed to be as follows: the woman's 'vital blood' is imagined as a mass of small red dots that are thought to be 'very hot'. At their contact with male emission, these dots first become 'heated', a stage during which the yellow male element predominates. This process is visualized as a bright yellow background upon which a number of moving luminous dots are projected. This visual image is designated as *noméri*, lit. 'to paint with fine dots', and is said to be a fleeting sensation perceived by both partners during intercourse. It is also said to be a frequent visual sensation at the onset of drug-induced hallucinations (Reichel Dolmatoff 1978a). But soon the red element increases in quantity and temperature, and now begins to 'cook' the man's semen, a process which, during at least the first month of pregnancy, is said to cause acute discomfort to the man. The respective imagery describes a swirling multitude of large luminous dots which now dominate over the red element. This image is called *dobéri*, lit. 'to paint with large dots', and is also said to be a hallucinatory pattern perceived during a deeper level of trance. Both *noméri* and *dobéri* patterns will flash in the imagination of the prospective father, who thus believes he is able to see how his semen is being 'cooked'. At this stage, the pregnant woman finds herself in a condition called *nomé kéeri*, 'woman-dreaming', an expression with a double meaning; in one sense it refers to the woman seeing the moving mass of red dots, but in another sense the term *kéeri* can be interpreted as the plural form of *kée*, a bundle or package, such as the leaf-wrapped fish that are put into the hot embers to roast, or rather, to steam. This practice is frowned upon because by eating this food couples are likely to have too many children. When speaking here of the woman as 'dreaming', what is meant is the imagery of the man introducing a 'bundle' of semen into her womb. During the respective rituals the shaman will chant: *mariré sorará yinyóra*, 'us-cooking-they are'. At birth the child is 'done', it has been transformed and thus enters into a new dimension of existence. It has become 'edible' and in due time will be 'eaten' by a member of another exogamic group.

In the second case, when menstruating does take place, the process is imagined thus: the man's semen initially did impregnate the woman, but her blood was too hot and she 'overcooked' the mixture before it could solidify into an incipient embryo. The mixture went stale, became putrid, and was eventually expelled; the potential life died, began to rot, and was finally ejected in the form of menstruation. To the Desana every menstruation signifies the death of a child; menstrual blood is a dead sibling of a living child and is being referred to as such.

Desana theories of conception imply a number of other aspects of importance. In the first place, every new life that is created by the fusion of yellow semen and red blood becomes the carrier of chromatic energies which now enter the wider circuit of birth and individual development. This circuit must be maintained because it is the very essence of the continuity of society and nature. In fact, man is *bogá*: he is part and parcel of the circuit; semen and blood must combine and must transmit the flow of parental energies. But this will happen only if the child was conceived under culturally prescribed conditions. Both parents should have observed all food restrictions: they should have eaten 'black' or 'red' game only if it was prepared according to specific norms. They should have eaten sparingly and should have consumed few foods that are thought to stimulate sexual activity. According to the Desana, all children should thus be carefully planned by procreating them only in conditions of ritual purity. If not, the offspring is likely to lack respect for tribal traditions; children will grow up into unruly adolescents, incestuous lovers, and, eventually, into social misfits.

Shamans believe that all life processes are the results of these chromatic energies. By this they mean not only all biological processes such as conception, gestation, birth, and the ensuing development of the individual through puberty, maturity, illness, and death, but also animal reproduction, plant growth, and the change of seasons. Into the same category of processes I shall include here transformations such as cooking, the fermentation of beer, the processing of bitter manioc, the firing of pottery, the action of fish poisons, the production of honey in a beehive, and many other procedures, all of which imply substantial chemical changes. Hallucinations, whether brought about by drugs or by endogenous means, such as sensorial privations, are also thought to be a most important result of colour 'energies'.

I have said that the liver is believed to be the organ that, during the approximately twenty-eight days of the menstrual cycle, accumulates and eventually discharges the 'rotten' blood, *dií nyíri*, lit. 'black blood'. The liver is called *nyéme turi*, 'darkish-section', an expression that refers to the moon, *nyamíri mahsó turi*. Sun is semen, and his sister, Moon, is a blood-bloated liver.

Menstruation is an event surrounded by anxieties that have led to a large body of restrictions. We have seen that 'living blood' eventually is being overcooked, turns stale, and begins to putrify. Just like a fruit, it passes from a state of ripeness, of being 'cooked and done', *bogë*, into overripeness, and hence turns *boári*, that is, a state of incipient putrefaction characterized by decoloration, odour, and flavour. This marks a state of great danger, because now an energy potential is seen to have failed, an expected input has been rejected, and the vital *bogá* circuit is in danger of being interrupted. This is especially disturbing because women themselves are held responsible for this precarious state. The Desana identify menstruation with the estrous cycle of game animals and say that women come in heat, '*gëyári diari*', like animals. It is believed that during these days a woman stands quite outside of human society, quite outside of culture, and has become a receptive she-animal which exposes society to shame and pollution. She is imagined as being completely cut off from all chromatic energies, except the sickly violet colour of lunar putrefaction, and now belongs to *vai-mëra turi*, 'game animal-system'; as a matter of fact, the woman has turned into an animal, *irá nomé vai-mëra waro dohpá*. And she herself is accountable; if she had obeyed cultural rules, she would have become pregnant, but by menstruating she has separated herself from all human conventions. As an estrous female she now immediately attracts the attention of all male animals, especially of rutting deer, and thus exposes herself to all kinds of dangers. Above all, the Master of Animals will persecute her and will endanger all members of her household. She is not allowed to go to the fields, for fear of animals attacking her. A menstruating woman is said to be similar to *perá*, 'beasts' or vermin such as snakes, frogs, crabs, or ants. All these evil-smelling animals bite or sting, that is, they are 'poisonous', but the main characteristic they have in common is that they all shed their skins, that they undergo a short-term metamorphosis after which they return once more to a normal state. Menstruation is said to be such a shedding of the skin, after which the woman returns, is 'reborn', to her human and cultural functions and becomes receptive once more. In her transformation she again acquires her colour energies and so becomes once more a vehicle for transmission in the great energy cycle.

I have mentioned that ripeness is called *bogë*. This is a key concept in Desana theories of energy and transformation, and it must be explained in some more detail. The term *bogë*, as applied to menstruation, implies pollution. It stands for the near putrid and is compared to filth, carrion, or rotten fish. It is said to be 'cold' and 'acid'. Its colour is, typically, said to be 'the colour of liver'. It causes not only repulsion, but is thought to be directly a pathogenic agent. But when applied to animals, fruits, and processed foods, *bogë* stands for the edible, the permissible. While blackness and redness in animals and fruits represent dangers and are said to have the odour of menstrual, estrous blood, or of musk, most brownish animals are *bogë*. It is the brownish animals the hunters pursue; they are transformed animals, animals that have been 'cooked' by *vai-mahsë*, and they are 'warm' and 'sweet'. They have reached a ripeness that makes them edible and profitable.

But all other foodstuffs must be transformed into *bogë* foods before they are fit to be consumed. To accomplish this, foods must be processed in various ways. In general terms, game animals such as tapir, deer, white-lipped peccary, monkey, and some others must be smoked. These animals are said to have gamy meat, with a rank musky or estrous smell. If anteater is to be eaten, it has to be smoked. Among birds, curassow and trumpeter bird are smoked. Practically all catfish, *vaipë*, are smoked, and so is caiman. All animals that contain 'fat', for example *pavá* fish or curassow, must be smoked with special care. Smoking is said to have several effects: in the first place, it eliminates all unpleasant odours; in the second place, the 'yellow' male component disappears and the meat turns red, a colour that, in this context, is desirable. These animals, most of which inhabit the *nëngë* environment of deep rainforest, are said to feed on oily and strong-smelling fruits that are thought to be harmful to men, under certain conditions. Smoking also eliminates fat, *ëye*, which is associated with semen and, although said to have feral smell, is believed to cause undesirable sexual potency. For this very reason, roasting is frowned upon, especially if done by young people, and only foodstuffs such as very small fish, small pigeons, and certain larvae, *pingárämë*, are eaten roasted.

But however well-smoked the game might be, it usually is also cooked before being consumed. As a rule, all *bogë* animals should be cooked carefully; game and fish should never be combined in the same pot, since this would amount to pollution. 'Black' brocket deer should never be combined with avocados because the strong male associations of both would make the consumer sexually too potent and he would engender twins. Larvae should not be eaten with meat or fish, nor should a certain piranha be eaten together with other fish, but can be consumed only with cassava bread. All 'black', 'red', and 'cold' fish must be smoked and then boiled, but *bogë* fish are boiled without being smoked first. A favourite *bogë* food is called *bahurí*, 'mixture', and consists of small brownish fish boiled with cassava starch until it forms a thick brown broth. 'Warm' wild-growing fruits such as *nyumú* (*Jessenia polycarpa*), *sorá* (*Anacadium occidentale*), *mahá vahsú* (*Hevea* sp.), *karé* (*Chrysophyllum vulgare*), *mëë* (*Phytolacca rivenoides*) can be cooked and eaten separately, but 'cold' fruits such as *sëmé* (*Dahlbergia* sp.), *neé* (*Mauritia flexuosa*), *mihí* (*Euterpe olercaea*), *ëngá* (*Orbignya* sp.), *vahsá* (*Hevea* sp.), *vahsú* (*Hevea* sp.), *toá* or *vivapichuna* (LG) must be boiled in cassava broth, *nyohká*, which is 'very hot'. Cassava tubers must always be left for three days in the shallow water of the creek before they can be processed into flour, bread, or starch. One Indian said: "Cassava must be transformed for three days to turn *bogé*, just like beer in a trough, or people at a ritual exchange". These are only a few of the innumerable restrictions and recommendations for preparing and combining different foods. When people are eating, a bystander will sometimes say: *mereké*, 'combine well!' A father will say the same to his son who is courting a girl, and it is significant that the verb *mererí*, 'to combine', should be so closely related to *pererí*, 'to contaminate'.

The reasons for most of these rules and restrictions are verbalized by many people as dangers to the consumer's health, but when pressed for details, people will say that the real danger in not observing all restrictions would be an uncontrolled increase in male and female sexuality and the procreation of too many children. This is said in a very matter-of-fact way and is emphatically corroborated by shamans who will add that the consequences of unrestricted food consumption would lead to rape, incest, and the seduction of prepubertal youths. To give another example, between new moon and first quarter sexual intercourse is prohibited; around and at full moon it is allowed, only to be prohibited again during the waning of the moon and the three nights of darkness. This cycle is geared to hunting and fishing activities; fishing is said to be most profitable in dark nights, between new moon and first quarter, but when the moon becomes brighter, hunting and fishing must be interrupted, to be resumed during the waning of the moon and during the dark nights. Shamans say that this programming is quite intentional, to keep the men away from their women at night. The older women support the shamans in their admonitions concerning these rules, and both are quite blunt about the birth control aspects of them. These are not dogmatic statements of extreme positions, but are common enough ways of expressing concern about population increase.

Cooking, *sorarí*, is a very important process indeed. The word is related to *suriro*, glossed as 'essential condition, specific state', and by cooking an important change in 'essence' takes place. Cooking is said to be a process of 'combining' things, *sorá bohkarí*, 'to-cook-to meet', is an expression often used in shamanic language. Water, heat, colours, and flavours combine and are transformed into energies which will pass on to the consumers and to their offspring. The word *bohkári* means not only 'to combine', but 'to make profitable', that is, edible. As a matter of fact, any raw and uncooked food would be *vihsíri*, 'polluted' or 'polluting', and would produce in the consumer a state which, far from being transitory, would require lengthy shamanic attention.

The process of cooking and boiling is said to consist of several successive phases. The first is called *sumu pori*, 'bubbles-forming', from *pori*, 'to bring forth' or 'to germinate'; the second is *sumu parí*, 'bubbles-floating', from *payári*, 'to float'; the next phase is called *nyairí*, by which the food is declared to be ready and done or 'eager to be eaten', as one Indian put it. During phase two, the floating bubbles are skimmed off with a gourd spoon because they are said to be 'like menstrual blood', especially when 'black' or 'red' game is being boiled. The expression *nyairi* deserves a few explanatory words. In the beginning of time, during the great World Fire, Tinamou hid in a gourd vessel and thus was saved from destruction. Analysis of this myth reveals that, after first fertilizing the world with the Flood, the sun now was 'cooking the world'; Tinamou was a phallic bird and the gourd vessel was the vagina of the Daughter of the Sun. When the bird emerged alive, it sang *nyairó-ro-ro*, an expression which was glossed by my informants as either: 'I am cooked', 'I am done', or 'I am saved'. The reason why Tinamou was the only survivor of the World Fire lies in the fact that this bird lays remarkably brilliant-shelled eggs of many different colours and hues; it thus saved the colour energies from destruction.

Opposed exogamic groups refer to each other as *nomé sori mahsá*, 'women-provide-people'; the verb *sori*, meaning 'to supply, to get ready, to deliver', is closely related to *sorári*, 'to cook'. The opposed group are 'cooking' their girls before exchanging them. The second day of a ritual exchange of women and food is called *boo-në*, meaning 'well-done day', in the sense of, by then, things being well cooked; on that day the nubile girls are turned over to the complementary exogamic unit, the beer is ready to be consumed, and the smoked fish and game are being exchanged. The same concept is expressed in the custom of turning over the young woman together with a younger sister or younger brother, *buhibó/penyamë*, who join their sister in her new virilocal longhouse and eventually, after reaching puberty, marry into it. During the three or four years this period might last, the children are under the care of their sister's father-in-law, who has to take care of their education in the traditions of his local group. This process too is referred to as 'cooking' and the common expression for it is *sorá ehó mahsúri*, 'to cook-to bring up', alluding to the sister or brother of the newly acquired woman being 'cooked', so he or she can eventually marry a suitable member of the longhouse.

The cooking metaphor always refers to the necessity of thus processing raw materials (food, women) proceeding from *other* social or geographical dimensions than one's own, before they can be used and eventually consumed. This idea is expressed in many aspects of Desana culture. To further illustrate this point I shall briefly describe some symbolic aspects of the manufacture of cooking vessels. Among the Desana, only women manufacture pottery and good plastic clay must be fetched by them from certain spots that lie outside their territory, but within either Pira-Tapuya or Tukano territory. Similarly, Pira-Tapuya women gather clay in Desana or Tukano territory, while Tukano women obtain theirs from Desana or Pira-Tapuya territory. The bluish clay is called *mata gamí*, 'crab clay', because of the property it shares with river crabs, turning from a bluish-gray to red, when being fired or cooked. After fashioning a circular base from a flattened coil of clay, about ten or twenty centimeters in diameter, the potter will form with another rope of rolled clay a hexagonal outline on top of this disc and begins to build up the vessel walls by coiling the ropes one on top of the other. The humid surface is then scraped with a short straight piece of wood called *mëhpëri*, a word having a phallic connotation, with which the raised hexagonal design and the coils are eliminated and the walls are smoothed. Next, the inside and outside of the walls are smoothed with a convex piece of gourd, *koa soropéro*, that has a female connotation. The pots are now left to dry for three days. On the third day their surface is burnished with a smooth, elongated pebble called *varári yee*, 'back-and-forth-copulator', from *vari*, 'to go', *áriri*, 'to come', and *yeéri*, 'to copulate'. The pebble, a very hard yellow chert, must come from the outside the Vaupés territory, generally from the region of the Apaporis River, or from a hill called *varári yeégë*, near La Pedrera, on the Caquetá River. The vessels are now decorated with incised or painted motifs surrounding the mouth of the cooking pot, the designs consisting of one of five or six named graphic symbols representing the birth-giving anaconda, a vagina, a 'cooking' design of the *noméri* or *dobéri* type, a clitoris ('pineapple-bone') design, or a motif indicating sprouting vegetation, that is, offspring. After the pots have been fired with specific firewoods, the inside is painted with the juice of the macerated green leaves of *Solanum quitoense*, called *ëhtoká*, and each vessel is now placed upside down over one of the three short tubular potstands of clay, *peamé yeéri*, 'hearth-penis', in explicit imitation of coitus. The firewood is arranged between the three stands forming another triangular pattern, so that the layout of the hearth is hexagonal, and the transformation takes place under the sign of the crystal. A fire of *muhí* leaves, the same that are used for thatch, produces a very thick black smoke which, combining with the plant juice, gives the inside of the vessel a permanent brilliant black colour. The vessel is now imagined as representing a colour sequence; once it is put upon the hearth, between the three potstands, the lower part is said to be yellow, because of the flames, the convex middle part is red because this part is 'boiling' and 'cooking', and the upper part has a greenish connotation, not in terms of colour, but in terms of the imagery of the sprouting forth of growth. The significant aspect is this: a woman's body is a cooking pot; Desana women paint around their waists a belt of black design motifs. On ritual occasions, nubile girls will add to this a so-called *vahsú* design consisting of a thick vertical line beginning at the umbilicus, rising between the breasts, whence it branches into bicornuate scrolls that encircle each breast and symbolize the sprouting *vahsú* (*Hevea* sp.) tree, with its milky latex. I might add here that each of the three phallic potstands represents one of the exogamic units: Desana, Pira-Tapuya, and Tukano, whose men are 'cooking' the woman/vessel. The entire image finds its idiomatic expression in the designation *uári soró*, 'big pot', for women in an advanced state of pregnancy: an alternative expression is *uári sarú*, the last word being derived from *saruári*, 'to become pot-shaped'.

A similar symbolic transformation is implicit in smoking fish or game. A tripod of wooden poles, called *vai këya*, 'fish-grid', represents the men of the three exogamic units. The firewood is distributed on the ground so as to form another triangle, the ground plan thus acquiring a hexagonal shape. The fish or game that are being smoked on the grid must come from outside the consumer's territory and is identified with the women of the complementary group, designated here as *vai-mahsá nomé*, 'fish-people-women', or *vai-mëra nomé*, 'game animal-women'. The entire tripod structure is imagined as having three coloured layers: the lower part is yellow, represented by the flames; the central part, the grid, is said to be red because there 'the food turns red' in the smoke; and the upper part from which the processed food is removed is *bogë*, the brownish colour of all edible foods.

The shamanic curing of illness is another process of transformation that eventually leads to the 'rebirth' of the patient. Most diseases are defined as an unbalanced condition of colour energies, in other words, of maladaptive behaviour. Although all human beings have the same proportion of energies, their specific intensities vary individually, according to circumstance. For example, if a certain colour in a man is diagnosed through the crystal as being 'weaker' than the woman's, the shaman will summon colours, temperatures, and odours to restore the balance. This process is called *bayíri*, from *ba-kë yíri*, 'to make eat' [the patient]; but this is meant in an abstract sense; the shaman will imbue some beverage, *bayíra*, with the necessary energies, after having obtained these from animal or plant sources, or from his crystal. This procedure is said to be, in every sense, a sexual impregnation, followed by the patient's going through the different phases of gestation and 'cooking'.

Food Restrictions, Preferences, and Ecology

I have repeatedly referred here to the fact that the Desana and their neighbours attribute to certain game animals undesirable qualities that tend to restrict their consumption, while others are exempt from such restrictions and can be consumed without any special precautions. In the case of restrictions we cannot speak of 'avoidances'. The so-called 'black' or 'red' animals are not avoided; they simply are hunted only very occasionally, and if so, their meat has to be processed in special ways, before it becomes fit for consumption. They are risky food, *bari guári*; their evil estrous and musky odours have to be eliminated by singeing, smoking, and cooking, and even then, persons such as menstruating or child-bearing women, prepubertal youths, or sick persons, that is, people who are involved in giving birth, or expect to be 'reborn', are not allowed to eat this kind of game. The game of restricted, although not tabooed, use consists mainly of tapir, deer, and white-lipped peccary. These offer large amounts of meat; they are fairly frequent in their forest environment; they are rarely pursued, however. The preferred game are 'brownish' animals, the *bogë* animals, that is, the 'cooked' and thus transformed game, and these are mainly paca, agouti, cavi, and armadillo. The problem of this hunting selection is of interest, and I analyse it in some detail below. The way the Desana themselves explain this situation is presented; I believe that their interpretation might have some bearing upon similar situations in other areas.

It is obvious that the two groups of potential game animals occupy different ecological environments; the restricted game inhabit the deep interfluvial forests, *nëngë*, while the unrestricted game inhabit open forest, *tara boa*, riverbanks, *dia vehkó*, and, above all, old clearings, undergrowths, and abandoned fields, *viado*. A look at the corresponding tables 1-5 shows that, apart from the three or four major species of restricted hunting, the forest environment is inhabited by other very profitable prey such as sloth, howler monkey, woolly monkey, curassow, tortoise, and others. To hunt these animals, even in remote forest areas, is certainly not a task fraught with dangers or implying extraordinary hardships. Neither the neotropical rainforest nor the neotropical game animals represent any real danger to a fairly competent hunter. White-lipped peccary might become aggressive and chase a hunter up a tree, but I have never heard of anything worse than a bad fright or a mauled dog. The idea of physically dangerous hunting grounds is utterly unrealistic.

When speaking of these large game animals the Indians again and again refer to their bad odours, and they identify these with estrous, musky, and menstrual smells. But why should all this deter a hunter? These animals are not difficult to hunt; they can easily be stalked, they present a large target, and they yield large amounts of meat. Why then should the Desana tend to almost ignore this formidable protein source and give preference to the meek rodents? The argument reaches back to the time of mythical cultural origins.

Most of the Eastern Tukanoan groups are newcomers to the Vaupés territory; their myths, tales, and genealogical recitals speak of migrations that penetrated up the Rio Negro and into the Vaupés, Papuri, and Tiquié drainages. Since each exogamic group has its own origin myth and claims its own spot of emergence, it is clear that considerable time-depth underlies the consolidation of the twenty or so tribes we have come to call the Eastern Tukano. But not only did different migratory groups arrive at different time periods; there already existed a native population in the Vaupés territory, which became partly assimilated by the invaders and partly continues to survive in a marginal situation. On the one hand, many interfluvial regions were inhabited by nomadic hunters and gatherers, archaic groups designated at present as Makú, remnants of which are still living in some regions. On the other hand, according to many traditions, some groups of horticulturalists such as the Tukano proper, or peoples with a strong emphasis on fishing, like the Pira-Tapuya, existed already at a time when other groups were only beginning to make their first forays into the Vaupés. Traditions referring to these migrations tell of how the newcomers routed the forest and river peoples and assimilated many of them, including a number of Makú groups, into their own emerging tribal structures. We may remember here that at the tail end of the Anaconda-Canoe the Makú servants were sitting.

Desana traditions are somewhat divided about their original point of emergence; some place it at the Ipanoré Falls, where the equatorial line crosses the Rio Negro, but some say it was at the falls of Wainambi, on the Makú-paraná, an affluent of the Papuri, and right in the centre of a traditional Makú territory. The Desana will reluctantly admit that they have a large Makú component, but still pride themselves in having a hunting and palm starch gathering tradition; they also feel somewhat uneasy in the presence of the Tukano proper, who never fail to claim primogeniture and autochthony.

The Tukano say that tapir is their ancestral animal. They do kill and eat tapir, but it continues to be a game that deserves a certain respect. Desana migration stories tell how they met Tapir at Ipanoré and were stopped by him; how they fooled Tapir and his ally, Howler monkey, and raped Tapir's womenfolk; how a Desana stole Tapir's female 'seed' and ran away to mark with it what was to be Desana territory. The stories go on, telling how they met Deer, Peccary-Women, Trumpeter-Women, Woolly Monkey, Tortoise, and all the rest, and how they overcame them by fair or foul means.

I must refer once more to the game animals and their present relationship to people. All forest animals are called *vai-mëra*, 'creatures-ancient ones'. I have mentioned already that the word *vai* or *va'i*, also meaning 'fish', is derived from *bari*, 'food', while *mëra* means 'old people', or 'the ancient ones'. The Desana say that 'all game animals were formerly people'. Now, Tapir is called *vehkë* in Desana, and this means 'father-in-law'. A certain local variety of large, very dark-coloured tapirs is called *mëë vehkë*, 'umarí-tapir', this fruit (*Poraqueiba paraensis*) being precisely the female 'seed' the Desana invaders stole from Tapir at Ipanoré. The Tukano proper are still called *vehkëa mahsá*, 'Tapir-People'. The white-lipped peccary is called *yehsé*, a term which, according to the Desana, means 'to copulate-passive female object'. They are said to be the foul-smelling womenfolk that eventually became incorporated into the Desana sib that at present is being called *yehséa mahsa*, 'White-lipped Peccary-People'.

Let me turn now to the other group of game animals, the rodents. Agouti is called *buí*, meaning 'son-in-law'. It 'belongs' to the Pira-Tapuya, just as Paca does, and so is a potential son-in-law of the Desana. Paca is called *semé*, and Desana men call their Pira-Tapuya spouses *semé-pagó*, 'paca-daughter of'. In an intentional play of words, they will also refer to them as *sëmé pagó*, '*Dahlbergia* sp.-daughter of', thus giving to understand that there exists an identification not only of women with preferred game, but also with certain forest fruits that are the preferential food of that animal, another chain of relationships that deserves study. Moreover, in myth these are the animals that talk. Tapir, deer, peccary, sloth, monkey, curassow, trumpeter, and tortoise; they all have their speaking parts in the tales that refer to the original settlement of the Vaupés area. Tapir speaks Tukano, Paca speaks Pira-Tapuya, and so on. But sometimes their language is incomprehensible and creatures like Trumpeter Bird must communicate by coarse cries and anxious gestures. Even the feeding habits of the restricted game animals express their 'otherness'; they feed on *sëmé*, *vahsú*, *vahsá*, *vahsúpë*, *poé*, *buhtí*, and other forest fruits, all of which are strong-smelling, flavoured, and oily.

The preferred game animals represent an entirely different picture. Paca, agouti, cavi, armadillo, and others are referred to as *mahsá tëróri mahára*, 'people-close by-belonging', or *poé tëoróri mahára*, 'gardens-close by-belonging'. They all share man's food in that they feed on tubers, roots, manioc peel, and pineapple. They are said to be attracted by smoke, because they feed on kitchen refuse; they are starch eaters, and so they have a pleasant body odour, and their meat is white and not strongly flavoured; it is *bogë*. These animals, too, talk, but they do so in the language of 'people'; they call out in Desana. And they, too, are women: *semé-nomé*, 'Paca-Women', belong to a Desana sib who marry Pira-Tapuya or Tukano men; *buía nomé*, 'Agouti-Women', belong to a Pira-Tapuya sib with whom the Desana intermarry; and *bohsó nomé*, 'Cavi-Women', belong to a Tukano sib that marries Desana or Pira-Tapuya men. At present, *pamú nomé*, 'Armadillo-Women', belonging to a sib of the Karapana tribe, marry into Desana sibs.

It will become clear now why the large game animals of the forest environment should be of restricted use. In the depths of tribal myths, we are told, events took place that have come to constitute a warning to all men, and grounds for condemnation of all animals; they are tales of nature against culture. Anaconda-Woman used to live in a lagoon on top of a hill near Sao Gabriel, from where she watched the Milky Way. Once, when she was menstruating and shedding her skin, her brother, Jaguar, attacked her with his blowgun and killed her. It is said that he raped her and so Anaconda, just like the incestuous Moon, became a '*maculata*', covered with large black *dobéri* dots, and ever since has had to live as an animal. Another tale is this: when the First Men were gathered to receive the divine gift of the narcotic plant that would forever provide them with a link with the invisible, divine world, the animals of the forest were with them, on an equal footing with people. But, under the influence of the drug they separated forever; while men understood the dazzling visions as a revelation, a moral teaching of profound relevance to the ordering of social relations, the animals were overwhelmed and lost all control. They began 'to eat their tails', *ira poréru bayóra*; they 'ate their own flesh', *ira bahsí dü bayóra*; in other words, they committed incest. And ever since their vital energies do not reach beyond the biological sphere, and only man is transcendental.

The meaning becomes clear now; procreation on the animal level condemns both partners to an animal existence. At menstruation, when women, by their biological condition, 'become like animals', they are likely to fall prey to dark animal forces that might separate them from culture altogether. In menstruating women, the Desana believe that the distance between humans and animals has disappeared. *Vai-mahsë* himself, a being that, often enough, symbolises man's animal nature and who is not bound by any times to the laws of exogamy, will be the first to find himself attracted by the women. The black animals once were humans; they want to be humans again and want to participate in men's colour circuit; but since they cannot attain their goal, they at least try to sting and bite the woman and to cause her abdominal pains with sharp claws, and fangs, and beaks, tearing at her body in dreams and nightmares.

A few additional remarks are in order here. I have mentioned the Desana belief that certain rocky hill formations deep in the forest are the supernatural wombs where game animals multiply and are being 'cooked' by the Master of Animals, who then periodically releases them to stray in the forest as *bogë* game. The Desana say that these are precisely the large game animals and that they formerly were 'people', but had been condemned to lead an animal existence in the hills and to serve as food to the Desana because they 'did not obey customs'. The humanoid beings that are thought to dwell inside these abodes as 'condemned' creatures are Desana who placed themselves outside all cultural conventions and so became animals. They are women who were attacked while menstruating; they are the incestuous, the deviants, those who renounced all social norms and so cannot participate in the human-solar energy cycle, but have to depend upon the hunters for the transmission of their vital energies. Although all animals that emerge from the hill-houses are *bogë*, sometimes a hunter will come upon a large male, an old tapir, or a deer that came along with the others to show them the trails and salt licks. Such an animal is *nyehkë*, an ancestor; it may be killed and eaten but, of course, it has to be smoked and cooked and prayed over before its meat will become *bogë*. Just as these 'ancient animals' of the deep forest regions are the providers of meat, so the Makú who live at present with or near the Desana are their providers, *ai gari korégë*, an expression meaning 'those who bring what is expected'; that is, those who bring *bogë* food. The Desana call these assimilated Makú by the name of *poyá*, meaning a person who has 'passed'; the singular form, in shamanic language, is *poyë*, and that, of course, means *bogë*; they have 'passed', in that they have become 'cooked'.

This also might explain why pregnant, lactating, or menstruating women must not eat big game, because the 'eating' would be equivalent to pollution from a noncultural source. The food restrictions of the prepubertal stage have the same origin: uterine or prepubertal development – in the preinitiation sense – are thought to be exposed to seminal pollution from uncultured beasts.

It may reasonably be said that all this does not offer yet a 'rational' explanation of why the Desana and their neighbours should prefer minor game such as rodents to the far more profitable large game of the forest. A perfectly sound argument advanced by many Desana is that the food situation, as it is at present, is so satisfactory that tiresome hunting excursions into the forest are really quite unnecessary. This seems to be true in all areas where shamans and elders apply traditional controls and restrictions. And this brings me back to some initial questions.

The large game animals can be eaten as long as the person has the necessary shamanic permissions and obeys the rules of culinary preparations. Still, edibility is determined in very abstract, symbolic terms, not only in shamanic thought but also by the layman.

One might call shamanism humbug but, after all, the proof of a sound ecological adjustment is in the eating. Wherever traditional values are still in force and where shamans control all or most aspects of food procurement, protein and other resources are plentiful among the Desana; food intake is adequate and the nutritional status of the Indians seems to be satisfactory. People can afford to be selective in hunting and fishing and do not have to go to great pains to obtain game, even for large family units. It is also true that shamans occasionally will not shy away from extremely harsh reprisals, if it should become a matter of upholding rules the high adaptive values of which are known and accepted by most leading individuals. A large number of food restrictions obviously constitutes an effective mechanism for realistic ecological adaptation, and by the use of the threat of illness, shamans have a powerful influence over people.

But as soon as shamanic controls are weakened or disappear altogether, game depletion sets in. Around mission centres such as Mitú, Yavareté, Fátima, Carurú, Santa Cruz, Vacuravá, and others, all on the Vaupés River, game animals have become very scarce because of increased hunting pressure. The same has occurred, or is occurring, at Teresita, Montfort, Pira-coara, and Uacari-coara, on the Papurí River; at San Javier, on the Cuduyarí; at Uahti-maá, on the Ti River; and at the mission station of San Miguel, on the Pira-paraná, not only have the missionised Indians come to disobey their traditional restrictions and have begun to overhunt, but the economic incentives offered by government officials, missionaries (both Catholic and Protestant), rubber collectors, and others who will buy game, fish, fruits, and raw materials contribute to the depletion of resources.

In areas like the Vaupés and Papurí drainages, where culture contacts and change have strongly influenced and modified traditional concepts, the large game animals are not tabooed, may be killed, and can be eaten; they are not actively hunted because there is no pressing need. But in other regions taboos do exist. The Makú of the Makú-paraná do not eat tapir; they can kill the animal and sell or barter the meat, but to eat it is forbidden. Among most Tukanoan tribes of the Pira-paraná drainage, tapir, deer, and peccary are tabooed, although these animals may be killed and the smoked meat may be sold or exchanged with groups that do not profess this taboo. This situation is due to the fact that here I refer to territories that only recently have been exposed to outside influences and where food restrictions still include taboos and avoidances.

One might predict that, in the near future, the Desana and their neighbours will eventually begin to actively hunt, and probably decimate, the large game animals of their forests, while the Pira-paraná tribes will adopt, transitorily at least, the attitudes that now prevail among the Desana. In a sense, paratotemic animals come to constitute a valuable food reserve. Once a year, in the *umarí* season, the Desana will organize a tapir hunt; the men will go off to the forest saying *nyehkë semára ya viígë*, 'ancestors-house of-we go', and a few days later will return with plenty of smoked meat.

But in any case, the problem of game resources will eventually depend on the confrontation between outside pressures and shamanic authority, and there can be little doubt about the outcome and the consequences. One Indian said to me: "When people lose their respect for animals, they soon will lose everything else."

Notes

1. Whenever these three names are mentioned, I refer to the exogamic group called 'Tukano' – not to the Eastern Tukano in general.

2. Part of the research on which this paper is based was made possible by a 1976/1977 Guggenheim Fellowship, which is gratefully acknowledged. I also express my gratitude to the officers and staff of the Smithsonian Tropical Research Institute, Canal Zone, Panama, for a 1977 grant for library research and consultation. For other references on the Tukano, see the bibliography.

3. I am thankful for the help of Dr Hernando Garcia-Barriga, botanist, and Dr Fred Medem, zoologist, both of the Universidad Nacional, Bogotá, in identifying several species.

4. I refer to the Pira-Tapuya and Tukano proper.

5. Note that *e* is pronounced like the *e* in *que*, *je* (French); *h* is pronounced like *ch* in *ach* (German). The letters LG indicate that the respective term is taken from lengua geral.

6. The term *buru* also stands for 'undergrowth' and is sometimes affixed to the names of certain animals, much like the term *nëngë* which is affixed when one wishes to emphasise the forest habitat.

7. Many edible larvae are found in rotten palm trunks, especially in *Euterpe oleracea*, *Mauritia flexuosa*, and *Oenocarpus bataua*. The largest larvae are found in the last two. Larvae (*mojojoi* in LG) are called *pingará* in Desana. They often belong to beetles of the family Curcolionidae: those found in *Mauritia flexuosa* are *Rhynchophorus palmarum*. The Indians also eat the beetles, *mimi-doro*. Insect foods are of considerable nutritional importance among the Desana.

8. Pronounced with a nasalized e.

9. Probably *Argiope* sp., a spider with black and yellow stripes. Interestingly, these spiders leave their prey for a time at the border of their net, before they start to feed on it, just as a Desana hunter who leaves his prey *outside* the longhouse, to be retrieved by the women.

10. *Plica plica* L.

11. From some vague references. I have been given to understand that the three dividing lines used to be, or still are, alignments of astronomical relevance. It is rather interesting to note that the dividing line, in fact *any* dividing line, is called *tabú* (plural *tabúri*), from the verb *tabuuri*, 'to delimit, to establish an obstacle to penetration'.

12. *Nyohká* is a broth of boiled manioc juice: it is called manicuera in lengua geral.

Tapir

TAPIR AVOIDANCE IN THE COLOMBIAN NORTHWEST AMAZON

I

The Eastern Tukanoan Indians are divided into some twenty tribes.[1] The main characteristic of social organization is language group exogamy; in fact, each tribe speaks its own language (Jackson 1976). Ideally – that is, according to shamanic precepts – these eighteen or twenty tribes are grouped into six phratries, each one consisting of at least three tribes that stand in a relationship of sister exchange. In this chapter I shall refer to the phratry constituted by the Desana, Pira-Tapuya, and Tukano proper, who occupy mainly the drainage of the Papuri river, a major western affluent of the Vaupés river.

Although it might appear to the superficial observer that these three tribes or, in fact, all Eastern Tukanoans,[2] share an essentially common culture based upon one single body of traditions, widespread resource homogeneity and a generalized inventory of material culture, there do exist marked differences owing to a variety of intellectual orientations and also to different local ethnohistorical traditions. The Eastern Tukanoans are not a homogeneous people who would have developed from a common stock, but they rather are congenerics of larger or smaller groups, some of which are remnants of older populations. Others, perhaps most of them, are descended from invaders, newcomers from other regions who, for one reason or another, had penetrated upriver and beyond the rapids and falls into this vast rainforest region that occupies a somewhat marginal position with reference to the wide floodplain of the Amazon Basin. From their traditions it seems that these different peoples met and mixed, raided each other or formed alliances, creating in the course of generations the kind of generalized culture that, when perceived only at its surface level, appears to be homogeneous.

There also is an apparent overall similarity in the origin myths of all these tribes. It is told by each group in its own particular version that the ancestors came from the east from where the sun rises, and that they slowly penetrated the land by travelling upriver. Another cycle of myths tells of a semi-divine being who carried a magic staff that he thrust into the riverbank to find a place where it would stand upright and not cast a shadow. He eventually found that spot on the equatorial line, and there he created mankind. Each tribe has a repertoire of hundreds of tales that refer to the deeds of the ancestors, to their courage, their determination, not to speak of their superiority to everything they encountered on their perilous voyage.

However, as one probes deeper into these oral traditions, if one discusses and analyzes the textual records with the help of knowledgeable elders, then quite another image beings to emerge. There exist, it would seem, two parallel traditions: one is that of a glorified mythical conquest; the other is the prosaic memory of hardships and fear. Above all, there are the origin myths of how the First People sprang forth miraculously and of how they settled the land and of how a group of agnatic brothers, already specialized as chiefs, shamans, singers, warriors, and servants, built their huge longhouses, danced and sang, and took possession of the land. This is the glory of the ancestors, the ancient ones, the wise shamans and fierce war chiefs who became the progenitors of distinguished lineages. But then another story emerges: the story of a few desperate, hungry men who penetrated into a strange country full of dangers. Among these dangers were 'other beings' that uttered incomprehensible sounds and lived in a strange way; these beings were hostile to all outsiders and were a threat to them. The story is one of struggle for survival.

I am referring here to the Desana, the Pira-Tapuya, and some others, but their case is far from unique; on the contrary, the Northwest Amazon has always been a region of change and movement. For thousands of years, wandering groups, raiding parties, and small bands of men have moved here and there, lost and expatriate, as the last survivors of some disaster, or for any other reason. On the individual level, survival was not too difficult because the tropical rainforest has many resources, even for people with a very simple tool kit; but on a social level, the level of reproductive sex and family life, the matter was far more difficult. If the wandering groups included some women, then most likely they were close kin and the problem of incest arose. The only choice left was the abduction of women from another tribe, and this, of course, meant violence. And so again, the myths and narratives are replete with episodes that, under the guise of cautionary tales, speak of abducted women, women found and lost, women who ran away, and women who would commit any kind of treachery. There exists, then, a large body of oral traditions that refer to the slow process of finding a mate. At first, there are references to incestuous relationships; then came the search for almost any mate from the outside, generally acquired by abduction and often enough preceded by the murder of the women's male kinsmen. Until, at long last, alliances began to be formed; groups of different peoples met and exchanged marriageable women and, eventually, elaborated a formalized ritual. There exists another large body of myths and tales that describe this process that leads from incest to exogamy, from chaos to order, from the violent abduction of any mate to ritualized sister exchange. This process is the all-pervading theme of Tukanoan oral literature.

It is here where, from the native point of view, the abstract problem of man-animal relationships arises and where animals are attributed with symbolic values. The point is that, in practically all of the texts I have collected among the Eastern Tukanoans, animals play the roles of people. Not that they turn into people or that people turn into animals; not that they descend from animals or anything like this; but that they are like animals. The animal image is used to describe 'other' people – not only 'other' women but other tribes.

According to traditions preserved in myths, tales, genealogies, spells, songs, descriptions of ritual, and so forth, several groups of people were already established in the Vaupés territory before the arrival of the Desana and other Tukanoan tribes. These people were the *behkára* and the *poyá*. The *behkára* were a large tribe of sedentary agriculturalists who lived in longhouses surrounded by manioc fields; the Desana called them 'Tapir People'. The *poyá* were nomadic hunter-gatherers who, in small bands, roamed the deep forests of the interfluvial regions, appearing here and there, on river-banks, near a longhouse, or a planted field, only to disappear again into the depths of the forest.

In the course of time the Tukanoans prevailed. They established themselves all over the Vaupés territory, and at present they can be found in the vast regions lying between the Vaupés river, the Apaporis, the Tiquié, and parts of the Rio Negro, mainly in Colombia but also in Brazil.

Although the modern Tukanoans derive their basic sustenance from their manioc fields, hunting and fishing are important activities, and fruit gathering in the forest constitutes another major source of food. In fact, emotionally, the hunt is a focus of many expectations and fears, gratifications and anxieties, of basic values and vague aversions that together constitute a very complex system of thoughts and actions. Among the many game animals of the Amazonian fauna, three stand out in nature as well as in the emotional world of the Tukanoan hunter: tapir, deer, and peccary. They are the largest mammals of the tropical rainforest, and they are fairly abundant and not difficult to hunt. Still, the Indians are reluctant to kill them and prefer to hunt paca, agouti, armadillo, tinamou and guan. One might wonder then why they should deprive themselves of such a plentiful source of proteins and fats as that offered by the three large forest mammals. There exist, of course, certain practical considerations: first of all, tapirs are not very plentiful in the forest, deer are found somewhat more often, and only peccaries can be said to be abundant. Tapirs, it is true, can be called by the hunter, but deer and peccaries must be tracked, often for long distances. To hunt them in the depths of the interfluvial forests is a matter of two or three days at least, and the lesser game animals can be found at short distances from residential compounds and the fields. Tukanoans agree that the large game animals would provide greater quantities of meat, but they add that the quality is poor; the meat is musky and fat, and it is not easily digestible. Many are forbidden to eat it; children, expectant mothers, and women who are still nursing a baby must not eat the meat of such forest animals as tapir, deer, peccary, woolly monkey, curassow, trumpeter bird, or tortoise.

Above all, the tapir must be avoided; it is the 'old man' (*bëgë*) of the forest, and only rarely will the more tradition-minded Tukanoans kill and eat it. I shall attempt here to analyze some of the reasons for this restriction, and in doing so I shall approach the question through a body of ethnographic observations backed by original texts collected during a long-term association with Colombian rainforest tribes.[3]

II

In the languages of the Desana and Tukano,[4] the tapir is called *vehkë*, in Pira-Tapuya it is *behkë*, and in all three languages this term also means 'father-in-law'.[5] The Tapir People that the Desana and Pira-Tapuya encountered when they first entered the Vaupés territory were called by them *behkára*, which is the same word; and, at present, *behkára* is the name the Desana give to the Kuripáko, a large group of Arawakan tribes that live north of the Vaupés territory, mainly along the Isana river. In fact, a subgroup of the Kuripáko is called *tapiíra*, and all of the Arawakan tribes living to the north of the Tukanoans are generally referred to as Tapir People. It must be added that in many myths and tales of the Desana and other Tukanoan tribes, the tapir is described either as a respected or as a ridiculed father-in-law figure.

Before going into the details of tapir imagery and symbolism I shall first describe the way in which the Desana view the zoological species. A tapir is seen as a huge and heavy beast, very powerful and fast-moving, but clumsy and quite inoffensive; only when wounded might a tapir bite a hunter, a predator, or a dog. Otherwise, it is a cunning, yet slow-witted brute. Tapirs will open trails in the dense underbrush that lead straight to the river's edge and, when frightened, will blindly rush along these tunnels to plunge into the water. They will not hide or silently scuttle away but will noisily overrun all obstacles on their trail. The tapir's large genitals are frequently commented upon by the Indians, and it is thought that tapirs are sexually very active owing to certain fruits they feed on. Indians often say that there is a close relationship between a person's or an animal's food habits and sexual behaviour, and since tapirs feed on acidic forest fruits and oily nuts, such as the fruits of the *mirití* palm (*Mauritia flexuosa*), they are said to be examples of sexual prowess. Tapirs relish sweet-tasting *umari* (*Poraqueiba paranensis*), a fruit that has a quite definite aphrodisiac connotation. They also eat *meré*, a forest variety of *Inga* sp.; *sëmé*, the large lentil-shaped fruits of *Dahlbergia* sp. trees; and *pubú*, a large round forest fruit of unknown identity. Other foods that the tapir eats are *vahsú*, *vahsá*, *vahsúpë*, all these being the fruits of different, latex-exuding *Hevea* trees, besides *buhtí*, *niá-dëhka*, and a number of other forest products. The fruits, pods, nuts, and kernels that the tapir finds lying on the forest floor have marked fertility connotations and are said to have a strong flavour (*mukúro*) and a yellowish fatty essence (*ëye*) that might be dangerous to a person's health, not perhaps in terms of mere indigestion but rather in terms of disturbing a delicate balance of odours, flavours, and 'colour energies' that are so important in Indian nutritional theories (Reichel-Dolmatoff 1978b. See essay 2 in this book). Since, in Tukanoan ideology, food and sex are equated, the tapir's feeding habits are linked to an image of voracious sexual appetites and great fertility, both being conditions that, from a native point of view, are morally condemnable but privately enviable. However, tapirs are praised for being very clean animals that spend much time in the water. They are said to have a strong, and rather human, body odour but to lack the sexually attractive odour that, according to the Indians, characterizes some other animals.

Sometimes the tapir is jokingly referred to as *vehkë gubutí* (literally, 'foot-blunt' or 'stub-footed'), an expression alluding to its hoofed feet but with the implicit meaning of 'used, worn out, senile, impotent'. Another common epithet for the tapir is *toró vehkë* (literally, 'package-tapir'). The word *toró* or *to'ó* means 'package, bundle, bulk' and refers to the size of a tapir's testicles; the word is related to *toári* (to sting), with the implied meaning that the expression *nomé toári* (woman-to sting) refers to copulation. Another word, *toróri*, means 'big-eared one' and is a common insult among men. In fact, tapirs have rather large ears that, in some stories, have a phallic connotation. Although a large penis is a shameful thing according to Tukanoans and all these allusions to the tapir's food habits and anatomy put ridicule and shame upon this animal, they are not devoid of certain admiration.

Desana-tapir symbolic relationships develop on several different levels and use many different images. In one important image Tapir is Thunder, a powerful being who lives, surrounded by his women-folk, in a huge longhouse high up in the sky. The Desana word for thunder is *buhpú*[6], and Thunder's wife is *bëhpë* (spider), a common metaphor for vagina; significantly, the Desana term for daughter-in-law is *behpó*. In a group of myths, the first Desana takes a dose of narcotic snuff and goes to visit Thunder by climbing up to the sky on a column of tobacco smoke. Thunder is asleep when he arrives, but the Desana youth talks to his wife; she wakens her husband, and a ritual conversation develops in which the youth and Tapir eventually form an alliance. Younger Brother Desana offers his sister to Elder Brother Tapir in exchange for one of Tapir's women. In this image, then, Tapir is respected and feared; he has the roaring voice of thunder; the visitor has seen that Tapir's longhouse is inhabited by many women; but he is also aware that Tapir distrusts strangers, and so the alliance with Tapir becomes a celebrated feat.

This is a stock situation in which matters are described as fairly simple: an audacious young man, a sleepy oldster, and in the background a bevy of giggling girls. In this type of story there often is an element of rainforest Boccaccio. But many other tales describe Tapir as a wily and distrustful creature, quite unwilling to make any sort of deal with an outsider and jealously watching over his womenfolk. Tapir is described as a glutton, an egoist loath to share his property. In fact, Tapir People are said to be very hostile to strangers.

In a number of tales connected with this general topic, Tapir is described in quite unmistakable terms as practising cultural norms that are strange and unknown to the Desana. One tale describes how a party of Desana raiders hide near a longhouse, watching in wonder a Tapir initiation ritual. In other stories fun is made of Tapir's incomprehensible language; his dances are described, his boisterous songs, his ornaments, even his hammocks and mats. In fact, from detailed textual analysis of a large body of origin and migration myths, genealogies, and other traditions, it becomes clear that when the Tukanoan tribes first entered the Vaupés territory most of it was inhabited by Arawakan Indians, whose culture, language, and physical type were different from those of the newcomers. The Tukanoan invaders raided the Arawakans for women; and these raids are described in the oral literature either as hunting expeditions in which the prey are the females of a certain species or as chance encounters between men (mashsá), the Tukanoans, and beings (mërá) – the 'others', the animal-like inhabitants of the forest.

Among the Eastern Tukanoans, male initiation rites that take place at certain times of the year – called yuruparí in the Amazonian vernacular – are centred upon the use of certain large trumpets which are played in pairs, traditionally near palms or other fruit-bearing trees. From the analysis of textual sources it seems rather improbable that this ritual complex is of Tukanoan origin; it seems rather to have been taken over from the Arawakan tribes. According to shamanistic precepts, the uncommonly loud sounds emitted by the trumpets make the pollen 'vibrate' and fall down; that is, the sounds make the pollen grains, which transport the male gametes, fall on the static female parts of the palm. Symbolically, shamans link this process directly to human sexual physiology. Whether this *is* a botanical fact or not, I am unable to say; but it quite definitely is a shamanic theory (Reichel-Dolmatoff 1981a). The Desana and their phratry members say that different sound waves will produce different effects upon pollen and that successful pollination can be produced only by a complex orchestration of the sounds from different pairs of trumpets, which, it is said, are associated with certain symbolically significant animals.

There are many tales describing how the Desana, by hook or crook, obtained these instruments, meaning that they acquired this fertilizing power. The gist of the story is that Tapir, that huge creature, formerly had a mighty voice, the force of which resided in the trumpets and in their power of pollination. But Tapir lost his voice; the Desana stole the instruments and left Tapir with the feeble whistling voice he has to this day, which is quite disproportionate to his body size. While Tapir pursued the thief, so the story goes, the other Desana raped his womenfolk; and when Tapir returned, voiceless and empty-handed, he was castrated and killed by the victorious Desana. At any rate, the abduction and rape seem to have met with a certain amount of encouragement from the women, and Tapir is pictured in these tales as a cuckold and a fool.

But eventually the situation began to change; soon the Desana began to acquire some of the cultural traits of the Tapir People. Once they had adopted the *yuruparí* complex, they took over certain ritual ornaments and songs and began to imitate Tapir in many ways. After a period of raids and abductions, more formal relationships were established with the Tapir People, and eventually the highly formalized sister exchange developed, as anticipated in the description of the Desana youth's visit to the house of Thunder Tapir and as it is practised today. Throughout the many interrelated episodes described in the oral traditions one can see how the image of Tapir changes from that of a dumb, uncomprehending beast of the forest into that of an ignorant cuckold, and, finally, into that of a 'person' (*mahsë*), a true human being of equal status, with whom from then on all relationships became subject to strict rules of exogamy and reciprocity.

From oral traditions and the commentaries that were elicited about them, one can deduce that this process of transfiguration was accompanied by a gradual change in descent rules. In the beginning, after the first contacts had been established and raiding had become less frequent, matrilineal descent and uxorilocal residence are mentioned. The highest-ranking Desana sib, for example, is descended from *boréka*, the *aracú* (LG) fish (*Leporinus copelandi*) 'caught' by the first Desana, who afterwards went to join her family. In genealogies, generations of Fish Women, Duck Women, and other water-related women are named and described; and the importance of uterine descent is mentioned. In mythical episodes Tukanoan men are described as living with their new in-laws. One cycle of myths tells in detail of the hard work to which Desana and other Tukanoan men were put by their new brothers-in-law, who made them work in their fields. In these contexts, mothers-in-law are often described as helpful and friendly to the foreigner, sometimes in exchange for sexual favours. One myth cycle tells of how, at one time, women actually owned the sacred trumpets and thus had authority over men. The gradual change to partrilineal descent is indicated in other tales, and it is no wonder that sometimes descent lines get badly entangled.

It is at this time that Tapir becomes incorporated into the Tukanoan genealogy. At present, practically all tribes consider Tapir as one of their ancestors, *bëhkëro* (T), a term in which we recognise the name *behkára*, the Desana designation for the Arawakan Kuripáko in recognition of the historical fact that it was

Aracú (LG) fish (*Leporinus copelandi*). Vaupés river, Mitú

mainly the Tapir People who first provided the Tukanoan invaders with women and so became their fathers-in-law and their ancestors. It is interesting to note that the Desana verb *vehkári* means 'to join, to aggregate, to bring together'; in other words, the cluster of terms for tapir-Kuripáko-father-in-law implies the idea of alliance and partnership, not necessarily on very friendly terms but in recognition of a historical relationship.

This relationship is also indicated in some idiomatic expressions that are found in shamanic texts referring to Tapir as an ancestor. One expression is *yurá vehkë*; *yurá* means 'thread, twist, interwoven object', and a literal translation would be 'twisted thread-tapir'. In discussing this term, several people rephrased it as *yurá seró vehkë*, which expands the translation to 'twisted thread-forked object-tapir'. Now, on the one hand any bifurcate object (*sero*), be it a forked branch, a bifurcation in the river, a forked house post, or a fork-shaped drawing, symbolizes a crotch with sexual associations. On the other hand, the term *yurá* (thread) refers to a 'line', a line of descent; and the translation is thus 'descent line-copulation-tapir', an expression that clearly indicates legitimate kinship with Tapir. Here we might add the following ethnographic detail: many women married to Desana men wear woven knee bands that are called by the very same name – *yurá seró vehkë*. The bands are adorned with a pattern of opposed triangles forming small hourglass designs that symbolize a male-female union. Another detail is that until quite recently Tukanoan girls were put into a first-menstruation enclosure constructed of six large tapir hides to symbolize their transformation into marriageable females, fit to join the Tapir People.

Another expression for Tapir is *nyamiri vehkë* (literally, 'nights-tapir'); in

Desana, *nyamí* is 'night' and *nyamíri* the plural form. According to the Indians, the word *nyamí* is derived from *nyaári* (to become transformed) and *miriri* (to become satisfied, saturated). The meaning of this expression was explained as referring to Tapir as a female element, the female counterpart in the marriage alliance. In shamanic language, Tapir Women (Arawakan women) are creatures of night; they inhabit the west, the regions of the setting sun. They are *nyamíri nomé* (nights-women), who transform and satisfy men. The Desana are *ëmëkóri mahsá* (Day People) because they come from the east, with the rising sun; and indeed the sun is their father and ultimately the creator. In these two idiomatic expressions, then, Tapir comes to stand for the exogamous union between Day People and Night People, between east and west, and whatever else might be associated with these two opposing but complementary concepts.

Although the Tapir is found in some forest areas and, at times, in the riverine environment, the Indians rarely hunt it. Among the Desana, Pira-Tapuya, and Tukano there exist no formal prohibitions to kill or eat tapirs, but people are reluctant to do so and will give numerous reasons why they are not being hunted. First, there is a strong belief that the spirits of game animals might try to harm the hunter and cause him or his family to fall ill. Apart from this, people will talk a great deal about the supposed dangers of eating tapir meat; it always has to be smoked and it is said to be difficult to digest, to be too tough, too strongly flavoured, too rich, or too fat. People say that one would need special permission from a shaman, a special spell or some other ritual protection. Needless to say, all these arguments are unconvincing; the fact remains that the largest game animal of the forest is rarely hunted. From a practical point of view this is of minor importance because protein sources are abundant in the Vaupés territory; there is plenty of other game to be had, and fishing, of course is a major food resource. So the problem of tapirs being restricted game does not affect the nutritional status of the community.

I shall transcribe here the words of a Tukano hunter, a young man who occasionally went out to kill a tapir and who gave me an account of his thoughts on tapirs and tapir hunting. I quote him at some length because this man, who is not a shaman, states in a very precise fashion what others have said in a less coherent way. This text is crucial to an understanding of tapir symbolism and avoidance.

The hunter first described how tapirs wander about and feed in the forest and then how they go to the river to visit their watering places. At this point he began to speak of tapirs as if he were talking of human beings. "When they go to drink water," he said, "they drink their beer and behave like people at home." He then went on: "Formerly, in the beginning, they too were progenitors; they too had descendants when each group of people [Tukanoan invaders] arrived; thus, some tapirs belong to the Barasana tribe, others to the Tuyuka, and others to the Bará.[7] Each group of tapirs had their properly named place of origin; they evolved like people." The text continues with a lengthy description in which the seasonal cycle of the tapir's feeding resources is compared to a common household routine. The narrator then said, "They [tapirs] are people like us; they have their houses, their tapir houses." The hunter said that by this he meant the supernatural abodes in hills and rock formations in the deep forest, where all game animals in spirit form are said to dwell under the care of the Master of Animals. I shall return to this image. The text continues: "But we kill them; we lie in ambush for them when they come to drink."

The narrator then established certain differences between categories of tapirs, some of which he described as zoological species, but compared others, which he called "true" tapirs (*vehköa varoo*), to human beings. He said, "Those that go to feed in our fields are not important; they merely steal food. They will sleep anywhere; they belong to the forest. But those that have houses do not go about like this, they stay in their houses… The tapirs that steal food from the fields are their servants… This is why we lie in ambush for them when they eat manioc… A tapir never knows in advance when he might go to a salt lick; he gets a warning from others; a tapir is like a person, I tell you. But if we think of this and ponder it, then tapir will see us in his thoughts. When we think of her [*sic*] she becomes aware of us [of our intentions] and knows… If we want to kill one, we must think of other things."

The hunter then explained in detail that, if one went for a tapir, one should always concentrate on its animal nature; otherwise the tapir would read one's thoughts. "If we think of a tapir as a person, the others will take revenge. This happens to shamans, but to an ignorant person like me, this won't happen. Tapirs take revenge only on those who think of them as people. His [the hunter's] children will fall ill. They [tapirs] take revenge and kill. So we kill her [*sic*] and eat her. If we were thinking like shamans, we would be eating human beings, but for us it is not dangerous to eat tapir."

After another description of how tapirs go to their watering places, the hunter explained that these locations, the same as salt licks, were like imaginary longhouses where tapirs gathered to talk, take coca, imbibe narcotic potions, and drink their fermented beer. "They go to their watering places," he said, "just like women drawing water," and drink "as if it were beer". The hunter ended his talk by saying, "They have various greenish beverages; this is their *yajé* [a hallucinogen].[8] If we were to drink the potion of the true tapir, we would turn into tapirs… and, transformed into tapirs, we would go to where they are and enter where they live."

The hunter's account throws new light on the problem of tapir avoidance. While this document provides a confirmatory context for the point I have made already, that a 'tapir component' is present in many Tukanoan tribes, a number of new elements have been added to the original situation. In the first place, there now are two kinds of tapirs: the zoological species and one that consists of transformed human beings who live in supernatural longhouses. The narrator commented that it was difficult to tell the difference between the two at sight and that there always remained a dangerous uncertainty. In the second place, man-tapirs were said to take revenge upon the hunter's family; and third, if a hunter should think of a tapir as a person, the tapir would read his thoughts and punish him; but if he took the tapir for an animal, no harm would come from killing and eating it. As we can see from the narrator's switching from he- to she-tapirs, male and female personifications are involved here and, in order to become a prey, a tapir must be thought of as 'someone else'. Reportedly both male and female tapirs appear in dreams, nightmares, and drug-induced hallucinations, sometimes to accuse the dreamer of overhunting, at other times in a context of social relationships and an atmosphere of intense anxiety. Shamans are much interested in patients' tapir visions and say that the visions mirror the quality of a person's social problems.

To get a truer perspective of these images I shall briefly summarize some general attitudes toward game resources, their shamanistic implications, and their psychological projections. The Indians believe that certain isolated rock formations, deep in the forest, are ghostly abodes wherein game-animal spirits dwell under the care of the Master of Animals (Reichel-Dolmatoff 1971). These 'hill houses', as shamans call them, have a womblike character; they are the places where game animals are said to multiply and from whence they emerge to roam in the forest; they are the spirit houses inside which a continuous process of gestation is going on. Shamans say that they visit these places during their narcotic trances because they must converse with the Master of Animals in order to ask him to release some of his charges so that the hunters may kill them for food. When shamans say these places are wombs and places of gestation, they mean that these are places of transformation, which can be recognised as such because, hovering over them, a spiral-shaped cloud formation or a large funnel-shaped dust devil can sometimes be seen. These spirals or funnels are compared to vaginae, entrances to the womb, which is the house inside the hill.

The cosmic fertilizing force that enters vertically into the house consists of what shamans call 'colour energies' (*dári*), which are said to be derived from the sun (Reichel-Dolmatoff 1978b. See essay 2 in this book). In the opposite direction, rising from the subterranean abode to the surface, run what shamans call 'wind threads' (*miru dári*), which transmit particular odours that emanate from the animals. As a matter of fact, the hunter who approaches such a hill can perceive the penetrating scent of certain aromatic herbs together with the musky estrous smell of game animals, such as tapir, deer, or peccary.

In a trance induced by hallucinogenic drugs, a shaman will enter a spirit house to negotiate with the Master of Animals, who is a jealous protector of his charges. The shaman will not ask for individual animals but rather for herds or troops of a certain species. He must always recompense the Master of Animals, and the payment consists of human souls. In fact, the shaman promises to kill a certain number of people, whose souls then enter the hill houses where they replenish and invigorate the energy of the game animals that have been released by their Master. Inside a hill house two categories of animals exist. One is formed by the spirit manifestations of the zoological species that multiply and breed inside the hill and are then released to fall prey to the hunters; the other category of animals consists of people who have been transformed, who are 'like animals' because during their lifetime they did not obey social norms, especially those related to exogamy. When these people die, their souls, instead of leaving this earth and returning to the dimension of solar energy, remain in *deyóri turi*, the 'visible world', and enter a mountain or hill, where they live in animal form. The purpose of their continued existence is two-fold: in part, their vital energy contributes to fomenting the community of game animals; and in part, they suffer punishment for their misconduct and are occasionally sent out into the forest, where a hunter might mistake them for fair game and kill them. As a precaution a hunter must always cut out the tongue of game animals, such as tapirs or deer, so they cannot tell their kin about their fate at his hands, in case his victim was a transformed human who went unrecognized. Another Tukano text of interest that refers to this matter says in part: "They [the hunters] are fearful and immediately after killing [the game] they cut out the tongue and throw it away because they [the game] would tell their kin. They [people] say that their spirits would tell them. The tapir of the true house would take revenge, they say. And I always do the same; rapidly we cut out the tongue of any tapir we are going to eat."

From a number of statements made by shamans and other people, it is possible, then, to summarize the situation as follows: Most people believe that there are two categories of tapirs – the common game animal and transformed people. If the prey is a common animal, there will be no objection to eating it if one follows the basic rules of smoking the meat and eating it sparingly. But if the prey is believed to have been a man-tapir, the matter is serious; cutting out the tongue may be a good preventive measure, but it is better still *not to think* that a tapir encountered in the forest might by any chance be a human being. Hunters are insistent that when killing the animal one should never think of it as human; one should banish this thought and think of the animal as a mere beast of the forest and never as a person to be killed. However, an ignorant person is not held responsible, the hunters added. The emphasis on this mechanism is such that one is led to think that the identification of a tapir with a male or female person is a problem that constantly preoccupies the hunter.[9]

Most interestingly, expert shamanic opinion differs quite notably from the point of view of the average hunter; shamans believe that all large game animals – not only tapirs, deer, and peccaries – are 'images of people'. One shamanic statement says, "When we kill a tapir we do think that we are killing a person, and so tapirs become our enemies." The same shamans and several others believed that they were being punished by tapirs for consciously killing them, and that the animals sent them illnesses, accidents, bad frights, and, what was worse, nightmares and visions of monstrous tapirs; but they added that these risks were inherent in their profession. They simply had to "kill people" by casting malignant thorns and splinters at the Kuripáko and by shooting tapirs in order to recompense the Master of Animals for the game he released from his abode to be taken by hunters. Indeed, many shamans say that *all* game animals, including game birds and certain fish, are transformed souls.

To Tukanoan shamans the entire animal world, most especially the game animals that inhabit the hill houses, is not a biological unit set apart from man but is an extension of man, of man's many self-images, of man's fears and expectations, of his good and evil tendencies. In fact, the animal world is a mirror that nature holds up to man, and shamans use precisely this imagery, expressed by the term *keori* (to mirror, to reflect, to produce an echo). One important aspect of the hill house or sacred-mountain image is that it exactly represents society; it is a longhouse unit, a human community. Another aspect is that each animal in the hill house represents a human personality trait. These collective images of analogues are very characteristic of Tukanoan shamanistic ideology, and I shall come back to this point. As I have said, there is never an identity relationship between a person and an animal; man never *is* an animal, but often is *like* (*dohpá*) an animal. Animals, by their particular odours, colours, and activity patterns, are metaphors of human beings; men can be understood only if seen through this similarity to animals. In one shamanic image a hill house is compared to a human brain: a structure divided into innumerable ventricles or compartments, each one occupied by a particular animal. But an animal never appears as a mere type specimen; it manifests itself under many different aspects expressed by a range of colours, a range of odours, a range of sounds and movements. These differences, according to shamans, are due to the animal's adaptation to different ecological environments; animals of the interior forest will have a dark coloration, but the same species will have a lighter colour if adapted to open forest. Somewhere in the hill house (or in the human brain) there will be a spot for, let us say, deer; but it may be a red deer, a darkish deer, or a brownish one; it may be a fawn, a rutting buck, or an estrous doe ready to be bred. It is the same with all animals; a tapir is not only a father-in-law image, he is also elder brother, swift runner, a graceful dancer, a solitary wanderer, a glutton a rank-smelling male, and a powerful ally. In this trance a shaman may see a hill house either as a womb or as a honeycomb, a beehive, or a mass of many-coloured butterflies. But whatever he sees in his imagination is always an extension of man, a projection of his mind. The circulation of animals to and from the hill houses, as potential food or as the condemned who must give their souls so people may eat, constitutes a complex model of ecological and psychological equilibria. Supernatural punishment may befall a hunter, fisherman, or gatherer not because he has killed or harvested but because he has been careless in combining the black-red-brown (*nyígë-diágë-borégë*) energies; that is, he has not taken care to transform the opposing principles into a balanced product. The options to kill, to overkill, or to avoid killing are a social behavioural code, and not merely a set of shamanic prescriptions aimed at preserving the biotic environment in terms of food resources.

Once a year, between December and February, in the *umarí* season, the men organize a tapir hunt. They go off into the forest saying, "*nyehkë-semára ya viígë*" (ancestor-house of-we go). This is the time of the year when tapirs can be found near *umarí* trees and at salt licks, places where they can easily be ambushed. This is also when they leave the deep forests and forage in secondary growth, where most 'edible' (*bogë*) animals are at home. In other words, the tapir becomes *bogë* at this time and offers himself to an alliance. Shamans set about to prepare the tapir's trails; through songs and spells and narcotic trances they open the doors of the hill houses (*ëhtëngë dihsipóro*) and 'open straight trails', pave them with potter's clay (*mata*) and yellow clay (*bahsí*), and put on them the sweet scent of *umarí* (Reichel-Dolmatoff 1978b:281. See essay 2 in this book). After a week or so the men return with plenty of smoked meat and baskets full of *umarí*, as if they were returning from an exchange ritual. But this is not a 'totemic' feast; it is, in shamanic terms, an ecological stock-taking and a balancing of books. The tapir hunt takes place in the dry season, the period of highest human infant mortality; and the children who die belong mostly to the age-group below three months of age called *diádu* (red ones). Bereaved parents openly blame the shaman for the deaths of their children and say, "He pays for our food with the lives of our children." Shamans will agree and say "We are eating our son" (*marí mahkëre baása*); but they rationalize infant mortality as a mechanism of population control and as part of the exchange pattern between people and tapirs, between the Tukanoans and the Arawakans. "It is an exchange of deaths," one commentator said and went on to explain that a dead tapir would enter the house of the hunter, whereas a dead child would enter the house of the tapir. Vital energy (*bogá*) runs in a circuit in which nothing ever is lost. The killing of the 'old ancestor' and the death of a child is a renewal, the expression of having achieved a balance. Soon the spawning season will begin; fish will be running, Orion is in the sky, and the tapir will be back in the darkest depths of the forest.

III

Symbolically, deer are closely related to the tapir. Two kinds of deer are found in the Vaupés territory; the most common is the brocket deer (*Mazama americana*), which lives mainly in the forest and in secondary growth; less common is the whitetailed deer (*Odocoileus virginianus*), which, although it prefers savanna country, in the Vaupés can be found in stretches of open forest. Both genera are designated as *nyamá*, in practically all Tukanoan languages. I mention later some other names that are important in explaining certain native categories.

Whereas on the social-psychological level the tapir represents one Arawakan component of the present Tukanoan population, the deer represents another local element toward which the invading Tukanoan tribes have developed a particular set of attitudes. Deer are not thought to be powerful owners of any desirable property; they are not feared for social reasons, as is the tapir because of his large household units, but deer cause another, very ambivalent, reaction. I shall first describe deer as viewed by the Indians in terms of their zoological characteristics. The main emphasis is on deer's 'cleanliness'. Deer feed on what is considered to be very 'pure' food, such as fresh sprouts, young green leaves, and sweet fruits like *umarí* and thus, as a species, have an inoffensive body odour that is said to be essentially human. What greatly attracts the Indians' attention is a deer's complex pheromonal system of chemical communication, by which signals are transmitted among members of the same species. Message-carrying pheromones are produced by the whitetailed deer, secreted by interdigital glands, tarsal and metatarsal glands, preorbital glands, a forehead gland and also excreted in urine and faeces. Whitetailed deer, if frightened suddenly from close by, will run off and repeatedly break wind, probably to mask the odour trail left by the interdigital glands and thus mislead predators and hunting dogs. All these chemical signals carry messages relating to territoriality, species and mate recognition, sexual attraction, scent masking, and other aspects of survival behaviour. Brocket deer are believed to have a similar communication system. The fact that deer are repelled by human menstrual odours has not escaped notice by the Indians, and is pointed out as further proof of deer's 'purity'.

These two aspects then, odour communication and territoriality, distinguish deer; and so we need to know more of native concepts that refer to these salient characteristics. According to the Indians, human beings have a general surface body odour called *sëríri* that is shared by all members of a phratry; for example, the intermarrying Desana, Pira-Tapuya, and Tukano all have the same *sëríri*. Moreover, since the Desana traditionally are associated with hunting and game, the Pira-Tapuya with fishing and riparian resources, and the Tukano with agriculture and field fruits, they are said to be distinguishable by their particular food odour called *omá sëríri*.[10] This also means that other phratries or tribal groups share the same *sëríri*, but have different *omá sëríri*. The word *omá* is related to the verb *omári* (to carry), so in this case the meaning is 'to carry an odour'. This was stated quite clearly: 'It is not the people who smell, but their food that smells through them.' Thus, Desana men are said to have the particular *omá sëríri* of forest game and smoked meat. Desana women are said to smell of the raw material from which the tumplines of certain carrying baskets are made; when wet it is said to have the odour of menstruation. The Pira-Tapuya are said to smell of fish and the Tukano to smell of roots, tubers, and other products of their fields. Apart from these permanent odours, people of both sexes emit odour signals in periodic cycles; these odours are called *poré suri*. This expression is derived from *poré*, a term that indicates dehiscence, a state of sudden, active sexuality, the bursting open of a seed vessel, and the spilling of pollen; the word *suri* is related to the verb *suurí* (literally, 'to mix, to combine', but here used to mean 'to copulate'). It is described as the perfume or ripe fruit or sweet roots and certain aromatic herbs. The quality of *poré suri* changes gradually according to the age of the person.

The same odour classification is applied by the Indians to all animals. In the forest, a hunter can distinguish the specific odour (*sëríri*) of tapirs, deer, peccaries, rodents, and other animals; apart from this he can perceive the particular odours (*omá sëríri*) of carnivores, herbivores, and animals that feed on fish. To these are added the estrous odours of the different species, mainly those of the large game animals. The specific odour (*sëríri*) is neutral, neither attractive nor repulsive; it merely identifies and so, possibly, warns the intruder. Within the same territory, for example, people claim to perceive what is called *mahsá sëríri*, an abstract odour, a term best translated as 'sympathy' or 'tribal feeling'. When travelling from one region to another – say from the Papuri drainage to the middle Vaupés river, or to the Pira-paraná – men continuously sniff the air and comment upon differences. It is said that on the Pira-paraná, people 'smell good' because they eat *bogë* food, here meaning that they eat animals that feed on sweet-tasting fruits; and on the Vaupés river, people are said to have a different smell from eating game and fish that feed on acid or oily fruits. The term *sëríri* can be used to describe a state of ripeness, the climax of growth, as, for example, when speaking of a well-developed manioc tuber; but when nasalized (*sëríri*), as in *sëridígë*, it may refer to an undesirable overdevelopment, a kind of overripeness that has the connotation of excessive fertility. In any case, phratry odour 'lays down a thread', as the Indians say; it marks a territory with *sëríri dári* (odour-threads) in the same manner that an animal (deer, rodent, feline) would mark its territory and establish odour trails and scent posts. Within a given phratric territory, therefore, one can also recognise *omá sëríri dári*, the threads or trails laid down by distinct exogamic groups, and occasionally one can perceive their *poré suri dári*, the sex attractant odours.

Deer mark their territories, and this is expressed by the specific names the Desana give to their deer categories. The common brocket deer is called *nyama-ka bohóru* (literally, 'deer-enclosure-brown'); a somewhat abbreviated designation would be *nyamá bohó*; the expression *kaa* (enclosure) stands here for 'territory'. Two slightly larger kinds of brocket deer are called *nyamá diágë* 'red deer' and *nyamá nyígë* 'black deer'. Whitetailed deer are called *nyama-ka saríro* (deer-enclosure-hourglass-shaped object), a name I shall analyze below. Although the Indians mention these three categories of deer, the principal distinction is generic; they say that brocket deer have a closed hoof and do not spread their digits, whereas whitetailed deer spread theirs wide open. Because deer hooves and their imprints are compared to the female sex organ, brocket deer are said to be 'chaste' and, therefore, a preferred prey, but whitetailed deer, which openly display their interdigital scent glands, are said to be promiscuous and dangerous to eat.[11] It is said that bucks in rut have a mating call, *poré poré poré*, related to the human *poré suri* condition of emitting sexually attractant odours; a person who hears this call in the forest is likely to fall ill and might even die (Reichel-Dolmatoff 1976b. See essay 7 in this book).

The Indians believe that what we would call an ecosystem is rather like a longhouse structure inside of which individuals of the same species acquire a particular colouring and a distinctive odour according to local conditions. This general concept of a home environment is called *vahpíkëro* (literally, 'that which accompanies'). Brocket deer are a case in point. They vary greatly in coloration; those living deep in the forest (*nëngë*) are very dark (*nyígë*), those living in an open forest environment (*tara boa*) are a reddish colour, and those living in secondary growth (*viado*) are a brownish colour (*bohóru*). Even the quality of their musky odour changes according to the particular environment. The small brocket deer of brownish colour (*nyama-ka bohóru*) are said to have almost no odour at all, and those of a dark or red colour, a rather unpleasant smell. Animals that inhabit different ecological systems or 'enclosures' are designated as *gahí turi vaimëra* (other-dimension-beasts) or, as the case may be, *gahí turi vai* (other-dimension-fish). But it is especially in the true rain-forest environment where the Indians distinguish the largest number of ecosystems according to soil conditions and, above all, to soil colour. They say, "Animals take on the odour and colour of their environment." The limits between ecosystems are said to be streams and creeks, watering places where, at certain times, animals of the same species meet and 'face each other' (*inyári*) across a stream. The Indians compare this image to a ritual meeting between exogamous units. The animals may vary in colour and odour, but they constitute a breeding population, just like a phratry. And it is there, at these liminal spots, that the hunters lie in ambush, waiting to make their kill. Animals of a dark or reddish colour are always said to be dangerous to eat, but animals of a brownish colour are *bogë*, a term that here indicates ripeness, edibility; it refers to something that has been 'cooked and done' and thus is preferential for eating. Hunting deer, especially whitetailed deer of the dark variety, is quite definitely restricted; hunting brocket deer is optional and is recommended only when the hunter goes after the brownish variety.

The division of the physical environment into a number of 'enclosures' or 'houses' establishes a set of rules for food procurement and permissibility. A person should eat only animals that feed on local food resources; should he want to hunt or collect animals in another environment (*gahi turi mahára* 'other-dimension-belonging') he will need a special shamanic spell (*bayíri*). This rule applies mainly to forest (*nëngë*) resources and, to a much lesser degree to open forest (*tara boa*), swamp forest (*tará*), or *mirití* swamps (*nee tará*), where shamanic permissions are thought to be less important.

Once more, the entire system is taken to be a mirror image of Tukanoan social organization. Exogamy is equivalent to exophagy; the game animals are, in all aspects, females, many of them territorial females; and only those that have been transformed from strange forest creatures (*mëra*) into true people (*mahsa*) can safely be espoused and brought into one's tribe. Only the dark deer of the forest are viewed as dangerous estrous females and must be avoided. Hunting restrictions and food prohibitions or preferences thus become matters of mate recognition and selection.

Native attitudes toward deer are highly ambivalent, as I have said; on the one hand, deer are seen as clean, sleek forest maidens, sweet scented and seductive; on the other hand, they are repulsive bitches in heat. Both tapirs and deer feed on forest products and not on what people grow in their fields; both may be clean, but there is a very definite 'otherness' about them; quite clearly they are *gahí turi mahára*, they belong to another dimension.

Deer are called *nyamá* and this term contains a cluster of meanings that is difficult to unravel. I shall quote some current interpretations given by a variety of native informants. I have mentioned that *nyaári* means 'to become transformed' and shall add here that it also refers to an 'object to be transformed'. The expression *nyaá* (nasalized) means 'nettle' and, in a wider sense, 'itch, sting', all words with a marked sexual connotation. Nettles are sometimes mentioned in curing spells and are used to sting the patient because, as some informants put it, "The itch of the nettle takes away the itch that caused the illness." In all these cases the Indians indicate that the root *nya* refers to sexual stimulation. Moreover, the word *nyamó* (D, T) means 'a so-and-so' and refers to a woman of doubtful reputation; it is quite definitely related to the bitch image.

All Vaupés Indians use a simple tripod for smoking game or fish that is formed of three long poles tied together at the top, with a triangular horizontal grid of parallel sticks placed approximately at half the height of the tripod. An identical tripod, but without the smoking platform, is used to support a round, shallow basketry sieve through which women knead the sodden mass of freshly grated manioc to extract the starch. Both kinds of tripod are called *nyamá* (deer). How shall we interpret the relationship between this artifact of daily use and the game animal? The Indians offer a variety of ideas: deer often stand on three legs, they say, alluding to the posture the animal adopts when rubbing its metatarsal gland over its head, with which it then marks a scent post of the territory. In fact, the horizontally uplifted hind leg is compared to one of the horizontal bars that form the triangular frame for the sieve, a bar that is the only movable one since it serves to adjust and stabilize the sieve. It is emphasized by the Indians that the

An Indian woman straining the sodden mass of freshly grated manioc to extract the starch

extraction of starch from grated manioc symbolizes the fecundity of women, starch being the key symbol of the fundamental female component of a new life. Others say that the odours of singeing and smoking game and those of estrous deer or menstruating women are very similar and equally repulsive. On a more abstract level, people say that both, deer and tripod, are agents of transformation; a deer is a transformed human female, a forest woman of another tribe who, in turn, can transform a man into a buck by sexually initiating him and taking him into her tribal unit. Tapir and deer meat become edible and permissible only after being transformed by smoke from a potentially dangerous essence into valuable nourishment.

What is feared and avoided by all Tukanoans is *ëye sëríra*, the smell of burning fat or tallow, which they compare to the musky smell of rutting animals. In fact, all forest animals that have a humanlike odour – tapirs, deer, monkeys – are also said occasionally to have the repulsive human odours associated with sex and menstruation. These are not cultural odours, intentionally produced by dietary and sexual restrictions, but the rank smell of nature. Smoke is the only means by which these odours can be neutralized, and shamans maintain that what really is involved here is tobacco smoke as a cleanser and transformer; smoke from wood is only a substitute. In other words, all forest animals that contain this fatty substance because of their feeding habits must be smoked, must be detoxified before they become edible – that is, before the women they symbolize are fit to become the spouses of Desana, Pira-Tapuya, and Tukano. Their pheromonal communications must be changed.

Once, when I was discussing the deer-tripod-woman homologation with a shaman, he took a stick and, with a few swift strokes, drew a tripod in the sand; he pointed out that, when looking at it upside down, it appeared to be like a female organ *and* like a deer seen from behind, standing somewhat knock-kneed but with the lower part of the hind legs spread far apart.[12] This, exactly, is the image people have in mind when calling whitetailed deer *nyama-ka saríro* (deer-enclosure-hourglass-shaped object). The hourglass shape, the outline of two triangles joined angle to angle, is a graphic expression of the concept of male-female junction, or, in other words, of a transformative act. The term *sariró* is also used to designate an hourglass-shaped potstand made of canes, a simple object of material culture that is imbued with a very complex symbolism.

Although the common designation for a tripod is *nyamá* (deer), the correct expression would be *nyamá seró*, which was explained in the following manner: *nyaári* (object to be transformed), *ma'á* (way), *seró* (forked object). As I have mentioned before, when speaking of *yurá seró vehkë* (twisted thread-forked object-tapir), all bifurcations have a sexual connotation. In the case of deer this is important because of two further aspects: One is the shape of the antlers; brocket deer have only two smallish tines, but whitetailed deer have four or six points. Antler is *sáro* in Desana, a term that is related to *seró* (forked object). Another aspect is the cloven hoof. Further associations would take us into the subject of funnel, cone, and spiral symbolism, which is very elaborate among the Vaupés Indians and beyond the scope of this discussion. The cloven hoof of whitetailed deer is imagined as a funnel, a vulva; in fact, the word *pe'eró* can mean 'cloven hoof, funnel or spiral', and, when pronounced *peró*, becomes a deer's mating call. Suffice it to say that the expression *nyamá seró* is translated by most people as simply "It's a woman." Moreover, shamans pointed out that the expression *nyaári mahsá* (literally, 'transformer people') is used in ritual address and refers to the 'other people', the complementary exogamous unit of wife-givers and, therefore, the transformers. The word *ma'á*, not only means 'way, trail, path' but also signifies 'passageway, entrance, manner, approach', all of which carry an implicit sexual connotation.

I have, so far, suggested a symbolic relationship through the chain of deer-tripod-estrous-odour-transformation-woman-of-another exogamous-unit. I now turn to another chain of interconnected meanings that relate to deer symbolism.

Potstand for pottery or basketry objects

In Desana, *nyamí* is 'night,' and in many contexts one can observe a play on words in *nyamá-nyamí*, or 'deer-night'. The tapir is sometimes referred to *nyamíri vehkë* (nights-tapir) or *nyamíri mahsë* (nights-person). His women being the complementary unit of *ëmëkóri mahsá* (Day People), as the first Desana invaders called themselves. Tapir's womenfolk, his spouses and daughters, are *nyamíri nomé* (night-women), but they are also designated as *nyamá nomé* (deer-women). According to tradition, the Arawakan tapir with whom the first alliance was celebrated had two daughters, *vehkë pora nomé*, who were deer; the younger one became the wife of the first Desana. Tapir also had two sons, *vehkë pagë pora*; the younger one married the Desana's younger sister. According to these traditions, Deer Women belonged to another Arawakan tribe that inter-married with Tapir People. These deer-tapir relationships were elaborated on by several informants in the following manner: In the night sky, deer are associated with the Pleiades (*nyamó*), which in other images represent a bunch of palm fruits or a female descent group. In the deer image, however, the Pleiades are called *nyamá mashsá gobe* (deer-people-origin), and the Indians see in them the tracks, hooves, and antlers of the animals. The reappearance of the Pleiades in the sky announces the ripening season of palm fruits. The Indians say, "Tapir depends on palm fruits for food; so he depends on deer." Further, deer are said to be the preferred prey of the anaconda; and since the self-name of the Pira-Tapuya is Anaconda People (*pinoa mahsa*), they too marry Deer Women. In fact, at present there exists a Pira-Tapuya sib called *nyamá pona* (deer-sons).

In summation, the following conclusion emerges: by abduction or formal espousal of the Tapir's women, the first Vaupés-born generation of Desana would have had deer mothers. Just as the Arawakan tapir had become a father-in law and a father figure, deer became a mother-in-law and a mother figure. In ancient times both were, as the Desana say, *maríre nyaári mahsá nomé* (our-transformer-people-women). It also seems that the territoriality of Deer Women was important in the contact period when they belonged to Tapir; but once virilocal residence was established, women became a fluctuating element, comparable to wandering peccaries, running fish, or migrating birds.

The concept of transformation is also expressed in the word for night, *nyamí*. The verb *nyamiúri* means 'to submerge oneself', with the implicit meaning of 'renovation' or 'refreshment' in both a physical and spiritual sense. The act of submersion is called *nyamiúro* and night, *nyamí*, is said to be 'a state of renovation,' during which spent energies are renewed.

The psychological basis of *nyamá-nyami* relationships was explained by some shamans and elders, but it is not common knowledge. The fundamental imagery is this: Deer Women are women of night and both sex and sleep are transformers. Both submerge (*nyamiúri*) people into other dimensions of consciousness. Drug experiences, too, are compared with this dimension, an important point because hallucinations induced by *Banisteriopsis* potions, taken during ritual gatherings, often contain incestuous visions in which the person becomes his own begetter by returning to the maternal womb and being reborn from it. The incest theme is closely connected to the *nyamá-nyamí* relationship. Here is a brief summary of a large body of myths that refers to this theme: A primordial father figure surprises his deer wife, *nyamí*, in adultery with a deer man called *nyamá*. He kills the man, castrates him, and transforms the severed penis into the belt of Orion. In some other versions the guilty couple are an incestuous mother-son pair or incestuous siblings. The theme is one of Day and Night, Sun and Moon, incest and eclipse; the deer woman is a seductive grandmother-mother-sister figure, and the deer man is a castrated hero. On the level of forest animals this is the story of Tapir and his Deer Woman, or the Arawak confronted by the Tukanoan invaders. In this manner a historical memory provides the screen upon which oedipal processes are projected.

An important point is that Tapir avoidance is largely based on fear, a very real fear of the forest-dwelling 'other people' whom the Tukanoan invaders encountered when they entered the Vaupés territory. Until quite recently Tapir was a very real and dangerous enemy. From genealogical accounts and migration stories it appears that many Tukanoan tribes arrived only five or six generations ago; and since there still exist Arawakan tribes in the area who are rather unfriendly toward the Tukanoans and who constantly are accused by them of all kinds of evil intentions, the memory of violence is easily refreshed by reciting tales of bloody encounters between the First People and Tapir. Raids accompanied by rape, castration, and cannibalism are still spoken of as events in the not too remote past. Moreover, the Vaupés territory is one of the few regions where there still exist sizable remnants of nomadic hunter-gatherers, the Makú Indians who are feared as poisoners and evil shamans. The Makú feel very much at ease in the deepest forests and are not afraid of forest animals, whereas the Tukanoans are always somewhat apprehensive in that situation. To the Makú the interfluvial rainforest is home; to the Tukanoans it is *vaimëra turi* (old beasts-dimension), in the sense of 'ancient ones-dimension', the domain of the legitimate autochthonous population.

Tapir avoidance at present in the Vaupés territory can be assessed thus: Along the Vaupés river, which in many ways is the most acculturated area, the tapir is occasionally hunted and eaten by Tukanoan tribes. In the Papurí drainage tapir hunting is less frequent; and the Makú of the Macu-paraná, a major affluent of the lower Papurí, never eat tapir, although some local Tukanoans might do so occasionally. However, the Makú kill and eat deer and, preferentially, hunt the white-lipped peccary. The Tukanoan tribes of the Pira-paraná hardly ever hunt and eat tapir because in their region the fear of the 'ancients' is still very much alive; some of the little-known nomadic forest hunters live not too far away, toward the southeast, and their magic is greatly feared. Neither do the Pira-paraná tribes hunt 'black' or 'red' brocket deer, white-lipped peccaries, or several other animal species. Many informants expressed this quite clearly by saying that on the Vaupés and the Papurí the interfluvial population had largely disappeared and that, therefore, 'their animals', namely, their women, could be hunted.

IV

The third animal I shall discuss in relation to tapir avoidance behaviour is the peccary. Two species are common in the Vaupés territory: the white-lipped peccary (*Tajassu peccari*), called *yehsé* (D), and the collared peccary (*Tajassu tajacu*), called *yehsé buru*. White-lipped peccaries roam in large herds of up to a hundred or more. They are omnivorous but feed mainly on roots and rotting fruits; like tapirs and deer, their preferred seasonal food is the fruit of *umarí*; occasionally they will even devour small reptiles. In cultivated fields they cause damage by uprooting manioc plantations, and they can devastate a large garden plot in a very short time. A troop of peccaries will leave behind it a well-trodden open trail and a penetrating odour. Their prominent musk glands produce a stench that can be noticed at considerable distances; the odour repels most other animals but attracts predators such as jaguars, who will closely follow a troop and attack the sick or old ones that straggle behind. Peccaries are often covered with infected boils caused by horseflies, and their flesh and intestines are infested with parasites. Collared peccaries are similar in most respects, but they have more solitary habits and do not herd together.

Most Vaupés Indians view peccaries as rather disgusting creatures. They are compared to savage forest women, foul smelling, always foraging and grunting, and openly promiscuous. Quite unlike sedentary tapirs and territorial deer, peccaries roam at large over wide areas and in many different ecological environments; they are nomadic gatherers who are at home in the deep forests but who will also forage in riverine environments, in secondary growth, and, of course in cultivated fields. All of these characteristics make them readily comparable to the Makú Indians, especially Makú women. The Desana, Pira-Tapuya, and Tukano often speak of these similarities, and in many myths and tales Makú-peccary comparisons are described in detail. In many ways, the Makú are still thought to be 'not quite human'; thus, peccaries constitute a continuum between nature and culture that is expressed in their occasional forays into cultivated fields. But again attitudes are ambivalent; on the one hand, peccaries are repulsive creatures, all-devouring and marked by a nauseating odour; on the other hand, there is about them a fascination prompted precisely by their uncontrolled behaviour and by their being delicious to eat when properly roasted or smoked.

From a body of oral traditions and from present ethnography, the historical origins of the peccary image can be reconstructed as follows: When the Tukanoan tribes entered the Vaupés territory they came upon wandering Makú bands with whom they found it far easier to establish some temporary contacts than with the sedentary and agricultural Arawakans. Makú women were approachable, and readily joined the Tukanoans; soon a strong Makú influence became noticeable, especially among the Desana and to a lesser degree among the Pira-Tapuya and the Tukano. However, once a formalized system of women exchange had been instituted between Tukanoans and Arawakans, Makú influence came to be considered somewhat shameful; descendants of Makú mothers were incorporated into Tukanoan social organization, as 'servant' sibs. The present relationship between some Tukanoan tribes and neighbouring Makú has been described as one of subservience, in which the Makú practically become the slaves of the Tukanoans (see Koch-Grünberg 1909). This is a dubious statement. Makú Indians will sometimes join a Tukanoan settlement and collaborate as hunters, basket makers, or experts in narcotics and poisons, but they are free to leave whenever they wish, and often enough they quietly disappear into the forest after having enjoyed a few weeks or months of a fish and manioc-based diet.

Tukanoan-Makú relationships have strong emotional overtones. Makú women are said to be legitimate marriage partners, but the slightest mention of having Makú ancestors will be met with violent denials, especially by the Desana, who are the Tukanoan tribe that appears to have the strongest Makú component.[13] But ambivalence prevails. The Desana say that women who, in their animal image, eat forest products (as tapirs and deer do) are outsiders but that those like peccaries, who steal and eat cultivated field fruits, are 'sisters', that is, they can be married.

Peccaries are called *yehsé* (D), a term said to be related to the Desana verb *yeéri* (to copulate). The meaning of *yehsé* was given as 'to copulate-passive object'. This etymology may not be too convincing, but since it was given by the Indians themselves, it expresses an attitude toward peccaries that corresponds to what many other informants have said in other ways about these animals. Because of their preference for oily, greasy food, peccaries are said to be prolific and to breed large herds, something that the Indians disapprove of. Uncontrolled multiplication; large families; and voracious, omnivorous appetites are condemned by most Tukanoans, who are ever so diet-conscious and preoccupied with population control. The white-lipped peccary thus constitutes a model to be avoided.

In some migration myths that describe first contacts with 'other people', Thunder's women are depicted as large herds of peccaries. A Desana youth asks Thunder to grant him the power to 'fulminate' some of them but is rejected.[14] At last, the youth finds Thunder asleep, castrates him, and thus acquires power over Peccary Women. There are other, similar tales that parallel the initial situation encountered with Tapir and Deer Women. The following statement made by a Tukano is to the point: "Tapirs are the Makú women of the Tukano, deer are the Makú women of the Pira-Tapuya, and peccaries are the Makú women of the Desana." When speaking of these ancestral relationships the Indians will use the term *pagësëmára* (ancestors) to designate their maternal origins. This term is formed by two elements: *pagë* (father) and *sëmé* (pod). The word for umbilical cord is *sëme-da* (pod-string), and *sëmé* is the large pod of the *Dahlbergia* sp. tree. In some Desana origin myths, Paca Woman (*semé*) was created form this pod (*sëmé*) when a Desana threw a dry pod on the ground and from the rattling seeds sprang forth a paca calling out *kekeke*. In those early times it seems that matrilineal descent and uxorilocal residence were the rule and that only when the Tukanoans began to displace and partially absorb the Arawakans and Makú did they develop their present patrilineal and virilocal system. I should add here that an alternative term for *pagë-sëmára* is *nyehkë-sëmára*, the first element having the meaning of 'ghost', in the sense of a revenant.[15]

V

The game animals the Desana and their neighbours prefer over any others are rodents, such as the paca (*Coelogynis paca*), the agouti (*Dasyprocta fuliginosa*), and the cavy (*Myoprocta* sp.). They are herbivores that feed mainly on tubers and roots found in abandoned fields covered by secondary growth or in cultivated gardens. Quite often they will approach settlements and rummage in the surrounding underbrush, or they will come to steal fruits the women soak in baskets that stand overnight in the still, shallow waters of nearby creeks. The Indians emphasize that these animals eat the same light, easily digestible vegetable diet that people consume, in contrast to tapirs, whitetailed deer, and peccaries who feed on a heavy diet of acidic, oily, and strongly odorous fruits. The rodents are starch eaters; they sit on their haunches, peel their food, and take it up with their paws, 'just like people'. Indeed, they all have digits, not hooves like the three forest species.[16] They have a pleasantly human body odour or, as is said of the paca, no odour at all. Still, they too have a well-developed pheromonal communication system and mark their territories, mainly by urinary odours. These rodents, together with the armadillo (*pamu*) and certain mice (*bii*), are said to be strongly attracted by human scent and to approach a hunter without fear.[17] They are also said to be attracted by smoke because it tells them that a field is being fired or that some kitchen refuse is near. They are *poé tërori mahára* (field-nearby-belonging) or *mahsá tërori mahára* (people-nearby-belonging). All of these preferred small game animals are said to be 'women' who do not have to be transformed by smoking to become edible.

The paca is called *semé*, the agouti is *bui*, the cavy is *bohsé*, and the armadillo is *pamú*, all of which are kinship terms and also the names of sibs.[18] The word *semé* (paca) is related to *sumú*, which signifies the white foam and bubbles that float on the dark waters near waterfalls and deep pools; these spots always have marked fertility associations, and the Indians speak of 'foaming' and 'bubbling' as procreative and birth-giving processes.[19] The expression *sumu-da* means 'bubble-thread', another term for umbilical cord. Among the Pira-Tapuya is a sib called *semé-pagó* (paca-mother). This is also the most common term that Desana men use to designate their Pira-Tapuya wives. Sometimes a slight but quite intentional change in pronounciation will make it *sëmé-pagó* (*Dahlbergia* sp.-mother), and, as mentioned above, the paca is believed to have been created from a pod (*sëmé*) of that tree. Another variant is the expression *sumu-dari pagó* 'bubble-threads-mother' or 'umbilical cord-mother'.

The agouti's name, *bui*, is a contraction of *buhí* (son-in-law; D, PT, T, U). There is a Pira-Tapuya sib called *buu mahsá* or *buhí mahsá* (Agouti People); they marry Desana women and are thus the sons-in-law of the Desana. The term *buhi-bo* or *buhí nomeo* means 'daughter-in-law' in the same languages. The cavy

The Meyú Rapids, Barasana territory. Pira-paraná river

is *bohsó*, a term whose etymology is not clear; the verb *bohsarí* means 'to favour, to please', and the cavy is often designated as a woman, a pleasant companion, and a housekeeper. Tame cavies are much-discussed pets in many households and like to hide in the tubular manioc squeezers that might lie in some dark corner, a habit that provokes oblique references to sex. The name is said to be related to *buhí*. Pacas and agoutis have no tails, but the cavy has a stubbed tail, the story of which is perhaps related to this animal's somewhat anomalous position. It is said that in early times the cavy, who then had a long tail, was an ally of the Desana; it stole Tapir's 'seed' and ran away with it to the Tiquié river. Tapir rushed after him and stepped on the cavy's tail with his heavy hoof; ever since, cavies have had these stubbed tails. There are many episodes in the oral literature of rodents stealing and scattering the 'seed' of Tapir, and they all refer to exogamous unions and virilocal residence. The armadillo is *pamó* or *pamú*, a name that is said to be related to *vamé* (mother's sister or father's sister; PT); in Uanana it is *vamanyó*. At present, some Desana marry Armadillo Women from the Karapana tribe, whose sib is called *pamóa mahsá* (Armadillo People).

In the present social organization, the other group of ancestors, those of the forest interior, is represented by *vehkëa mahsá* (Tapir People), a Tukano sib; by *nyamá pora* (Deer Sons) and *nyamá kamónoa mahsá* (Deer-ear People) two sibs of the Pira-Tapuya; and by the Desana sibs of *nuhpí pora* (Curassow Sons) and *moabore pora* (Trumpeter-bird Sons). In each tribe there are several sibs that have associations with the ancient Arawakans and with the Makú; it is worth noting that the higher-ranking sibs of the Desana and Tukano require certain ritual services from neighbouring Makú, such as the preparation of cigars for ceremonial smoking. In fact, the Cubeo, Uanana, and Tariana, tribes who figure prominently in the Vaupés territory, were originally Arawakans who have become Tukanoanized during the last few generations.

VI

To summarize, it is essential to understand that all these symbolic and sib-related animals never stand alone as mere visual images but that they always form part of their wider biological context, which includes feeding strategies and food habits, locomotor patterns, activity patterns related to reproduction, territorial behaviour, social interaction, and – above all – pheromonal communication. Within a species, the Indians take into account local ecological adaptations with reference to coloration and local feeding resources. In man-animal relationships to plants, the Indians take note of local variations in colour, odour, flavour, size, shape, surface texture, digestibility, and other characteristics always with the stated purpose of correlating certain human groups or particular biological conditions (age, reproductive cycle, etc.) with specific environments and the above-mentioned characteristics of their particular animal or plant populations. Kin relationships are seen not only among animals but also among plants. For example, all fruits growing on trees are said to be the 'daughters' of tubers; first came the root, the stock, and then came the offspring in a sequence that leads from below the ground to above the ground, passing through the transformational dimension of the soil surface that is man's domain.

Within a phratry, food plants and their multiple associations are magically owned by individual exogamous tribes, who exchange them among each other according to traditional rules. For example, the Desana are the owners of *patabá* palm fruits (*Jessenia* sp.), which they exchange ritually with the Pira-Tapuya, who in turn give them *umarí* (*poraqueiba sericea*) and *meré* (*Inga* sp.); the Desana also give smoked game in exchange for smoked fish and for fruits such as *toá* (*iua pichuna*; LG), *sëmé* (*Dahlbergia* sp.), and a variety of *Hevea* fruits, such as *vahsú* and *vahsú-bëgë*. The Pira-Tapuya exchange fish, *babassú* palm fruits (*Orbignya* sp.), and *poé* (*Pouteria ucuquí* R.E. Schultes), a fruit that according to myth served the first Desana as bait to catch the first Fish Woman. The Tukano own and exchange *assai* palm fruits (*Euterpe* sp.). The exchange chain consists of *women*, together with their food-producing and processing activities and odour associations; of *animals* and their feeding habits and odour associations; and of *vegetables* and their odour, and flavour associations. To this must be added all the attributes of colour, shape, size, surface texture, seasonal availability, ecosystem, and many other associations, all of which have to be carefully balanced in the exchange system. All these foods and attributes are, of course, common property in everyday life; and since they exist all over the Vaupés territory, they can be harvested by anyone. Only at a ritual exchange will each group give and receive according to magical ownership. It is clear, then, that the significance of hunting, fishing, and gathering goes far beyond their economic purpose. Their symbolic importance is paramount. Symbolic animals are only a link in this chain, one image among many, and cannot be isolated from the totality of nature.

The Tukanoan concept of ancestral animals is based upon the historical fact that they, the Indians, actually are, in part, descendants of previously established populations whose women they raped or abducted and that these women were initially compared to certain animal species. These comparisons never were (nor are they at present) formulated in terms of a human-animal identification, but were based to a large degree on pheromonal recognition, which in turn was related to food habits and other activities. Among the Tukanoans, a person is *like* an animal because he or she smells like one.[20]

What might appear to be totemic animals are the remnants and reminiscences of former inhabitants with whom, in earlier times, there was considerable intercourse. These people became transformed, in the eyes of the newcomers, from beasts of the forest into wife-givers and, eventually, into allies and thus into a category of lineage founders. The true ancestors were the original invaders; and all myths, migration stories, and genealogical recitals emphasize this over and over again. The indigenes, however, were compared to beasts that had a disagreeable but human body odour; that were mostly herbivores; and that had certain human behavioural patterns, such as ritual, the use of fire, and an articulated, although incomprehensible, language. These beings became 'edible' by smoking them in order to mask their peculiar odour. It is understood that 'smoking' meant much more than a mere culinary process: it was cultural transformation that ultimately was a hallucinatory experience induced by tobacco smoke and other narcotics administered by shamans.

The historical situation seems to have provided the screen upon which many psychological problems were projected, related to incest, rape, 'father-in-law' imagery, along with the desire to find a cultural balance and to assure survival. Tapirs, deer, and peccaries came to represent these conflicts, the solution being the rodents.

But this, I admit, is highly conjectural and demands a much more detailed analysis of the original texts than can be attempted here. So I should add that tapir avoidance is also based on a deep-seated fear of the Arawakans. To insult tapirs, or any of the large game animals of the deep forest, by hunting them would be to defy not only the ancestral tradition but also the surviving Arawakans. Although the Tukanoans maintain a complex symbolic trade relationship with these Indians, the Kuripako and their shamans are greatly feared. Tukanoan shamans magically 'kill' Kuripáko to pay the Master of Animals for the game he releases; the Kuripáko have similar beliefs, so they do the same: their shamans 'kill' Tukanoans, and their game animals are transformed Tukanoan souls. If, as in one commonly used shamanic image, game animals are women, then we understand that the traditional exchange ritual between the Arawakans and Tukanoans continues to be acted out in the spirit abodes of the hill houses.

It is true that shamans do talk and sing a lot about animals and to animals and that animals figure very prominently in their ideology and practice. However, at least in the Vaupés territory, all this preoccupation with animals is not concerned with the zoological species and their economic importance but with their symbolic value. At times, shamans become quite annoyed if someone gives too much weight to the mere biological and economic aspects and will unequivocally insist on the semantic value of animals. Animals are images, they will say, that represent abstract concepts in a cognitive system which includes all of nature and which in the last resort, goes far beyond it.

Notes

1. On the term 'tribe' see Introduction, footnote 1.
2. When speaking of Eastern Tukanoans or Tukanoans, reference is made to all Tukanoan tribes of the Vaupés territory; when speaking of Tukano or 'Tukano proper', reference is made to a distinct tribal unit within the Eastern Tukano.
3. For background literature, see among others, Koch-Grünberg, 1909; Reichel-Dolmatoff 1971, 1975, 1976b (see essay 7 in this book), 1978b (see essay 2 in this book). I wish to express my sincere gratitude to the John Simon Guggenheim Foundation for a 1976-77 Fellowship.
4. The language of the Tukano proper (or, simply, the Tukano, as I shall call them) has become a lingua franca but, in any case, all Vaupés Indians speak several languages of Tukanoan stock (Sorensen 1967). I shall use the following abbreviations in parentheses: D for Desana; PT for Pira-Tapuya, T for Tukano, U for Uanana, LG for lingua geral, the Amazonian vernacular. The pronunciation of *ë* is similar to the of *e* in *que, je* (French); *h* is pronounced like *ch* in *ach* (German).
5. In Desana, father-in-law is *behkë* if he is a Pira-Tapuya; otherwise the term is *meagë*, and *meokë* in Tukano. In Desana, mother-in-law is *vanyó*, and *meokó* in Tukano.
6. The name of thunder, *buhpú*, is said to be related to that of a ritual trumpet called *mëhá*, the sound of which is very loud. A shamanic commentary says, "The House of Thunder is a house of transformation."
7. The Barasana live on the middle course of the Pira-paraná; the Tuyuka on the middle course of the Rio Tiquié; and the Bará, on the head-waters of that river.
8. *yajé* (LG), a leafy jungle vine (*Banisteriopsis* sp.) from which hallucinogenic potions are prepared. See Reichel-Dolmatoff 1975.
9. A lengthy Tukano text, speaking of dream symbolism, says, "When we dream of killing our father and of weeping over it, there will be plenty of food." All this, of course, takes us dangerously close to *Totem and Taboo* (Freud 1918).
10. This specialization is not symbolic; it is a fact that among the men of each tribe certain activities predominate.
11. Deer hoof rattles are provocative because of their odour associations. Deer bones are used in the manufacture of such ritual objects as skull flutes, straight tubular flutes, and bone spoons for taking powdered coca leaves mixed with *cecropia* ash.
12. *nyamá paréye* (nasalized), literally, 'deer-to skin', an obscene term for coitus.
13. This was already observed by Koch-Grünberg (1909, I:241). The self-name of the Desana is *wira*, commonly translated as 'wind' or 'Wind People'. However, not the meteorological phenomenon is meant; the name is related to *vihíri* (nasalised), 'to sniff, to smell'. Several informants said that it referred to both a peculiar body odour and sniffing at that of others.
14. 'To fulminate' is a synonym for copulation.
15. When people hear a strange noise in the forest, they will mutter *nyehë*, the expression is said to be derived from *nyéri* (evil, black) and the root *ëh*, which signifies a process of transformation or the result of one.
16. There is no consistency in the number of digits; the paca has four digits on its forepaws and five on its hind paws, and the agouti has four on its forepaws and three on its hind paws.
17. This is doubtful; the paca, for example, does not respond to a hunter's call and is rather difficult to hunt.

18. Paca, *semë* (D, PT, T, U); agouti *buí* (D), *bu* (T), *buu* (PT, U).
19. See Reichel-Dolmatoff, 1971. These spots are the 'waterhouses', the supernatural abodes of all aquatic animals, and correspond to the 'hill houses' of terrestrial animals.
20. These considerations go far beyond ethnography. It would be most interesting to obtain analyses of the chemical constituents of certain emotion-charged foods, such as *umarí*, groundnuts, honey, *Dahlbergia* and *Hevea* fruits, and others. A study of individual sensibilities to certain categories of odour and flavour might also shed some light on native concepts of mate selection and exogamy.

Two tapirs confronting each other

IV

A Hunter's Tale from the Colombian Northwest Amazon

Introduction

Among the Tukanoan tribes, man/animal relationships can be seen to develop in several different but interrelated dimensions.

On the most obvious level, animals are food; they are killed and eaten, be they game animals of the forest, fish of the river, or insects and larvae collected along the trail.

On another level, animals are seen as models of and for human behaviour; for example, the territoriality of deer, the organization of social insects, or the flight patterns of birds may provide metaphors that people use when talking of themselves or of others, and may become an integral part of the shamanic idiom. In fact, mating behaviour, feeding strategies, pheromonal communication, or other forms of social interaction among animals constitute models that are pointed out in myths, tales, and daily conversations.

On still another level, animals may appear in dreams, in nightmares, or in drug-induced hallucinations, where they come to stand for people and, through them, for abstract concepts. They may represent a certain person, such as a parent, a spouse, or an adversary, or they may represent a vague collective notion, such as 'women', 'elders', or 'ancestors'. Sometimes the dreamer himself will be able to establish the identity of the animal apparition, but more often, especially if the dream or the hallucination should have produced a state of intense anxiety, a shaman will be consulted, who will analyze the imagery and explain its meaning to the dreamer.

When speaking of these different man/animal relationships the Indians will say: "Animals are just like people." This expression, however, is not meant to say that people and animals are thought to be equivalent in any sense. In the first place, the Indians will point out that animals are essentially different from men in that they do not fully participate in the cosmic energy circuit of which human beings form an integral part. An animal's spirit essence remains on this earth after its death, while man's spirit returns to the great cosmic energy source that lies beyond earthly existence.

In the second place, what distinguishes animals from men is that people, 'real people', are exogamous, that they obey incest laws, and that they have learned to control their procreative sexual activities and their normative food intake; animals, in turn, are promiscuous, prolific, and voracious, and these traits set them apart from humans.

Now it is certain that there will always be some people who 'behave like animals', because they disobey the rules of society, and these deviants, after their deaths, might have to adopt animal shape and thus find themselves confined to the earthly energy circuit of animals. Yet even this does not mean that they are transformed in all their essence; there is no belief in transmigration of the soul; they continue to be 'people' and even if they should now appear under the shape of a jaguar, a deer, or a bird, their motivations and goals will still be wholly human and not like those one would expect from an animal.

The particular reasons for which certain animals are being selected by the Indians from among a multitude of others, and are made to represent concepts such as paternal authority, sexual gratification, illness, aggressiveness, digestibility, and so on, depend to a large degree upon some salient anatomical or physiological characteristics and less so on the behavioural patterns of the animal in question. It is true that specific behaviour becomes important in certain intellectual elaborations, as when it can be compared with human social and economic activities, but on a more primary level the symbolic nature of animals is determined above all by their particular odours, shape of genitalia, surface colours, and flavours when prepared as food. The peculiar smells of mammalian musk glands, of fish, of ants, or of specific birds play a most important role in linking certain animal images to emotion-charged situations in infancy, puberty, and maturity, and these associations find their expressions in many aspects of native attitudes.

It would, in fact, be difficult for an outsider, used to establishing categories according to his own cultural tradition, to keep these different animal images apart. Any attempt to do so is bound to fail because the imagery is poly-metaphoric and the 'meaning' of a certain animal will depend upon details of context, of local tribal tradition, individual experience, shamanic or lay interpretation, and many other aspects, making it nearly impossible to isolate, say, the food aspect from the maternal image, or the ethnological aspects from moral considerations.

One point, however, is clear; among the Tukanoan tribes there is no totemism in the sense of a mystical identification of man and animal; no mysterious message is being conveyed between species. Animals are a stark reality to the Indians, no matter how they are perceived and conceptualized – as proteins, social models, or nightmarish projections.

The Text

We now turn to a document, a native text I recorded in the field and which I have translated here from the Tukano original. The narrator is a young man, a proficient hunter whom I had met on several occasions and who, at that time, was travelling with me in the forest. This, then, is not a shamanic text, but an informal conversation in which several dimensions of thought are combined into a hunter's attitude I found to be fairly common among Indians who were not overly concerned with esoteric lore but who, nevertheless, represented a traditional way of life.

I knew that among these Indians there existed restrictions on hunting certain animals, such as tapir. Not that tapirs were tabooed or venerated in any sense, but one could notice a certain wary attitude among men whenever the matter of tapir hunting was brought up. Actually, people hardly ever seemed to hunt tapir. But one evening I overheard my Tukano companion when he told some other Indians how he went about hunting tapir; and this was how I was able to record his tale.

1. "There are large tapirs around here. Tapirs with their young. These tapirs roam everywhere when they are feeding. Sometimes they feed on palm fruits, and in our fields they feed on tender leaves. Sometimes, during the dry season, they go to the mineral licks; there they have their spots where they lick the briny earth and drink water. They drink it as if it was beer and they behave just like people when they are at home."

2. "Formerly, in the beginning, tapirs too were our ancestors. When the different people immigrated here, tapirs too founded lineages. Thus, some are related to the Barasana tribe, others to the Tuyuka tribe, and others to the Bará tribe. They all have their places of origin, with their proper names. This is why one still speaks of the many spots where tapirs left descendants. They developed just like people, and this is why tapirs are people; they are persons. That's what tapirs are."

3. "And this is why, when they go to drink water, they really are drinking beer made of palm fruits. They go to the watering places when the dry season begins and when the water level goes down. They also have their ritual exchange gatherings and invite each other to drink beer. This is why they go to their particular watering places and this is what they drink. They also have their fixed days, because they are just like people; they have their houses, their tapir houses. But we kill them, we ambush them."

4. "Those tapirs that feed in our fields are not important; they simply steal food. They will sleep anywhere in the forest; but those that have houses do not wander around like that. They stay in their houses. They leave them only on occasions. The tapirs that steal food in our fields are their servants. They feed on

manioc from our fields. The manioc they steal they take to the others and from that they make the beer they drink. They are looking for seedlings. The other tapirs are their masters; but these work for them."

5. "So we ambush them when they come to eat manioc. It's about this time of the year that they come. They come out at about this time; sometimes they come out a bit later or when the moon is down. This is when we ambush them. If they don't come, we call them by whistling. He answers the call and when he approaches we kill him with a large bullet. We shoot to kill but sometimes we miss. Sometimes we hit him in the head; or, at times, we hit the forelegs or sometimes we shoot at the tail end and hit him through the anus, right down to the heart; then he dies instantly. Sometimes we make a kill but sometimes we miss and he gets away; all this may happen when one goes hunting. When we want to kill several we go to the mineral licks and watch them and there we hide on separate stands and lie in ambush."

6. "Female tapirs, too, come, even in the daytime and in the late afternoon. In their own way they are 'drawing water', just as our women do at this time of day. But when dusk comes and we get drowsy, they don't come anymore. Shamans say that 'they are drawing water' just before dusk. This is why we ambush them there, thinking that at that time she [sic] will come down to the river as if it was a landing place, and so we can kill her."

7. "A tapir never knows in advance when exactly he might go to a mineral lick; he gets a warning from others. A tapir is like a person, I tell you. But if we think of her [sic] then she will see us in her thoughts. If we think of her she will become aware of our intentions and then she won't go down to the water; she will have a foreboding and will know. If we want to kill her we must think of other things. I tell you, should we not think of something else but only of her, we won't be able to kill her. But otherwise, we will make a kill. Else we make enemies and the other tapirs will take revenge. But this happens to shamans, not to an ignorant person like me. Tapirs take revenge only on those who think of them as people. Then the hunter's children will fall ill, I tell you. Tapirs take their revenge and kill."

8. "So we eat the dead tapir. If we were thinking like shamans, we would be eating a human being, but for us it is not dangerous to eat tapir. So we can hunt tapir. All those who hunt tapirs say so. They hunt according to their needs. They kill one and eat it, just like that."

9. "Occasionally, when they go to kill those that come down to drink at the salt licks, there will be many of them; one comes to know them individually and to distinguish them. One knows when they will come down and one can observe many of them and they leave many tracks, without fear. During the daytime we watch how many of them come down to the water and it is like a greeting of sorts. So we go off contented, I tell you. When many of them come down they go in pairs, or maybe three of them, but not more. The same happens at dawn

and then the jaguars, too, come down; they all go down to the water to drink. There are jaguars, deer, birds, parakeets, parrots and pigeons, all drinking that beer."

10. "Tapirs have their various greenish beverages; this is their hallucinogen. If we were to drink the potion of the true tapir, we would turn into tapirs; if we drank of these waters, I tell you. It would be noxious for us, and transformed into tapirs we would go to where they are, and enter where they live."

General Commentaries on the Text

Before commenting upon some specific points of the text, let me summarize some native ideas on energy flow and balance. The Indians believe that the spirit essence of all game animals is concentrated in certain hills in the forest where they lead a ghostly existence under the protection of a supernatural Master of Animals, whose phallic character is elaborated in many tales. The inside of these hills is imagined like that of an enormous longhouse. Periodically, in a drug-induced trance, shamans will penetrate into these womb-like abodes and will converse with the Master of Animals and ask him to release some of the game, to be killed then by the hunters. In return the shamans must replenish the energy potential that has been diminished by hunting, and this they accomplish by magically killing a number of people whose spirit essence will then enter the long-houses, in the shape of game animals. Those whom the shamans kill, that is, whose deaths he claims to have caused, are persons who, according to shamanic judgment, have disregarded some important social norm, such as the rules referring to incest, exogamy, and reciprocity.

The supernatural dwellings are thus inhabited by two categories of animals: the various zoological species that, eventually, are being hunted and killed, and the '*people*' who 'behaved like animals' and who now are being punished by finding themselves exposed to the danger of being sent out into the forest where they might be killed by the hunters.

To this we should add the following observation. The lonely hills are thought to be shamanic power sources but also danger spots where a person might become the victim of a shaman's or a spirit animal's displeasure. For this reason these spots are avoided by hunters and so they have become important game reserves; they are sanctuaries where game animals are abundant and quite tame. In this manner, the native idea that these hills are the womb-like breeding places of game animals has a quite realistic basis.

The average availability of game animals as food resources depends upon the quality of animal imagery and this, in turn, is largely determined by the effectiveness of shamanic power. Overhunting of a certain species usually means that people, for one reason or another, have ceased to operate with the symbolic image of that animal. For example, shamanic control of hunting and fishing usually consists in threats of illness. A person who does not feel well or who is obviously ill will consult a shaman who then questions the patient about the kind and quantity of game he has consumed and, subsequently, about dreams, nightmares, or visions in which animals may have appeared to him in a threatening or seductive manner. According to this information the shaman will point out the need for restrictions in hunting or fishing and, as a rule, these admonitions will be taken into account by the patient.

But there are a number of other possibilities; for example, the person may be ignorant or indifferent and might simply continue to hunt that particular species; or, if he fell ill, he might have rapidly recovered and so decided to disregard the shaman's orders.

There remains the further possibility that the shaman himself might have taken no particular interest in the patient's complaints and might even have failed to ask him about dreams and visions. It may happen, then, that a few men or a local community will seriously affect the availability of game through a number of quite unforeseeable personal and local reasons. Perhaps there *is no shaman* in the neighbourhood, or perhaps some young men who have worked for rubber gatherers or missionaries have come to flaunt tribal customs.

Now once a certain game animal becomes scarce, this is attributed to 'other people', to neighbours, to other tribes or to evil shamanistic manipulations. Scarcity is always blamed on the 'others' and so gives rise to, or intensifies, social conflicts.

As long as people are under shamanic control by the threat of illness (in reality, the threat of overpopulation and hunger), animal imagery will be vivid; people will constantly talk of animals, they will dream of them, they will feel threatened by night phantoms or by monstrous visions during their periodic narcotic trances; or they will feel elated by the prospects of a successful hunt, after a period of ritual abstinence.

However, from texts and conversations it becomes quite clear that *this imagery is not really concerned with animals as such*, but with projective mechanisms in which *animals represent people*. Deer, peccary, rodents, or fish will appear as seducers, as succubi; a hunter on his stand or a fisherman in his moored canoe will fall asleep and dream of being seduced by game animals that take the shape of forest women or of strange creatures that dwell in the depths of dark pools. These female images are taken to be the women of 'other people', of non-Tukanoan tribes. While the devouring aquatic creatures can be interpreted by us as maternal images, dream tapirs are threatening father figures.

I must emphasize here that these symbolic associations are *not* formulated only by the ethnographer, but are described as such by the Indians themselves.

The hunt, then, provides a stage upon which many social and psychological conflicts can be acted out. The ghostly longhouse with its inhabitants is a mirror image of society; it is one's home, one's family, one's neighbours and allies. To hunt in the forest is to court and to kill and eat one's opponents, one's competitors and oppressors. But let us return now to the text.

Analysis of the Text

Already in Section 1, after a few scene-setting commentaries, the narrator introduces the idea of animals behaving 'like people', and in Section 2 he states that tapirs had been founding lineages. This statement refers to ethnohistorical traditions according to which the Tukanoan tribes are newcomers and recent invaders of a territory originally inhabited by Arawakan Indians, people who were culturally and linguistically quite different. These Arawakans, some of whom continue to live farther to the north, had been designated as Tapir People, by the Tukanoans, and the descendants of mixed marriages were thus said to be of tapir ancestry. On a deeper level one might suggest that the 'founding of lineages' refers to a father image.

In Section 3 the narrator distinguishes two categories of tapirs: those that are supernaturally associated with the Arawakans, *and* the zoological species, the 'unimportant ones' as he calls them, who are said to be the servants of the others. This subservience provides the key to the identification of this category. In the interfluvial forests of the Northwest Amazon there still exist groups of nomadic hunter-gatherers, the so-called Makú Indians, who formerly raided the manioc fields of the sedentary and horticultural tribes. Even today the Makú continue to occupy a marginal position of what may be called subservience to several Tukanoan tribes. Wandering bands will steal manioc tubers or seedlings, or sometimes will stay for a while at a Tukano settlement and help in the daily work in house and field. The two categories of tapirs are thus identified with two different, but more *ancient*, tribal societies which eventually were superseded by the Tukanoans. The yearly round of fruiting seasons provides a further comparison; whereas tapirs feed on certain fruits that drop from trees, and will gather them near these trees, people prepare from the very same fruits a fermented beer which they consume during ritual gatherings.

Section 5 speaks in a quite matter-of-fact way of some practical aspects of hunting but, beginning with Section 6, the narrator approaches the latent problem of psychological projections. Referring mainly to *female* tapirs the hunter now makes some erotic innuendos that focus on the landing place located near a longhouse, where women go to fetch water, bathe, and gossip. In Tukano thought, landing places are spots with a high emotional content; they are points of articulation, liminal zones where opposite principles meet and interact, and the comparison with mineral licks or mudholes were the animals are wallowing is frequently elaborated in myths and tales.

In commenting upon tapirs having presentiments and becoming aware of a hunter's thoughts, the narrator now apparently changed the subject and began to speak of dreams. He mentioned that male tapirs would appear in dreams in a threatening manner, being of gigantic size and having huge genitals, while female tapirs would appear as strange and beautiful women who led the hunter astray and seduced him somewhere deep in the forest. When the man awoke from his dream he would realize that the tapir woman of his vision had not been a stranger at all, but rather a close and forbidden relative; he would then fall ill with a high fever and waste away.

These remarks of the hunter are highly significant and may be complemented here by some additional textual statements made on this occasion. Part of this complementary text says: "Before going to hunt, we have dreams. If we dream that we kill game, it will come true. We dream that we kill it and butcher it; if we dream like this, it will come true." I must add here that the term 'to butcher' (*bërëose*) has a sexual connotation in Tukano.

The text continues: "If we dream that we touch a woman, we shall kill deer. Sometimes we dream of a woman we cannot seduce; then the prey will escape us. If we dream that we kill a person and that we weep because of what we have done, there soon will be food to eat."

At this point I interrupted the narrator and asked him to what person he might be referring. His blunt reply was: "We dream that we are killing our father."

Conclusions

The relationship between food and sex in our hunter's tale is, of course, not surprising, nor are the obvious Oedipal projections and the occasional cannibalistic implications. Of interest, though, is the particular manner in which these problems of survival have been intellectualized and integrated into the shamanistic world-view, and how this conceptualization comes to constitute not only an effective guide to resource management, but also a guide to mental sanity, by providing an outlet for many psycho-social tensions. The concept of the supernatural longhouse replete with game, under the care of the Master of Animals, is not only a shamanistic response to the pressing ecological problems of the physical environment, but also to human conditions. A true balance can be found only within the framework of the homologation of cosmos-house-body.

To identify a game animal with a human being, with explicit aggressive intentions and implicit sexual ones, leads, according to the Indians, to punishment by illness. This idea is being fostered by all shamans who try to create and maintain guilt feelings through which they can control game depredation. The killing of most large game animals, such as tapir, deer, or peccary, is, therefore, always restricted by shamanic controls.

At the same time, shamans are fully aware that hunting provides an occasion on which aggressive tendencies may be acted out. In establishing a workable balance between conflicting feelings and actions, shamans play a truly fundamental role in that they take it upon themselves to deal with the feared Master of Animals who, in the context of his supernatural community, appears as the great shaman of all game animals.

There exists, then, a dualistic society of People and of Animals, the relationship between whom is similar to that which exists between two exogamic units. Just as Man the Hunter acts out his part and stalks his prey in the forest, so the game animals become the actors in a play staged by shamanistic ideology, the purpose of which is to provide a guide for survival.

In the Amazonian rainforest, when man is talking *of* animals and *to* animals, and is listening to their voices, *he is conversing with himself*, and the topic is physical, social, and psychological survival.

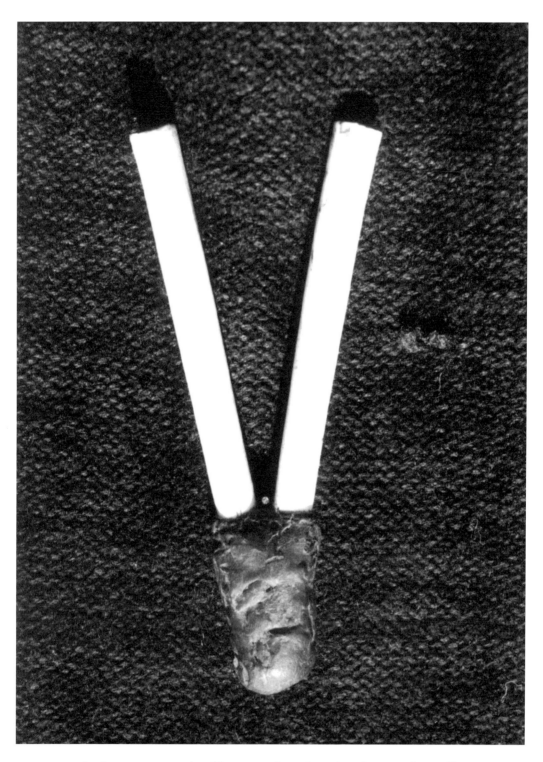

An instrument made of bones and used to absorb narcotic snuffs

V

Some Source Materials on Desana Shamanistic Initiation

The detailed study of aboriginal texts that refer to shamanic ideology and practice constitutes a rich field for ethnographic research which, however, in the case of most Colombian Indian societies, has remained largely unexplored. This is all the more unfortunate because in many regions of this country traditional shamanistic knowledge is rapidly disappearing. Subsequent tentative reconstructions from hearsay, of what 'the old people' did or said, are bound not only to lack significant detail, but also to miss that particular mark of authenticity which only the native speaker's active involvement and personal convictions can lend to a textual document. It is saddening to realize that every year that passes sees the irretrievable disappearance of a body of human knowledge and experience that might have enriched the intellectual and spiritual life of modern man, if only the indigenous possessor of this knowledge had been given the opportunity to record it for posterity.

But even in those cases where textual materials have been recorded, it is obvious that literal translations of texts, however voluminous the material may be, are likely to miss many implicit meanings and thus tend to present the reader with a rather one-sided and possibly quite erroneous view. The people, animals, plants, landmarks, and actions that make up the body of most shamanistic texts, are only metaphors for a dense network of conceptualizations that constitute the essential premises of the shamanic world-view, and it becomes therefore necessary to assess the cultural value of each of them, in order to be able to comprehend this network. It follows that, quite apart from exact transcriptions and translations, texts should be accompanied by extensive notes and commentaries based upon particularized and repeated discussions with knowledgeable native informants; interpretive inquiry should extend to every part of the document, no matter how ordinary it might appear. It is only in this form that a text can come to constitute a truly useful instrument for research and, at the same time, will do justice to the complexity and profoundness of the aboriginal culture.

For the present discussion I have selected two short texts of the Desana. These texts refer both to shamanistic initiation, but differ in that Text I contains only a brief description, in an almost colloquial style, of an initiate's first experiences, while Text II enters into many details of shamanistic practice and, furthermore, presents most of them in the particular shamanic idiom and in the context of specific spells. These spells are pronounced by the master-shaman during the initiation and can, occasionally, be repeated, should the particular state of the newly initiate demand it.

The texts were dictated by an elderly Desana shaman, known to me for many years, who occupies a highly respected position among his people, and who agreed to discuss at length every section and scene, in the company of several other men. Since practically all Vaupés Indians are multilingual, the texts and many related topics were also discussed by me with several Pira-Tapuya, Uanano, and Tukano proper, informants, some of whom occupy shamanic status. The transcriptions and translations, together with the commentaries, were checked at several successive stages of progress and I believe that, in this manner, a reasonable degree of exactness in the rendering and interpretation has been achieved. In translating I have taken care to give, in the first instance, the commonly accepted literal meaning of words, while alternative and implicit meanings are given in the section on Notes and Commentaries. All sentences are numbered so as to facilitate cross references between the English translation, and the commentaries. Words that were not spoken but that complete or clarify a turn of phrase, are distinguished with square brackets.

Among the Tukano tribes it is customary that next to the narrator should sit a man who closely follows the thread of the recital and who then rapidly rephrases the last few words of a sentence, in a rhetoric question which, in turn, is being acknowledged by the speaker, with an affirmative *aa*. For example, the narrator might finish a sentence by saying: "...and then he returned home", whereupon the other will immediately add: "Did he return home?", being promptly answered by the narrator: *aa*, meaning 'yes, he did'. Since these repetitions do not contain any additional information I have deleted them in the English translations. In my transcription of the Desana language, *ë* is pronounced like *e* in *que* (French), while *h* is pronounced like *j* in *rojo* (Spanish). The letters LG indicate that the word is taken from *lengua geral*. The exogamic group called Tukano is designated by me as 'Tukano proper', in order to avoid confusion with the wider Tukanoan Linguistic Family.

Before turning to the textual analysis a few introductory remarks are in order, to provide the reader with some general guidelines to an understanding of the texts, previous to their detailed interpretation.

Among the Desana and their neighbours, that is, the Pira-Tapuya, Uanano, Tukano proper, Tuyuka, and some others, shamanistic initiation is a process of transformation the different stages of which are conceived as being patterned, in all essence, after the successive stages of intra-uterine development, but are observed in reverse and condensed in time: the initiate symbolically dies and must then be reborn into a new existence, that of a shaman. In the preceding training period the apprentice has had to submit to a very rigorous discipline. In the course of many months or even years of instruction, under the guidance of one or several shamans who either are members of the apprentice's local group, or whom the apprentice periodically visits, the aspirant to shamanic office has acquired a large body of esoteric knowledge consisting of plant and animal lore, drug use, cosmology and mythology, genealogical traditions, together with the knowledge of specific ritual procedures. During this preliminary period the novice has been introduced into the hallucinatory dimension of narcotic drugs which, according to the Indians, provide the principal mechanism of communication with the other world. Once the apprentice has mastered this knowledge and has given proof of his readiness to submit to the rules of abstinence that dominate a shaman's life, his master, occasionally even two or three experienced shamans, will proceed to the formal initiatory ritual. For this purpose the apprentice and his teachers must retire to a remote spot in the forest where they go to live in a temporary shelter, a hut that contains only the barest essentials: a few hammocks, a hearth, some cooking vessels, but hardly more. No women are allowed to approach and all visitors are excluded.

The small group of men will live in isolation for several months, subsisting on some boiled manioc starch, but little else. At night they will sing and dance, under the influence of different narcotic drugs, and after about two months they will barely be able to walk and then will spend most of the time in their hammocks, their postrate emaciated bodies convulsed, their faces contorted, their hoarse voices chanting endlessly to the rhythm of their gourd rattles.

This scene, of dead or dying shamans, of skeletal beings in a remote spot of the forest, appears occasionally in Desana imagery: in tales, dreams, and hallucinatory states. It depicts the first stage of portentous events; a man has to die before he can be reborn from himself, and shamanistic initiation is, fundamentally, a process of death and subsequent rebirth.

Sometimes the process of initiation is compared by the Desana to a man's life-span, condensed into an abbreviated time-dimension. The 'death' of the initiate is marked by his skeletonization and his falling into a deep trance. This state has been brought about by the combined and escalated effects of several narcotic beverages and snuffs, the active psychotropic agents of which are mainly Bufotenine and Harmine. By saying 'combined' I mean that the master-shaman systematically administers a sequence of specifically prepared drugs, the effects of which are known to him from experience, and which he can modify by dosification and certain admixtures. This means that the nature and intensity of the trance states are by no means a mere chance product of intoxication, but are carefully manipulated by the leading shaman. The 'death' of the initiate is symbolized by his 'leaving this world' and by his ecstatic, bird-like flight into the clouds, but he soon returns once more from this vertical dimension, and the next stage of his experience consists in a highly abstract, but still earthbound, dimension, at the mouth of a symbolic river and at its headwaters.

River symbolism, in Desana thought, is very complex and I shall mention here only some of its fundamental aspects, while leaving a full discussion to the analysis of Text II. In shamanic metaphorical topography, all rivers of the Vaupés territory are said to run from West to East. They are compared to the outstretched bodies of anacondas, mythical vehicles that, in the beginning of time, carried people all over the land, to settle them on the riverbanks. The courses of the rivers, the same as the bodies of these mythical snakes, are imagined to be sectioned into socio-geographic units separated by rapids or falls. The true generative power of a river lies at its mouth; it is there where the river has its 'beginnings', while the headwaters are its 'end'. But these extremes are reversible, they are interchangeable, in that life may be compared to the *ascent* of a river, from the birthgiving East to the life-ending West of the headwaters; or to the *descent* of a river, from spiritual rebirth at the headwaters, to a new life in another dimension.

However, metaphoric thought does not cling to one single easy analogy; Desana shamanism will make use of any number of other images that, in an interchangeable fashion, may come to express a process of transformation. Intra-uterine development, plant growth, hallucinatory trance, the process of cooking, or the firing of pottery, these and many others combine into one single imagery, that of transformation from one essential state into another, the imagery of creation, of continuity.

In the course of the discussion that follows, I shall repeatedly refer to these distinct, but combined, strands of metaphoric thought and shall, whenever possible, try to amplify some of their intricate patterns.

I shall turn now to the analysis of Text I which, as I have mentioned already, contains a brief description of some aspects of shamanistic initiation. The English translation is followed by Notes and Commentaries.

Text I

1. Their master [shaman] first absorbs the snuff and he has practice in this. 2. They prepare snuff, plenty of it. 3. This done, they blow it into their nostrils. 4. One dose into this nostril and another dose into the other. 5. Once they have absorbed it, they grind another bit. 6. What? It [the snuffing tube] is [made from] a Harpy Eagle bone. 7. The powder is put into the bone [tube] and they give them a dose into this nostril and another dose into that one. 8. This done, they administer some *Virola* bark; here one dose and there another, not more. 9. This done, they throw into the air some white down feathers and now, singing, they rise.

10. This done, we have, first of all, the rattle that is adorned with oropendola feathers. 11. Inside it are quartz crystals. 12. The handle is made from a piece of *sëmë* wood. 13. Another [suitable] wood is that of a *paakaroyoagë* tree. 14. [From] the red part of that fallen [tree].

15. The cloud rises up high and they grasp it, all the while singing and shaking their rattles, and they absorb [the cloud]. 16. Once they have absorbed it, they are ordered to swallow what has been given to them. 17. Having done so, they continue. 18. Absorbing [more] snuff they continue in this state of suspension; it is dangerous.

19. Then they take the splinters. 20. These splinters appear quite inexplicably. 21. They take these splinters and introduce them into their arms.

22. This done, they merely sit and look toward the East where the sun rises, and they see the *vëavëa* birds approaching. 23. There are large Harpy Eagles and small ones. 24. They are singing, and then they [the shamans] shake their rattles: thi-thi-thi. 25. This done, they disappear once more.

26. Next they drink 'fish *yajé*' from small gourd cups. 27. They drink only one cup. 28. It is very strong; I myself have taken it; it is very strong. 29. That day we became overpowered and everything was turning around us, and the soul was strangely deranged. 30. If they are strong, they can stand it; but it is very bad. 31. The ordinary *yajé* is not so bad, [but] this one is awful. 32. This is what they do.

33. When they are thus engaged they have a [woman] brought to them who has recently been taken ill. 34. They observe her and see drops of water, this being an indication that they must asperse her with water. 35. They see these drops of water falling. 36. When they thus fall, they asperse the patient with water. 37. While thus splashing water [over the patient], the splinters and thorns drop off. 38. When the sun is over there, before noon, they stop.

39. During all this time they must be fasting. 40. They put some manioc starch on top of the broth and drink this. 41. When they are thus engaged, they fast and for one month they eat nothing but broth. 42. Later on they may eat some small fish. 43. In this way they acquire their power. 44. After having pronounced a spell, they now may eat and he [the master shaman] has thus shown them what they have to do.

45. This is how the old people used to do it, and this is the way they still do it; that is all.

Notes and Commentaries to Text I

1. The text opens with the scene when the master shaman administers a specially prepared narcotic snuff. The Desana term *viho* is used to designate several varieties of snuff; here it refers to a snuff prepared from the resin that is contained in

Harpy Eagle

A group of dancers. The lead dancer carries harpy down feathers. Pira-paraná

the inner bark of a jungle tree of the genus *Virola*, a Myristicacea, several species of which (*V. calophylla*, *V. calophylloidea*, *V. theidora*) are found in the Vaupés territory. For details see Reichel-Dolmatoff 1975: 20ff; Seitz 1967: 335-336; Schultes 1954: 248-250.

2. In the preparation of snuff from *Virola* bark, several admixtures are used by the Desana, according to the occasion or the desired effects. These additives may consist of powdered tobacco, powdered coca leaves, the ashes of Cecropia leaves, or dried and shredded stems of *yajé* (LG) vines (*Banisteriopsis* sp.). For shamanistic initiation the snuff is mixed with the white powder shaved off a small (12 cms.) stalactite. These stalactites are designated as *abe yeru*, 'sun-penis'; in fact, the narcotic snuff is said to be a divine semen. The snuff alluded to in this section is prepared with this stalactite powder, added to a *Virola* base.

3. Narcotic snuffs are usually absorbed through a V-shaped instrument made of two short tubular bird bones through which the consumer himself blows the powder first into one nostril, and then into another. In shamanistic initiation, as in certain other rituals, the master shaman will sometimes use a somewhat longer and straight single tube to blow the snuff into the initiate's nostrils, with a very sharp puff.

4. The text says *goa*, 'bone', meaning that each time a 'bone-full' is being administered. I have translated this as 'dose'. The term 'bone' has here a phallic connotation; it transmits a seminal matter.

5. The act of grinding or scraping refers to the salactite powder.

6. This is an interjection; someone had put the question to the shaman, of what kind of bone the tube was made of; *gaa* is the Harpy Eagle (*Harpya harpyja*), a very powerful bird of prey. In the Desana mind this bird is closely associated with shamanism, and its soaring flight is likened to narcotic ecstasy. Its erectile crest is compared to a shaman's feather-crown, and its piercing cry: *keeeee-ye*, is a shaman's call. Jaguar, Harpy Eagle, and Anaconda, are the Desana shaman's avatars.

8. This refers to another admixture based on *Virola*.

9. The yellowish-white down feathers (*vihto*) of the Harpy Eagle carry seminal connotations and are often used as adornments, or are manipulated in shamanistic rituals where they represent a fertility concept. In the present case the act of actually swallowing these little downy feathers, combines the concept of seminal impregnation with their fluffy cloud-like quality; however, it was made clear by all informants that the initiate does not assume harpy shape.

10. Shaman's rattles are often adorned with the tail-feathers of the oropendola bird (*Icteridae*), whose yellow colour symbolizes solar and male fertility. The name of this bird is *umu*, which is closely related to *ëmë*, meaning 'day', or 'sun'; it is a solar bird, prominent in mythology.

11. When rhythmically shaking a gourd rattle for hours at a stretch, the tiny sharp quartz crystals it contains will ignite the minute particles they shave off the

soft interior walls of the gourd, and eventually smoke, or even sparks, will emerge from the small holes or slits of the rattle. This phenomenon has been described by Wilbert (1974: 92), to whom belongs the credit of having first observed it, among the Venezuelan Warao. In the present case, the crystalline particles are interpreted by the Desana as semen, while the hollow body of the gourd rattle is said to be a womb. The production of fire, by the rhythmic shaking of the instrument, is an act of uterine creation, or re-creation, if performed in a curing ritual when the rattle is being used as a healing wand. The minute particles are called *marari* and constitute, as we shall see, an important element in the process of transformation.

12. The handle of a shaman's rattle penetrates the entire body of the hollow gourd and is thus likened to a phallus. It must be made from one of several very special woods taken from a tree that has lain submerged for a long time at the bottom of a deep pool in a river, and that is very hard, smooth, and of a black or reddish colour. The text states that the wood must be *boa merera*, literally, 'grown rotten', meaning that it must be seasoned, cured. The two woods mentioned here are *kare* (*Chrysophyllum vulgare*) or Star Apple, a tree the fruits of which have a seminal connotation; and *sëmé*, a leguminous tree (*Dahlbergia* sp.), the pods of which have an uterine connotation. In a trance state the apprentice imagines that he dives into the water, to obtain the wood for the handle of his rattle. This ritual immersion is a standard practice in initiation. It is interesting to observe that, while ordinary rattles have a straight, rod-shaped handle, a shaman's rattle usually has an asymmetrical, forked shape, rather like a deer antler. This may be significant and there is some suggestion of an intentional similarity, but I have no further evidence.

13. This is another wood, from an undetermined species; it is said to be very hard and of a red colour, the Spanish vernacular name being *palo de sangre*. The name of the tree, *paakaroyoagë*, is derived from *pari*, 'to beat', *karo*, 'long stemmed', *yoa*, 'elongated', followed by the masculine suffix *-gë*.

15. A shaman's ecstatic flights are said to reach different altitudinal levels; some only extend to the low-lying layer of dark rain clouds; others reach above it, where white cloud-layers are suspended; others may attain the Milky Way, and still others go beyond it. When asking the shaman about the nature of the white cloud layer, he said that it consisted of 'the white essence of the Harpy Eagle', explaining that it was a state of insemination, of impregnating whiteness. The initiates had to 'absorb' this whiteness and thus become saturated with generative energies. They could keep suspended only if they continued to agitate their rattles.

16. At this point, the shaman explained, the initiates were penetrated with the seminal 'whiteness' and now the master shaman ordered them to meditate on this state. They had to assimilate ('swallow') the experience and now remain in a state of acute awareness of their new command over generative powers. The

term which I have translated here as 'assimilate', is *uhuri*, a verb that can also mean 'to absorb' or 'to smoke'. It is related to *ëhëri*, a verb that implies an act of transformation. The shaman explained once more that the saturation with the 'white' generative power constitutes a process of insemination.

17. The insemination stage ends here and the initiate goes on to a new experience.

18. The expression *gëadëaro* has been translated here as 'dangerous'; it has the alternative meanings of 'strange', 'incredible', 'imposing', or 'difficult'.

19. The acquisition of pathogenic splinters and thorns is an important part of shamanistic initiation; they are used mainly against personal enemies.

20. That is, the master shaman supplies them by sleight of hand.

21. The shaman places the small black splinters on the inside of the initiate's left forearm, and then 'pushes' them into the flesh, with a symbolic gesture. These splinters can be cast at a person, however distant, with a violent movement of the arm (Reichel-Dolmatoff: 1975 80).

22. Here begins another stage. The *vëavëa* birds are imaginary creatures and are described as being similar to grey herons. When a shaman has visions in which large flights of these birds appear near a lagoon, he knows that the rainy season is approaching. The 'natural' counterparts of these birds are certain small grey herons, called *vava*.

26. The so-called 'fish *yajé*' is probably a species of *Banisteriopsis* or, perhaps, a combination of different species. No botanical determination is available; it is said to be used only by shamans (Reichel-Dolmatoff 1975: 151-152).

28. Here the narrator refers to his own initiation.

31. By this, *Banisteriopsis caapi* and *B. rusbyana* are meant.

33. Correct diagnosis of an illness is supposed to be part of an initiate's tests.

35. The appearance of what seem to be brilliant drops of water, is said to be a frequent phenomenon in these trance states.

37. The pathogenic splinters are being washed off.

39. The term *vera* means 'starch' but, in this context, it is a fertility word, the same as *poga*, 'flour', which is related to *bogá*, 'energy'. The initiate ingests seminal foods, in order to become impregnated with generative powers.

43. What has been translated here as 'power', is the term *beharo*, an alternative meaning being 'rank'. The word is related to *behsu*, 'arrow', and the corresponding verb, *behari*, means 'to touch', 'to collide', 'to acquire rank', 'to arm oneself'. Arrows are symbolic power tools of transformation; a touch with an arrow bestows rank and power upon a person; this is expressed in the root *-eh*. (cf. Section 16, *ëhëri*).

45. *mëragea*, 'the old ones', 'the ancestors'. The narrator emphasizes that their traditions continue and that shamanistic initiation is still the same as in the past.

While in Text I the narrator had used a simple, descriptive language, in which he employed common denotative terms, Text II is replete with covert meanings and develops the theme of shamanistic initiation on a very abstract level. Although the reader will easily recognize many similarities of expression, he will soon be able to distinguish the subtleties of the specific shamanic idiom.

Text II

1. There is a *Virola* bark tree the leaves of which are red and green on the underside. 2. They prepare [the snuff] on a clay dish. 3. They prepare it on the crab dish. 4. This thread is annointed with milk and with *tooka* sap; with firewood from the shrimp tree, with firewood from the bat tree, and with firewood from the *puikaro* tree; always in accordance with these classes of firewood.

5. These *Virola* barks, these luminous spots, they penetrate into us and make us dizzy. 6. These dishes they touch and anoint with *miratavá* leaves; they cool the dishes, they cool them, and when they take hold of them they remove the luminous spots; they anoint these dishes with *tooka* sap and with milk and, taking hold of them, they manipulate them and control them. 7. Taking hold of them they control them, they control the luminous spots; they destroy them by taking hold of the luminous spots and by cutting them off; by taking hold of the luminous spots and by removing them. 8. [They do this] so that the luminous spots will not make us dizzy.

9. Then comes Day-Person, the *aracú* fish, and his dish for *Virola* snuff. 10. This snuff is called the snuff of the penis of the sun. 11. This is called the snuff of the sun. 12. It is like a metal dish. 13. It consists of firewood from the *puikaro* tree and from the bat tree; this firewood pertains to mankind. 14. This is the dish for the preparation. 15. Because of these heats, the game animals of the forest are considered to form part of humanity. 16. They are the game animals.

17. These dishes they anoint with milk and with *tooka* sap, to be reborn, [and they touch them with] the leaves of *miratavá*, and so they control them. 18. So that this dish will not make us dizzy on that day, so it won't make us dizzy. 19. So it won't affect us. 20. They take hold of them and throw them away. 21. They oppose their helpers and destroy them. 22. They anoint these luminous spots with milk with *tooka* sap, to be reborn, and they control these threads and destroy the luminous spots and throw them away.

23. They take hold of these luminous spots and push them away and destroy them.

24. After this come the round particles of *Virola* snuff; they contain the same seminal power as macaw [feathers].

25. So that these luminous spots will not make us dizzy, they take hold of them and control them by taking hold of them. 26. The dizziness produced by these luminous spots, they dominate it with the odour of *bayapia* leaves; this

dizziness overpowers us and makes us feel nauseous. 27. So that these luminous spots will not make us feel nauseous and will not make throb our hearts, they control the luminous spots. 28. Taking hold of the luminous spots they resist them, destroy them, and throw them away. 29. So that the swelling will not grow, they take hold of them, bite them to shreds, and throw them away. 30. They take hold of the growing swelling, manipulate it, shake it, and throw it away.

31. Next comes the crystalline snuff. 32. They anoint the luminous spots and the luminous threads with milk and with *tooka* sap, and so they will not make us dizzy, they take hold of them, control them, and destroy them. 33. So that [the evil] will not increase, they take hold of it, bite it to shreds, and throw it away.

34. There also is *carayurú* starch. 35. There is that *carayurú* starch. 36. This overpowers the seminal essence. 37. They control the seminal essence. 38. Taking hold of this seminal essence they control it; taking hold of it they destroy it. 39. The odour of *bayapia* leaves makes us dizzy. 40. They take hold of these luminous spots, they destroy them and cut off the energy of the current. 41. So that the swelling will not grow, they take hold of it, bite it to shreds, and throw it away.

42. Then there is that thread of fever. 43. From the limit of the headwaters to the limit of the rivermouth extend these threads. 44. That thread is the course of the sickness; it has a red, a black, and a white [section]. 45. These threads make us see luminous spots, and make us dizzy. 46. This combination of threads makes us feel nauseous.

47. They anoint these threads with milk, they make them reborn; they anoint them with *tooka* sap and they control these threads with [the coolness of] *bayapia* leaves and, taking hold of them, they control them. 48. These threads grow in us. 49. So that this swelling will not grow, they take hold of them, manipulate them and, taking hold of them they control them. 50. They take hold of them and control them; they take hold of the luminous spots and destroy them; they cut them off and, taking hold of the luminous spots, they throw them away. 51. So that the swelling will not continue, they bite them to shreds and throw them away. 52. They manipulate them, shake them, and throw them away.

53. Next comes the jaguar plant. 54. That, too, exists. 55. That plant, too, belongs to the shamans. 56. It belongs to the same group.

57. So that the growing luminous spots will not make us dizzy, they take hold of them and control them; taking hold of them they cut them off; taking hold of the luminous spots they cut them off and throw them away; taking hold of the luminous spots they cut them off, bite them to shreds, and throw them away. 58. Shaking them they destroy them and throw them away.

59. They do the same with 'fish *yajé*'. 60. They drink it. 61. It is the *yajé* of shamans.

62. Next comes that poisonous vine. 63. This flame is divided into red, yellow, and white [sections]. 64. Flames have a dark outline. 65. This outline makes us feverish and makes us dizzy. 66. It makes us feel nauseous. 67. They anoint it

with milk and with *tooka* sap, and with the threads of *miratavá*, and they take hold of the luminous spots and control them. 68. Taking hold of the luminous spots they control them, cut them off, and destroy them. 69. So that they will not make us dizzy, they anoint them with milk and with *tooka* sap; taking hold of them they manipulate them and they cut off the energy of the current. 70. This is the spell against our malaise. 71. This spell takes a long time.

72. Next comes our *yajé* vine. 73. There is a knotty vine, a fish-poison vine, a taro vine, and a *too* vine. 74. This is how they are called. 75. There is a vessel, a vessel and gourd cups, and a clay dish. 76. There is a clay vessel, for the *yajé*. 77. This vessel has designs painted on it with yellow clay. 78. The vessel has zigzag designs painted on it. 79. There is a little stirring rod of knotty vine. 80. This little rod makes us dizzy because of the movements of the luminous points; they anoint it with milk and with *tooka* sap and, taking hold of it, they manipulate it and control it. 81. So that the luminous spots will not make us dizzy, they manipulate them and control them; they take hold of them and control them; taking hold of the luminous spots they tear them to shreds and throw them away; they take hold of the luminous spots and destroy them by cutting them off. 82. So that the [evil] will not increase, they take hold of the luminous spots and throw them away; they take hold of the luminous spots and destroy them; taking hold of them, they bite them to shreds, and taking hold of their particles they destroy them and throw them away. 83. And so there won't be the energy of the liquid, they cut it off.

84. The odour of *bayapia* leaves is our adornment. 85. There is [an odour] of red branches, white branches, and green branches. 86. There are agouti leaves, red and black ones; there are agouti leaves.

87. So that they will not make us dizzy, they anoint them with milk and with tooka sap; they manipulate them and control them. 88. They take hold of them and control them; they take hold of the energy of the liquid and cut it off to destroy it. 89. They destroy the luminous spots and throw them away; they push them away and, taking hold of them, they destroy them and throw them away. 90. Here it ends.

Notes and Commentaries to Text II

1. On *Virola* see Text I, Notes and Commentaries, Section 1.

2. *siburi*, 'to condense', 'to concentrate (by boiling)'; cf. below, Section 3.

3. *gami mata*, 'crab-clay'; this expression pertains to the shamanistic idiom of transformation. Among many Vaupés tribes the manufacture of pottery obeys rules according to which each exogamic group (Desana, Pira-Tapuya, Tukano proper, etc.) must obtain its potter's clay from the territory of its complementary unit. This clay is then called *gami mata* because it shares an obvious character-

istic with crabs, in that it is transformed by heat and from a bluish-grey colour turns red under the influence of fire: this process is referred to by shamans as 'the way of the crab'. In fact, there is a double meaning attached to this, in that *mata* means clay, but *maata* is derived from *maa*, 'way', 'trail'; therefore, *gami maata* means 'the way of the crab', a process of transformation. The small clay platter on which the narcotic snuff is being prepared is, of course, itself a product of this transformation and, in Desana logic, thus enhances the transformative power of the narcotic.

The shamam and the other commentators took pains to point out that the verb *siburi* (cf. above, Section 2), although it meant 'to condense', in the sense of 'to prepare', had the implicit meaning of 'to make perfect', 'to make adequate'. This 'perfection' refers mainly to the specific brownish colour of the snuff, a colour that expresses its 'edibility', a quality designated as *bogë*. For a detailed discussion of this concept, see Reichel-Dolmatoff 1978b (Essay 2 in this book). The action, they said, did not refer to a technical, physical preparation, but to a process of spiritual purification.

4. This sentence contains references to several rather complex ideas. The text states that 'that thread' (*iri dare*) is being anointed. The term *da* (plural, *dari*) means, literally, 'thread', 'string', 'vine', but can also stand for 'line', 'filament', 'series', anything 'strung together' in a sequence and that constitutes a chain, a conduct that transmits an influence, an energy; this may be a narcotic vine, a flying spark, or a ritual necklace. In the present context the word *da* was said to refer to a series of very small luminous elements which are imagined to circle around a centre, similar to sparks flying from an open fire into the dark, and tracing a glowing trail or 'thread'. This image, apart from being taken from the observation of a fire at night, of glowing embers or a torch, is patterned after certain photic sensations perceived under the influence of a narcotic drug, which are quite independent of an external light source. In his commentaries the shaman explained that these glowing threads constitute a communication between the beholder (in this case, the initiate) and the ecstatic dimension he is about to enter. This communication, according to the shaman, is awe-inspiring and its impact must be assuaged by anointing. As I have mentioned elsewhere (Reichel-Dolmatoff 1976b. See essay 7 in this book), in this and in other spells, a sexual impregnation is being enacted, and the anointing with milk (human breast milk) and the sap of the *tooka* plant, is an essential part of this procedure. The plant is a Melasomacea, probably *Tococa guianensis* Aublet, or *Clidemia* sp. What is being anointed here is the dish or, rather, in the shaman's words, 'the power of the dish'; this dish is seen as a female element impregnated with seminal snuff.

The expression *mahsukaa* is derived from *mahsari*, 'to cure', with the implicit meaning of 'to create', 'to re-create', 'to renovate', 'to make (or become) reborn'; but in an important shamanistic metaphor the verb is linked to *mahsuri* and thus is made to signify 'to make perfect for use'.

The different kinds of firewood represent, according to the shaman, three distinct but related, heat-producing (that is, transformative) principles. The 'shrimp tree' (*Pourouma cecropiaefolia* Mart.) has phallic and seminal associations; its wood is whitish, with red veins, similar to a river shrimp, a food which is said to be aphrodisiac. The 'bat tree' exudes a red latex and its wood burns very fast, producing great heat; the name alludes to blood-sucking bats and to Desana theories of conception according to which the human embryo is formed by a mixture of male semen and female blood (see Reichel-Dolmatoff 1978b, essay 2 in this book). The *puikerogë* tree is a leguminous (?) tree of the open forest environment, which is said to be similar to a *sëmé* tree (*Dahlbergia* sp.), except that its fruits are not edible. Desana women manufacture from its inner bark a carrying strap for their food baskets, and this bark has a very peculiar, pungent odour which men compare with menstrual or estrous smells. To say of a woman that 'she smells of *puikaro*' is a standard insult, meaning to say that she 'displays a behaviour fit only for animals' (Reichel-Dolmatoff 1978b, essay 2 in this book). The commentators went on to explain that every time heat was being spoken of as being produced by different woods, what was really meant was the range of colours of yellow and red flames. The main problem, they explained, consisted in combining male (yellow) and female (red) elements, and in balancing their respective 'energies' (*bogari*) in the act of insemination.

This passage, then, describes the various sensations of the initiate who, in the first stage of a *Virola* trance, enters into the process of transformation.

5. The expression *iri nomeri* is glossed here, initially, as 'these luminous spots'. While by *dari*, multicoloured luminous streaks or fleeting 'threads' are meant, the word *nomeri* means, in a general sense, 'to paint with fine dots'. However, in shamanistic metaphoric language it can also mean 'to ejaculate'. It refers to the image of a large number of small moving, yellow and red dots, approximately in equal proportion. These glowing dots represent the life-creating combination of male and female components, during the first three months of pregnancy. Semen and blood are mixing in an environment of increasing heat but, the shaman commented, it was not yet sure if the embryo would survive. He added that the visual perception of *nomeri* dots was always superceded by a phenomenon called *marari* (singular, *mara*), a mass of luminous particles similar to powdered quartz crystals (cf. Text I, Section 11).

Here, however, another meaning of the term *nomeri* must be mentioned. Woman, in Desana, is *nomeo* (plural, *nomea*) and the root *nom* contains several meanings that range from 'scintillating', 'exciting', 'colourful', to the description of states of intense affection, of passion, and of love. To convey a general idea of these meanings, I shall quote some textual expressions. For example, when a man says of a woman: "She made me see stars" (*nomeri inyakë yiakuma*), literally: 'luminous-spots-see-she me made' he is not referring to a love affair, but simply wants to say that she 'circled around him' and that she 'shone upon him', and 'illuminated' him with her presence. Another man said: "Women are like sparks from a fire; they shine briefly and then they are gone." In both examples quoted here, the men see themselves as luminous centres surrounded by *dari* threads and *nomeri* dots.

Taking into account this interpretation of *nomeri*, the meaning of the initial sentence would change from 'these luminous spots' to 'these women'. In fact, the commentators of the text explained that 'it is the women who make us dizzy', in the sense that they formed a disturbing and dissociating element, because of the promiscuous tendencies that are being attributed to them. The process of 'perfecting' (*siburi*) consists, therefore, in the careful blending of yellow and red procreative energies, into a state of 'controlled temperature'.

Before going further, I must explain that the luminous sensations referred to here by the terms *dari*, *marari*, and *nomeri*, are said to be characteristic of the initial stages of a narcotic trance. They are believed to manifest themselves not only under the influence of *Virola* snuff, but also of *Banisteriopsis* concoctions, or of any other hallucinogenic preparation. Technically, these sensations are called *phosphenes* and can summarily be described as subjective light patterns which illuminate 'flash-like' the visual field, but which otherwise are independent from an external light source. The perception of these patterns is entoptic, that is, they are not the result of mere visual, retinal observation, but are generated mainly in a neuronal system which includes the retinal ganglion network together with the cortical and subcortical range. Being thus originated within the eye and the brain, these light patterns are common to all men; they are inbuilt (see, among others, Eichmeier and Höfer 1974; Reichel-Dolmatoff 1969, 1978b [essay 2 in this book]; Siegel and West 1975). Even in quite 'normal' states, these phosphenes, which may be latent, can occasionally be triggered by certain environmental sensorial stimuli, and then may suddenly project themselves upon normal vision. For example, the Desana often compare sexual intercourse with a hallucinatory experience and state that, on these occasions, they will perceive *marari* and *nomeri* patterns. The same phenomenon is said to occur on other emotion-charged occasions such as nightmares, erotic dreams, during prolonged fasting, a sudden fright, the sound of a certain musical instrument, or the perception of a certain smell. These inbuilt reactions, then, form important models for chains of associations.

Lastly, the word *me'biriri*, mentioned in this section, describes the effect of the drug upon the initiate, in terms of 'penetrating' into him, and of making a disturbing and essentially seminal impact upon his mind.

6. To alleviate this very unsettling state of the initiate, the shamanistic spell now introduces a 'cooling' element in the form of fresh *saviru* leaves. These are described as the small, fleshy, and very green leaves of a luxuriant jungle tree called *miratavá* (LG), the very hard wood of which is used for canoe-making. In this spell, the shaman touches with these leaves the 'hot' clay dish which contains the

snuff, and thus 'cools' it. The shaman commented that this dish, made of 'crab clay', symbolized the male and female elements, the state of transformation, of 'being fired'. But here the shaman and the other commmentators mentioned another aspect; the specific name of the *saviru* tree stands here for the generalized concept of *saveri*, referring to an initial, unripe state of plant growth. Among the 'energies' (*bogari*) contained in the shamanistic plants called *tooka* or *toon-da* (Melastomacea) exists a triadic division of the growth stages of their fruits, into *saveri-da* (unripe, green, and conical in shape), *yëbëri-da* (ripe and rounded, of a somewhat reddish colour), and *kare-da* (almost over-ripe, and of a yellow colour). This sequence is also comparable to the developmental stages of the human life-span. In the present case, it is thc *saveri-da* stage that is being alluded to, thus indicating an incipient and, essentially, 'cool' state. The fresh fruits and leaves touch and 'move' the initiate, exercising a soothing and cooling action over him. After much elaboration of this theme, the shaman stated that the 'coolness' of plant growth was a figure of speech; what was meant was 'the coolness of sexual passion', of a perfect blending of 'heat' and 'colour', which had to be accomplished quite beyond the physical level. He added that, by touching the dish with milk and *tooka* sap, the disturbing aspects of the *nomeri* dots were eliminated.

The expression *veapi-yuu* is yet another rather characteristic shamanic term which is frequently employed in exorcising or purifying formulas; it is derived from *veari*, 'to take out and put on a side', and *yuuri*, 'to make disappear', 'to suppress', 'to make descend', 'to eliminate'. These spells often contain the expression *tuunyari*, from *tuuri*, 'to push', and *nyari*, 'to hold'; I have initially glossed it as 'to resist', 'to oppose', 'to interrupt'; however, the commentators emphasized that, apart or, rather, above this overt meaning, stood the concept of moral 'control' and pointed out that 'coolness' dampened all passions and that the expression *tuuneanuguri* implied the idea of 'orientation', of the channeling of all drives into culturally sanctioned directions. Another characteristic idiom is *taameyuukakoma*, derived from *tari*, 'to cut', 'to divide', 'to destroy', and *meyuri*, 'to throw away'. All these are typical shamanistic power words by which evil is being banished.

8. The initiate's state of 'dizziness' is described by the term *tuusororo*, from *tuuri*, 'to push' (cf. above, Section 7), and *sorori*, 'to move in circles', 'to mill around'. In the metaphoric idiom of shamans, *tuuri* also means 'to impregnate', 'to copulate', while *sorori* means 'to cook', 'to boil'. The shaman explained that the dizziness referred to the initiate's condition of uterine gestation, of his being 'cooked'. (For details on this symbolism, see Reichel-Dolmatoff 1978b, essay 2 in this book.) Here again, the term *nomeri* acquires the meaning of 'women', of female sexuality, and the shaman explained that what he had meant to say was: "...so that women will not disturb our social life...". In saying this he used the expressions 'to interfere' and 'to unbalance', as equivalents of 'to disturb'. He

added that one might recognize the specific meaning of the term *nomeri*, by its pronunciation; if the second syllable was nasalized, it referred to women.

9. This section refers to *Virola* snuff that has been mixed with the powdery shavings from a stalactite. The term 'Day-Person' refers to the sun and, in a wider sense, to the Desana who refer to themselves as *ëmëkori-mahsá*, 'day-revolving people'. The *boreka* fish (*Leporinus copelandi* Steindachner), or *aracú* (LG), is the mythical ancestor of the highest-ranking Desana sib, called *boreka pora*, '*boreka*-sons'. Further discussion added the following details. The commentators explained that here a scale, a sequence was being referred to. First came the sun, the personification of the divine creator, associated with 'white energy'; the sun was the fundamental principle in a moral sense. Second came mankind, represented by the Desana and by *boreka*, their mythical ancestor; third was the narcotic snuff. On this the commentators elaborated by saying that *viho* (snuff) was derived from *vihiri*, 'to absorb', but that it also meant 'to sniff', 'to scent', 'to desire', alluding to attractive female odours or to estrous smells. They said that men should not be like dogs following a bitch in heat, but should try to 'perfect' their passions. In saying so they translated the expression *siburi* as 'to filter', 'to distil', indicating that it stood for a purifying action; the 'dish', they said, had to be purified.

10. *abe yerú viho* means, literally 'sun-penis-snuff'. In one of many shamanistic images, the penis of the Sun Father is said to be a stalactite. According to myth, this snuff is the semen of the Sun, and was obtained, in the beginning of time, by the Daughter of the Sun, *abe mago*, in an incestuous union with her father (cf. Text I, Section 2). Referring once more to the term *vihiri* (cf. above, Section 9), the shaman said: "He who feels desires, goes in search [of gratification]". He explained that *vihiri* meant 'to desire', 'to search', but that it also meant 'to move around'. He went on to say that *abe yeru viho*, 'sun-penis-snuff', meant 'sun-penis-copulation' and referred to the seminal aspect of the snuff.

11. *ëmëko viho*, 'day-snuff', a synonym for 'sun-snuff' (cf. above, Section 10). In an additional comment the shaman emphasized the need to control all passion. "People must obey the rules", he repeated several times.

12. *daata*, from the Spanish *lata*, a tin plate. The reference to a metal dish is metaphorical; metal grows hot very rapidly and then becomes difficult to handle, to control. One commentator said: "Some people are too easily aroused by women; they don't control themselves". Another said: "People get heated up like a tin plate".

13. Here the shaman explained that the heat from firewood, contrary to that of a hot tin plate, could readily be controlled. The expression 'this firewood pertains to mankind', is a shamanic turn of phrase meaning that the heat given off by these woods, that is, their generative and transformative energies, now 'cooks' the initiate; it transforms him and so creates him anew. The shaman added a few words to the effect that it was 'befitting', it was 'convenient for

mankind'. He added that excessive heat might do great harm.

14. This alludes to the idea that the snuff on the tablet or dish has been 'condensed' and 'purified' by these different heats.

15. As I have shown elsewhere (Reichel-Dolmatoff 1978b, essay 2 in this book), the game animals of the deep rainforest environment (tapir, brocket deer, collared peccary, spider monkey, etc.) are identified with the ancient inhabitants of the interfluvial regions, who were present *before* the Desana arrived in the Vaupés territory. The shaman pointed out that, although they were 'not quite people', they possessed 'heat energies'.

16. To this the shaman commented that game animals do not contain 'excessive' heat (because of their estrous cycle) and that 'controlled' heat does not produce *nomeri* illusions. He added that only increased heat, that is, uncontrolled human passion, will lead to unsettling *nomeri* states.

17. The shaman explained that by 'these dishes', he had been referring, not to snuff dishes, but to an abstract concept of 'receptacles' or, rather, 'sources', represented by the game animals. These animals, by their reproductive activity, constitute a source of energy for people, but their 'heat' had to be controlled with milk, *tooka* sap, and *saviru* leaves, that is, with elements taken from nature. The phrasing here is somewhat obscure. Here the expression *masuu* is being used again (cf. Section 4).

18. The shaman and his companions discussed at some length the concept of 'source' (cf. above, Section 17). He said that, initially, there were several sources but that, one by one, they had to be purified and brought under control until there was 'full agreement', and they all formed one single source; this had to happen 'on that day' (*ëmë*), meaning, 'in our universe'.

The verb *tumahiri*, 'to overturn something', refers to the evil influence of uncontrolled sources of energy; the shaman called them "sources of excessive heat".

21. The expression *mahsa gumure* has been glossed here as 'helpers'. The term *gumu* is usually applied to the main rafter of a longhouse, and means 'foot', 'support', 'origin'; it is related to *kumu*, 'shaman-priest'. In this present context, *mahsa gumure* can mean 'people of support', in the sense of allies or assistants, but the shaman explained that it had two further meanings, one being that of 'offspring', the other being that of 'consequences', in the sense of proliferation. He said that this was the covert meaning of this expression. The other commentators added that not only the 'dizziness' must be dominated, but also its 'offspring', that is, all other unpleasant sensations that might arise from it.

22. The meaning of *iri nomerore* is figurative; the shaman referred to it as 'a state of desires' that had to be canalized. He added that milk and *tooka* stood for 'controlled whiteness'.

24. The expression 'round particles' refers to two related aspects; one concerns crushed fragments of stalactite, of about 2cms. diameter, the other refers

to a new phase of visual phenomena, called *doberi*. This term means, literally, 'to paint with large dots'; it is a phosphene that follows upon the *nomeri* stage and which consists of the entoptic illusion of large moving spots of a dark-red colour, which begin to absorb the yellow element which was still present at the *nomeri* stage. According to the shaman's commentaries, the *doberi* stage begins after the third month of pregnancy, when both husband and wife will occasionally perceive these dots, as a fleeting sensation. By then the foetus is growing and the process of 'cooking' is well under way. The text also alludes to the red and yellow fecundity and fertility symbolism of certain colourful macaw feathers. The expression *mahsa pora ahpaka*, lit. 'people-male descendants-have', was commented on by saying that it meant: 'they [the *doberi* spots] signify that all belong to the same people, to the same descent group'. The shaman elaborated on this by saying that it excluded all adolescents who were sexually inactive; to procreate, a youth had to be 'condensed' (*siburi*) and at that stage only the young people could be called *mahsa pora ahpaka*.

25. The shaman paraphrased this by saying: "So that these energies will not dominate, they must be directed".

26. *bayapia* is a leguminous (?) tree with thick fleshy leaves that are said to exude a strong, sweetish smell. The name is related to *bayari*, 'to chant', 'to enchant', and to *piari*, 'to emit a strong (but pleasant) odour'. The commentators said that it was an arousing female scent, an intoxicatingly attractive odour. The plant figures prominently in shamanistic spells.

27. I have translated *tuunërëra* as 'to throb'; the word means lit. 'to pant' and is related to *tuuri*, 'to push', and *nërëri*, 'to persecute', 'to harrass'. It is a shamanistic term used to describe the panting of a jaguar, a condition which is said to be symptomatic of jaguar transformation, when the shaman begins to contort his body and pants as if out of breath. This behaviour marks an advanced state of intoxication. The narrator elaborated on this and compared this state with 'young men running after women'. "Our hearts should not be obsessed by them", he said. He added that this state was also related to masturbation. (For details on jaguar transformation among the Desana and their neighbours, see Reichel-Dolmatoff 1975.)

29. The expression *bëgamerero*, explained the shaman, had several meanings, one of them referring to a steady process of growth, of increase in size; *bëgari* is 'to grow', and *mereri* (strongly nasalized) concerns the particular form this growth process is taking. Several alternative meanings are: pathological cellular growth, pregnancy, or tumescence of genitalia, all three associated with a state of 'throbbing' and 'panting'. The shaman said that the 'swelling' and the 'excitement', whatever their nature, had to be controlled. When commenting on the expression 'biting to shreds', he said that evil substances had to be 'devoured'. The image of 'to wide open the mouth and to bite', he explained, signified an act of fecundation and, thereby, of control. The swelling had to be 'torn

to bits' (*nubturi*), so it could be fitted into society and subordinated to its norms.

31. *dehko viho*, lit. 'water-snuff'. Some commentators explained that by this term a 'transparent' snuff was meant, a snuff that had an admixture of very finely ground rock crystal. Crystals are important shamanistic power tools, and crushed particles of rock crystal, called *marari* (cf. Section 4), are sometimes used in certain ritual preparations. Rock crystals are supposed to contain powerful seminal forces and are the shaman's principal instruments of transformation (Reichel-Dolmatoff 1978b, essay 2 in this book). To this the shaman added a very different commentary, by saying that the term *dehko viho* referred to *vehko mahsa*, that is, 'water people', meaning the women of such exogamic groups as the Pira-Tapuya, Uanano, or *Vai-mahsa*, who traditionally are said to be river dwellers and fishermen. He explained that by mentioning this 'snuff', reference was being made to women with whom marriage was permitted.

33. 'To bite' is equivalent to 'control' (cf. Section 29).

34. This refers to all women of childbearing age, and to the need to 'control' them. *Gurunya* (*Bignonia chica*) is a shrub from the fruits of which a red dye is prepared; in LG it is called *carayurú*. The expression *gurunya vera*, 'Bignonia starch', equates 'starch' with 'essence', that is, with the energy of female generative power. The shaman explained that, by now, the large *doberi* dots that had developed out of *nomeri*, were turning a very dark-red colour.

36. These dark spots now dominate completely the yellow spots. The shaman said that this 'control' was in agreement with cultural norms.

37. By this is meant that the process of gestation and of 'cooking' is steadily advancing.

40. This section refers to male sexual abstinence. In the expression *dehko boga*; lit. 'water-energy', the word for water stands for 'transparent liquid' and, in shamanistic metaphor, for semen. At this point, the shaman and the other commentators explained at length that, what has been described so far, was a transformative process which was symbolized first by the appearance, in the initiate's mind, of minute luminous particles (*marari*), which eventually developed into *nomeri* phenomena; these developed into *doberi* dots which, in turn, were accompanied by an evil seminal current that had to be stopped. They explained that this referred to the prohibition of intercourse during this stage of pregnancy. It must be added here that the term *doberi* is occasionally used to describe masturbation or *coitus interruptus*.

41. The term *dia merero* means literally 'water (or river) sediments'; from *merehari*, 'to deposit sediments (dregs)'. The commentators explained that this meant 'to become dense', 'to become compact', referring to advanced pregnancy.

42. *nimakërida*; from *nima*, 'poison', *këri*, 'to possess', *da*, 'thread', 'vine'. The shaman explained that "these threads are very hot" and that they envelop cores or bodies which are formed by a feverish substance; he described this as a glowing point from which heat and light were radiating. Another commentator

added: "Some people fall ill because of abstinence; this is the cause of their fever-ish states".

43. The complexity and subtlety of symbolic meanings increases in this and the following sections. In certain shamanistic metaphors the courses of rivers are compared to life-conducting veins or to nourishing umbilical cords. Each river is thus conceived as a 'thread' which is divided into a number of longitudinal sections. The life-force of a person is identified with the course of a river and, in this particular case, the feverish state of the initiate is said to 'stretch like threads' from the headwaters to the rivermouth, forming a 'contaminated' (*vihsiro*) area. In fact, the shaman said: "Within this area the *dari* threads turn round and round. Such is man; this area is man"

This concept of 'area' requires some comment. The hexagonal shape of shamanistic rock crystals provides, among others, a spatial model of varying dimensions. The all-important concept of 'limits', of strict and straight dividing lines between abstract and concrete areas of prohibition and permissibility is, remarkably enough, called *tabú*, in Desana. The plural is *taburi* and the word is related to the verb *tabuari*, 'to establish limits', and this, in turn is related to *taberi*, 'to cut off'.

In the shamanistic worldview, the entire Vaupés territory or any given part of it, can be divided or, rather, *is* divided, by a grid of adjoining, or somewhat sep-arated, hexagonal spaces. Natural models for this grid pattern are, apart from the crystal, several horny plates of the shell of the land tortoise (*Geochelone den-ticulata*), a honeycomb, a wasps' nest, or a pineapple. The dividing lines (*taburi*) between two adjoining hexagons are designated as *dari*, but not in the sense of 'threads', but of vertical planes, the same as the region of the rivermouth, which also lies within a hexagonal enclosure. In between lies an open space, so to say, where lies the main course of the imaginary river, and along this trajectory run the *dari* threads which represent the life-force of the person that lives along that particular river. This life, in the in-between area, develops between two *tabú* planes which cut perpendicularly across the river, just below the headwaters and just above the deltic region. These two hexagons constitute, according to the model of the shaman's rock crystal, two clearly delimited *areas of transforma-tion*, the one at the rivermouth being somewhat larger than that on the headwa-ters. Since in shamanic topography all rivers run from West to East, toward the rising sun, the hexagon of the rivermouth is associated with birth, while death, followed by rebirth, occurs at the headwaters. We understand now what the shaman meant when he said "this area is man".

44. The shaman now commented that the river represents the course which the feverish state of the initiate is taking. This course is formed by three threads carrying red, black, and white energies which combine into one single current. He elaborated on this and said that within the hexagon of the headwaters is a small hexagonal area which specifically controls all alimentary and, metaphori-

cally, all sexual activities of the individual. The same he said was true of the larger hexagon at the rivermouth, which also included a small, and equally specialized, hexagonal area. He went on to say that on the headwaters, food and sexual restrictions were "so severe that the *taburi* lines were like flames, black and white flames". He said that this was necessary because on the headwaters people ate 'pure' wild growing fruits such as *vahsu* (*Hevea* sp.), *sëmé* (*Dahlbergia* sp.), the fruits of the *Uasai* palm (*Euterpe precatoria*, in Desana, *mihi*), and of the Jessenia palm (*Oenocarpus bataua*, in Desana, *nyumú*), which made them sexually more active than those who lived on the lower stretches of a river.

45. The shaman mentioned once more that these threads produce different colour sensations. However, by this he did not refer to lineal 'threads' but to *tabú* threads, that is, to prismatic planes. He explained that these planes were like many-coloured flames, indeed like curtains of flames, shaped like a series of lancet arches. Each of these elongated, flame-shaped arches showed the same colour sequence, from inside to outside: yellow-red-dark blue. He added that only shamans and the initiate could see these fiery curtains.

46. Here and in the six next sections follows the stereotyped formula of the exorcizing spell.

53. The term *yee* (plural, *yeea*) means both 'shaman' or 'jaguar'; and the related verb *yeeri*, means 'to copulate'. The plant *tadëhka* is an undetermined hallucinogenic plant which is said to be used only by shamans; it is said to have a strong and pleasant odour. Although it grows in the forest, shamans often cultivate it.

56. *mahsa pora ahpaka*, 'people-male descendants-have' (or 'belonging'); some commentators said that what was meant here was that it pertains to 'the same essence', the same descent group. Others added that the expression referred to those who were resolved to practise abstinence. The reaction to a narcotic potion prepared from *tadëhka* (cf. above, Section 53) was said to be decisive; high-ranking shamans (*kumua*) became abstinent, but common shamans (*yeea*) were less restricted.

59. 'Fish *yajé*' is said to be used only by shamans, and to distinguish itself from other hallucinogenic plants, by the particular colours of the visions it produces. The symbolic value of these colours, however, depends upon the specific exogamic unit to which the person belongs. The flaming curtains of each *tabú* division, are each differently coloured.

60. "They drink in the luminous threads", the shaman commented.

62. Here the term *nimakërida* (cf. above, Section 42) has been glossed as 'poisonous vine', following the shaman's indications; he added that a certain *Banisteriopsis* species was meant by this. The division of vines into red, yellow and, eventually, white components, refers to two concepts: first, the shaman explained, the three colour threads run along the vine in its entire length, containing male fertility, female fecundity, and white, undifferentiated solar energy;

second, the hallucinogenic potion is prepared from different sections of the vine, according to the age of the plant. Each section is said to produce visions in which predominate specific colours, that is, represent specific dimensions of the hallucinatory sphere as determined by shamans. The shaman added that this narcotic plant greatly affected users who had been 'too abstemious'; the swirling *dari* threads caused them great discomfort.

63. Desana shamans are much interested in the structure of open flames and in the chemical processes that develop in different parts of them. In the process of burning, shamans will distinguish different zones or 'stripes' (*pame*) which are related to their theories of colours and energies, and when speaking here of the 'dark outline' of a flame, what is meant is the bluish mantle that surrounds the bright red flame. This mantle is called *nyiri da*, 'black-thread' or 'dark-thread', and the shaman explained that by this term the dark blue part was meant, and that it constituted a different energy zone into which the initiate was about to enter.

The shaman now explained in sweeping images what had happened so far.

The master shaman and the initiate had established themselves in a small hexagonal area lying between the large hexagon of the rivermouth and the somewhat smaller one of the headwaters, but not on the river itself, rather at some small affluent of the middle course. There the initiate had 'died'; but his spirit-essence had gone to the rivermouth where he penetrated the fiery *tabú* door and submerged himself into the primeval waters of the Lake of Milk (*ahpikon dia*). Passing through the *marari-noeri-doberi-dari* stages of transformation, he had penetrated through a flaming, vaulted *tabú* door into the hexagon of the headwaters. This marked his rebirth into a new life, that of the shaman he was going to be, and from there he returned to his local group, to his own people. His initiation had ended in rebirth from himself.

The term for 'flame', as used by the shaman, is *dihpame*, a word that deserves comment. While *pame* means anything composed of parallel elongated elements, stripes, bands, the fingers of a hand or the reeds of a panpipe, the root *dih* refers to something liquid or, rather, fluid. This, then, does well describe the 'striped' colour effect of a burning flame. But let us go a step farther. In shamanistic topography the headwaters of a river always lie between hills, the very same hills which are said to be the uterine abodes of the game animals (Reichel-Dolmatoff, 1971; 1975; see 'Houses of the Hills'). Near these hills is imagined to be a lake, the same as near the rivermouth, conceived as 'Houses of the Waters' where all aquatic creatures have their abodes. Lakes or lagoons are called *dihtaru*; the root *dih* refers to the fluid, 'striped' or layered condition of water, to varying depths. The shaman explained that each particular depth of such a lake had its distinct colour energy, and that these lakes were 'filters' or 'doors', *dihsiporo*, through which shamans passed into other dimensions of being. The shaman's scheme was therefore conceived in two dimensions: the vertical 'door of flames', at the *taburi* limits and, behind these – be it at the rivermouth or at the headwaters – a horizontal 'door of water', both doors being imagined as being encircled or outlined by rainbow-coloured bands. Rainbows, of course, are always 'doors' and always mark a *tabú* line.

One final observation before returning to the text: the Desana term used to designate a hexagonal space is *saré*, with the second syllable strongly nasalized, meaning 'fence', 'fenced in space'. It is derived from *sarisari*, 'to fence in'. But *saré* is shamanic shorthand for *dihpu mahsa sari*, lit. 'head-people-fence', a denotative expression which, metaphorically, means 'authority-exogamic unit-law'. This then is one of the principal meanings of the hexagonal pattern, next to its meaning as 'area of transformation', 'point of origin', or similar expressions. The shaman said that a hexagonal space was 'a fenced-in spot whence people emerge', but he was quick to point out that each *tabú* line was a 'law' that referred, above all, to the relationships between certain exogamic groups. The birth-giving river-mouth is such a hexagonal spot, and so is the region of the headwaters, the sources. It will, perhaps, not come as a surprise that a newborn child's fontanelle is also designated by this term: *dihpu mahsa sari*.

65. Here the shaman commented: "The heat of these coloured outlines produces fever; there is too much energy".

67. "…the threads of *miratavá*" stands here for the cooling action of the ointments. The text designates these leaves (or leaf) as *pudaa*, lit. 'leaf-thread', that is, 'leaf-energy' (see above, Section 6).

72. According to myth, each exogamic group, or even each sib, is the owner of a certain species of *Banisteriopsis*. It is doubtful however if these can be botanically distinguished since Vaupés Indians often classify plants by their effects upon man rather than by their morphological characteristics. The term *too* and *tooka* refer to the same plant; *–ka* is the diminutive form.

73. Three of five *Banisteriopsis* vines mentioned here are associated by the Desana with other plants, but remain botanically unidentified in our systematics. They are: 1) *kuripi daa*, 'knotty' vine; 2) *ma da*, [fish] poison vine; 3) *duhtu seré da*, taro (*Colocasia* sp.) vine; 4) *mere da*, guamo (*Inga* sp.) vine; 5) *too da*, tocoa (*Melastomacea* sp.) vine. In some other shamanic spells of the Desana, vine No. 1 is called *kuurikë da*; vine No. 3, *duhtu puu* (leaf) *sere da*; vine No. 4, *merepi da*; and another vine, *karepi da*, is added, from *kare* (*Chrysophyllum vulgare*). (See Reichel-Dolmatoff 1975: 150-154, 158, 180-181.)

77. The designs are painted with a certain yellow clay called *eboboho*; from *ebo*, a certain clay, and *boho*, 'dry', 'condensed'. The colour has a seminal connotation.

78. The 'zigzag' design is an approximate translation. Desana pottery decoration consists of incised, rarely painted, design motifs which encircle the upper part or the mouth of cooking pots. The individual design motifs have, almost always, sexual connotations. The underlying idea is that the manufacture of pottery is a process of transformation (cf. above, Section 3), patterned after the

stages of the life process: insemination ('mixture'), pregnancy (consolidation by swelling), and transformation by birth that is, by firing. The vessel is conceived as a woman; from her womb emerges the child, analogous to cooked food. The mouth of the cooking vessel is therefore marked (one might hesitate to say, decorated) with a horizontal band of specific motifs. In the present case a row of Y-shaped incisions is meant, this being a graphic shorthand symbol for clitoris. The Desana name of this design is *sera goa*, 'pineapple-bone', an euphemism for clitoris and a metaphor which is related to the bone-soul complex of revival and resurrection. The incisions should be made with a little elastic stick from a *tooka* plant, an implicitly phallic element. I shall add here that Desana women paint around their waists a girdle of the very same design motifs, thus identifying their bodies with life-giving cooking vessels.

80. The shaman alluded here to the sexual connotations of this act; the *yajé* vessel is a female body and the stirring rod has a phallic character.

82. Meaning 'our essence'.

83. The shaman commented: "The seminal liquid must be controlled".

84. The verb *ma'mari* has several alternative meanings; 1) to adorn oneself; 2) to embellish oneself and make oneself look younger by applying body paint, aromatic herbs, and by wearing adornments; 3) to become rejuvenated, to be reborn in a spiritual sense; 4) to become worthy of something. The shaman took pains to explain that, on a deeper level of understanding, it is this last concept that is being referred to here.

85. The word 'branch' is here the common, literal translation. The term *kee* (plural, *keeri*) refers to the central vein of a leaf, in this case, of *bayapia*. This vein is said to contain a sweet-smelling sap that, to the Desana, is the essence of enchantment. The shaman's comments indicate, however, that by *keeri*, a descent group is meant, a 'branch', as he called it, 'of people of the same odour'. (For Desana odour classification see Reichel-Dolmatoff 1978b, essay 2 in this book).

86. 'Agouti-leaves'; this expression was commented upon thus: 'Agouti-Women' (*buia nome*) belong to a Pira-Tapuya sib that intermarries with Desana men who belong to a certain sib. The women (leaves) are a cooling, soothing element.

Summary

The two texts I have presented in the foregoing pages contain a brief description of some of the experiences a Desana shaman's apprentice is said to undergo in the course of his formal initiation. The initiation itself is described as a carefully prepared narcotic trance which is meant to be a slow rebirth, by consecutive stages, of the individual who first must suffer a symbolic death, after months of severe deprivations and the frequent ingestion of highly toxic drugs. He then must be reborn from the bones, from a skeletonized state.

However, the neophyte's psychic voyage does not lead him into a dimension where he has to confront spirits or initiatory demons, nor does he receive a secret message. During his trance, the initiate is expected to become aware of his existence, to meditate, and to watch his own reactions to the various drugs he ingests. The entire sequence is described as an ecstatic metamorphosis, a dream world of colours and shapes, projected by an intoxicated mind.

As has been said at the outset, a number of parallel but interlocking symbolic models are involved here. One is human foetal development which begins with an act of insemination by the Sun, and ends in rebirth; it is symbolized by the Sun-God's semen on a clay dish which, in itself, is a transformed object; and by the penetration of the fiery door of flames at the thresholds of the river. Another model is the process of cooking, another that of firing pottery, and equally present is that of plant growth. The entire transformative sequence is also comparable to the succession of neurophysiological sensations perceived during an advancing state of drug-induced trance, and many of all these states and conditions have a strong sexual resonance. It would be mistaken to try to interpret shamanic initiation only in terms of one single model; in the metaphysical universe of Desana shamanism a multiplicity of secondary models is being superimposed or incapsulated, forming a train of images that are interchangeable, although the theme of rebirth forms the recurrent and fundamental motif.

Returning once more to the problem of the textual sources, it is clear that a summary reading of a literal translation alone, would have missed some of the most important meanings; these only come to light in the commentaries. It is remarkable how much crucial information is condensed in certain passages which appear to be deceptively short statements but which, when discussed in detail, yield important clues to the interpretation of the text. In this manner, a few words, sometimes said quite casually, will open to the native listener a complex chain of visions and associations, but will be meaningless to the outsider, unless he is assisted by knowledgeable informants, and has an adequate grasp of the wider cultural context.

In closing I should add that I am quite aware that the two texts offer hardly more than a superficial glimpse of shamanistic transcendence, but even so they constitute a kind of document which, unfortunately, is rare in Colombian ethnography, and which soon will become impossible to obtain.

EDITOR'S NOTE: A transcription of the original Desana texts can be found in Reichel-Dolmatoff, 'Some Source Material on Desana Shamanistic Initiation', *Antropológica*, Caracas, No. 51, 1979, pp55-59.

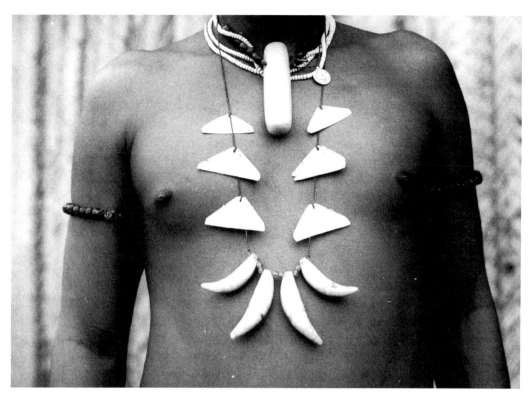

A cylinder of white quartz and a necklace with jaguar teeth and 'silver butterflies', insignia of shamanistic power

VI

Desana Shamans' Rock Crystals and the Hexagonal Universe

Quartz crystals, or translucent rock crystals, have played a major role in shamanic beliefs and practices at many times in history and in many parts of the world. They have frequently been found in prehistoric contexts: they are mentioned in many early sources; they were prominent in Old World alchemy, witchcraft, and magic, and they are still in use in many traditional societies. American Indian shamans and healers use rock crystals for curing, scrying, and many other purposes, and their ancient use in the Americas is known to us from archaeological reports.

In the search for detailed descriptions of the significance and use of rock crystals among South American Indians, however, little precise information becomes available. This is surprising because upon closer inquiry among some present-day Colombian Indians it appears that rock crystals continue to be important ritual objects which incorporate and integrate a wide range of cosmological and other concepts.

In this essay I discuss the use made of these crystals by the Desana Indians.

Crystals and Energy

All shamans of the Eastern Tukanoan tribes count translucent rock crystals among their most treasured possessions. These crystals are the principal power objects of shamanistic practice and are surrounded by a complex body of lore.

Crystals of different sizes, sometimes up to fifteen or twenty centimetres in length, and of varying degrees of purity, are found in several localities in the Northwest Amazon. Many crystals come from the territories lying to the north of the Vaupés, from the Guainía, Isana, and Inírida rivers, and it is worth keeping in mind that the well-known quartz-encrusted manioc graters that are traded by Arawakan Indians over much of the Vaupés area come precisely from this northern region that borders on Venezuela and the upper reaches of the Orinoco.

Among the Desana and their neighbours, most large crystals of recognized

149

significance are inherited from father to son. A shaman will keep his crystals in a little box (*behepu komoro*) made of carefully plaited strips of the yellow spathe of a palm tree.

All rock crystals are of hexagonal structure, and in this recurrent phenomenon the Indians see an element of predictability, of continuity. The hexagon thus provides an important model for a large number of Desana concepts referring to primordial energy, to lasting generative powers, and to transformation. Hexagonal shapes, wherever they occur in nature, are always thought to be imbued with powerful generative forces.

One of these basic models is the land tortoise (*Geochelone denticulata*), called *kuri* in Desana,[1] a reptile which is fairly common in the rainforest. Several of the horny plates on top of its dome-shaped carapace are of hexagonal shape and, from a shamanic point of view, represent power units related to rock crystals. The carapace is imaged as being studded with these hexagonal elements. The hexagons on a tortoise shell constitute an explanatory device that can be 'read' in a spiral, counterclockwise fashion and that contains condensed information on cosmogony and the origins of Desana social organization (fig. 1). Of the six adjoining plates, plate 1 represents the Son of the Sun Father (*abe mangë*), who personifies male seminal energy, while plate 2 is the Daughter of the Sun (*abe mango*), representing female fecundity. From the primordial incest of this sibling pair sprang the first 'human' child, called *ërera*, represented by plate 3. The name derives from the verb *ërerí*, 'to be drowned, to be out of breath, to be overwhelmed', expressions that are used in this context to refer to a newborn creature struggling for breath and survival. Plate 4 is called *vahpikëra*, literally 'the combined ones', a term that refers to a group of four: the Sun Father, the siblings, and their offspring, who now come to constitute the so-called Sun People (*ëmëkori mahsa*), the first Desana, represented here as the direct descendants of the Sun. Plate 5 is designated as *yuhu mohoto*, 'one hand', meaning a basic social unit, a nuclear family, while plate 6 is *yuhu mohoto gahi mohoto yuhuro*, meaning 'one-hand-other-hand-one', an expression that can be translated as 'five fingers of one hand plus one finger of another hand', a Desana image that refers to the extension of the basic nuclear family by marriage into another basic unit.

The tortoise symbolizes stability, longevity, astuteness and protection, and figures in many myths and tales. In a cluster of other images, however, the tortoise is seen to turn into a trickster and transformer, a womb-like figure marked with vagina-shaped signs. In fact, its name (*kuri*) has the alternative meanings of 'bundle, package, swelling, pregnancy'. The tortoise's habit of feeding on carrion, together with its gripping bite, suggest an insatiable female of indiscriminate appetite. Irrespective of the particular metaphor, the recurrent hexagonal element on the carapace constitutes, in the minds of the Indians, a model of regenerative powers.

Other hexagonal shapes in nature, all thought to be imbued with specific fer-

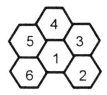

Figure 1. Interpretation of hexagonal plates on tortoise shell

tility and transformative powers, are honeycombs, wasps' nests, certain spider webs, and even pineapples, whose slightly protruding buds are compared to hexagonal inward-pointing crystals, while the bulk of the fruit is interpreted as a female element. In all these forms, then, the Desana see nature's 'memory'; they perceive in them the predictable manifestation of a certain form which, in their minds, is associated with a number of all-important characteristics that can be observed in a shaman's rock crystal.

I have described in some detail (Reichel-Dolmatoff 1978b, essay 2 in this book) the empirical observations on which Desana shamans base their beliefs in the powerful energies they attribute to rock crystals. A few points of this particular aspect are summarized here.

Desana shamans say that rock crystals are condensed solar energy and that they were created by the Sun. They are called *ëhta bohoru*, 'stone-condensed' or 'stone-transformed', and are thought to contain concentrated 'heat energy' (*ëhëri boga*). The Indians elaborate this concept by saying that the crystal is the Sun Father's penis (*abe yeeru*) or that it consists of crystallized semen. In some shamanic contexts the crystal is referred to as a female element and is directly designated as a womb or a clitoris. This hermaphroditic quality is important in order to understand Desana theories of transformation and the interconvertibility of energies.

The colours of the prismatic spectrum visible in a crystal under certain light conditions are believed to contain beneficial or harmful forces. Whereas yellow signifies male fertility, red stands for female fecundity, green for plant growth, and violet for putrid matter. Shamans claim to be able to distinguish more than thirty different hues in a rock crystal's reflections, all of them being interpreted in terms of 'energies' (*bogari*) which have to be balanced, combined, opposed, transformed, or otherwise manipulated, with the primary purpose of preserving a steady rate of human, animal, and plant fertility and growth. All living beings are said to contain these chromatic energies, and any organic dysfunction is believed to manifest itself in subtle changes in hue, intensity, and value. The shaman is able to observe these pathogenic modifications by looking at the patient through a crystal, or by touching his body with it. After having diagnosed an imbalance, a cure can be effected by calling upon the crystal's energies to reestablish a balanced relationship in the patient's organism. The crystal is thus a handy diagnostic tool which, in combination with an extensive body of spells and songs, is of prime importance in curing practices and in aggressive practices in which a shaman might try to harm a person by willfully altering the balance of his or her colour energies.

Crystals and Space

On a more abstract level, Desana shamans will use rock crystals as a kind of television screen. The underlying ideas are these: in a drug-induced trance the shaman will imagine himself as standing inside a huge man-sized crystal and looking out upon the territories of the three exogamic groups which transitionally intermarry; the Desana, Pira-tapuya, and Tukano proper.[2] His vision will penetrate the forests, the rocky hills, and the walls of houses, and thus each crystal face will turn into a screen upon which he can watch not only people and their actions, but also their respective animal and plant resources. (For more on this process, see Reichel-Dolmatoff 1978b, essay 2 in this book.)

Rivalling shamans often engage in violent contests, but all fighting is acted out in a hallucinatory dimension, the two contestants lying in their hammocks in a deep trance.[3] During these fights each shaman imagines himself as standing encased in a crystal which serves him on all sides as a protective armour. Next to him stands his adversary, also enclosed in a crystal. Both are thought to stand upon hexagonal shields, and the ensuing struggle involves an attempt by each contestant to unbalance his enemy, to knock him over, and to make him and his crystal lose their firm footing on the shield. In attack and defence, one must never offer the enemy a flat prism face, but always a vertical edge where two prism faces meet. The contestants imagine themselves to be pushing and thrusting at close range. This violent jostling is designated, in shamanic idiom, as *ëhta boho yee tukare maha beo*, literally, 'crystal-penis-shake-topple over-throw down', a highly significant expression.

The idea of a hexagonal space being enclosed by six windowpane-like transparent walls is most important in shamanic ideology. According to shamanic concepts, sacred space is hexagonal in outline, and it is in this dimension where all essential transformations are thought to take place. The first such spatial extension consists of the traditional tribal territory. The origin myths of the Tukano Indians tell that the tribal ancestors proceeded from a region lying toward the East, somewhere in Brazil, and eventually embarked in huge canoes shaped like enormous anacondas which then took them upriver, into the Rio Negro-Vaupés territory. Inside these serpent-canoes the First People sat according to phratry and rank. Each anaconda is imaged as divided longitudinally into six sections: the point of the serpent's head carried the guiding creative 'whiteness' of the Sun Father; behind it came the section where chiefs were sitting;

behind the chiefs sat dancers and singers; behind these came the warriors, and these in turn were followed by shamans, while the tail end was occupied by servants. At certain spots along the rivers people disembarked and settled, and this slow penetration of the riverine system of the Vaupés constitutes the main theme of a large body of origin myths. It so happened that there were six original anacondas which, outstretched as rivers, began to enclose the future tribal habitat between the Rio Negro, the Vaupés, the Apaporis, the Pira-paraná, the Tiquié, and the Papurí rivers. At each corner of the hexagon, where a serpent's head met another's tail, lies an important landmark in the form of a major fall or rapids.

Just as our geographical concepts are based upon the idea of a grid of coordinates, Desana shamans conceive of the entire Tukanoan territory as divided into a grid pattern of adjoining hexagons of varying sizes, all of them lying within the all-embracing hexagon formed by the six original anacondas. At any given spot, large or small, where a process of transformation is taking place, a shaman might establish one of these imaginary enclosures, for example, around a hunting or fishing territory, around a certain field, or around a maloca where a ritual is being performed. To establish the central point of such a transformative hexagon is called *ahpiri*, a fertility term. By the same token, all landmarks that are associated with events in the mythological past are said to lie at the centre of such a hexagonal space.

I am speaking here of areas, of certain well-defined spaces, and this concept requires some comments. The Desana often emphasize the need for well-defined limits, be it in a physical, topographical sense, or in the sense of recognizing clear-cut dividing lines between the tangible and the abstract, the permissible and the forbidden. This concept of boundaries and bounded space, of setting limits to lands and customs, is called *tabú* in Desana. By *tabú* the Desana refer to a divisory line, to a space enclosed by several of these lines, to a prohibition, to a restrictive law, or to a set of norms, indeed very much as we would use the Polynesian term. I have no explanation for this similarity. In fact, *tabú* is a good Desana word;[4] the plural is *tabúri*, and the word is related to *tabuári*, meaning 'to set a limit', and this, in turn, is related to *tabéri*, 'to cut off'. Desana shamans explain that a rock crystal, or any other hexagonal shape or space, is enclosed by six *tabú* limits. These limits are the six lateral planes of the prismatic structure of the crystal and, in the case of a hexagonal territory, these boundaries are imagined not as lines, but as invisible vertical planes that form an enclosure.

The three imaginary lines that separate the three exogamic units from each other – as observed from inside the crystal – are designated as *tabúri*, the same as the six anacondas that enclose the Vaupés territory. The concept of 'crossing a *tabú* line' (*ta'riri*) signifies 'to enter another *tabú* system' (*gahi tabú turi*), that is, to choose a forbidden marriage partner; in order to choose the right partner one must 'sight along a *tabú* line', a procedure called *paríri*. The three units, Desana, Pira-Tapuya, and Tukano proper, stand in a complex relationship of reciprocity, not only in relation to the exchange of women, but also with respect to food exchange, the exchange of raw materials or of finished artifacts, to the ownership of certain ritual practices, and to many other aspects. It is said that formerly all Tukanoan tribes were organized, theoretically at least, in similar triadic constellations of phratries. For example, the exchange of women is visualized by the Desana in the following image: three men, each one representing an exogamic unit, stand with outstretched arms, hands touching, and thus forming a hexagon. Each man's right hand represents a son, while with his left hand he offers a daughter. This image is elaborated in myths, genealogical recitals, and shamanic spells and is called *paríri*, literally, 'to contact', but here meaning 'to sight along a line', that is, along a *tabú* division.

The principal significance of the hexagonal pattern, as derived from the rock crystal, is that it is a model of social organization and of the laws that govern it. The hexagonal form itself is a dynamic constellation of two basic principles; in Desana graphic symbolism two different types of triangles are distinguished: a male triangle pointing upward and a female triangle pointing downward. The hexagon represents the superposition, the combination of these two triangles, that is, the union between the male and female components of the three exogamic groups. These and related ideas are contained in a body of concepts which find their verbal expressions in several root metaphors. I attempt to analyze some of them.

The Desana word used to designate a hexagonal shape or space is *saré*, meaning 'fence' or 'fenced-in space'. The idea is that of a closed body of norms, a coherent set of rules of behaviour. *Saré* is shamanic shorthand for *dihpu mahsa sari*, literally, 'head-people-fence', a descriptive expression which, metaphorically, is translated by the Desana on two levels; on the crudest phsyiological level it means 'phallus-people-vagina', whereas on an abstract ethical level it means 'authority-exogamic unit-restrictive norm'.

Another root metaphor which is used in referring to hexagonal space or form is contained in the expression *kama vehe dihpuru*, literally, 'harpy eagle-dead-head'. This is a well-known expression that figures prominently in certain mythological cycles which extol the dangers of disregarding exogamic laws. In brief, a younger brother's amorous adventures have led to his 'crossing a *tabú*' and his subsequent banishment by his elder brother to 'the headwaters'. In great fear the culprit exclaims: *yëe ii tabú përë vagë yë dohpaa yigëkuri yëë*, 'What shall I do when I arrive at that *tabú*?' After he has settled down in the 'other *tabú*' ('*gahi tabú*'), this hexagonal territory becomes known (and feared) as 'Dead Harpy Eagle's Head.'

The expression *kama vehe dihpuru* must be analyzed word by word to unravel its multireferential meaning. On one level of interpretation, the word *kama* is said to be derived from *gaa*, 'harpy eagle', a bird with marked solar and seminal associations. But, the commentators say, the word can also be derived from *kaa*, meaning a fence or an enclosure, and *kaa-maa* would come to mean 'fence-way'. It also might be related to *gamá*, 'to reach puberty', or to the Uanano word *kamáa*, 'to love'. The term *vehe*, all commentators agree, is derived from the verb *veherí*, which has the following meanings: 'to kill, to fish, to cohabit, to inseminate'. They added that the verb *veheri* was related to *vihiri*, 'to absorb, to smell, to sniff, to become contaminated, to establish illicit relationships'. The noun *dihpuru*, in turn, means 'head', but can also mean 'phallus', 'authority', or 'law'. My Desana commentators translated the aforesaid expression on various levels: (1) 'Harpy eagle-dead-head', (2) 'boundary-trail (line)-norm', (3) 'pubis-path-insemination', and (4) 'exogamic unit-communication-law'.

This cluster of metaphors is so important in Desana thought that it is expressed in a number of material objects, with the explicit purpose of constantly reminding people of the rules of exogamy. For example, *kama vehe dihpuru* (here translated literally as 'Dead Harpy Eagle's Head') is the name of a hexagonal firefan (also used as a potlid), of a Cat's Cradle figure, and of a children's game traced in the sand. When making a fishnet one begins with three parallel strings which are then knotted together to form three triangles called *kama vehe dihpuru*; the individual threads that enclose each triangle are designated as *tabúri-da*, '*tabú*-threads'. The points of these triangles are then tied to a flat wooden crossbar which forms the baseline for the body of the net and is called *vehe digë*, 'to fish-thing male'. The other extreme of the net, called *tiari-da*, 'finishing-thread', again consists of three triangles called *kama vehe dihpuru*.

Another example is this: in a traditional Desana maloca the three most important ritual objects associated with transformation are the shaman's stick rattle (*yeegë*), the large box (*komoro*) containing his feather ornaments, crystals and other paraphernalia, and the painted clay vessel (*gahpi soro*) in which hallucinogenic potions made of *Banisteriopsis* vines are being prepared. These objects should be displayed on a framework of sticks placed between the first two main posts on the left side of the maloca. This ritual display is called *kama vehe dihpuru* and, in this case, the translation is emphatically, 'exogamic unit-communication-law'. The three objects hang from a horizontal pole designated as *kama vehe peyari gumu*, 'exogamic unit-to raise-ridge pole'. I might add here that the three-pronged lower end of the phallic stick rattle is also called *kama vehe dihpuru*, and it symbolizes the male elements of the three intermarrying units.

Finally, the same term, *kama vehe dihpuru*, is used to designate a hexagonal outline crossed by three axes (fig. 2). The shamanic interpretation is as follows: the three triangles lying above the A-B axis represent a mythical elder brother of the first Desana intruders (1), a younger brother (2), and their sister (3). These three are *maríya mahsa*, 'our people'. The three triangles lying below the A-B axis represent three tribal groups that were already established in the Vapués territory before the arrival of the Desana: the Tukano proper (T), the Uanano (U),

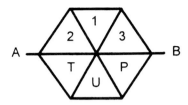

Figure 2. Hexagonal scheme of social units and side view of longhouse

and the Pira-Tapuya (P). These three are designated as *gahi mahsa*, 'other people'. In some texts this original dualistic scheme receives a certain amount of elaboration. But eventually, the commentators' interpretations continue, the Desana established the following formal relationships: elder brother married a Uanano woman, younger brother married a Tukano proper woman, and the Desana girl married a Pira-Tapuya and went to join his *tabú*. In this manner the six triangles began to represent the present-day tripartite grouping of (male and female) Desana, Pira-Tapuya, and Tukano proper, the Uanano not being accounted for any more.[5]

In another image the three triangles above the horizontal axis are compared to a rock crystal lying on one side, the upper half visible and resting on the ground, and the lower half invisible and underground. The upper part symbolizes a maloca;[6] in this image the basal part of the crystal, which carries the principal cluster of 'colour energies', is identified with the 'male' frontal part of the structure, whereas the pointed end corresponds to the rounded 'female' part of the house. An additional comparison with a land tortoise identifies the reptile's head with the male section of the maloca. The entire crystal-maloca-tortoise image is designated as *maríya tabú*, 'our *tabú*', or 'our law', and is imagined to have its invisible underground counterpart, called *gahi tabú*, 'other *tabú*', meaning that it represents the tripartite mirror image of the three complementary units.[7]

Crystals and Transformation

That rock crystals contain a spectrum of brilliant colour which, in the Desana mind, contains procreative energies means that the crystal and its shape are elements of transformation. Hexagonal shapes are, therefore, associated with ideas, traits, or objects which, in one way or another, imply a process of transformation.

Let us first take a brief look at human anatomy. The pelvic region of the body, both male and female, is conceptualized as hexagonal in shape, this being a region of procreation and gestation. Lumbar vertebrae are said to be hexagonal and cervical vertebrae triangular; in fact, the crystal as a shamanic centre or axis of observation and insemnination is sometimes compared to a human spine, and even a shamanic stick rattle is occasionally visualized as a spine. Furthermore, a hexagonal design, on the blade of a paddle, for instance, graphically represents a vagina, and an abstract representation of a uterus is also hexagonal in shape. Similarly, a newborn child's fontanelle is described as a hexagon.

Desana material culture is replete with hexagonal patterns, although they are rarely used as a decorative device and rather constitute a structural feature. A few outstanding examples are mentioned here.

A Desana hearth consists of three hollow cylindrical potstands of clay that support the cooking vessel or griddle. The three potstands are said to be phallic elements and to represent the men of the three exogamic units; the cooking vessel or griddle is female and the fire, which is the transforming agent, is composed of male yellow and female red flames. Because a hearth is an important point of transformation, its layout has a hexagonal shape in that the firewood is arranged (theoretically, at least) in a triangular pattern within the triangle formed by the three potstands (fig.3). A similar transformation is implicit in the act of smoking

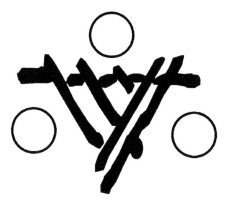

Figure 3. Hexagonal ground plan of hearth: potstands and firewood

fish or game on a roast. The Desana construct a tripod of wooden poles symbolizing the men of each exogamic group. Again, the firewood is distributed on the ground so as to form another triangle, the ground plan thus acquiring hexagonal shape.

Some further examples are these: the damp white mass of grated manioc has marked fertility associations, the same as many other grated fruits. For fermentation, that is, for transformation, this mass is always kept in a large leaf-lined funnel (*kai sariró*) with a hexagonal mouth. White manioc starch is another element with fertility associations; when being transported, it must be packed in elongated baskets (*vera dëhka*) of hexagonal shape, about thirty centimetres in diameter by fifty centimetres in length. Fish poison consisting of a coarse mass of macerated leaves and vines is placed into the shallow waters of a river in three

Potstands of clay to support cooking vessels upon the hearth

large hexagonal containers made of sticks. The act of poisoning fish is, of course, one of transformation.

Although apparently circular in shape, the ritual shield of traditional Desana warriors is conceived by the Indians as hexagonal. Its name *vábero*, is derived from the verb *vari*, 'to go', followed by a particle of negation. This name is explained as meaning 'area of not-going', or rather, 'of not-penetration', and it was added that this hexagonal artifact represented the defense of *maríya nihkú*, 'our land'.

During pregnancy the womb is imagined as a hexagonal 'crystal', with the foetus 'sitting' on a hexagonal 'shield'. In childbirth the infant is supposed to emerge at an angle between two adjoining crystal faces. Difficulties in childbirth are said to be caused by the infant's insufficient strength to 'separate' the two crystal walls.

During the period when Desana girls undergo the rituals connected with their first menstruation, they are isolated from other household members in a special enclosure of hexagonal shape.

The Desana bury their dead in a canoe which is cut in half so that the other half will serve as a lid. The cross-section of such a coffin is therefore more or less haxagonal.

Crystals and the Image of Order

Based on what has been said here about crystals, it becomes clear that the hexagonal model represents a major principle of organization among the Tukanoan tribes of the Colombian Northwest Amazon. Among the Desana and their neighbours these crystals are certainly not mere objects of irrational shamanic manipulation. On the contrary, their recurrent shape is taken for an image of order; their scintillating colour spectrum is taken for an image of dynamic change. In both aspects they can be seen to contain an enormous amount of condensed, multireferential, and tightly structured information, and thus they serve as models for a wide range of human activities.

One might wonder, then, about other regions, other cultures. Among the Kogi Indians of the Sierra Nevada de Santa Marta, in northern Colombia, rock crystals and the hexagon constitute a major religious focus in which 'colour energies', the sacred number six, and the sun = crystal = fertility sequence play an important part.

Emeralds, too, have a hexagonal structure, and we know from the early Spanish chroniclers that they were of great religious importance among the Muiska Indians of the Colombian highlands. According to a Muiska myth recorded at the time of the Spanish Conquest, the daughter of a local chieftain was impregnated by the divine sun and eventually gave birth to a huge emerald. The stone burst open and from it emerged a child which grew up to become the great chief Goranchacha.

There is some indication among widely separated Colombian Indian societies (Kogi, Muiska, Tukano, and others) that the hexagonal pattern is related to native astronomical concepts, to fixed points of observation, to lines of sighting, to the rising and setting points of celestial bodies. These observations, in turn, seem to be related to territorial divisions and to social organization. It is quite conceivable that the mineral wealth of the Andes and the Amazon has provided a set of recurrent models on which native thinkers have constructed their cosmic interpretations, in a vast variety of images, but in a great similarity of form.

Notes

1. In my transcription of the Desana language, *ë* is pronounced like the *e* in *que* (French), and *h* is pronounced like *ch* in *ach* (German).
2. By the term *Tukano proper* I refer to the specific exogamic unit known by that

name: when writing only *Tukano*, I am referring to the Eastern Tukanoans in general.

3. On the use of hallucinogenic drugs among the Tukano, see Reichel-Dolmatoff (1975, 1978a).
4. The equivalent term in Tukano proper would be *teo*: in Uanano, *tanyë*.
5. The exact nature of the 'first' contacts and the early phases of exogamic relationships are the subjects of much speculation by the speakers of the various groups. There exist many different and, sometimes, quite contradictory traditions.
6. On the symbolism of the maloca or longhouse, see Reichel-Dolmatoff (1971, 1975).
7. This is strikingly similar to certain concepts of the Kogi Indians of northern Colombia; see Reichel-Dolmatoff (1975, 1978).

Tatuyo boy with ritual stick-rattle

VII

DESANA CURING SPELLS: AN ANALYSIS OF SOME SHAMANISTIC METAPHORS

Among the Desana Indians, the ritual pronunciation of highly formalized spells constitutes one of the main procedures in the curing of illness, and is practiced not only by shamans imbued with recognized healing powers, but also by certain unspecialized male individuals who, for a number of personal reasons, have gone to the trouble of learning and applying these spells. But not only are these spells thought to exercise a therapeutic action upon a diseased organism; many of them also constitute a prophylactic measure meant to neutralize or prevent certain imminent dangers that threaten people's health.

This paper discusses some aspects of the nature of these curing spells and considers some of the relationships they appear to have with the wider context of Desana society and culture. I frequently refer to two previous publications of mine that deal with the Desana, or with Tukano culture in general, and, for simplicity's sake, shall occasionally use the abbreviations AC and SJ for *Amazonian Cosmos* (1971) and *The Shaman and the Jaguar* (1975), respectively.

Desana Theory of Disease

Although the Desana are sedentary horticulturalists who derive most of their daily sustenance from their manioc fields, hunting and fishing are important activities in the food quest, and also loom large in their emotional world. Desana men like to see themselves in the role of hunters, and their relationships to the animal world are elaborated not only in myth and ritual, but also in daily allusions in which animals play a prominent part. There is great interest in animal behaviour, in animals as bearers of good news or harbingers of evil, and the habits of animals are often taken as models of adaptive behaviour in terms of survival under adverse conditions. The animal world is thus constantly referred to, and acquires its importance not only from its being the all-important protein source, but also because it provides an almost infinite range of models, images, and metaphors that serve to illustrate behavioural patterns and rules of the most varied kind.

Animals play a major role in Desana theories about the origin and nature of disease, and animals are thought to be instrumental in causing and curing it. In the first place, the game animals of the forest are thought to take revenge upon the hunter by causing him illness; as a matter of fact, the malevolence of the game animals is believed to be the largest single cause of illness, and for this reason the maintenance of viable relationships between society and the animal world becomes a major field of elaborate ritual attitudes.

I shall first refer in some detail to the native theory of disease. The specific bodily or mental conditions that, according to the Indians, constitute ill health and that manifest themselves through weakness, acute discomfort, nausea, pain, fever, organic dysfunctions, psychiatric disorders, and a number of other symptoms are almost always believed to be caused by an outside influence. The pathogenic agencies fall essentially into two categories: (1) the ill will of other people, and (2) the malevolence of animals, above all game animals and fish. Apart from the pathological conditions mentioned above, one may include here such accidents as sudden falls, a dangerous cut, a broken limb, death by drowning, snakebite, painful insect bites, and so on. All these mishaps and calamities affect the state of a person's health, as well as such states as soul loss and object intrusion.

These illness categories may be chronic or acute: they may strike suddenly, or develop slowly over long time periods: what they all have in common is that they are thought to be the consequence of the willed malevolence of outside forces. In Desana disease theory it would be meaningless then to search for such categories as diseases caused by 'magical' or by 'natural' agents. There can be only one environment, one context in which the individual exists, and in this context seen and unseen disease agents mix and mingle in a very complex combination of pathogenic forces.

I am not concerned here with native ideas about illnesses caused by personal enemies who, for any number of reasons, might wish one ill; this causal theory is well attested to in Desana culture and does not, as far as I am aware, distinguish itself greatly from the broad general ideas common to many tropical forest Indians of the Amazon Basin. What I am concerned with here is the concept that illness is a punishment, a revenge by which the game animals gain retribution for the persecutions they suffer at the hands of the hunter.

Illness is called *dore* in Desana, a word that according to my informants, designates the outcome of an intention. Thus, the result of an intense desire or wish – for good or evil – is *dore*. This noun is said to be related to the verb *doreri*, 'to command, to order, to send', so that the word *dore* acquires the meaning of 'remittance', in terms of a consignment or a gift. An alternative meaning of *doreri*, however, is 'to change into something in imagination', and this idea of transformation is, from what I am told, related to another verb, *dorori*, and its two meanings: 'to paint with spots or stripes' and 'to disguise'. Another, related term, *dorora*, refers to spotted things and, according to the Desana, spotted things are of an evil nature: they form a category that includes animals like the jaguar, the stingray, the electric eel, a number of snakes, and certain wasps and spiders. The idea that spots are stigmata or maculae is derived from a large body of myths and tales that refer to incest, an act that, in Desana religion, represents Original Sin. The spots on the moon's face are said to be the imprint of the blood-stained hand of the moon's daughter, who had rejected her incestuous father, and the close relationship between the moon and the jaguar is partly based upon their common spottedness (SJ, pp. 127-128). The related verb, *dore-yeeri*, means 'to make someone fall ill' and contains the root of the verb *yeeri*, 'to cohabit'. My informants explain that, in the concept of disease, three components are present: the idea of a remittance, transformation by 'painting', and sexual impregnation by defilement.

Here, I must refer once more to the problem of disease categories. The Desana establish two very broad divisions: illnesses that, because of their fairly clear symptoms, can be diagnosed with some accuracy, such as smallpox, bronchitis, amebiasis, malaria, and those that are not readily recognized as well-defined entities, because they manifest themselves by a large number of rather vague signs and symptoms such as headaches, fever, nausea, insomnia, sharp localized pains, infected boils, incipient blindness, nightmares, and so forth. The first category, then, consists of a group of rather serious ailments the cause of which will generally be attributed to the ill will of humans, that is, of a personal enemy. These illnesses will eventually receive treatment over prolonged time periods, and in most cases the patient will be put under the care of a recognized healer.

The second category is an entirely different matter. The manifestations of ill health such as weakness, pains, fever, dizziness and so on are *not* thought to constitute an illness in the sense of a well-defined syndrome, but are seen for what they are – as isolated symptoms – with the consequent fear that these might, at any moment, develop into a major illness. This category, therefore, causes considerable anxiety, because the patient is in a state of great expectancy and continuously watches out for the slightest change in the development of his ailments. It is this category, of ill-defined but extremely bothersome symptoms, that is generally thought to be caused by the game animals. Their revenge does not consist in punishing the victim with immediate violent sickness, but in causing lingering ills, that is, in generating an anxiety-charged state of ill health and disabling weakness for which there can be no precise empirical treatment, because the symptoms are too vague and too varied. It is, of course, a fact that the average person living in the rainforest under poor sanitary conditions and deprived of all modern medical services, will very frequently develop this or that disquieting symptom and will thus live in an almost permanent state of apprehension, if not outright ill health. The disease category described above can thus be said to be endemic.

The pathogenic agents the game animals are thought to use against their persecutors and consumers in general are many. The most common ones are imagined as short and thin wooden splinters (*vahka*; plural, *vahkari*) or thorns that are shot off by the animals as if they were tiny invisible arrows. Other disease-carrying agents are thought to consist of diminutive fragments of quartz, bushels of hair, small feathers, decaying leaves, or the rotting residues of other vegetable fibres. All these diverse objects fall into a number of subdivisions. The needle-sharp wooden splinters can come from a large number of trees, and those of very hard wood are more feared than others. Hair is thought to be highly pathogenic and generally is imagined as an entangled mass, a wad of bushy or stringy matter. Most dangerous is monkey hair, especially that of certain monkeys of nocturnal habits, but tapir hair, deer hair, or jaguar hair are also mentioned as potential disease carriers or producers. Feathers are imagined as little curved elements, rather like tiny sprouts or shoots, and not as isolated large objects, nor as small bundles. In both cases – hair or feathers – the exact provenance is of importance, and even the precise location on the body of the specific animal is of concern to both the patient and the healer; hair from the tail, down feathers, whiskers, and so on, must be clearly identified by the shaman in order to accomplish a cure. Some fish bones as well as scales, teeth, or the sharp spines and stings that characterize certain species are dangerous pathogens. The gall bladders and swimming bladders of certain fish are also mentioned. Ants, wasps, termites, and other insects that might inflict painful stings or bites are spoken of as potential pathogens. All dirt, mud, and rotten organic matter are thought to contain the essence of disease, or to be a vehicle for it, especially swampy soils collected from stagnant puddles on the trail near a house. In many cases a shaman will readily recognize additional categories by referring to a seemingly endless number of specific characteristics enumerated in terms of shape, size, colour, origin, and so forth. Colour categories will often be mentioned when speaking of a specific agent, for example, 'white splinters', 'red splinters', or 'black splinters', and when speaking of water and its different degrees of transparency, the practitioner might refer to 'white water', 'red water', 'muddy water', 'black water', and so on. The formal description of a pathogenic agent, given in a ritual context, can therefore be extremely lengthy and detailed.

Apart from these concrete, tangible objects which are 'shot' into, or otherwise introduced into the victim's organism, there are certain specific aspects of animal behaviour that are believed to have a pathogenic effect upon humans. For example, there are certain small fish that do not swim in a straight line, but move in rapid zigzag movements. These fish are said to 'entangle' the veins of people, and to cause dizziness and exhaustion. Other fish that swim with very slow and lazy movements are said to cause drowsiness. The nests of certain oropendola or cacique birds (Icteridae), or even the voices of certain songbirds, are thought to produce illness, and to have one's hearing impaired by the shrill sounds of unknown and unseen animals may eventually develop into a serious ailment.

These pathogenic agents, however, cannot be introduced into the human body by the vengeful animals themselves, but must be manipulated by spirit-beings that act as intermediaries. The Desana believe in supernatural personifications that are closely associated with the animal world, and that often are described as the protectors and representatives of the local fauna. The most prominent of these beings is the Master of Animals, called *vai-mahsë*, 'Animal-Person', who is imagined as an anthropomorphic being, a phallic dwarf, who lives among the animals and is their constant companion and guardian. He is not associated with a certain species, but *all* animals are thought to stand under his care (AC, p.80ff).

All this is imagined as happening in a dimension of an Otherworld wherein animals are socially organized and behave very much like humans: they talk, sing, dance and otherwise go about their daily routine like rational beings. The spirit-forms of these animals are supposed to reside inside isolated rocky hills that rise here and there in the forest, and these 'houses', as they are called, are avoided by people. In the case of fish and other water creatures, the abode of their spirits or masters is thought to be at the bottom of deep and dark pools that form below waterfalls or cascades. *Vai-mahsë* is thus imagined to exist in many personifications: as a Master of Game Animals, a Master of Fish and, in quite general terms, as an overall spirit-protector of all species, or indeed of all nature. Within one central concept of a 'Master of Animals', there are thus many, and quite often the term is pluralized as *vai-mahsa* and thus reference is made to groups of 'masters' or to their individual families.

I have mentioned that the animals themselves cannot take any direct action against the hunter and his family, and that they must act through *vai-mahsë*. They may 'shoot their arrows' or foretell evil by their voices or behaviour, but their malevolence has to be substantiated, so to say, by their master who then makes effective their threats.

The specific ways in which the diverse pathogenic agents afflict the victim's organism are the following: splinters are thought to enter the body at practically any spot, and then to wander about causing intense local pain. The same occurs with particles of quartz. Hair, especially the entangled bushels that are frequently mentioned, is said to obstruct the respiratory system (*dyihsë*, 'obstruction') and to become lodged in the throat or chest where it will cause a wide range of troubles, from a persistent cough to acute attacks of asphyxia. Decaying organic matter (*marari*), dirt, swampy water, or similar agents are thought to penetrate the skin and to become lodged in certain organs (liver, heart, kidneys) where they cause swellings, fever, and putrefaction. All these objects or substances are thought to fly through the air like arrows or darts, being flung at the victim from afar by his aggressor, and although their trajectory is almost always invisible to the eye – except to the shaman's – it is said that occasionally one might see the flying object, and that sometimes its impact can immediately be felt and even heard.

A greatly feared omen of ill health is when the game animals appear in a hunter's dreams, because then their behaviour is thought not to be as obvious as it is in nature, but has to be deciphered by correctly interpreting their actions and appearances. Game animals or fish might appear as women, as witch-maidens trying to seduce and abduct the hunter, or they might appear as monsters, as huge predators in feline, reptile, or bird shape. Animals will also commonly appear in a number of other states and, of course, during narcotic trances induced by hallucinogenic drugs (SJ). In most of these cases the person will consult a shaman or an elder and will ask him to interpret the disquieting visions which, often enough, are accompanied by feverish states or other vague symptoms of an approaching illness. But not only will the game animals appear in a hunter's dream; occasionally the Master of Animals himself will visit the sleeper and, in a nightmarish and tumultuous scene, will invite him to partake in his food and drink consisting of noxious brews he forces upon his benumbed victim. Since Desana hunters are highly sensitized from having to undergo a series of rigorous purification practices such as dieting, emetics, sexual abstinence, insomnia, and other privations, the anxiety caused by these dreams seems quite remarkable.

Although often enough the patient himself will diagnose his illness from dreams or hallucinations in which the offended animals voice their complaints or, at least, appear as mute accusers, in many cases a shaman or an experienced healer will be consulted. The practitioner will question the patient on his dreams, his food habits, and his experience as a hunter and will thus establish a first diagnosis. This may be followed up by the healer taking a narcotic drug, generally a *Banisteriopsis* potion, in order to consult with the Master of Animals or to hear the complaints of the game animals. Sometimes both healer and patient will take such a drug, and then discuss the patient's visions in search of clues.

The Curing Spells

Desana curing spells consist of narrative recitals of varying length, spoken by the practitioner in a fairly loud, always audible, voice. The word for spell is *bayi* (plural, *bayiri*), and to pronounce a spell is *bayiri*, or *bayi uri*, 'to invoke' or 'to call'. They are said in the native vernacular language, without using any exceptional terms, and do not contain any unintelligible passages, so that the patient can always understand what is being said. There seems to be no restriction as to time or place for the saying of a spell: the practitioner usually sits on a low stool in his or his patient's house, and bystanders are tolerated as long as they are silent and respectful.

No divine powers are implored in these spells: they are not prayers *(goa mëë bayari*, 'god-songs'), but represent a direct communication between the practitioner and the forces for evil. While describing in the spell the pathogenic agents, the illness, and the preparation of the healing action, the voice of the shaman is kept fairly even and often becomes rather monotonous because of the lengthy repetition of names, places, colour, or other details. Some spells are 'rattled off', one might say, in a very routine manner, but most of them are said slowly, in a clear and even voice, and with proper emphasis on certain key words. The voice rises when mention is made of how the essence of the illness is being grasped and held, and once this essence, or the disease-carrying object, are being banished, thrown away, or otherwise destroyed, the corresponding words are emphasized, the passage being accompanied by violent gestures of the hand. Sometimes there is a sudden accumulation of words or a doubling of vowels whereby each sentence is finished in a long drawn-out manner.

I have very little information on how the Desana account for the origin of their curing spells. From some disconnected fragments it would appear that, until shortly after the Creation, only the animals knew the spells, and that human beings were quite ignorant of them and thus suffered greatly from all sorts of calamities, because they had no effective protection against many ills and accidents. According to some myths it was the daughter of the Sun, a rather ambivalent divine personification, with certain attributes of a Culture Hero, who introduced the first spells, especially those connected with childbirth and burials. Some of my data suggest that certain spells were revealed to people by animals, often in a dream or during a narcotic trance. Unfortunately there is little else I can add.

There probably exist hundreds of spells, and some practitioners have a very large repertory indeed, but most adult men know only a certain number of them, limited to their personal needs or preferences. But there is interest in learning more spells from older men, even if there is no immediate reason for doing so. A knowledge of spells gives security and carries prestige: a person who knows many spells will call them his 'weapons' and will feel 'armed' against dangers.

All tape recordings were made in the field, at night, and in the presence of few people. In the texts I have recorded, my informants took care not to pronounce the spells in the first person, because a direct manner of address might needlessly have summoned the spirit-helpers of a practitioner, or might have attracted the attention of some malevolent forces. To avoid this, they said the spells rather as if they were describing the actions of a third person, that is, of an unidentified shaman. The *words of power* that are thought to carry the true force to heal, or anathemize, however, were always said in the way in which they would have been pronounced in an actual curing ritual. They were called out as an order, an exorcising command, pronounced in a sharp tone of voice, and never failed to impress the audience.

When reciting a spell, the practitioner is expected to do his best to avoid errors or forgetting some words or names, but even shamans of renown are not unreasonably strict about this matter. The validity of a spell is not impaired by some occasional fumbling for words, or some frantic repetitions while trying to remember what comes next. As we shall observe farther on, the sequence of a spell is sometimes interrupted by exclamations, asides, or by stereotyped phrases in which the authority of tradition is called upon. Expressions like: "This is what the old people said!" are inserted here and there to give additional weight to the recital, and often each sentence ends with an affirmative *aa*.

Once a preliminary transcription had been made, the texts were discussed in detail with a number of informants who were asked to provide explanations, comments, etymologies, or information on the animals mentioned in the spell. It is my impression that these commentaries, coming from several people, constitute a valuable aid to a better understanding of the spells. The texts of the tape recordings were translated by me directly from Desana into English, without the medium of the Spanish vernacular. Since I am not a linguist, it is quite possible that I have committed errors, not only in the transcriptions, but also in the translations, but I believe that what I am presenting here is an acceptable rendering of the original. In the course of this work I have had to decide whether to make a quite literal translation, or whether to use here and there words that would best fit the context. For example, according to the adjoining matter, the expression 'he said' might be translated as: 'he replied', 'he asked', 'he ordered', 'he wondered', and so on. I have chosen to use the same word over again, however, just as the Desana do, even if this makes for monotonous reading, but I am fully convinced that this form of translation conserves much better the flavour and the intensity of the original.

Words that complete a sentence, but that were not actually spoken, were inserted by me and are distinguished with square brackets, and so are, occasionally, a few explanatory interpolations. A question mark in parentheses means that I am not certain about the correct translation. The division into sentences is based upon the original texts, and I have added only the punctuation; in a few places I have corrected evident slips of the tongue. Except for these minor amendments, I have made no alterations whatsoever in the texts.

I should like to add here that, while illness-producing spells are generally not revealed to outsiders, those that are meant to heal are not considered secret by the Desana. In this manner, no breach of confidence is being committed by me in disclosing them in published form.

Texts and Comments

In the following pages I quote several texts that, in the Indians' own words, state some of the points I have made so far. I begin by quoting a shaman giving a short description in which animals and human beings are compared. This, of course, is not a spell, but an informal statement that might serve here as an introduction to the main topic of this study.

Text I

1. In the House of the Hills, they [the game animals] live like people. 2. They are people like us. 3. Like us they prepare *chicha* [beer] in their houses, and drink it. 4 [To quote an example:] The animals were looking for fish in the creeks. 5. When they had gathered fish from the creeks, they ordered chicha to be prepared. 6. Even if they are animals, they are like people. 7. Being like people and bringing with them some fish, they made a *dabucuri* [feast]. 8. The women gave them all sorts of chicha. 9. Also at a *dabucuri* they behave like people. 10. [The narrator explains] What they call: 'To cut out the tongue'. 11. [Let us say] a tapir goes down to the watering place to bathe. 12. Look! Just as we do – going down to fetch water. 13. Back and forth they [the women] go fetching water. 14. Another woman goes to fetch water: she too fetches water. 15. Another prepares manioc and this one, she prepares [a dish of] *manicuera*. 16. They go to collect firewood, and they cook and drink.

17. But we kill the people [beings] who go to the watering place, such as the tapir. 18. Be it deer or tapir, we kill them when they go to fetch water. 19. Having killed them we cut out their tongue and bury it in the ground. 20. If we did not cut out their tongues, they would tell their kin.

21. And so they [the animals] come to kill us, or our children, or others. 22. They, too, are many in their houses. 23. They kill us with their splinters, with wooden splinters. 24. Therefore we cut out their tongues and bury them, because they would comprehend and tell. 25. Their weapons are wooden splinters: of *saviri* wood, of wood from the canoe tree, of *puuyoagë* wood, of *borepugë* wood, of *bohseru* wood: these are the weapons they kill us with in revenge. 26. They are armed with arrows; therefore we cut out their tongues and bury them.

Comments

The following comments are meant to explain some specific aspects of the text and follow the numbers of the individual sections.

1. The expression *ëhte yuhkë* literally means 'stone-tree' and alludes to the subterranean, cavelike dwellings of the animal spirits in the deep forests. My informants always translated this expression as 'hill-houses' or 'hill dwellings'.

2. Here the narrator beings to tell a short episode in order to illustrate his comparisons.

7. In *lengua geral* (LG) a *dubucuri* is a ritual gathering of two or more complementary exogamic groups, during which gifts, usually certain foods, are exchanged.

15. *manicuera* (LG) is a common food preparation.

22. That is, they are powerful in their own way: they are very numerous.

25. *saviri*, from *savi*, 'knot, swelling, pregnancy'; a tree the wood of which is

extremely hard, heavy, and durable, and which is used for houseposts. These posts are called *saviri bora*, the last element (*bora*) being a synonym for penis. The name of the *puuyoagë* tree is derived from *puu*, 'leaf,' and *yoari*, 'long,' with the male suffix *-gë*. The tree called *borepugë*, literally 'white-leaf,' is the Cecropia tree (*Puruma cecropia folia*). The underside of the large leaves is a whitish colour, and the five-lobed leaf recalls the mythical scene when the Daughter of the Sun, in the throngs of her birth pangs, grasped a leaf that was lying next to her on the ground. The name of the *bohseru* tree is derived from *boho*, 'dry', and *seru*, 'bark'.

This short description states quite clearly, and in rather sympathetic terms, the way in which the game animals become the victims of the hunters and how, in revenge, they try to harm their persecutors with their wooden splinters.

Another description refers to the behaviour of certain animals that appear here as evil omens and foretell disease.

Text II

1. Deer are like people. 2. Like men, like men. 3. When they make a sound like a small child, it foretells evil for us. 4. The sound is: oeee-oeee-oeee. 5. They [people] say: 'An evil spirit is calling: it is a deer.' 6. They say they are like people. 7. People do talk about this – they do talk. 8. It is an omen. 9. That is the way they are.

10. [My] dead brother saw some. 11. He had climbed [a tree] to pick some *vahsá* fruit. 12. It grew high up, high up. 13. It is called *tara vahsa*. 14. While eating up there, he looked down and there stood two large deer. 15. When they arrived they blew on their musical instruments, just like people, and the sound was: poreperu-perupere-poreperuu-peru, and then they danced backward (?). 16. 'What are they doing there?' he said [to himself], while watching from above. 17. 'This is an evil omen for people' [he thought]. 18. He watched in silence. 19. They were stamping their feet. 20. They were dancing together, the two of them. 21. The same way we do when copulating. 22. [They called] poreru-poreru-poreru-peru-peru-peru, and then they danced backward. 23. Three times they did this. 24. 'Watching them I became afraid' he said [afterward]. 25. After a while they went away. 26. One after another they left.

27. This is why they are an evil omen to people. 28. Deer are people. 29. My father too heard them. 30. It happened near our field. 31. There they called: oe-oe-oenene, in his direction, he told us. 32. They were deer.

33. This is why evil things happen to us. 34. Illness is approaching us. 35. That is the way they [deer] are. 36. There is another [animal], the marten. 37. [Its cry is] hii hii hii hii, and then people will say: 'An evil spirit is crying!' 38. But evil spirits never cry. 41. They are foretelling our disgrace. 42. The nocturnal monkeys, those that had been evil people, when they pass by, people say they

foretell our [disgrace].

45. All these animals. 46. That is why they cry at us. 47. They cry and cry and they say: 'Your hair will become messy'. 48. [And then] we [become] sad and bloodless. 49. That is what they say when conversing. 50. That is what the nocturnal monkeys foretell, our disgrace. 51. 'He will perish' [they say]; [he who is] adorned with our hair; he will perish.

Comments

On the basis of the foregoing text we can extend our commentaries and we observe, first, that the voices of animals do not directly *cause* illness in humans, but that they only prognosticate it. Secondly, it appears that not only game animals such as deer foretell ill health by their insistent calls, but also animals that are not hunted, such as nocturnal monkeys, rats, martens, or parrots. The deer mentioned in this text can be identified by the description of its call as a Mazama deer: when frightened, these animals stamp their fore-feet sharply on the ground, sometimes simultaneously with both legs, but sometimes holding aloft one leg and then changing rapidly from one foot to the other. The term used in this text to describe the stamping is *gubukëma*, from *gubukë*, 'to beat time by stamping with the foot'. During certain dances, Desana men posture and stamp in a highly formalized manner called *guburo moari*, 'foot-to-do-stamp', and the reference to the 'dancing' of the two deer is therefore not a casual comparison.

11. The *vahsa* (*vahsu*) tree (*Hevea pauciflora* var. *coriacea*) is a rubber tree with edible fruit that ripens during the rainy season and has for the Indians a male, seminal connotation, because of the mucilaginous texture of its flesh. The *vahsu* tree is 'male' in Desana thought, a phallic tree whose milky sap is often compared to sperm. It was this fruit the man was gathering when he watched the deer copulating.

22. The sound poreru encodes many sexual significations: *poreru*, 'tail', *porero*, 'penis', *pore*, 'clitoris', *poreri*, 'to become erect', and the cry is often quoted when the sexual activity of deer is mentioned. Their blowing on a musical instrument refers to an instrument made of a deer skull (*nyama dihpuru*), which is played at certain dances.

36. The mammal called *mahsë vehe*, 'person-old,' is the grey-headed *tayra* (*Tayra barbara senilis*), a large marten that derives its Latin and Desana epithet from its grey head. To this can be added its somewhat stumbling gait, similar to that of an old man. Although omnivorous, this animal is known to be very fond of sweet foods such as honey, pineapple, and sugarcane, and this preference makes it a rather lecherous old creature in the eyes of the Desana, because sweet foods symbolize women and sex. The tayras are among a number of animals that have a *baculum*, which, in the opinion of the Indians, makes them symbols of male potency. The nocturnal monkeys are said to have been people in ancient

A dancer tying rattles round his ankles

times, but were punished and degraded because of their blatant incestuous behaviour.

37-38. It is mentioned here that, when hearing the cry of the tayra marten, people will say fearfully: "An evil spirit is crying!" The narrator of this text is a highly respected old shaman and he adds quite bluntly: "...evil spirits never cry: it's the animals that cry". This no-nonsense statement might suggest that there exists a difference between popular belief and formal shamanistic belief, at least on that point; to the shaman, animals are not spirit-beings, they are biological facts, but they can become the *tools* of spirits. They themselves have no supernatural power, but they can become the instruments of such forces.

A third text will suffice to complete this introductory section, in that it explains how the Master of Animals can be appeased, so he will not serve as an intermediary and executor of evil.

TEXT III

1. The Master of Animals, in his personification of an anaconda, is furious when women bear children. 2. The fish, too [are furious]. 3. Also the jaguars of the forest. 4. The *boraro* the same. 5. They become furious when they [the women] are that way.

6. In his [the Master's] house, they [the shamans] take care of him by preparing him food. 7. In the House of Sand, of rough stone, they take hold of him and look after him while he is sitting there. 8. They give him to eat from a gourd-vessel with starchy flour, with *pari* fish, with manioc flour, with *vahsu* flour, with termite flour, with red ant flour and, taking hold of him, they turn him around and make him sit down. 9. Having eaten this, they [the Masters] sleep well. 10. While they are thus unaware, they [the menstruating women] can bathe [in the river].

11. The Masters of Animals of the forest [must be taken care of] in the same way. 12. In his abode, they [the shamans] take hold of the lizards, the toads, and the butterflies and, turning them around, they make them sit down. 13. They [give] them the same [food]. 14. Their attention must be diverted so that [the women] can eat. 15. Grasping the mat [with] the fiery reflection of *anatta*, they take it to the river (?). 16. The [sap] for head scrubbing too [must be] from a red tree and from a white tree. 17. Also in our house [must be done the same].

18. When this has been done, they fast. 19. They do not chew sugarcane, to avoid toothache. 20. When they chew sugarcane, they [the worms] gnaw at our teeth. 21. They do not eat salt either. 22. Nor do they eat *ëhtoka* fruit. 23. [All] these things make our teeth rot. 24. For this reason the old people prohibited them.

25. This lasts for two weeks. 26. So that they can eat [again], they now kill the beasts and banish them. 27. Also the fruits. 28. They do the same with the fish and, destroying their gall bladders they banish them. 29. They must taste and eat shrimp pepper, small pepper, large pepper, and water pepper. 30. They must eat this with the meat.

Comments

A few comments are called for here to clarify some aspects of this description.

1. The Desana say that the Master of Animals is always greatly concerned about human sexuality, and that he is very resentful when women give birth to children. In part, this attitude is due to the fact that any increase in population size becomes an additional danger to the game animals (*AC.* p.147).

2. The *boraro* is a male forest spirit that is, in many ways, similar to the Master of Animals. In lengua geral this being is called Curupira (*AC.* p. 86ff: *SJ.* p. 182ff).

7. As we shall see farther on, the different 'houses', or abodes, of the Master of Animals or of animal spirits are often described in some detail.

12. The two lizards mentioned in this text are *saveroa* (*Plica plica* L.), one of *vai-mahsë's* personifications, and *Oroka soaga*, of uncertain identity (*AC*, pp. 80-81, 103, 116).

15. The 'fiery mat' represents an important magical object that is mentioned in several spells, but is very difficult to explain. On the one hand, the word *imikeyaru* can be used to refer to a mat woven of reeds, or some kind of esparto, with fairly wide interstices, but it can also mean 'fence' or (fish?) 'trap'. On the other hand, *imika* means 'smoke'. Some informants described it as having the bright red colour of Guinea peppers, but others said that it was 'the colour of colostrum or of yellowish milk'.

16. This refers to the lathery sap of a jungle tree, probably *Solanum mammosum*, which is used as a kind of soap, especially to wash one's hair with.

20. It is commonly believed by the Desana that toothache is caused by the gnawing of tiny worms.

22. The *ëhtoka* fruit (*Solanum quitoense* Lam.) is very sweet and astringent.

I shall proceed now by quoting a spell that is said to cure an undetermined illness caused by splinters that have been sent by various birds, upon the request of the Master of Animals. This is a relatively short spell, but it is rather characteristic of a large number of curing spells in that it refers to the manner in which the pathogenic splinters are neutralized, an important point in shamanistic healing.

TEXT IV

1. The splinters are looked for and found at the door of the House of Thunder. 2. White splinter, red splinter – it is adorned with the fuzz of the Harpy Eagle. 3. By leaving [with us] the splinters, they cause illness. 4. To banish the splinters, they are anointed with milk and with *tooka* milk, and are thrown away. 5. They are banished to the Netherworld. 6. The fuzz makes us dizzy.

7. The *eoka* eagle [said]: 'I too have my splinters!' 8. When the splinters get into the blood, they cause us pain. 9. The splinters were gathered at the door of the House of Thunder. 10. To throw them away, they anoint them with milk and with *tooka* milk. 11. So the fuzz will not penetrate into us, they gather it up and [throw it away], so it will not make us feverish.

12. The eagle of the manioc gardens said: 'I too have my splinters!' 13. The earth splinter – he had adorned it with fuzz. 14. The splinter is anointed with milk and with *tooka* milk, and is thrown away. 15. Seizing the splinter, they send it to the Netherworld. 16. There, in the Netherworld, the splinters disappear in the decay. 17. The swallows too have their splinters, their adornments. 18. These splinters they anoint with milk and with *tooka* milk, and they take hold of them.

19. This done, they throw them into the Netherworld. 20. There, in the *mëë* river, they are crushed.

21. Their fuzz makes us dizzy: they do [all] this to avoid this. 22. When they do this, the illusions disappear.

Comments

It is stated here that the splinters are gathered at the door – literally the 'mouth' – of the House of Thunder, a concept I must try to explain briefly before referring to the further contents of the spell. Thunder (*buhpu*) is represented by Thunder-Person (*buhpu-mahsë*), a male spirit-being closely associated with the Sun-Father (*pagë abe*), and the Thunder-Jaguar (*buhpu yee*), three personifications that occasionally overlap in Desana religion. A shaman's apprentice must visit the House of Thunder in a narcotic trance induced by hallucinogenic snuff and must obtain from Thunder-Person the tools of his office consisting of a gourd-rattle, a pair of copper ear-pendants, a number of pathogenic splinters and – most important – a set of 'thunderstones', pebbles of different sizes, shapes, colours, and textures, which are used in the curing of illness (*AC*, p. 78; *SJ*, p. 51-53). Some of these stones are of translucent whitish quartzite. The shiny ear-pendants Thunder-Person wears produce lightning, a phenomenon that is described by some informants as 'a sudden glance of the sun'. But lightning can also cause disease because it 'makes the quartz shatter'. It is believed that lightning consists of a tangible object, a projectile, a thunderbolt of quartz hurled by Thunder-Person at some victim on earth. Thunder-Person will do so only upon the demands of a shaman who wishes to destroy an adversary or his house, and wherever lightning strikes, a shaman will immediately search the ground for diminutive quartz splinters, in order to neutralize them with spells, or to 'throw them back' at his enemy. The statement then in this text, that the pathogenic splinters are being 'gathered at the door of the House of Thunder', refers to this general context of ideas.

2. The splinters are described as being 'adorned' with fuzz or down of the Harpy Eagle, and this introduces another aspect of Desana disease theory. I have mentioned already the use of pathogenic feathers, and I should add here that the word for feathers, *poari*, is the same as that used for body hair, hair of the head, or fur; in each case, the exact meaning has to be inferred from the context. But the term 'fuzz' (*vihto*) is more specific. It refers, for example, to the white down from the underside of a Harpy Eagle, a King Vulture, or to the fine white hair from the underbelly of a jaguar. All three are thunder-animals in Desana cosmology, and while the jaguar is mainly associated with a life-giving, fertilizing energy, the Harpy Eagle is thought to be a destroyer of illness, while the King Vulture, being a carrion-feeder, is a cleansing agent wherever impurity is present. The Desana see in this thin, fluffy texture a male seminal substance that repre-

sents a principle of fertilization. For certain dances, Desana men cover their heads with large masses of downy white cotton wads or bird down, both signifying fertility. While discussing the word *vihto*, my informants compared this downiness or floss with the tiny hairs one can observe on leaves, the stems of tender plants or on the body of insects, that is, they related this fuzzy appearance to the biological concept of pubescence. These fuzzy particles (*vihto këri*) have a very ambivalent nature in Desana thought; sperm and germ are easily equated and can represent a principle of benefic fertility and growth, or they can represent a principle of evil, which defiles and destroys the matrix wherein it develops. The decisive factor is the law of exogamy, a point I shall refer to later on. For the moment I want to say this: the process of falling ill is generally taken to be the consequence of an insemination, in the sense of the patient having become impregnated by an impure, life-destroying force (*AC*, pp. 175-187).

4. We now arrive at an important point in the curing ritual: the anathema, the expulsion of the evil, unclean substance. The disease-carrying agent, often the disease itself, is 'anointed with milk and with *tooka* milk, and is thrown away'. Milk refers to breast milk (*ahpiko*), and we thus enter a dimension filled with complex symbolic meanings.

According to Desana myths, mankind arose from *ahpikon dia*, the River of Milk, the main axis of Paradise, located under our earth. On its eastern side is the Lake of Milk into which flow all the rivers of our earth. This unworldly domain of milk is a life-giving and life-sustaining region which has its celestial counterpart in the Milky Way, which emerges like an enormous frothy river that runs from east to west, and on which float all unclean, pathogenic residues that have been carried up there by the vultures and other celestial scavengers. Milk, the supreme life-sustaining substance is, according to the Desana, similar to semen, the supreme life-creating substance.

The *tooka* plant – so far botanically unidentified – is described by the Indians as a small jungle plant the leaves of which are bright red on the underside and have a greasy, oily texture: the blackish fruits or berries are said to have a sticky sap considered 'very sweet' and 'like honey'. The sap of *tooka* is also designated as 'milk' and is compared to semen. The root *too* has three meanings: a cluster of fruits, a generation, or descent.

The place to which the splinters or other matters are banished and thrown away, is the 'Netherworld' or, more specifically, a lake located just above the mouth of the River of Milk. This river empties into the waters of the Beyond, into a paradisiacal realm, a land of milk and honey, where the souls of people who have lead a virtuous life are said to reside after death. Every living thing that travels along this stream of life must pass through this lake, which is described as a kind of sluice or 'filter', before entering the great waters of *ahpikon dia*. This lake, set at the end of life and the beginning of rebirth, is called *dia gorosiri*, from *dia*, 'river', and *gorosiri*, 'place of return', also called 'place of death'. My informants said: "The animals that cause illness go as far as *dia gorosiri*; there they disappear, they vanish." The verb 'to vanish', used in this context, was *mëhtari siriri*, from *mëhtari*, 'to divide', 'to become diluted', and *siriri*, a word that can be translated as 'to intercept', in the sense of 'putting an end to something', signifying death.

20. It is mentioned here that the splinters of the swallows are destroyed in the *mëë* river, another stream of the river system of Paradise. The fruit of the *mëë* tree (*Poraqueiba sericea, umarí* in LG) is edible and sweet, and has a highly emotional meaning to the Desana, being the symbolic female, fecundity counterpart of the male, fertilizing *vahsu* fruit.

The idea of the lake being a 'filter' is very elaborate and somewhat obscure. It is thought that the waters are inhabited by enormous ghostly piranha fish and other scavengers that shred to bits all evil flotsam that is carried down on the river. The unclean substances are sifted through woven mats, sieves, or baskets and, finally, disappear in the huge mass of rotten leaves and branches that has accumulated at the outlet of the lake. There are floating islands and 'houses' (*gorosiri vii*) inhabited by spirit-beings, and when speaking of these waters of death one has the impression that what is being described is the mouth of a large tropical river – perhaps the Rio Negro or the Amazon – a desolate expanse of muddy water, carrying with it dead trees, islands of floating vegetation, and the stench of decay.

To go a step further, I shall quote now a spell by which abducted souls may be recovered.

Text V

1. This is how the peoples of the headwaters steal souls.
2. There is is a rope of black monkey hair, and a rope of white monkey hair.
3. The splinter of the *caimo* tree has a veil of hair. 4. These hair ropes are tied to the head. 5. This splinter pierces our souls. 6. When we feel this, we must pronounce this spell.

7. These ropes of black monkey hair and of white monkey hair, and the splinters, are anointed with milk and with *tooka* milk, and after anointing them they are thrown into the *mëë* river. 8. They are buried in a heap of leaves in the River of Milk. 9. The veil is anointed with milk foam and is grasped and taken away and banished. 10. The piranha of the Lake of Milk, the piranha of the waters, the piranha crusher of leaves receives it and thus it is banished.

11. Then comes the black monkey. 12. There is a black monkey garment, a black monkey garment. 13. The red monkey is called *bogë* and the black monkey is called *nyii*. 14. There is a splinter with a garment of hair, a splinter of the *caimo* tree, a white splinter. 15. We feel these splinters are piercing us. 16. The splinters are banished by anointing them with milk and with *tooka* milk. 17. The

splinters are thrown into the lake at the River of Milk. 18. After anointing it with milk and with *tooka* milk, the garment is seized and taken away. 19. In the lake of the River of Milk the piranha bites it and crushes it.

20. Then Night-Person comes once more, dressed in a garment of hair. 21. Then there are the night monkeys with red fur, with red fur. 22. The black splinters of the *sëmé* tree are covered with a garment. 23. The splinter is anointed with milk and with *tooka* milk and, having been anointed, is taken away. 24. The garment is taken away and the piranha crushes it in the River of Milk.

25. The night monkey is the brother of the piranha. 26. He too has a black garment and a red garment. 27. The splinters of the black and red *sëmé* tree are wrapped into the garments. 28. He takes away the splinter by anointing it with milk and with *tooka* milk. 29. He throws it into the heap of leaves in the lake of the River of Milk. 30. The piranha crushes the garment and the splinters.

31. Then his grandfather [the Night-Person] comes again. 32. There are also the Marten-People with their garments of hair. 33. There are some with a black garment and some with a red garment. 34. The splinter comes from the bow tree and is wrapped up in the garment. 35. It is a black splinter and it is anointed with milk and is banished. 36. In the lake of the River of Milk the piranha crushes it.

37. After this comes the garment of hair of the *gahki* monkey. 38. The splinter of the bow tree is wrapped into this garment. 39. After anointing it with milk, the splinter is thrown away. 40. By anointing it with milk it is banished to the lake of the River of Milk. 41. There the piranha receives it and crushes it by biting it.

42. If we do not know [all this], it would kill us.

43. After this comes the *seegë* garment of hair. 44. There is a black garment of hair and a white garment of hair. 45. There is a black *dohtogë* splinter and a red one. 46. The splinter is anointed with milk and with *tooka* milk, and it is thrown away. 47. The splinters are thrown into the heap of leaves in the lake of the River of Milk. 48. The garment too is anointed with milk and is taken away and banished. 49. The piranha of the River of Milk crushes it by biting it.

Comments

This text introduces us to a fundamental concept of Desana disease theory: the idea that illness is a state that is symbolized by a kind of 'garment', a vestment, a veil, that is defiled or contaminated. But before occupying myself with the discussion of this aspect, I shall rapidly comment on some minor points that are mentioned in this spell.

The expression *dihpari mahare* means literally 'headwaters-belonging to', a locution which refers to people that live in relative isolation on the upper reaches of a river. The term is usually employed in a rather derogatory fashion and combines two implicit meanings: that of backwardness and that of magical aggressiveness. In the case of this particular spell the Cubeo Indians of the Querari River were alluded to. Section 2 mentions the name of a monkey, *meresiamë*: this is a small animal of a brownish colour (gen. *Saguinus*) the Desana name of which is derived from its predilected food, the fruits of the *guamo* (*Inga spuria*) tree: *mere*, 'guamo', and *siari*, 'to enjoy'. The tree mentioned in section 3 – *karegë* – is called *caimo* in vernacular Spanish and is an important fruit tree (*Chrysophyllum vulgare*), the sweetish fruit of which is highly appreciated by the Indians. Both fruits – *guamo* and *caimo* – have marked male sexual connotations and encode spermlike qualities. In section 5 it is not quite clear whether reference is being made to the monkey hair ropes being tied to the back of the head, which would be the usual way of wearing them, or whether they are imagined as being wrapped around the head in a painful manner. Ropes or strings of monkey hair, interwoven with hair from girls' puberty rituals, are tied on the back, or on top of the head, to a short jaguar bone, and form an essential part of male ceremonial attire during dances. They represent virility and I shall refer to this particular symbolism later on.

The 'heap of leaves' mentioned in section 8 makes reference to the large mass of rotting leaves and branches that often obstruct the rivers or creeks. These densely entangled accumulations of decomposing organic matter are, in the mind of the Desana, a kind of drain, a sewer where all decaying and unclean things are being caught and eliminated. Decaying leaves and other vegetable matter in decomposition that float on rivers or in lagoons are closely related to Desana concepts of pollution. These supposedly pathogenic substances are said to be effectively eliminated by such aquatic scavengers as piranha, or other voracious fish, that appear as spirit-helpers of the shaman. Carrion represents one of the worst forms of pollution on land, and is eliminated by vultures (Cathartidae) and other carrion-feeding scavengers. Section 20 mentions Night-Person, a concept that more often appears in a pluralized form as Night-People (*nyamiri mahsa*), a category of spirit-beings thought to represent Death, and who have the characteristics of psychopomps. They are thought to be the 'souls' or 'ghosts' of the dead, who inhabit the so-called Dark Region of the West (*AC*, pp. 66-67). The *sëmé* refers to a leguminous tree of very hard wood, the pods of which contain large lentil-shaped fruits that are eaten or can be made into chicha. The Tayra-People or Marten-People mentioned in section 32 are the grey-headed tayras I have described in commenting on Text II.

I shall turn now to the central concept I have mentioned above. Beginning with section 9, reference is made to a 'garment' which is being anointed with milk and with *tooka* sap before it is being taken away and eliminated. In Desana *suriro* means 'dress', 'clothing', a 'covering', and the verb *suriri* means 'to dress' or 'to cover oneself'. This can refer to most any kind of clothing, be it Indian or European, be it a tailored garment or a simple piece of cloth. A ceremonial bark cloth mask, like the ones used by the neighbouring Cubeo Indians, is called *suriro*, and so is a shirt made from trade cloth. But *suriri* also means 'to become wrapped up', 'to be entangled', ensnared, confused, and the noun *suriro* thus comes to signify a state of being an 'aspect' in terms of a specific physical, psychological, or mental condition of the person. Thus, to be in love is *gametarari suriro*, to be happy is *muhku miriri suriro*, to be furious is *gamekëari suriro*, to be under a spell is *bayiri suriro* (SJ, pp. 95-96). In all these cases, the underlying idea is that the person is in a 'state of', that is, has been covered with some special quality which, only on the most simple metaphorical level can be interpreted as a piece of cloth, a wrapping, a sort of skin or shell that envelops the person. To be sick is *doremoari suriro*, and the meaning is precisely that the patient is 'wrapped into' the illness, that he is wearing what I have called the 'garment', or 'veil', of disease. I may add here that, while the verb *suriri* means 'to dress', 'to cover oneself', the related verb *suri* means 'to paint', 'to anoint'.

The following text describes a very different situation. This is a short spell against dream-visitors, Thunder-People who come carrying illness.

TEXT VI

1. He comes with his tobacco from the Snake River of Milk. 2. He comes with 'water tobacco,' with '*sai* tobacco,' and with 'day tobacco.' 3. He comes with his train of followers. 4. They come with Thunder. 5. Seeing this, he [the shaman] must know what they [intend] to do to you. 6. He stops the sons of his people and makes them return to the river. 7. At the Snake River they seize their tobacco and take it away from them.

8. They also come with their tobacco from the headwaters of the Snake River. 9. *So that Thunder will not come, I change this spell.* 10. He also comes with his train of people. 11. They, too, carry water tobacco and *sai* tobacco. 12. Thunder comes also with day tobacco. 13. Therefore, by anointing it with milk, he takes it away. 14. Stopping them he takes away their tobacco and sends it to the mouth of the river.

15. They say this spell when there are many bad dreams. 16. At this side [north] is the electric eel [female]. 17. She too arrives with her tobacco. 18. She too comes with her day tobacco, water tobacco, and *sai* tobacco. 19. They anoint it with milk and with *tooka* milk and disarm her. 20. After having taken away their weapons, they make them go back to where they came from. 21. They pronounce this spell when there are bad dreams.

22. At this side [south] is the Snake River of Women. 23. She too arrives with her tobacco. 24. She too [comes] with her day tobacco, water tobacco, and with her train of followers. 25. He disarms them by anointing it with milk and with *tooka* milk. 26. He stops them and turns them around and sends them back to where they came from. 27. When he does this, he also banishes the train of people. 28. Making them turn back, he cuts off the train of people.

Comments

The significance of the different kinds of tobacco is not clear, nor can I add any information on the whereabouts of the Snake River. Undoubtedly, this spell is a mere fragment of a much larger invocation. While the narrator was speaking, there was far-off thunder, and he became uneasy and changed the wording (section 9).

The next spell describes how the shamans placate the Master of Animals by visiting him in his abodes, in this case in different subaquatic 'houses', and by offering him food.

Text VII

1. He [lives] in the House of Green Stone, of the frog. 2. In the Frog House of Stone; he has the quality (power ?) of quartz. 3. His ear-pendants are white, they are white. 4. His ear-pendants rub against his cheeks. 5. Seizing the ear-pendants, they take them away. 6. They take away the power of the quartz. 7. They make him sit down with his back turned, when they leave the house. 8. Sitting in there with his back turned, they give him his gourd vessel with groundnut manioc, with *vahsu* manioc, with *mëë* manioc, with sweet potato manioc. 9. [And] a gourd vessel with those [edible] ants; they [all belong to] the Master of Animals. 10. This is what he has for food; they light his cigar and, sitting there, they make him fall asleep.

11. After the House of Green Stone comes the House of Quartz. 12. The one of the House of Quartz also wears ear-pendants, he wears ear-pendants. 13. He has ear-pendants like red fire, he is adorned with red ear-pendants, fire-red, red ear-pendants with the power of quartz; they take away these ornaments and give him to eat from his gourd vessels with groundnut manioc, with termite manioc, with ant manioc. 14. They make him sit with his back turned and, sitting there, they make him fall asleep. 15. While his attention is thus diverted, one must go down to the landing place to wash.

16. After the House of Quartz comes the Stone House of the Frog. 17. After the House of Green Stone comes the House of Quartz. 18. In that house he is adorned with ear-pendants like pale fire. 19. The quality of the quartz is like pale fire, yes; seizing this they take away [this quality], they take it away; seizing him they turn him around and make him sit down. 20. He sits with his back turned and they give him his gourd vessels with manioc of his house and with groundnut manioc; and seizing him they make him fall asleep sitting there, and they make him forget.

21. After the Stone House of the Frog comes once more the House of Green Stone. 22. The one of that house also wears green ear-pendants that have the

power of quartz. 23. They cure this by anointing the quartz with milk and, seizing them, they take away his ear-pendants. 24. Seizing him they take away his ornaments and they turn him around. 25. Having turned him around, they give him to eat from his gourd vessels of groundnut manioc and *vahsu* manioc and, sitting there, they make him forget.

26. After this comes once more the Stone House of the piranha, the house of the grinding stone (?), the one they call the House of the Piranha. 27. White Fish-Person is there; in that house too he wears white ear-pendants: these are the ear-pendants he uses. 28. Again the quartz is white and, seizing the power of it, they take hold of the quartz and take it off: while he sits there they give him his gourd vessels with manioc, with groundnut manioc, with *vahsu* manioc, and thus they make him forget. 29. Thus they [the shamans] divert their [the masters'] attention from us people.

30. After this comes the one of the Sand House. 31. There is the House of Lightning Teeth, the house they speak of. 32. They say it is the House of Lightning Teeth. 33. He also wears ear-pendants like dark fire, like dark fire. 34. The dark ear-pendants, the dark ones, have the power of dark fire, of dark fire. 35. They cure this by anointing the quartz with milk and with *tooka* milk and, taking hold of them, they take them off; seizing them they take away his ornaments. 36. Taking hold of him, they turn him around and, sitting there, they make him sleepy and forgetful, and they give him to eat from his gourd vessels of groundnut manioc, of *vahsu* manioc: they give him to eat, they give him to eat. 37. They make him forgetful and while he sits there eating, he forgets about us, about us.

38. After this comes the Sand House once more, his Sand House. 39. The Sand House is his, it too is his, it too. 40. Again, he [has] his house of sand, his white house, they are his. 41. His ear-pendants are yellowish-red and his quartz, too, has the quality of redness, the quality of redness. 42. The one of the white house has ear-pendants of white power. 43. They cure this by anointing it with milk and with *tooka* milk, and they seize this power and take it away and, taking hold of him they turn him around and make him sit down: they give him to eat from his gourd vessels of manioc, so that he will pay no attention to us; he pays no attention to us while eating.

44. After this comes the Land House once more, the Land House, yes; now comes another matter.

45. The Clay House is his, isn't it? He too wears green ear-pendants, he has ear-pendants, ear-pendants. 46. Green ear-pendants that have the power of quartz. 47. They take away [that] power and, making him sit down quietly they have him sit there quietly, and they give him food from his gourd vessels of *vahsu* manioc, and of termite manioc; they turn him around and they make him fall asleep.

48. After this comes the Yellow Clay House, his house of crab clay (?). 49. They take off his ear-pendants and they take off his adornments of quartz: they

give him to eat from his gourd vessels of *vahsu* manioc and *pari* fish manioc and, sitting there, they make him fall asleep: they make him sit quietly.

50. Once again there is the Yellow Clay House, the yellowish-red one. 51. They call it yellowish. 52. This is his house; his ear-pendants are red and that one too, and the quartz has a red quality. 53. Seizing him they take off his ornaments, they take them away, they take them away, and taking hold of him they turn him around and they give him to eat from his gourd vessels of manioc, of *vahsu* manioc, of *pari* fish manioc, and they make him sit and fall asleep. 54. While eating thus he sits turned around.

55. Here is the end of this: after the House of Yellow Clay comes the White House, and what they paint it with is called *bore*. 56. This is his house: this too has the power of white quartz and again [he wears] white ear-pendants; seizing them they take them away, and taking hold of him they turn him around and make him sit down. 57. Making him sit down they turn him around and, sitting there, they make him fall asleep, and they give him food from his gourd vessels of *vahsu* manioc, of *pari* fish manioc, and of ant manioc; they give him food. 58. There it is, the White House: what they paint it with is called *bore*.

59. [And] this they say about the reddish one. 60. He is of this house, he too; turning him around they make him sit down and they take away his ornaments. 61. Seizing the ornaments they take them away, and they give him manioc to eat, and they make him sit down and turn around and, taking hold of him, they make him fall asleep, they lull him to sleep.

62. After this there is – again-again – that house, his Clay House: it is part of the land, part of the land. 63. Its power is a white power, a quartz power, that power. 64. The ear-pendants too, the ear-pendants, the ear-pendants; they take off the ornaments and, turning him around, they make him sit down, and they give him food from his gourd vessels of groundnut manioc and termite manioc, and they make him sit down and lull him to sleep.

65. This is the food of the Master of Animals. 66. This is what the Masters of Animals have for food; they ... yes.

67. After this comes again – what house? His House of White Starch; he wears the same ornaments, the same ones. 68. The power of quartz, too; the ear-pendants too, the ear-pendants; seizing them they take them away and taking hold of him they turn him around and make him sit down and make him fall asleep they give him food from the gourd vessels of termite manioc and *vahsu* manioc, and they make him fall asleep.

69. After this comes once more that land of his, of the frog – once again. 70. It is the same with him there – they take away his ear-pendants and, entering his house, they take hold of him and make him sit down: making him sit down they lull him to sleep. 71. They give him to eat from his gourd vessels of manioc, of *vahsu* manioc, termite manioc, and ant manioc, and taking hold of him they make him fall asleep.

72. When the ear-pendants of the Master of Animals touch one another, the sound is: tai tai tai: they anoint them with milk and throw them away.

Comments

In many Desana myths, spells, or descriptions of ritual, mention is made of ear-pendants, an adornment to which great symbolic importance is attached. At present these objects consist of brass shotgun shells cut in half lengthwise and highly polished, but in the past they may have consisted of gold, or an alloy. Great powers are said to reside in them, and to deprive someone of his ear-pendants is to make him helpless and utterly defenseless. Should the concave, groove-shaped side of the pendant turn toward the face of the bearer, this would be taken as a sure sign of approaching death, and the degree of health or energy of the owner is said to be expressed by the intensity of the brilliance of this adornment. From many mythical contexts it would appear that the ear-pendants are male symbols and that their power is, essentially, a sexual power. In the foregoing text, the Master of Animals is stripped of his sexual power attributes, but at the same time he is given a number of foods that, among the Desana, have strong fertility associations: *vahsu* and edible insects are 'male' foods, while *mëë* and sweet potato are 'female'. This inversion expresses the idea that vai-*mahsë*'s sexual powers are unclean and must be neutralized by the 'pure' food administered by the shamans. The seminal connotations of quartz have been mentioned earlier and it remains to point out that an important fertility symbolism is contained in the many colour terms employed in this text. The power of 'pure' male fertility is measured by a scale of yellow hues which the Desana perceive in flames, liquids, feathers, cotton, and a great many other substances. Greenish hues are taken to be evil.

I hope that what I have said so far is sufficiently explicit to serve as an introduction to an understanding of the essential nature of Desana curing spells. I shall quote now a fairly long spell that is used to cure a sickness which the Desana call *bëa-ari*, or 'numbness', and which, according to my informants, is characterized by fevers, chills, somnolence, and a general state of listlessness (*AC*, pp. 182-183). In the case presented here, the symptoms are attributed to the actions of a certain fish.

TEXT VIII

1. Numbness is like that – numbness. 2. The head of the *ahki* fish, the small spotted one, does this and entangles our veins. 3. It entangles them; we have seen that it does not swim in a straight line, but in zigzag, and in doing so it entangles our veins and drags them along.

4. Therefore it is cured by anointing it with milk and with *tooka* sap – cold-resisting person, cold-person – his adornments they invoke – of the black waters,

the red waters, and the white waters. 5. They cure us by anointing it with milk [while] grasping and straightening out the veins he has entangled. 6. They straighten them, they straighten them, they straighten them out, and they deliver them at the lake of the rivermouth.

7. The *ahki* fish does this, the slightly larger one, the one of the creeks, yes, the one of the creeks. 8. His kind exists in black waters, in red waters, and in white waters.

9. They cure this by anointing him with milk and with *tooka* sap – cold-wet-people, cold-people; so it won't entangle our veins they take them and smoothen them by straightening them out, and they deliver them in the House of Fish. 10. Therefore, by returning there he drags them along while straightening them out. 11. Therefore we say to recover, he straightens them out by going [there]. 12. This is what they say when conversing. 13. Given this afterwards, to the *ahki* fish of the river (?). 14. This is the river of our origins.

15. They are black, red, and spotted. 16. They are in black waters, in white waters, and in red waters, and the ones of the black waters are black, the ones of the white waters are white, and the ones of the red waters are red.

17. They cure [this] by anointing it with milk and with *tooka* sap – agents of cold – so he won't entangle our veins, and then, grasping them they smoothen them and send them away and, straightening them out they deliver him (?) at the House of Fish.

18. Next comes the *përisero* fish of the black waters and the white waters, and they invoke the red, the white, and the black one.

19. Anointing it with milk and with *tooka* sap – agent of cold, agent of cold-people – [and] so it won't entangle our veins, they grasp them and straighten them out, there, in the House of Fish.

20. [Next comes] the *deyë* fish, yellow fish in its house, the house of the *deyë* fish, that house is of quartz, of white quartz, of dark green quartz, of yellowish quartz; there it has its abode.

21. Grasping it they straighten it out and deliver it. 22. They invoke the *ama* fish next, the *ama* fish. 23. They are of the black waters, the white waters, and the red waters.

24. They cure it by anointing them with milk and with *tooka* sap – agent of cold, cold-people – [and] so it won't entangle our veins they grasp it and straighten it out, and banish it to the House of Fish, the House of White Quartz, of Greenish Quartz [and] grasping it they deliver it. 25. Thus, by going there, they straighten it out.

26. It is the same with the *pava* fish. 27. The *pava* fish of the red waters, the white waters, and the black waters: its frothing waters are our river of origins. 28. When it [the fish] looks for food it swims in zigzag, in zigzag. 29. It gets in and out, in and out: that is what it does.

30. They cure it by anointing it with milk and with *tooka* sap – agent of cold,

agent of cold – and so it won't entangle us they grasp it and, straightening it out, they send it away. 31. By going there he straightens out the veins. 32. [In] that house of red clay, house of yellow clay, of green pottery (potter's clay ?): in these houses they live.

33. The house of the green *deyë* fish is green: the house of the red *deyë* fish is red: and the house of the white one is whitish.

34. They cure this by anointing him with milk and with *tooka* sap and, grasping it they straighten it out and deliver it. 35. Therefore, by going there, they straighten it out.

36. It is the same with the *sai* fish, the same. 37. The *sai* fish, when looking for food in the river, entangles us: it is like this – it enters and passes on to another lake: this is how he does it.

38. They cure this by anointing it with milk and with *tooka* sap – agent of cold, agent of cold-people – and so it won't entangle us they grasp him and, sending him away, they straighten it out. 39. Therefore, by entering, he straightens it out. 40. It is of the clay house, of the sand house: they cure it by anointing it with milk and with *tooka* sap: and so it won't entangle us they grasp it and straighten it out and deliver it.

41. The *mëgasibamë* fish is like that, yes, the black *mëgasibamë* fish, and then there is the *mëgatogëro* fish and the *sëiperoru* fish.

42. They anoint them with milk and with *tooka* sap: they entangle us, they do – cold-agent people, cold-agent; so it won't entangle us, so it won't entangle us – cold-agent of the clay house – it is the spirit of the clay house.

43. There are the splinters of the yellow tree, the oropendola tree, the *varikateagë* tree; there is a black spirit and a green spirit. 44. There is also the spirit of the *miratava* tree. 45. They are the spirits of trees. 46. In these trees they have their abodes.

47. They cure this by anointing them with milk and with *tooka* sap: entering into these houses they entangle them. 48. Agent of cold, agent of cold-people: grasping it they smoothen it and straightening it out they send it to the House of Fish. 49. Therefore, by going there they straighten us out. 50. 'They enter [by] going there' they said when conversing: 'Yes, that is what they did.'

51. It is the same with the *sai* fish, the same. 52. It also belongs to the same spirits. 53. He is the spirit of the rotten branches of the *sëmegë* tree; he too, of the same. 54. The hollow trunk, too. 55. There he dwells. 56. The palm tree with the red inner pulp, with the white inner pulp, from there he is, in them he dwells, in them he is hidden (?). 57. In the holes of the rotten palm trees. 58. There are his abodes, his abodes.

59. They anoint them with milk and with *tooka* sap – agent of cold, cold-people – and grasping them they smoothen it and straighten it out, and they send them away. 60. There he drags them to straighten it out.

61. The *pava* fish is the same, also the same – there he is. 62. His house of

stone, his house of porous stone, also the house-hole in black stone, the house-hole in grinding stone – there he is. 63. The house-hole of quartz is his. 64. Leaving it, he entangles our veins as if playing; they cure it by anointing it with milk and with *tooka* sap; and so he won't play with us – agent of cold-people, cold-people – they grasp him and they smoothen him and by straightening him out they smoothen him and deliver him inside. 65. He straightens us out by descending. 66. They do this, those [fish] that have horns.

67. Then there is the spirit of the *mandi* fish, the *mandi* spirit, yes, he too is black, red, and white. 68. He comes from the beaches of red sand, of white sand. 69. When he is looking for food, he too entangles us, he entangles us, he entangles us.

70. They cure it by anointing it with milk and with *tooka* sap and they straighten it out so it won't entangle us. 71. It is the same with the *mandi* fish. 72. There is a small *mandi* fish and a large one. 73. They call it 'gourd vessel'. 74. It is the same with the *yahkëtemë* fish. 75. They cure it by anointing him with milk and with *tooka* sap; grasping it they smoothen it out and they send him away, straightening it out. 76. They cure it by anointing it with milk and with *tooka* sap and they straighten it out so it won't entangle us. 77. It is the same with the *mandi* fish. 78. The *sika* fish, the big one they call *kora sai*, yes. 79. There are *kora sai* fish of the red and the white creeks: also thrown up (?) on the beach: they do the same to us. 80. They too have horns: they cure them by anointing them with milk and with *tooka* sap: so they won't entangle us they grasp them and smoothen them and, while straightening them out, they send them away. 81. Their white sands, their black sands, their red sands – grasping them they smoothen them, and grasping them they deliver it downward. 82. There they live. 83. This is what they say.

Comments

I shall turn first to the disease of 'numbness' which is the object of this spell. The verb *bëari* can have the following meanings: (1) 'to benumb'; (2) 'to cover, wrap up, provide with a defence'; (3) 'to hide something in the dark or in the shade'; (4) 'to wind string on a ball'; (5) 'to dominate'. In the context of the manifest translation of this spell, the word was rendered as 'to benumb' and in describing this state, the Indians, on the one hand, referred to the idea of drowsiness, torpor, and inactivity. On the other hand, they said that the person was 'wrapped up', 'tied', or 'entangled' by some sort of strings, fetters, or something like thin cloth. This image of the patient becoming a helpless bundle might explain the other meanings of the word, which obviously refer to an act of 'covering' and isolating. The root *be* indicates a principle of inactivity or lack of energy: *beami* and *bero* are particles of negation: *bereri*, 'to abstain from' (food or sex), *behsu* 'enmity, death': *behtari*, 'lazy', 'inactive'; *beralu*, unclean matter.

The first agent of this illness is the *ahki* fish. This fish swims rapidly, zigzagging among other fish, and this behaviour is the model for certain fertility dances in which the men form a file and imitate these movements of the fish by weaving in and out of a file of dancing women. The name of the fish is related to the word *gahki*, a common synonym for penis. It is by its rapid to-and-fro movements that this fish is said to 'entangle the veins' of people. Now the word for vein is *vaada*, but this word also has the meaning of 'tracks' or 'trail'. The root for both – vein or trail – is *maa*, 'trail', followed, in the first instance, by the element *-da*, meaning 'string', 'vine', or thread'. The meaning thus becomes clear: the sex act (represented by the fish) leads the person 'astray': it debilitates and diminishes his energy.

In this spell the many different kinds of fish are occasionally designated as 'cold-people' or 'agents of cold', referring to their subaquatic habitat. In section 4 it is said that the 'adornments' (*buya*) are invoked. The noun *buya* has three meanings: (1) male dance ornaments, (2) cotton, (3) a quality or power, mainly sexual. The interrelationship is this: many ornaments used during dances consist of cotton strings or flocks to which, because of their white or yellowish colour, a seminal significance is attached. This symbolism is well known to the men and whenever these dance ornaments are spoken of, there will be more or less explicit comments on their associations with male fertility. This also explains expressions such as "The Harpy Eagle has his ornaments" and "The jaguar is adorned", referring to their white down or fur.

It is unfortunate that so little is known about the fishes of the Desana territory, and that I cannot offer ichthyological identifications of the species mentioned in the spells. All I can do in this case is search their names for clues to their importance, because it is quite clear that every single species mentioned in the spells expresses a very specific form of behaviour, or serves to convey a particular idea. For example, the name of the *perisero* fish seems to be derived from *periri*, 'to contaminate a woman', meaning to pollute her by having illicit intercourse with her. The second element of the name is related to *sëriri*, 'smell', 'scent', an emotion-charged term that indicates a powerful olfactory attraction between the sexes, expressed, for example, in the locution *game sëriri*, 'to mutually understand one another'. In the name of the *mëgasibiamë* fish, an armored catfish, the first element is *mega*, (edible) 'ant', while *siba* refers to rotten, unclean matter: the name was translated as meaning 'he that devours rotten things' and the impurities implied by that were associated with the ants, a male food. The *pava* fish (*Platystoma* sp.) also feeds on carrion. The name of the *megatëgëre* fish combines the word for 'ant' with an element related to *teagu*, 'to catch'. Among the Desana and most Tukanoan tribes, edible ants are 'male' food, with aphrodisiacal attributes. The 'Houses of Quartz' in which these and other fish are said to live allude to the seminal connotations of this mineral. Finally, the wood of the *miratava* (LG) tree mentioned in section 44 is very hard and is used for canoes.

The following spell continues the treatment of 'numbness' and similar states.

Text IX

1. The deer of the white country is white. 2. It takes part in benumbing us. 3. This is cured by anointing it with milk and with *tooka* sap and is taken away. 4. So he won't become benumbed, they take it off and send it away. 5. They take it away.

6. He [the deer] causes the earthworm to froth at the mouth, to froth, to froth. 7. At the mouth of the white earthworm, of the white earthworm. 8. They cure this by anointing it with milk and with *tooka* sap, and they cut off its head. 9. By cutting off its head, they cut off the flow of liquid.

10. The red deer is of the red land; the one of the black land is black – they are the black deer. 11. So they will not take part in benumbing us, they anoint them with milk and with *tooka* sap and, seizing it, they take it away. 12. So the colourful lights will not make us dizzy, they seize them and take them away. 13. Grasping the colourful lights they take them away: seizing them they cut them; seizing the lights they destroy them. 14. So the worm will not spout foam, they cut off its head and, anointing it with milk and with *tooka* sap, they cure us by sending the severed heads away. 15. They cut the stream of liquid; they cut the stream of liquid.

16. The black deer is from the country of black starch, and so is the red deer. 17. So that the forest-dwellers will not make us benumbed, they cure it by anointing it with *tooka* sap and, seizing it they take it away, seizing it they destroy it. 18. So that the colourful lights will not make us dizzy, they grasp the lights and they cut them off. 19. Cutting off the lights they set [things] in order and take them away.

20. So that the red worm will not foam at the mouth, they anoint it – agent of cold – and cut off the head. 21. They cut its stream of liquid. 22. He is the representative (?) of the 'day deer', of the earth. 23. The black [deer] is red. 24. So they cure it by anointing it with *tooka* sap, and they take it away. 25. So that its colourful lights will not make us dizzy, by grasping it they take it away. 26. Grasping them they take them away, and they cut off the colourful lights. 27. They take away the lights, they take them away.

28. So that the worm of the Houses of the Hill will not spout foam, they anoint it with *tooka* sap and they cut off its head. 29. They take away the liquid.

30. The deer of the clayey forest is red. 31. They are red and black, red and black. 32. So they will not make us benumbed they anoint them with milk and they take them away. 33. They seize the colourful lights and hold them and, seizing them they destroy them, and seizing the lights they cut them off. 34. So that the white worm does not make us froth, they cut off the head and, seizing the current of the liquid, they cut it off.

35. This is the deer of the yellow clayey forest. 36. They are red and black, red and black. 37. So they won't benumb us, they anoint them with *tooka* sap and, seizing them they put them in order and hold them: and seizing the colourful lights they cut them off and take them away and destroy them. 38. They cure it by anointing the white worm with milk and with *tooka* sap and so they won't froth foam, they cut off their heads. 39. Having cut off their heads, they take away their flow of liquid, their flow of liquid, their flow of liquid.

40. The black deer is from the clayey forest. 41. It is red. 42. They cure it by anointing it with *tooka* sap and so they won't make us benumbed and their colourful lights won't make us dizzy, they seize the lights and hold them and, grasping the lights, they take them away.

43. They destroy the lights. 44. So that the black worm won't make us froth, they cure it by anointing it with *tooka* sap, and so it won't make us dizzy they cut off their heads and send them away, and they cut their flow of liquid by seizing it. 45. Next comes the *buisikamë* fish.

46. The *buisikamë* fish is from the black waters, and the one from the black waters is black. 47. So he won't make us dizzy, he won't make us dizzy, they cure it by anointing it with *tooka* sap, and then hold it. 48. Seizing it they hold it, and seizing it they cut the head and holding it they take it away. 49. Seizing it they hold it; seizing it they cut off the head; seizing it they take it away.

50. The red *buisikamë* fish is of the red waters. 51. So it won't make us dizzy, they cure it by anointing it with milk and with *tooka* sap, and they cut off its head and, seizing it they destroy it and take it away; seizing the lights they cut them off.

52. The *buisikamë* fish of the white waters is white. 53. They anoint it with *tooka* sap so it won't make us dizzy, and they cut off its head and, seizing the colourful lights they cut them off, and seizing them they hold them and take them away.

54. They seize the stream of liquid and cut it off. 55. They seize the colourful lights and cut them off. 56. There is the *buisikamë* fish of the muddy waters. 57. They cut off their heads and destroy their streams of liquid and, seizing it, they put it in order and cut it off. 58. *This is what I am telling you, and there is still more; they shall cure the illnesses that exist; therefore listen to me.* 59. *There is more and more!*

60. The *mëgasibame* fish comes once more. 61. The *mëgasibame* fish is red, red and white, and white and black. 62. So it won't make us dizzy they cure it by anointing it with milk and with *tooka* sap, and hold it and cut off its head, and seizing the colourful lights they cut them off, and seizing them they take them away.

63. So they won't make foam they cut the stream of liquid. 64. They wash it with starch water. 65. There are black, red, and white *meganyimë* fish. 66. So it won't make us dizzy they cure it by anointing it with milk and with *tooka* sap:

so they won't froth they cut their stream of liquid and they cut their lights: they cut their streams of liquid, yes, and seizing it they put it in order and take it away: seizing it they put it in order and take it away.

67. They seize the lights and take them away. 68. That is the way it is. 69. There are red, black, and white *suipero* fish.

70. So it won't make us dizzy they cut off its head and, seizing it they destroy it; they cut the colourful lights and the stream of liquid. 71. Then there is the *pooro* fish, the black one, the red one, and the white one, and so they won't make us dizzy they anoint them with milk and with *tooka* sap and thus cure it and seizing the colourful lights they hold them: seizing the colourful lights they cut them: seizing the stream of liquid they cut it and putting it in order they take it away.

72. So that the *unyu* fish, the red and the white one, won't make us dizzy, they cure it by anointing it with milk and with *tooka* sap, and so it won't make us froth foam, they cut its stream of liquid and its lights; seizing the lights they cut them.

73. Seizing the lights they take them away; seizing them they take them away. 74. They wash its stream of liquid with starch water. 75. That is the way it is; that is the way it is.

76. There are black and white *nyumuyamë* fish. 77. So it won't make us dizzy they cut off its head, they cut off its head: they kill its beasts and, seizing its lights, they cut them; seizing them they cut them and here it ends, here it ends, here it ends.

Comments

The following comments may be added to this text. The enumeration of several differently coloured deer, living in diverse environments, is not a meaningless elaboration, but is based upon the observation that the local *Mazama* deer have developed distinct protective colourings. The behaviour of the earthworm is described as spurting or sputtering a whitish liquid, as indeed these animals do as a defensive action. The verb in question is *sumuri*, from *sumu*, 'foam', and has the following meanings: (1) 'to froth', 'to ooze'; (2) 'to ferment'; (3) 'to fertilize', 'to impregnate'. All informants gave a sexual interpretation to the worms.

The 'colourful lights' mentioned in several instances are called *nomeri*, a term usually reserved to describe hallucinatory images or, at least, flashes of bright colours produced by narcotic potions. By *nomeri*, 'figures' or 'illusions' are meant, and, in general, the colourful patterns that are perceived *before* deep hallucinatory trance sets in.

Several fish mentioned in this spell have somewhat ambiguous names. The name *pooro* is related to *poori*, a verb that can mean 'to distribute' or 'to procreate', and the *unyu* fish was created, according to myth, from the penis of an emasculated adulterer.

The noun *vera*, in section 16, is translated here as 'starch' by my informants, but can also mean: semen, spawn, or any whitish secretion. The verb *vara* in section 19 has the following meanings: (1) 'to set in order'; (2) 'to mould or polish'; (3) 'to copulate'.

The following text is said to cure people who are 'benumbed' and 'confounded,' and who suffer from headaches.

Text X

1. The *gahki* Monkey-People confound us, the *gahki* Monkey-People; they are Monkey-People he [the Master of Animals] turns into; this is why they confound us. 2. They cure it by anointing him [the monkey] with milk and with *tooka* sap, and they cut off his head and kill his beasts – his head – they cut it into bits; they destroy his bile, they destroy his heart. 3. They tear his bones into bits. 4. *Kura* peppers, water peppers, *vahsu* peppers, shrimp-head peppers, he is tasting them; eating his bones he makes it disappear.

5. Then comes the *seegë* monkey, the black *seegë*, the yellow *seegë*, the *seegë* of the vine. 6. He cures it by anointing it with milk and with *tooka* sap; they take away his life, they cut off his head and they crunch his heart. 7. They crunch his bones.

8. The *poreturu* monkey comes next, *poreturu*, *poreturu*, the black and the yellow one. 9. [Then] the red *gahki* Monkey-People come, and the yellow ones; they anoint them with milk and cut off their heads. 10. They cut off the head, they crunch its head, they destroy its bile, they crunch its heart, they crunch its bones. 11. Shrimp-head pepper, big pepper, water pepper, *vahsu* pepper, *kura* pepper, he is tasting them and he destroys him by devouring his bones. 12. They take his life, they kill his beasts, they kill him.

13. Then comes the black *vau* monkey, the black *vau* monkey, and the yellow *vau* monkey. 14. The black *guamo* monkey and the yellow *guamo* monkey – they cure it by anointing them with milk and with *tooka* sap, and to take his life they cut off their heads, they cut off their heads, they destroy their bile, they destroy his heart, and they destroy the bones. 15. They are tasting *kura* pepper, long pepper, water pepper, and by eating them they destroy him, they devour his bones, they kill his beasts by devouring them, and devouring them they destroy him.

16. After this comes the *guamo* monkey, the *guamo* monkey, the *guamo* monkey, and it is the same.

17. Those night monkeys, those beasts they kill, yes; they anoint them with milk and with *tooka* sap, and so they will die they cut off their heads, they destroy their heads, they destroy their bile, and they destroy their hearts and bones. 18. He is tasting *kura* peppers, water pepper, long pepper, *vahsu* pepper, shrimp-head pepper, he is eating them; he devours their bones, he destroys their

beasts, he takes away his life.

19. He finishes with the mammals: now come the birds.

20. The curassow comes now. 21. That old (?) confounds us. 22. They are transformed people: that is why they are like that. 23. They cure it by anointing him with milk and with *tooka* sap: they cut off his head and kill him. 24. They destroy his bile and destroy his heart and destroy his bones. 25. He is tasting shrimp-head pepper, long pepper, water pepper, and he destroys him by devouring his bones, and he kills him.

26. It is the same with the *tinamou*, the one with the red head that calls: voooo; the *tarapia* with the spotted head, and the *boaro*; he cures it by anointing them with milk and with *tooka* sap and, in order to kill them, he cuts off their heads, and he kills their beasts, and he destroys them, they destroy the bones. 27. He is tasting shrimp-head pepper, long pepper, water pepper, *kura* pepper, and by devouring his bones he destroys them.

28. After this comes the white curassow, the white one; it is the same with the white curassow.

29. There is a black river curassow and a white river curassow, and it is the same with them; he cures by anointing them with milk and with *tooka* sap, and he cuts off their heads and destroys their bile and their hearts; he destroys their bones. 30. He is tasting water pepper, long pepper, shrimp-head pepper, and so he kills them and, seizing his beasts, he kills them.

31. Then he gives his vessel to the black duck, the black duck – they are his kin. 32. He cures by anointing their heads with milk and with *tooka* sap, and to take their life he cuts off the head and he destroys it; he destroys the bile and crunches his heart, and crunching his bones he destroys them. 33. Long pepper, *kura* pepper, he is tasting them and by eating them he makes him disappear, by eating he makes him disappear, by eating he makes him vanish, and devouring his bones he kills his beasts. 34. So they say when conversing.

35. The toucan bird is the same; he greatly confounds us. 36. They feed on the impurities of worms; that is why they do us harm. 37. By feeding on unripe fruits they do us harm. 38. He cures this by anointing them with milk and with *tooka* sap, and he cuts off their heads and destroys their bile, and by crunching his heart he destroys it, and he destroys the bones by crunching them. 39. Does he kill the beasts? Doesn't he?

40. The large toucans and the parrots, they all do the same; they greatly confound us. 41. They do this by feeding on unripe fruit. 42. They cure it by anointing them with milk and with *tooka* sap, and he kills the beasts, he kills the beasts.

43. Also the [other] curassows are like that, because they feed on the impurities of worms. 44. This is why it does harm to us, why it is harmful. 45. They cure this by anointing them with milk and with *tooka* sap, and to take away their lives they cut off the head and by crunching it they destroy it: they destroy his bile, they crunch his heart, and by crunching his bones they destroy them. 46. He

tastes *kura* peppers, water peppers, shrimp-head pepper, and by eating them he makes them vanish; by crunching their bones he makes them vanish; this they said when conversing.

47. This done, they give them to eat and they prepare (?) all the foods: all of them, yes; and did they kill all the beasts?

Comments

Monkeys always have strong sexual connotations and the name of the *gahki* monkey means literally 'penis.' The Desana think that they are unclean animals, incestuous and lewd, and in most contexts they stand for uncontrolled sex.

All toucan birds are said to be closely related to the mythical origins of the Tukano Indians, as implied by their name. Because of their large and very prominent beaks, a phallic symbolism is attached to them, and they are said to be ancestral beings. This does not mean, however, that these birds cannot be hunted and eaten; as a matter of fact, they are a fairly common prey of the hunters. Toucans are gregarious and noisy birds and are rather omnivorous, but they are particularly fond of the hard-shelled *vahsu* fruits and are thus associated with the seminal interpretation given to the latex of the rubber tree. The intestinal tract of these birds is short and they defecate continuously, thus becoming the symbol of elimination, similar to the cock of the rock (*Rupicola*), another very colourful bird mentioned in some spells and said to be a companion of the Master of Animals.

Curassows are important game birds and are sometimes kept as pets in Indian houses. At first, their apparent importance in the context of this spell seems difficult to explain: these birds are neither carrion-feeders, nor am I aware of any fertility associations they might have, and their inclusion in the spell seems to be somewhat cryptic. But, as usual, when one goes into the details of animal behaviour, one soon discovers that the Indians never use an animal metaphor without some valid reason based upon sound observation. Curassows feed on the fruits of an Apocynacea (*Maloetia tamaquarina*) which are very poisonous to humans. As a matter of fact, it is said that, should a dog eat the bones of a curassow, it would immediately die, because it is precisely in that part of the body where the poison is concentrated. Curassows then are cleansing agents; they are immune to poison dangerous to man, and thus they are destroyers of a principle of impurity that is connected with ingestion.

In this and other spells, the gall bladder of certain animals is mentioned as an organ that has to be eliminated. Gall is *nima* in Desana, a word that can also mean 'poison'; this can refer to arrow poison, fish poison, honey, certain narcotics, and other substances. The bile is the essence of 'bitterness', a concept I shall discuss later on, and stands here for an unclean principle. Again, this idea is closely related to the Indians' preoccupation with bodily secretions and pollution through illicit intercourse. Indeed, one might speak here of the 'toxicology of sex', as conceived by the Desana.

The spell mentions a number of different peppers the shaman is 'tasting' and then eating to make the charm effective. The ingestion of strong peppers is a common ritual practice for hunters, and it is possible that this acts as a deodorant and thus diminishes the person's scent. As can be seen now, the above spell is mainly concerned with pollution.

I shall quote here one last spell which is said to call an illness called *mesiari*, 'unconsciousness'.

Text XI

1. There is a ball of feathers of the Sweet Potato [Eagle], a *yoho* catfish conical tangle of hair. 2. The yarn has a rope of entangled (?) disease. 3. The yarn is made of the Harpy Eagle's down.

4. That makes us dizzy and makes us fall down and become unconscious. 5. With this ball of feathers of the Sweet Potato [Eagle] he takes with him all evil.

6. There is a ball of feathers of the Sweet Potato [Eagle], mixed with the feathers of the black oropendola bird, and a tangle of feathers of the [macaw] of the *caimo* tree. 7. They mix all this together when they want to harm us. 8. This comes together with the thread of Harpy Eagle's feathers. 9. This causes in us unconsciousness. 10. This is related to the down ornaments. 11. The other [the *caimo* tree] is related to the matter of bitterness. 12. These garments they anoint with milk and with *tooka* sap, and thus they throw them away. 13. With milk they destroy these garments, and they go down shaping [them] with milk. 14. All this they throw into the Netherworld. 15. There the piranha destroys it by crushing it with its teeth.

16. Next comes the garment made of feathers of the Sweet Potato [Eagle], mixed with feathers of the black oropendola bird. 17. The garment is made with catfish impurities. 18. The thread is made with the down of the Harpy Eagle. 19. They anoint these garments with milk and with *tooka* milk, and throw them down below. 21. They throw them into the Netherworld, into the *mëë* river. 22. There the piranha that crushes leaves, goes biting them to bits.

23. This garment of deadly mould is made of the impurities of *cumare* palm fibres. 24. The garment is made of the deadly mold of *sëmé* tree branches. 25. It is adorned with worms (?) of the black oropendola, of the macaw of the *caimo* tree, and of the crane, of all whose feathers the garment is made. 26. The thread of the garment is made of the feathers of the Sweet Potato Eagle. 27. This makes us confused and makes us ill. 28. They anoint them with milk and with *tooka* milk, and they take hold of them. 29. [Anointing it] with milk they take hold of it and banish it to the Netherworld. 30. They throw it into the *mëë* river, in the Netherworld. 31. There the piranha that crushes leaves, bites it to shreds.

32. The garment is made with the worms (?) of the black oropendola and the

red oropendola. 33. The garment is also made of the impurities of *cumare* palm fibres. 34. The garment is adorned with the worms (?) of the smoke crane and the red oropendola, and the thread is made of feathers. 35. They anoint these garments with milk and with *tooka* milk and take hold of them. 36. They throw them into the Netherworld, into the *mëë* river. 37. There the piranha that crushes leaves, bites them to shreds.

38. Once again the garment is made of mouldering leaves. 39. The garment is adorned with the feathers of the smoke crane that feeds on small fish. 40. The garment is mixed with tapir hair and with toad hair. 41. They anoint the garment with milk and with *tooka* milk and take hold of it. 42. In the River of Milk the piranha that crushes leaves is shredding it to bits. 43. That is all.

Comments

The term *meseari* which is used here to designate the illness is derived, according to the Indians, from *mepiri*, 'to fall down', and *siari*, 'to faint'. It is described as a state of utter exhaustion, a comatose condition in which the patient is in extreme danger.

In this spell (Text XI) animal agents combine with pathogens of plant origin into deadly garments the shaman must banish to the Netherworld. Although this is a relatively short spell, the composition of the different garments is complex and I shall refer point by point to their individual components.

1. The so-called Sweet Potato Eagle is, according to my informants, a bird of prey that can often be seen hunting for mice or lizards near fields where this plant is grown. A 'ball of feathers' could mean the entangled mass of undigested matter thrown up by birds of prey representing an 'unclean' substance. On the other hand, the sweet potato plant is a vine and thus represents the concept of 'entanglement', which is the cause of the pathological condition described above. Many catfish, like the *yoho* mentioned here, are said to be unclean animals because they feed on rotten matter. The expression 'conical tangle of hair' was said to refer to female pubic hair.

6. Oropendola birds and other icterids encode a number of meanings. On the one hand, they are said to destroy all noxious insects with their strong beaks and to keep their nests very clean; on the other hand, their purse-shaped nests suspended from branches of high jungle trees are compared with human testicles (*AC*, pp. 179, 186, 196-197).

10. At this point, the practitioner makes reference to two different categories of pathogens, one consisting of the feather/hair complex of impurities, the other of a certain quality of taste, in this case of 'bitterness'. The terms 'sweet' or 'bitter' can be applied to foodstuffs, mainly fruits or honey, but can also be applied to men, by classifying them according to the quality of semen, that is, of their exogamic compatibility.

23. The *cumare* palm (*Astrocaryum*) produces long yellow fibres of a silky texture that are used in the manufacture of many artifacts. Skeins of these fibres symbolize semen and life-giving fertility, but a skein of rotten fibres is thought to impregnate in a life-destroying manner. The diseases that float on the Milky Way are compared to a stream of rotten fibres (*AC*, pp. 43, 48, 176).

25. I am not certain here of the correct translation of the word *pigëri*, but I believe it refers to those tiny gnawing worms that are believed to cause toothache.

This selection of curing spells will suffice to show the range and scope of this particular ritual behaviour. It now remains to interpret the spells within the wider context of Desana culture.

Discussion

The spells can be discussed on several levels and I shall begin at the simplest one, that of the average patient who has a spell said over him, or that of the average lay practitioner who says a spell meant to cure or to prevent an illness. On this elementary level, the interpretation is plain: the words of the spell attribute the illness to certain animals or spirit-beings and describe the pathogenic substances in terms of splinters, bolts, or some other everyday, tangible object. In the spell, this object is grasped, held, and thrown away. It is extracted, and is violently expelled and banished to a faraway spot, beyond the confines of this earth. In the case of spells referring to the Master of Animals himself, the procedure is equally simple: he is visited in his abode and his power objects are taken away from him. He then is given all kinds of special foods and, while sitting and eating, he is quietly being turned around toward the wall and is made to fall asleep. The imagery of spells, the gestures that accompany it, and the hypnotic repetition of certain words or phrases in a loud voice are impressive indeed, and sometimes the shaman will heighten this effect by suddenly producing a tiny splinter, a hair, or a grain of sand – seemingly extracted from the patient's body – and, after showing it briefly to the patient and his family, will violently throw it away. The whole procedure of a curing spell is understandable to the patient, who rarely will question the healer nor worry about the details of the spell.

Most patients will readily recognize the simple sexual connotations of the spells. The seminal symbolism of fruits or plant juices, the phallic attributes of certain animals or of *vai-mahsë*, are well known to all and are continuously referred to in daily conversation. This fertility symbolism is nothing strange to the patient because the entire Desana universe is conceived in terms of biological growth and decline.

On a somewhat higher level of interpretation, however, it becomes necessary to attempt to unravel some of the more complex meanings of the metaphoric lan-

Cumare palm fibres

guage in which the contents of the spells are expressed. In the briefest possible outline, the concepts involved are these: the game animals are thought to impregnate their victim with the germs of illness, in a sexual-seminal manner, and the illness itself is imagined as a placenta-like cover in which the patient is enclosed as if it were a shroud. The healer's task is to pierce this cover by enacting a treatment that will culminate in a recovery that is, in all essence, a rebirth.

This highly condensed outline calls for detailed discussion in which the available evidence can be analyzed and evaluated. I shall list here the main aspects to be examined:

1. Transmission of illness interpreted as sexual impregnation
2. Illness conceived as placenta-like cover
3. Recovery interpreted as rebirth

Desana cosmological theory is based upon the recognition of solar energy and is conceived in the following terms: the earth and mankind were created by a phallic Sun-Father; the entire universe functions because it is energized by a fertilizing power (*boga*) that is contained in the sun's rays and imagined as a seminal current or stream in which shades of yellow light combine with heat into a powerful reproductive life-force. This cosmic libido is thought to be creative in both a germinal, biological sense, and in the sense of occasionally leading to spiritual illumination by a penetrating flash of yellow luminescence perceived during states of mental dissociation induced by narcotic drugs. The cosmic energy consists of two opposed but complementary forces, however: a 'white *boga*' and a 'black *boga*', sometimes identified with male and female principles, sometimes with an antagonistic coupling of positive and negative aspects within one single principle. In all essence, procreation and reproduction are thought to be life-sustaining only as long as they are culturally controlled – by the rules of exogamy or by elementary ecological considerations – but they become life-destroying as soon as they disregard these norms. The norms include very strict exogamic marriage rules, sexual repression, dietary restrictions, and many other deprivations that combine into a strongly integrated mechanism of controls.

Although the Desana universe has an overall dualistic structure, it is *not* dominated by a strict polarity, but there is rather an elaboration of certain *scales* of value, of progressive steps and degrees of intensity. For example, the colour symbolism depends upon the many different hues the eye might perceive within one single tint; that of liquids will depend upon their transparency, viscosity, and taste: that of food, upon innumerable qualities and associations that range from mythical origins and provenance, to culinary preparation, caloric value, digestibility, smell, and so on. Similar concepts are applied to the physiology of sex, and semen is said to range in intrinsic quality between 'very sweet' and 'very bitter', quite apart from considerations of colour and texture. This specific scale refers to the permissibility of the act, that is, to the relative position the two partners occupy within the exogamic system. What is prohibited is 'bitter' or 'rotten', and the consequences of a transgression are defilement, decay, and decline.

We must keep in mind these ideas while recapitulating briefly the nature of the pathogenic agents that were mentioned in the curing spells. The following enumeration shows the different substances that are thought to be related to the idea of sexual impregnation.

Splinters: Arrows and blowgun darts and, by extension, sharp splinters or bolts, are phallic symbols among the Desana. This is expressed in native dream interpretation, in mythical passages, and in the conversations of hunters. Many pathogenic splinters are said to come from trees that have a strong sexual connotation such as bow tree, *caimo* tree, *sëmé* tree, *dohtogë*, *miratava*, and 'yellow tree'. We also recall here that the splinters are 'adorned with fuzz', or with a 'veil of hair'.

Fibres: Many vegetable fibres, especially those of a whitish or yellowish colour, have seminal connotations. Skeins or strains of *Astrocaryum* fibres are directly said to symbolize semen. Any rotten mass of fibres, leaves, or other plant remains are 'unclean' and are thought to represent a pathogenic seminal matter.

Hair: Body hair, especially entangled masses of monkey hair, symbolizes pubic hair and is often associated with the idea of illicit sex. The name of the common *gahki* monkey is a synonym for penis, and monkeys in general are said to represent uncontrolled sex behaviour. The name of the first Desana man in Creation, was *gahki*. The ropes of monkey hair that are used as dance ornaments represent virility, but they can become dangerous weapons. The expression 'to choke on monkey hair' alludes to illicit sexual intercourse.

Feathers: The fluffy white or yellowish down feathers of certain birds are said to represent a seminal essence. White down or fuzz is sometimes glued to the phallic rattle-stick, or is woven into fine threads that are used as dance ornaments.

Quartz: Translucent quartz crystals or splinters, or opaque quartzite splinters, have strong seminal connotations. They represent solidified semen. The cylindrical quartz pendant of the men is called *abe yeeru*, 'Sun's penis'. Lightning is sometimes interpreted as a sexual impregnation of the earth, through thunderbolts of quartz.

Dirt: Semen, produced in illicit sex, is sometimes compared to 'dirt' and is said to 'contaminate' the woman. All bodily secretions, if coming from a forbidden or 'contaminated' sex partner, can be classified and used as pathogenic 'dirt', that is, representing pollution.

Dreams: The game animals are said to appear in erotic dreams, seducing or even raping the sleeper. The Master of Animals causes nightmares and sometimes appears in women's dreams as a sexual aggressor.

Animal behaviour: The sight of copulating animals is said to cause illness in the casual beholder. The behaviour of many of the animals mentioned in the spells has sexual connotations: the *Mazama* deers 'dance' and cry: *poreru* (Text II), the sweet-loving martens and monkeys, the *unyu* fish that was created from an emasculated man's penis, the fish swimming in zigzag, the salivating worms, and others. The acts of stamping, treading, and 'dancing' have fertility connotations, and so have, of course, the spawning of fish, or a colony of purse-shaped birds' nests. A very important aspect of animal behaviour is their relationship to what, to men, represents pollution. The carrion-feeders are cleansing agents and thus occupy an important place in the theory of disease. Among them are the vultures and some hawks, the felines, tortoises, and beetles and, in the waters, the crocodilians, the piranha, many catfish, the crabs, and the tadpoles. All these animals are benefic and some of them can be eaten, but there are subtle differences and doubts especially in the case of fish.

We come now to the second point: illness interpreted as a garment, a placenta-like veil. The disease is interpreted here as a cover, a wrapping, a tangle of threads or ropes that restricts and hinders the patient, and isolates him from the vital environment. In commenting on Text V, I have mentioned that the term *suriro*, 'garment', is related to the verb *suriri*, 'to cover', 'to dress'. But there exist at least two more meanings: *suriri* may stand for 'to entangle oneself', 'to lose oneself', or, by deriving it from the root *suri*, it might mean 'to cast one's skin', as for example, when speaking of a snake. The 'garment of disease' can thus be interpreted as an isolating veil, an entangling thread, or a skin (*gahsiru*) to be shed, to be cast off.

In the spells, this 'garment' is treated in a very specific way. First of all, it is anointed (*suu*) with two substances: milk, that is, human breast milk, and *tooka* 'milk' or sap, a sticky plant juice that is described as being 'very sweet' and somewhat oily. Breast milk is, first of all, an infant's nourishment and all informants would agree on that, but *tooka* sap or 'milk' always stands for semen. It is 'like honey' and in Desana both semen and honey are designated by the same word, *mome*.

In Desana the verb *mahsëri* means both 'to cure' and 'to be born'; *mahsuu* means 'revived', from *suu*, 'anointed', 'painted'. *Mahsë* is man, a living being, a person. The all-important power formula that is central to the spells is *ahpiko suu mahsuu, tooka suu mahsuu*, 'milk-anoint-revived, *tooka*-anoint-revived'.

In the case of diseases thought to be caused by personal adversaries, the curing process consists of piercing the 'garment' and this is generally accomplished with the help of animals which, because they have sharp teeth or beaks, are invoked to assist the healer in tearing off the isolating wrapping. Since diseases are, in essence, 'rotten matter', animals that feed on carrion are invoked (*AC*, pp. 178-179). In the case of diseases attributed to the vengeance of game animals or their masters, this seems not to be the case, but here it is the shaman himself who 'takes hold' of the garment and then 'throws it away'. This is the central part of the curing process, the climax of the spell, and the words describing this exorcizing action are explosive and violent.

The Otherworld (*dohkamaha turi*, 'below-belonging-level') of the Desana consists of two different regions: one is *ahpikon yeba*, the Land of Milk, with its great waters of *ahpikon-dia*, the River of Milk. This is Paradise, a blissful country lying toward the East, and bathed eternally in a green light. There also flows the *mëë* river, the river of *vahsu*. The opposite aspect of the Otherworld is the so-called Dark Region – what I have called the Netherworld – a land lying toward the West, and which consists mainly of the great lake called *dia gorosiri*, 'water-place-intercept'. This lake, as I have mentioned earlier, is designated as a 'filter' through which must pass all things that arrive there by way of the river, on their way to *ahpikon-dia*. The term *dia gorosiri* has some four different meanings: it can refer to a mouth of a river, that is, to that part of the river where, as the Desana see it, lies its true 'power': it can refer to a place of origin, perhaps of mythical beginnings: it can also mean 'place of death', cemetery, or burial, and it can mean vagina or womb, sometimes called 'place of return'. The meaning implicit in these interpretations is that of transformation, and as a place of transformation, of purification, and the filtering of unclean substances, it is there where such scavengers as the voracious piranha fish, the 'shredder of leaves', has its abode, and where the masses of mud-coloured decaying vegetation – in opposition to the evergreen land of *ahpikon-dia* – sift and absorb everything that floats on these dark waters. Beyond these filters and sluices (*dia tauro*), lies the place of rebirth where, once the period of incubation under the shaman's guidance is over, the patient sheds his old garment and is reborn into the Lake of Milk.

The foregoing interpretation of the garment, its disposal, and the rebirth of the patient was offered by the Indians themselves, that is, by the practitioners who had dictated the spells. Not only did they know and point out to me the alternative meanings of the key words but, when asked for comments, they rearranged them into a new interpretative framework in which the concept of rejuvenation or of 're-formation', as some called it, became paramount. I doubt if the average Desana layman would readily recognize these metaphors. He would probably be aware of most of the synonyms, but I do not think that he would combine them into a new form, beyond that of a curing ritual meant to restore his bodily well-being by extracting the substance of evil.

There exists another level of interpretation and I shall turn now to certain aspects of Desana cosmology that are of interest in quite another dimension of their culture. According to the Indians, the universe was created by the phallic Sun-Father who, after forming a three-layered cosmos, created man, animals, and plants. The creative power of this divine force is imagined as seminal light and heat that cause plants to grow and animals to multiply. This seminal energy is thought to form an all-embracing circuit in which the entire cosmos participates, but which is limited in its quantity in such a manner that people may remove what they need for their survival, only if they reincorporate an equivalent into this energy circuit. This life-force is imagined mainly as sexual energy and the entire system is derived from the model of sexual physiology so that it requires a constant rebalancing by personal energy retrieval. For example, the killing of animals diminishes the energy capital which must then be replenished by such personal deprivations as sexual abstinence and dietary restrictions.

Among the Desana hunting is an activity that has a strong erotic component. The hunt is conceived as a courtship in which the hunter attempts to seduce his prey by making himself attractive and harmless. The game animals are thought to 'fall in love' with the hunter and to submit to him by adopting an essentially female attitude. The hunter himself has to undergo a ritual period of preparation lasting for a few days during which sexual abstinence is mandatory and only certain foods may be consumed. The body must be cleansed by bathing, emetics,

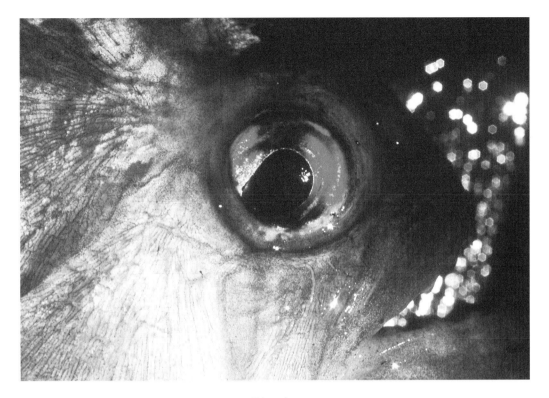

Piranha

and the absorption of strong pepper juice through the nose, and the hunter should not have had any dreams with an erotic content. All in all, the ritual prerequisites for a successful hunt are so many that rarely will a man go off into the forest without being somewhat apprehensive about some minor breach of the prescriptions. Since all these preparations and conditions are meant to make the game animals well-disposed toward the hunter, any contrary behaviour is thought to cause their malevolence which immediately turns into a threat to the hunter's health.

Since I have dealt elsewhere with this aspect of Desana culture (Reichel-Dolmatoff, 1976a, essay I in this book) I shall summarize here only some of the main points. In the rainforest territory inhabited by the Desana, carrying capacity is defined by the Indians largely in terms of protein resources: game, fish, and certain wild fruits. In order to maintain the settlements or individual communal houses for long time periods in one spot, overhunting must be avoided, and the most effective mechanism of control is the threat of illness caused by angry game animals and their spirit-protectors. The commonality of motivation to follow the rules is based upon the fear of disease and death. Desana disease theory, as related to hunting, has thus a highly adaptive significance. But apart from keeping people from overhunting, the spells also tend to act as a control to population increase by emphasizing the dangers of sex and pollution.

In the case of the curing spells I have presented in this article, it is quite obvious that the shamans are not much interested in this illness category as a function of biology. This is quite clear from the description of the diseases as *states of energy loss*. The shamans are concerned about the person's having upset an aspect of the ecological balance and make it their task to correct this social malfunctioning. It follows that the curing spells are an important tool in the management of natural resources, and that the shaman's influence extends in a very benefic way into many aspects of ecological adaptation.

It is quite clear that the spells do not contain any *rational* element; they do not cure the disease, nor do they alleviate the particular symptoms, except perhaps, in a very superficial way. This biological aspect of the illness is being taken care of by the old people of the patient's household, by the womenfolk who prepare potions and poultices and easily digestable foods. The shaman, apart from his spells, generally limits his intervention to ablutions with water and to the blowing of tobacco smoke. In other words, in the strict sense of medical practice, the spells are *not* connected with the healing of a pathological condition, but stand apart as a mechanism of social adaptation. After all, the disease-causing animals are *people*.

The spells provide a context in which the *prohibitions* of Desana society acquire stark significance for the individual. They are not gibberish spells, nor are they expressed in a highly esoteric language: the patient can follow them word for word and, what is more, he can understand the actions that are described by the words, because they refer to everyday matters, to fish and game, food and sex, the forest and the river. Indeed, into the confused and confusing world of dream and reality in which develop man's relationships to animals and plants, *the shaman has brought order* by naming, categorizing, locating, describing, and by taking the situation in hand.

Spells are documents in a class all their own; they are based on cosmology, but hardly relate to mythology. They are more direct than myths; they represent direct communication, direct intercourse with spirit powers. I would not know of any other formalized cultural expression of quite that immediacy. They are truly creative acts.

Conclusions

In the course of analyzing the spells contained in the present article, I recognized many implicit meanings that I had known already from my previous work on Desana cosmology, mythology, ritual, dream interpretation, and other materials I had recorded. Since I was thus fairly familiar with the specific characteristics the Indians used to attribute to many animals and was acquainted with the fundamental principles of Desana disease theory and curing practices, most spells were easy to understand and fell into a pattern that was consistent with other aspects of the native culture. Reflecting back on the contents of these spells, and on what the Indians themselves took to be their essence and true power, however, I have found myself confronted with a certain cluster of images that, because of their persistent associations, invite some speculation. I am referring to the symbolism of milk and honey.

As used in Desana myth and ritual, the word *ahpikon* means human breast milk. The word also encodes another meaning, however, one related to semen. The root of the word is *ahp* and it is interesting to trace it in a number of contexts. In the first place, we find this root in several words referring to human sexual anatomy and physiology: *ahpiri*, 'breast', 'womb': *ahpiru*, 'nipple'; *ahpirito*, 'testicles'; *nyahpi*, 'sweet potato', whose fruit is commonly compared to a female breast; *yahpi*, 'vulva'; *yahpiri*, 'to suckle to satiety': *gahki*, 'penis'; *gahsiro*, 'placenta'. In the second place, the root *ahp* is related to the hallucinatory sphere which, among the Desana, has strong sexual overtones (Reichel-Dolmatoff 1969). Thus, *ahpi* means coca (*Erythroxylon coca*) and *gahpi, Banisteriopsis caapi*, a narcotic jungle vine. A third context is provided by words that describe a creative act. Thus, *ahpiri* is 'to create,' 'to found', 'to establish'; the expression *ahpi yuhpë*, 'created-he', referring to divine creation, is a standard mode of speech in Desana myths and in them the creative act is a sexual act, performed by a phallic being. Finally, *ahpari* means 'to be essential'.

From what I have been able to understand in the course of many conversations with the Indians, the milky substance mentioned in the spells can mean both breast milk and semen. The latter, however, is usually designated by the word *mome*, 'honey'. To this must be added a third substance which is emphasized in describing the *tooka* plant, and that is an oily component found in the leaves of this plant. As a matter of fact, the leaves are sometimes used to cleanse the skin of one's face, because of their slightly greasy surface. The patient is thus anointed with milk, honey, and oil, and this act can be interpreted, from the available evidence, as symbolizing a fertility/rebirth ritual. The fusion of the two concepts and their encapsulation in a state outside of ordinary time leads to the patient's transformation.

Since milk – whatever it stands for – is the key symbol, it strikes one as a rather unusual simile in a tropical rainforest environment where cattle or goats are unknown. I have briefly glanced at some Old World sources in search of parallels, and I think it is interesting to summarize some of my findings.

In the Old World the ritual use of milk has been discussed by several authors, Usener (1913) and Wyss (1914) among others, both of whom have studied some of the available evidence for Greece and Rome. It seems that in practically all cases where milk was used ritually, the reference is to cow or goat milk, while human milk is mentioned only very rarely and then in connection with folk medicine (e.g. *Plinius*; see *lac, usus in medicina*). In this manner, the authors, when speaking of the ritual use of milk, take for granted that only animal milk could have been meant.

In Greece milk was above all an offering for the chthonic deities and spirit-beings, for Pan, the Nymphs, or for the Erinyes, but certainly not for the Olympian gods. These and other divinities received, among other things, offerings of wine, but the spirits of Nature received 'sober' offerings (*nephalia*), mainly consisting of a mixture of milk and honey (*melikraton*). This constituted an important form of offering to the spirits of the dead, and also to the Erinyes who were the personifications of vengeance on those mortals who had broken a taboo. Combined offerings of milk, honey, *melikraton*, and oil, designated as *meiligmata* ('appeasements'), were mainly made to placate the malevolence of all these spirit-beings. Oil and ointments were also among the offerings to the Manes of the dead.

Another context for the ritual use of milk was provided by the pre-Hellenic mystery cults. All these were connected with fertility and with the dead, and in the initiation rituals, milk was the nourishment of those who were spiritually reborn. Milk was the *symbolum immortalitatis* and of rebirth in the cult rendered to Attis and Cybele; milk and/or honey had ritual uses in the Dionysian Mysteries, in the cosmic religion of the Pythagoreans, and in the cult of Isis.

In the mystery cult of the Roman fertility goddess Bona Dea, related to Faunus, and worshipped only by women, wine played an important role, but its name was tabooed and, in the ritual language, had to be called *lac*, while the corresponding vessel was called *mellarium* (*Wyss* 1914:22). The offering Aeneas made upon his arrival in Italy consisted of wine, blood, and milk (*Verg.* Aen. V, 77), and it is of interest to observe here that the expression '*novum lac*' might refer to colostrum.

The question of why these substances should have acquired this widespread importance in the Ancient World is barely touched upon by these authors I have consulted. Wyss (1914:63) writes: "The idea that milk, as well as honey and oil, would appease and mollify the anger of the chthonic deities and the dead, because of their natural properties, cannot have been the motivation of their use", but he offers no alternative explanation, and only adds vaguely that "...the true motives lie in the natural development of human circumstances". He refers in passing to the possibility that 'primitive peoples' might have attributed 'magical-demoniacal' effects to such bodily secretions of animals and humans, as saliva, urine, and semen, but he seems to feel rather uneasy about this and soon drops the matter. He rightly attributes the milk offerings to the spirits of Nature, however, to a very ancient cultural substratum.

Sheep seem to have been the first milk-producing animals domesticated by man, and at Shanidar (Iraq) the evidence goes back to about 9000 B.C. The domestication of cattle developed in the next 300 years. The aurochs was probably domesticated in Greece and on Crete by 6000 B.C., and longhorn cattle existed in Egypt at least from the fifth millenium. Dairy farming, however, is a later phenomenon: in Mesopotamia it goes back to ca. 3000 B.C., but in Europe the earliest evidence appears only around 1000 B.C. (Cole 1970: Bender 1975: Ucko and Dimbleby 1969).

At Çatal Hüyük, the great Neolithic site in Anatolia where the domestication of cattle can be dated to about 6000 B.C., the fertility goddess who was the centre of religious activities is frequently found associated with bulls, human breasts, and symbols of birth and the continuity of life. The combination of a bull's horn with a modelled human breast is here most suggestive. Cole writes: "Such symbols nearly always appear on the west walls: but on the east walls, below which the dead are buried, there are symbols of death in the form of wall paintings of vultures and the jaws of such scavengers as pigs, foxes and weasels" (1970:50-51). The painted representations of vultures show these birds sometimes standing on human legs, suggesting a masked shaman performing a burial rite. A series of other wall paintings at Çatal Hüyük represents hunting scenes in which the hunters, wearing leopard skins, are seen touching the tails and tongues of the game animals. It is of special interest to note that, at Çatal Hüyük, the fertility goddess appears also in the role of 'Mistress of Animals', and then closely associated with the leopard, a feline that seems to have occupied a very important position in the religious life of the inhabitants.

All this points to a much earlier level of cultural evolution and clearly goes back into Paleolithic times.

I think it would be mistaken to believe – as some authors seem to – that the preoccupation with fertility and increase began or, at least, was greatly intensified, when Neolithic farmers started to worry about their crops and herds. I really cannot believe that a fertility symbolism such as that appearing at Çatal Hüyük is in any way a consequence of agriculture and the domestication of cattle. From Paleolithic cave paintings, sculpture, and much other evidence, it is quite clear that fertility rites were an essential part of the world-view of the Early Hunters, and that these rituals often contained sexual elements of the crudest order.

It is there, in that dimension, where I would suggest that one might look for the roots of the curing spells I have discussed in this article. The similarities between their core metaphors, and the few examples I have mentioned from the Old World cannot be brushed aside as vague coincidences or Jungian archetypes.

It is also quite obvious that the parallels do not stop short at the ritual use of milk and honey, but that the spells I have presented here contain many other elements that can be compared with the culture of the Early Hunters of Europe and Asia. So as not to list here a large number of traits that could easily be assembled let me mention just one major concept, that of the Master of Animals.

The Master of Animals of the Amazonian rainforest Indians, that supernatural woodsman, with his staff, his flute, his knowledge of herbs, and his hidden abodes where he dwells with his flock of deer, tapir, and peccary, is, in essence, a shepherd. He is the good shepherd who looks after the propagation and the well-being of his charges, who defends his animals against predators, who cures them when they are sick, and who roams with them over the boundless forests, or gathers them into the protection of the 'Houses of the Hills' – just like people.

On the level of hunting societies, be it in the Old World or the New, this supernatural personification generally represents a principle of procreation, of fertility, often expressed in its most elementary terms. On that level, the Master of Animals is sometimes a phallic being or, in female form, a monstrous succubus, and his universe is that of womblike abodes, seminal plant juices, and a host of 'male' or 'female' representations that fill the earth, the Otherworld, people's dreams and visions, in fact, every dimension of existence and imagination. In the Old World, on a more advanced level of cultural evolution, the Master of Animals begins to turn into a shepherd, more benevolent now, more domesticated so to say, perhaps closer to men because now, they too have become shepherds and herders.

In presenting a series of curing spells of the Colombian Desana Indians, I have not entered an obscure territory of savage customs and crude superstitions, but rather I have tried to explore a dimension that contains many landmarks familiar to the Western mind. If I am correct in suggesting that the central concepts and formulations of these spells are of Old World origin, and that they were introduced to America by the Early Hunters who crossed the Bering Strait from Asia, it would be of interest to make a more detailed study of the continuance and persistence of other shamanistic metaphors that, because of their vital importance to cultural adaptation, might succeed in spanning millennia, while maintaining all their powerful imagery and immediacy.

EDITOR'S NOTE: A transcription of the original Desana texts can be found in Reichel-Dolmatoff, 'Desana Curing Spells', in *Journal of Latin American Lore*, 2(2), Los Angeles, UCLA, 1976, pp203-219.

A Barasana headman offers a narcotic potion. Pira-paraná river

VIII

Brain and Mind in Desana Shamanism

This essay presents, in an abbreviated form, a body of shamanistic knowledge of a group of Amazonian Indians, with reference to certain neurobiological and biochemical phenomena and to their relationship to cognition and social behaviour. I am speaking here of the Desana.

Introduction

The Desana, numbering about 600 individuals, live mainly on the affluents of the Vaupés River. The traditional settlement pattern is one of scattered long-houses, called *malocas* in the local Amazonian vernacular, which are large and well built, and are occupied by several nuclear families. Although these Indians and their neighbours, such as the Pira-Tapuya, Tukano proper, Tuyuka, and other Eastern Tukanoans, are at present horticulturalists and cultivate bitter manioc for their staple food, for the Desana the hunt is the preferred activity, and fishing is considered supplementary. Both activities – hunting and fishing – are subject to a large body of restrictions which try to control overhunting, the excessive use of fish poisons, or any other activity which might lead to the deple-tion of resources. These institutionalized restrictions are effective and constitute a highly adaptive set of rules which are enforced by shamanic threats of illness, should the hunter or fisherman exceed himself.[1]

The physical geography of the Vaupés territory is characterized by certain landscape features which constitute what one might call ideological positions of support. By this I mean recurrent landmarks which, because of their conspicu-ous nature, lend themselves to imaginative speculation and which, at the same time, provide visible and striking points of reference for categorisation, and for the ordering of the universe and of man's ideas about it. I shall refer here to two of these characteristic aspects: the deep pools in the rivers, located near large waterfalls, and the isolated rocky hills that rise like dark islands over the flat, monotonous horizon of the forest. The pools and falls are said to have been the stopping places of ancestral migrations; they mark traditional boundary lines, and they are associated with mythical and historical episodes described in oral literature and commemorated in petroglyphs engraved on huge boulders. The true focus, however, of shamanistic interpretations concentrates on the idea that these pools are what the Indians call 'houses'; they are the spirit abodes of the Master of Fish. At the bottom of these pools are said to dwell enormous ana-condas, water serpents which are both life-giving and life-destroying monsters. This image of subaquatic 'houses', each one topped by the spiralling vortex of a whirlpool, is interpreted by the Desana as a female element, as a womb inside which cosmic and telluric forces procreate and gestate fish and other water crea-tures. In the Time of Creation it was people who were gestated there; from these pools emerged the first men who subsequently took possession of the surround-ing lands.

A similar, and complementary, interpretation is given to the rocky hills that rise here and there over the forest, mainly in the interfluvial or headwater regions. These hills or small table mountains are the isolated remnants of the ancient geological formation designated as Guiana Shield and have steep, almost vertical slopes, interrupted by crevasses, caves, and rock shelters. Many of these spots are archaeological sites. In the caves abound the bones of game animals consumed by ancient hunters, and on the walls of some of the rock-shelters one can see pictographs painted in red and ochre representing the very same animals, sometimes accompanied by abstract, geometrical designs.[2] These accumulations of prehistoric faunal remains, mainly of mammals, have given rise to the belief that the hills are the supernatural lairs of game animals, of the spirits of deer, pec-cary, rodents, and others which continue to lead a ghostly existence inside the hills, under the care of the Master of Game Animals. This 'master' is imagined as a dwarfish being, sometimes in animal disguise, who might suddenly and threateningly appear to a hunter who has ventured too far into the forest. The Master is a supernatural gamekeeper who watches over his charges, so the hunter will not diminish the animal population and exterminate certain species. The hills are avoided by hunting parties and, in consequence, have become veri-table sanctuaries, a fact which tends to reaffirm the initial idea of the hills being supernatural gathering places of animals.[3] In shamanistic imagery these hills, too, are designated as 'houses".[4] They are imagined as longhouses occupied by a multitude of dormant animals which occasionally are awakened and released by their Master and made to roam outside where they may fall prey to the hunters.

But on another and far more important level of shamanic abstraction, the hills are said to be 'heads'; they are skulls, human skulls, an idea based in part upon occasional finds of burial caves of prehistoric populations. Whereas in the case of the pools shamanic emphasis is placed upon their character as wombs, in the case of the hills the emphasis is on their character as skulls.

I shall begin by referring to the womb aspect. The Desana's comprehension of female internal anatomy, the menstrual cycle, and of gestation and birth has been enhanced occasionally by the observation of abortions, accidents, violence in warfare and, perhaps, in the not too distant past, by cannibalism. But above all the Desana are passionate hunters, and the butchering of animals is almost a daily occurrence. The killing and butchering of female animals, especially of large pregnant females such as tapir, deer, or peccary, always provide an occasion for detailed observation and lengthy discussion of foetal development, gestation periods, number of offspring, and similar subjects. Hunters always discuss these matters, be it at the kill site while butchering the animal, or later when talking about their hunting experiences.

Shamans say that inside the human womb the embryonic-foetal unfolding goes through a series of developmental stages or way stations which are imagined as a chain of contiguous ventricles. Shamanic spells describe in detail the characteristics of each stage, from conception to birth, tracing the 'travels' of the foetus, during which different physical, mental, and spiritual qualities are said to be acquired. The succession of these stages has been well observed and is described in terms of growing consciousness according to the gradual development of sense organs, to the intake of nourishment, and to the acquisition of independent movement of limbs. Many shamanic spells which are said over pregnant women, at childbirth, or during illness refer to these aspects in an attempt to influence and guide these processes. Shamans believe that songs, spells, tobacco smoke, prolonged rattling sounds, and strict dietary prescriptions for the childbearing woman are essential to the normal development of a new life.

The symbolism of the 'hill houses' as skulls, is based, of course, upon entirely different premises because knowledge of brain structure and speculation about brain functions are very different matters indeed. But again, from the millennial experience of hunting and warfare the Desana have acquired much practical knowledge about the anatomy of the mammalian brain. For example, they have noticed the similarity between monkey brains[5] and human brains, and every hunter, indeed every member of a household, has seen innumerable brains of large rodents and all kinds of other animals. Moreover, the Indians have observed that certain types of brain damage will affect behaviour in many different ways; a wounded animal may become paralysed from brain injury, or it will be seen to make unilateral convulsive movements. On many occasions, brains and injuries to the brain will be exposed to view when clubbing an animal to death with a stick or a stone; on other occasions a skull will crack and expose the brain during the process of smoking a carcass over the fire. Observations on the human brain are, at present, mainly based on accidents, as, for example, a fall from a tree, or a falling tree while clearing a field or during a storm. In the past, warfare would have provided considerable information, especially since the Desana and their neighbours used – and still use – very heavy hardwood clubs with a blunt cutting edge, which were aimed at the head. Survivors from heavy blows to the skull must have offered a wide range of clues to the relationship between brain injury and some aspects of human behaviour.

In addition, the Desana are avid consumers of many different hallucinogenic drugs of plant origin.[6] On almost all ritual occasions the participants consume narcotic drugs, so that direct biochemical processes come to influence behaviour. Moreover, shamans as curers use the trance states of their patients for diagnostic purposes, and, in general, all hallucinatory visions are openly discussed, scrutinized, and interpreted. To the inherent complexity of these trance states one must add the following consideration: all intense drug experiences of the Desana develop in an enriched environment; after a period of sensory deprivation the participants are gradually introduced to music, colours, and changing lights, which furnish a specific environment for each category of ritual.

The professed aims of drug consumption are twofold: in the first place, the participants believe they see mythological scenes and iconographic images which vividly confirm existing beliefs about tribal origins and the traditional nature of social and religious institutions. In the second place, narcotic trance states are enhanced by environmental stimulations and are used to induce specific states of consciousness which correspond to socially and individually adaptive behavioural norms. In other words, by using physicochemical mechanisms, and thereby altering the level of sensory awareness, shamans try to manipulate brain functions. In summary, hunting, club-fighting, and monitored drug use constitute a sound empirical basis for neurological appreciations.

Images of the Brain

I have said that on one level of shamanic interpretation, a hill is a house, and that on another level it is conceptualized as a skull. In order to trace this imagery, we shall examine, first of all, the ground plan of a traditional Desana maloca[7] (fig 1). The house may be some thirty metres long and fifteen metres wide, with the men's door located in the centre of the straight front wall, and the women's door opposite it in the centre of the semicircular back wall. The huge roof almost touches the ground and is supported by a number of strong vertical posts. Along the side walls are located several individual sleeping compartments divided by interwoven palm leaf walls, each cubicle being occupied by one nuclear family; there may be as many as eight or ten. A longhouse is imagined as having a longitudinal axis which divides it into a 'male' and a 'female' half. Most ritual objects are kept in the left half, that is to say, the half lying to the right when entering through the men's door, and the shaman himself has his seat there. But ritual is performed rather in the anterior central area which is a 'male' and public part. The peripheral area in the back is a 'female' and restricted part which

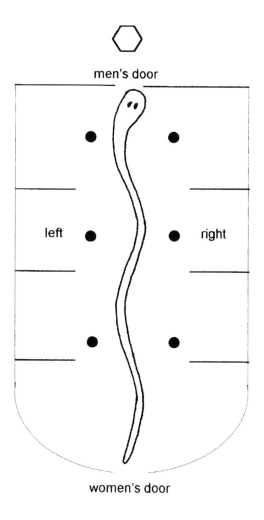

Figure 1. Ground plan of a maloca

has no ritual functions. Here food is processed, women, children, and dogs crouch around the fires, and the floor is littered with household utensils and garbage.

The central axis of the longhouse is imagined as an anaconda lying stretched out between the two doors. The Desana say that in the beginning of time their ancestors arrived in canoes shaped like huge serpents. The passengers were agnatic brothers who were sitting by order of birth, and from them the different sibs are descended. Each serpent was divided into a series of 'compartments', so to speak (fig. 2). At the tip of the head was a hexagonal rock crystal[8] representing the energy of the Sun Father who was guiding the anaconda. Next came Chiefs, followed by Shamans; then came the Dancers, then Warriors and, finally, Servants. Stretched out along the longitudinal axis of the house, the snake

Small anaconda

divides into five major sections, with the sixth point of reference, the rock crystal, just outside the men's door which, traditionally, looks toward the east. It is clear then that the longitudinal, ritual distribution of a longhouse represents not only specialization, but also life-stages, that is, developmental stages from infancy to advanced age.

The structure of a so-called hill house is imagined just like that of a longhouse, but on a much larger scale. Inside the hill are compartments, all occupied by the major species of game animals; other animals sit on rafter sand ledges; some crouch in corners while others hide under the roof. All of them are half asleep, as if benumbed. A huge anaconda is stretched out in the middle; there are other monsters, such as jaguars and poisonous snakes, evil forest spirits, and all kinds

Figure 2. The ancestral anaconda; the five agnatic sib founders are: 2, Chiefs; 3, Shamans; 4, Dancers; 5, Warriors; 6, Servants. They are guided by the divine rock crystal

of vermin. Another, important category of spirit-beings that occupy the hill houses are the 'other people', the doubles, the *Doppelgänger* of every person alive.[9] Some of the compartments are like geodes, globular bodies in a limestone matrix, coated inside with countless inward-projecting crystals. An occasional beam of sunlight might fall through the roof into the dark interior and project a slanting column of smoke and swirling odoriferous dust, as if rising skyward. All these spirit-beings are creatures of darkness which thrive under the care of the Master of Animals. Whenever the need arises, in the world of ordinary human beings, to obtain more game, more food, shamans will establish contact with the Master by addressing spells and songs to him and will ask him to release some of his animals. When he opens the door of his ghostly house, however, some noxious animal, some evil spirit, or the double of a living person might escape, too, and this is likely to cause some disgrace in the world of men.

The imagery of the water-houses is similar. They, too, are seen as large abodes divided into many recesses and chambers occupied by many-coloured fish, crabs, snails, frogs, snakes, and other water creatures. Slanting sunrays will penetrate into these depths, illuminating chains of glittering bubbles among which schools of multicoloured fish may be seen flitting by. Some of these chambers are set with brilliant crystals that glimmer with hidden reflections. And all these creatures are 'little ones', beings that develop and grow in these pulsating depths, and then well up to the surface as if the waters were giving birth to a part of nature that is essential to man's existence. It is clear from this description that the domains of the Master of Animals are conceived as hallucinatory dimensions; it is the drug experience which provides the atmosphere, both enchanting and frightening, in which these vital creative processes are developing.

The problem of maintaining viable relationships with the Master of Animals constitutes a central point in shamanic practices. The Master is a wily creature; he is highly ambivalent, a seducer who might appear as an incubus or a succubus. He incites people to incest; he tries to abduct women, or to lead lonely hunters astray. But at the same time he is man's friend and ally, because he is the game-keeper who protects vital resources for the ulterior benefit of people.

The Other Dimension

When speaking of these parallels between a longhouse and the abodes of the Master of Animals, in his double manifestation as Master of Game and Master of Fish, the Desana use certain idiomatic expressions to refer to these equivalences. One recurrent shamanic expression is *gahí vii*, meaning literally, 'other house'. When I first heard this expression and enquired about its significance, I understood that a house with two rooms was being referred to, and further commentaries made me believe that a two-storied house was meant, such as the

Indians might have seen at the mission stations of Mitú or Yavareté. So when I first heard of the 'other house', or the 'double house', I interpreted this on the simplest level of comparison and, at best, thought of a symbolic division of a house into two longitudinal sections, an image which I knew to be applied to a longhouse. In fact, I was told that "*it is where the other people are*", and so I made no further inquiries. When my knowledge of the language improved and discussion began to reach a more abstract level, however, I noticed that shamans were employing the term *gahí turí*, which could be glossed as 'other-dimension'. In fact, *gahí vii* and *gahí turí* eventually turned out to be interchangeable expressions. It took the better part of two years to break this code. When I finally learned the meaning of *gahí vii* and asked my informants why they had not told me long before, they characteristically answered: "*You never asked us.*"

From the analysis of a large body of shamanic and other texts which I have recorded and discussed in the field, as well as from thousands of hours of subsequent discussion with Desana informants, it has become clear that the concept of the 'other house', or the 'other dimension', refers to the two hemispheres of the human brain. This formal comparison is accompanied by a considerable amount of native knowledge of brain functions and functional differences between the two cerebral hemispheres. Let us see first how Desana shamans look at the human brain. The two hemispheres are said to be essentially symmetrical; in Desana, the terms 'right' (*diáye*) and 'left' (*kupëpë*) have little or no directional importance, but imply hierarchy. Thus, what we call the left hemisphere is called 'side one' and is more important than 'side two', or our right hemisphere. The great fissure is seen as a deep riverbed; it is a depression that was formed in the beginning of time (of mythical and embryological time) by the cosmic anaconda. Near the head of the serpent is a hexagonal rock crystal, just outside the brain; it is there where a particle of solar energy resides and irradiates the brain. The fissure can also be seen as a stream, a great current of *bogá*, or cosmic energy. In many shamanic images human existence is compared to a river, and the great fissure is this life-giving and orienting stream (fig. 3).

The whole brain mass is called *dihpú ka'í*, literally, 'head-mind'. The term *ka'í* can be glossed as 'essence of awareness'; it is related to the verb *kaiári*, which means 'to think and become aware of something, to become conscious'.[10] The convolutions of the brain[11] are called *kaë* and are seen in terms of compartments and cavities. Each compartment is said to be a 'deposit' that contains images or qualities. For example, a *kaë* ventricle can be compared to a small inlet, a backwater, untouched by the great *bogä* current, whereas others are designated as *vii tëró*, literally 'house-neighbouring', by this meaning that they constitute separate but interrelated units within the brain. In a way, each *kaë* is a diminutive brain by itself, but the totality of *kaë* is *ka'í*, what we would call the mind. The mind in the brain is thought to be the main organ of human cognition and behaviour. As a unit, each *kaë* contains a specific quality (*buyá*), image (*keori*), and colour

EAST

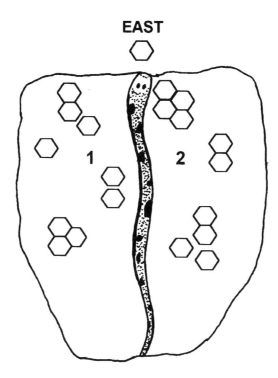

Figure 3. The human brain. The left hemisphere is referred to as Side One, and the right as Side Two. The fissure is occupied by an anaconda. (Redrawn from Desana sketches.)

(*gohséri*); it contains the particular odour of people (*mahsá sëriri*) related to concepts, such as honesty, amiability, and spirituality; or it may lack a particular odour and thus indicate undesirable personality traits, such as unfriendliness, coolness, and a withdrawn character.[12] In other words, all sensoria are highly specialized, although interrelated. The concept of visible, tangible nerves is lacking, and shamans speak instead of *dári* or 'threads' that convey luminous impulses from one *kaë* to another.

In order to visualize and intellectually comprehend the enormous variety of specific qualities (*buyá*) contained in the *kaë* ventricles, shamans have created a number of vivid images that make it possible to establish categories of brain functions, as understood by the Desana. In one image the human brain is compared to a huge rock crystal sub-divided into many smaller hexagonal prisms, each containing a sparkling element of colour energy.[13] In another image the brain is formed by a bundle of pencil-shaped hexagonal tourmaline crystals standing closely packed side by side; each crystal contains a sequence of colours which, from bottom to top, express a range of sensibilities. In another image a brain consists of layers of innumerable hexagonal honeycombs; the entire brain is one huge humming beehive, a wasp's nest, or a termite's nest, whatever the particular insect may be. Each tiny hexagonal container holds honey of a different colour, flavour, odour, or texture, or it houses a different stage of insect larval development. Another image shows the brain divided into hexagonal columns, those of the left hemisphere having the widest possible range of colours, while those of the right showing only yellow, red, and blue; in this manner, the left side contains a combinatory potential, and a commentator said that it "... *contains colours we don't even know the names of*". Each column varies in intensity from top to bottom. A brain can be seen as a bouquet of flowers, a fluttering cluster of butterflies, a glistening swarm of tiny tropical fish, or a quivering mass of multicoloured frogs.[14]

Each *kaë* compartment has its specific name, for example, 'the yellow place', 'the place of rough stones', 'the place of clay', 'the place of crystal'. References to mineral forms are frequent, especially since the brain is sometimes compared to a geode, the inside of which is lined with a multitude of sparkling crystals. Colour references, too, are frequent, and the Indians point out that while 'places' are called *gororí*, by shifting the stress to the second syllable, as in *goróri*, the word comes to mean 'flowers'. Since flowers have many different shapes, colours, scents, and textures, they combine many of the features which characterize the topography of the brain. In this manner, the Indians say that each sensorium is a 'state', a 'state of mind', and so what I have called 'places' might also be called 'states".

Apart from these sensoria there are other divisions, some with complex meanings. The precise significance of such a 'state' enclosed in a brain ventricle can be understood only if one has a good knowledge of Desana metaphors. For example, there is a certain *kaë* compartment which is said to contain a widowed woman, some grains of maize, and a lot of black ants. The metaphors are these: on the one hand, maize kernels symbolize male sperm, but on the other hand, maize planted in the rainforest is of poor quality. The same is true of black ants; they, too, have a seminal connotation, but they are not very nourishing. Therefore, if a widow eats maize and ants, that is to say, if she does not resume her active reproductive life, she will remain childless. The entire cluster of metaphors thus refers to the social uselessness of widows; since widows are a liability in Desana society, they have their specific spot assigned to them on the map of the brain. Another example is this: the 'place of rough stones' is located in the left hemisphere and is occupied by large mammals of yellow, black, and red colour, each animal representing a certain 'state of mind'. In fact, each area is subdivided into three sections which are associated with a range of colours that represent different energizing principles derived from the sun. A last example contains a group of metaphors which are similar to ours and need no comment; it refers to a 'yellow place' located in the right themisphere, which is inhabited by birds and young people. One of the informants pointed rapidly to different areas on an outline of a brain he had drawn and said: "*Here it is prohibited to eat fish; here it is allowed; here one learns to dance; here one has to show respect-ful behaviour*." Other *kaë* compartments are occupied by individual links of interrelated chains, a phenomenon which can be illustrated by the following example: a *kaë* might comprise a number of certain small fish which are the favourite food of a certain aquatic bird. The fish own the remedy for certain diseases, but are willing to surrender it only in exchange for certain conditions under which the bird must promise not to pursue his prey.[15] These few examples show that this mapping of the brain is extremely complex; nevertheless, it does not constitute an esoteric knowledge that would be shared only by a few initiates; on the contrary, many people who are not shamans seem to know about it.

Lateralization

The two cerebral hemispheres are said to have different but complementary functions. The left hemisphere is called *ëmëkóri mahsá turí*, meaning 'Sun-People-dimension', alluding to the dimension of the Sun-descendant first ancestors. It is male and dominant and is associated with the concept of 'elder brother'. The left hemisphere is the seat of the cosmic energy of the Sun and contains all the 'colour energies' shamans believe to be inherent in the rock crystal. It is the seat of all abstract shamanic wisdom and of the divine laws laid down by the Sun Father, the creator of the universe. It also is the seat of all shamanic utterances, of spells, songs, and recitals, of all words of power. It is the seat of music and dreams and, most importantly, of hallucinatory visions of abstract geometrical patterns. The left hemisphere represents the principle of moral authority, of law and order. It is the model of all intellectual and spiritual endeavours. Each *kaë* compartment is controlled by what shamans call *pesiró*, powerful abstract thought. The left hemisphere also contains *inyamahsíro*, 'intuition'. In other words, the left cerebral hemisphere is dominant for all higher functions.

The right hemisphere is called *mahsá turí*, or 'human-dimension'. It is female, subservient, and is associated with the concept of 'younger brother'. It is that part of the brain which executes, which puts into practice what is pre-established by the model of the left; it contains *pesirinyé*, the manifest expression of abstract thought. The right hemisphere contains all practical affairs; it contains the living tradition of the ancestors, all their customary rules and rituals. It contains everything pertaining to women, to animals and plants, to illness and death, to physical nature and biological processes. It is the seat of all pictorial, figurative hallucinations, of colourful and dramatic imagery. And what is 'intuition' (*inyamahsiró*), on the left, becomes *yimahsíri*, 'skill, know-how, specialization', on the right.

In general terms it can be said that everything that is believed to exist on one side of the brain is also present on the other side; there exists the concept of a mirror image. The difference lies in the idea that the left side harbours the ideal, the abstract model, while on the right side is the human potential to put that model into practice. It is precisely this dichotomy which is meant when shamans use the figure of speech expressed by the term *gahí vii*, the 'other house'. And more than that, *maría turí* means 'our dimension, our world', while *gahí turí* is the 'other world'. The question arises: which is real? Shamans say: *mári ariri kéro dohpá inyarí*, 'our-existence-dream-like-appears', but they will add that dreams are visions of a reality that is precisely *gahí turí*, the 'other dimension'. In death men return to that 'other side', to the left hemisphere; but only if they have lived according to the moral norms dictated by that side will they awake into a state of reality, upon returning to their left hemisphere. It is this duality that is expressed by *gahí turí*.

I have mentioned that the Desana do not think of 'right' or 'left', but refer to the two hemispheres as 'one' (our left) and 'two' (our right), always conscious of hierarchy. Their image is that of two parallel sets, two columns, so to speak; the left column is called *arimetáro*, 'abstract-first', and the right column is *arimetángë*, or 'existential-first'. When enumerating specific districts or compartments of the brain a person will refer first to the left hemisphere and will say, for example, 'women-food-fighting'; but when referring to the right hemisphere the speaker will say 'women-other dimension', 'food other dimension', and so on.[16] An important difference between the two hemispheres is that the left is associated with *mahsíro*, 'wisdom', while the right represents *mahsíri*, 'knowledge'.

The Workings of the Mind: Consciousness

The two cerebral hemispheres are said to be coordinated, not in a mechanical sense of cog-wheels or the like, but in a manner called *pee yíri*. This expression means 'to hear-to act' and implies the need for the mind to become aware and to listen to what the left hemisphere demands, and then put this demand into practice. This process of gaining awareness, of acquiring consciousness, constitutes the most important function of the human brain; it develops under the guidance of shamans, but must eventually be put into motion by the individual. It is not an automatic, inbuilt process, but consists of a cultural conditioning; after an initial socializing period oriented by shamanic ritual, it must become an individual discipline practised in solitude.[17]

On a very simple metaphorical level, this process is compared to a river crossing; the central fissure of the brain must be transversed from left to right. The image is that of a broad, swift-flowing river from which a number of stones or rocks protrude over the surface of the current, providing precarious footholds for the prospective traveller. Some of the stones are flat and offer a fairly firm footing, but others are angular and slippery. They are set at irregular intervals and the crossing thus becomes a problem of judging distances, evaluating surface features and stability, and a number of other, often unforeseeable qualities of these stepping stones. But this is a simplistic metaphor; it becomes more complex when the shaman makes one realize that the river, after all, is the body of the anaconda and that the stepping stones are the dark circular markings on the snake skin. Furthermore, since the huge serpent is moving and the glistening dark spots are half submerged, it is difficult to gain a firm footing on one spot and to accomplish the crossing by a series of well-coordinated steps or jumps. It is important never to attempt a straight crossing, perpendicular to the river's current; the shortest distance is not the most desirable, and a crossing must be pondered in detail, each move being thought out beforehand.

And still, as long as shamanic imagery speaks of a river or an anaconda, the left-to-right relationship, that is, the problem of gaining awareness, is not a too difficult one; this still is a highly simplified image, almost childishly straightforward. A far more complex picture emerges in the following shamanic conceptualization: the great fissure which separates the two halves of the brain is not a mere cleft with an overall equal width, but is a wedge-shaped space, wider at its frontal part and diminishing toward the occipital region. Within this wedge-shaped or, rather, cone-shaped space, two intertwined snakes are lying, a giant anaconda (*Eunectes murinus*) and a rainbow boa (*Epicrates cenchris*), a large river snake of dark dull colours and an equally large land snake of spectacular bright colours (fig. 4). In Desana shamanism these two serpents symbolize a female and a male principle, a mother and a father image, water and land, devouring darkness and energizing colour display. One could elaborate indefinitely on these chains of associations; in brief, they represent a concept of binary opposition which has to be overcome in order to achieve individual awareness and integration. The snakes are imagined as spiralling rhythmically in a swaying motion from one side to another. This rhythm, shamans say, is predictable and marks a daily, monthly, and yearly pattern, so that the 'crossing' must take into account the particular sway of the two gyrating serpents.

The left hemisphere is thought to be the seat of the 'power of personality', *pepí turarí*, a term meaning 'to feel-force'. In the right hemisphere this expresses itself as a physical and spiritual state of well-being, a state which must be achieved by *pepíburi*, literally 'to feel-not', meaning that the concept of personality should not be made understandable intellectually, but must remain a highly abstract and 'unfelt' concept. The term *turarí* (or *tularí*) refers to a moving dynamic force without which the immanent *bogá* energy would not be able to express itself. The concept of *bogá* can be compared to a skein of fibres floating in the wind or in the water. "*If it moves with the current, it acquires meaning; bogá must be set in motion by the abstract force of tularí.*" The potential energy of bogá is present in both cerebral hemispheres; it is "... *like a brilliant* (gohsëri)

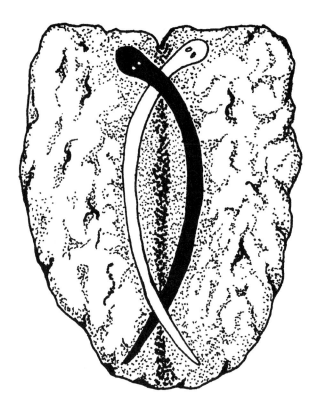

Figure 4. The human brain. The fissure is occupied by an anaconda and a rainbow boa. (Redrawn from Desana sketches)

and hot (ahsirí) *fire; it contains a transformative energy. But only its hot component transforms.*" To this the following statement was offered by another commentator: "*A person's particular personality consists of his pepíri bogá and his turarí bogá; pepíri is intelligence that is concerned with material things, but it also contains pepiró, the capacity for abstract thought. The quality of pepiró influences the (right) hemisphere. This is why there are people who think.*" In elaborating this train of thought one of the commentators added: "We call this *irá pepíro aríya*, 'they-to feel-it were'." This expression was glossed as '*They understand (intellectually)*', and was amplified as '*This would be their abstract inspiration*', the latter term being understood as equivalent to 'light, energy, fountain, water'.

When a shaman addresses an audience and wishes to call its attention to the abstract dimension of the left hemisphere, he will use the standard phrase *váro pepí doakeeeé*, an expression which, when translated literally, means 'well-to feel-be seated'. This can be glossed as '*enjoy yourself; leave your world behind and enter the abstract dimension*'. He will chant the last syllable in a long-drawn call, *doakeeeé*, and will then add the question, *doarí? 'Are you seated?*' Another shaman then chants the response, *doáa ii ëmëre*, '*Seated I am-that-day in*,' which can be glossed as '*I am enjoying this day*'. The meaning of these ritual formulas is an exhortation to stop operating with the right hemisphere and to enjoy the 'other dimension' of the left hemisphere.[18] This process of leaving the right hemisphere and finding a restful place in the left one is called *óreri*, 'to escape, to break loose'. The corresponding shamanic image is that of a horizontal sigmoid scroll (fig. 5); the left right-hand spiral (*oréro*) represents the left cerebral hemisphere, and the right right-hand one (*oréro*), the right hemisphere. Both are imagined as gyrating conical or cylindrical helices, and the person must – by an act of concentration – try to break away from the attraction of the right hemisphere and let himself be envoled by the left hemisphere. It is understood that this return to the left hemisphere is also a return to an intrauterine state of gestation and transformation, from which the individual is reborn into the practical life of the right hemisphere once the ritual is over. The process itself is called *oréro*, 'the breaking away, the loosening', and it is this that shamans demand from their audience (fig. 6).

In this manner, then, the human mind is continuously engaged in the task of fulfilling the demands of the left hemisphere. The degree to which this can be accomplished depends upon the individual's awareness of cosmic energies and upon the person's willingness to obey the moral order promulgated by shamans. The individual brain is permanently exposed to stimulations coming from the

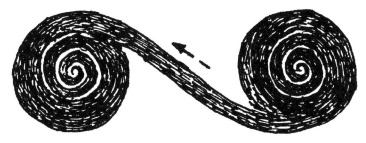

Figure 5. The human brain. The two right-hand spirals represent the two cerebral hemispheres. (Redrawn from Desana sketches)

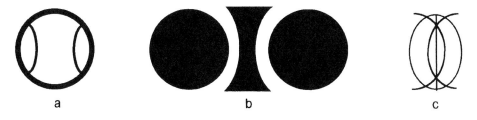

a   b   c

Figure 6. The human brain. Three abstract representations. (Redrawn from Desana sketches)

Desana and Pira-Tapuya Indians dancing, near Mitú

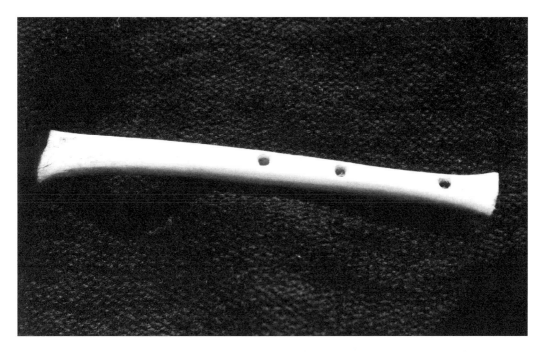

Bone flute (above). A musical instrument (*puridú*) hanging on a longhouse wall (below)

outside world, and the person must learn to interpret the many messages that are received by the brain. In addition to nature's messages, the brain is being stimulated by shamanic manipulation on many, if not all, occasions when a ritual is being performed. Indeed, shamans claim to be specialists in brain/mind relationships. The entire range of environmental sensorial stimulations, of drug use, altered states of consciousness, relaxation, and meditation constitutes a focal area of interest to the Indians, not only to shamans but to most adults who already have acquired a large body of knowledge of neurological processes by observing the effects of psychotropic drugs, together with their personal reactions to a variety of environmental stimulations.

A normal natural environment, such as the forest, a riverbank, or a cultivated field, transmits certain signals, called 'energies' (*bogári*), of which the recipient may hardly be conscious unless his awareness has been heightened, for example, by food restrictions before going to hunt. But in an enriched social environment these energies are intensified and orchestrated by monitoring devices. This control can consist of a single person, such as a shaman who speaks, recites, or sings; or it can consist of a group of coordinated dancers and singers accompanied by instrumental music; in any case, effective control will consist of the framework of traditional rules which guide the ritual. In practically all these situations the participants consume narcotic drugs, so that direct biochemical processes come to influence behaviour. The chemical components of many of the plants from which these drugs are prepared are fairly well known, but the fact remains that the Indians use many admixtures and combinations, and of these and their effects very little is known. Precise dosage constitutes a vast body of shamanic learning of which, unfortunately, our knowledge is still very scanty.

Although the general nature and content of hallucinations induced by these substances have been described by several authors, these descriptions do not do full justice to the Indians' categories of perception, which are likely to cover a much wider range of states of consciousness, as well as many different intensities of imagery. I have mentioned that all intense drug experiences of the Desana develop in an enriched environment; after an initial period of deprivation consisting of sexual abstinence, dieting, insomnia, and controlled breathing, the participants are exposed to vocal and instrumental music, to the sight of bright colours, to different odours, and to scheduled lighting changes accompanied by certain prescribed motor activities. The aim of these stimulations is to induce very specific states of consciousness which correspond to, socially and individually, adaptive behavioural norms, as formulated by the left cerebral hemisphere, the spokesman of which is the shaman. By using physicochemical mechanisms and thus altering the level of sensory awareness, shamans try to activate certain potentials in one or the other hemisphere, and to trigger specific behavioural responses.

The Desana have some twenty musical instruments, mostly wind and percus-

Tatuyo Indian playing a pan-pipe outside the longhouse

sion, a selection of which is played on ritual occasions. Each instrument is associated with a certain ritual, a certain time of day, a certain age-group, and a certain animal. Furthermore, the sounds of each instrument are classified by colour, smell, and temperature and are said to produce specific types of vibrations which, by affecting a particular part of the brain, transmit to the audience a specific, culturally coded message. For example, a particular large flute is played only by adult men; its long-drawn sounds are said to have a male odour, a very strong yellow colour, and a very high temperature; the melody is said to be of a merry kind and is associated with the image of a multitude of fish running upriver to the spawning beds. The vibrations produced by the sounds are said to trigger a message which refers to child-rearing, especially to breast-feeding during the first year of life. Another example is this: a small whistle is blown by adolescent boys early in the morning when they bathe in the river before dawn. The odour of the tune is said to be male, the colour is red, and the temperature is hot; the tune evokes youthful happiness and the taste of a fleshy fruit of a certain tree. The vibrations carry an erotic message to a particular girl.

And there exist other mechanisms. Shamans as curers and, in a sense, as confessors will give to their patients a hallucinogenic drug and then will ask them to describe their visions. Moreover, they will sometimes ask the participants in a drug ritual to describe their visions. On other occasions, people who are, or were, under the influence of a drug will consult a shaman about their experiences. All this means that shamans eventually acquire a profound knowledge of the nature of altered states of consciousness and of human projective mechanisms.

Shamans declare that their main task consists of converting the abstract thought patterns of the left cerebral hemisphere into images which can be perceived, understood, and acted upon by the right hemisphere. This fundamental process can be described thus: within the mind exists a faculty called *gunyáro*, a term we can gloss as 'memory'.[19] Since memory will fail, it has to be refreshed, meaning that flagging behavioural rules must be enforced from time to time. In order to do this an abstract idea lodged in the left hemisphere must be converted into an image (or, shall we say, an icon) which then is perceived by the person in the right hemisphere. The person will recognize the image, which is precoded and which stands for a cluster of condensed information which now makes the person fully conscious of the specific demands of the left hemisphere. The process of image formation is called *gunyári*, 'to create in one's imagination, to transform',[20] and the image or icon itself is called *gurunyá*, a word which, surprisingly, means 'facial paint'.[21] As a matter of fact, the term refers to certain red design motifs with which people paint their faces or bodies or some manufactured object.

To perceive these images or motifs is called *inyagoróri*, literally 'to see flowers' or 'states' (as I have mentioned before). This expression refers to what have been called phosphenes, that is, to luminous sensations perceived as subjective images, independent of an external light source. These luminous patterns originate within the eye and the brain and so are common to all men; they are neurally inbuilt. They can be induced by chemical agents, such as drugs, by external stimulation, and by sensory deprivation.[22]

I shall explain this process in greater detail. The term *veréri* means both 'message' and 'to speak, to communicate, to convey an abstract message'; *verérinye* is 'communication-thing', and can be glossed as 'mechanism of communication'. A telephone, radio, musical instrument, facial paint are such *verérinye* or means of communication. The shaman himself is a transmitter, a *verégë mahsë* (or *veverí mahsë*), a 'communication-person, a speaking-person'. This means by which the abstract message (*veréri*) is transformed into an action is called *vërëri*; this term refers to 'open things, orifices'; for example, *vërë* is a gaping mouth, or a hole from which ants emerge on their nuptial flight; *vërëri* refers to the 'disposition to act', as one informant put it. Once this transformation has been achieved and communication has been established, a state of *gaméro* has been reached, meaning that now a mutual understanding exists. The next step is action, and this is expressed by the verb *väräri*, 'to break away'. The entire scheme can be represented thus:

gunyáro	*gunyári*	*gurunyá*
vereeri	*vërëri*	*väräri*
influence	transformation	activation
idea	icon	action

Further discussions of this process led to the formulation of the following native ideas. The abstract concept located in the left hemisphere is an 'impulse', an 'instinct' which must be put into practice by transferring it to the right hemisphere. In order to achieve this transition the person '*must make himself strong*',[23] and this is an act of self-fertilization. This state leads to a 'birth', a coming into life of a moral action.[24]

In other words, shamans will intentionally induce colourful phosphenes which, as I have shown elsewhere,[25] are culturally coded and serve as visual reminders of recommended forms of thought patterns and behavioural norms. These abstract motifs, which at the same time can be described as elements of decorative art, are coded with reference to social organization, marriage rules, and many cosmological concepts. Shamans distinguish two categories of phosphenes: linear forms and closed forms. Linear forms, for example, lines (straight, zigzag, dotted, undulating, radiating, etc.), pertain to the right hemisphere, while closed forms, such as circles, squares, diamonds, spirals, or U-shaped labyrinths, pertain to the left.[26] The linear forms are *gurunyá* and can be exteriorized as decorative motifs, but closed forms are contemplative devices that express highly abstract thoughts and cannot be referred to as 'designs'. They are *gurunyá dohpá deyóri*, 'design-like-similar to', but they cannot be drawn with stark, simple lines; "*One can imagine them, but one seldom draws them*", a commentator said. In fact, one rarely sees a closed form, such as a spiral or a diamond, used as a decorative motif. Shamans will trace them in the sand, or draw them on objects, but there they have the function of contemplation objects, not of simple reminders of marriage rules. It was also pointed out that closed forms were "*states... that appear and disappear*", and thus were far more difficult to identify and reproduce than the linear motifs.[27] When discussing this process of left hemisphere phosphenes being carried over to the right, one informant made the remarkable observation that "*... in the left hemisphere exist thoughts and ideas which it has not been possible yet to convert into images that might be perceived and fully understood by the right hemisphere.*" This observation is very much to the point, because shamans say that the entire spiritual development of man is a quest (*amakuriró*)[28] which always leads from the abstract to the material and, by way of the latter, back to a fuller understanding of the initial abstract idea.[29] The suggestion that the icon might have preceded the idea is not acceptable to shamans, because in their view the universe contains a highly abstract ethic which, necessarily, precedes the image.[30]

The truly important point is that a shaman will never attempt to explain the *gunyáro/gunyári/gurunyá* process, in that many words. He will never expound or elucidate, nor will he ask leading questions or, in any other way, try to influence an individual to directly recall a problematic event. The person himself must become aware of it (*kaiári*, 'to realize the truth'); he must practise *pe mahsíri*, 'to listen-to know', by following the shaman's words, even if he has heard them many times before. A shaman merely speaks, recites, or chants, but by intently listening to his seemingly endless repetitions, one or the other participant will eventually be led back to a crucial point, a moment of awareness when long-forgotten, isolated elements suddenly fall into place and begin to form a significant pattern. The abstract *pe mahsiro* of the shaman must trigger the groping *pe mahsíri* of the listener; and it is here where his choice lies, where he can exercise his free will.[31] It may take years, in fact, it may take a man's whole life, before he reaches this moment of truth. The shaman will be deaf to all questions; it is the questioner himself who must hear the answers to his problems, over and above the din of the shaman's voice.[32]

By administering drugs, or by providing various kinds of external stimulations, shamans use at least four fundamental mechanisms to serve as initial guides to meditation. These mechanisms are called:

1) *inyagorórikë yimá*, 'to make one see, and act accordingly';
2) *pe gorórikë yimá*, 'to make one hear, and act accordingly';
3) *vihí gorórikë yimá*, 'to make one smell, and act accordingly';
4) *ke gorórikë yimá*, 'to make one dream, and act accordingly'.

Shamans thus try to induce specific moods or states of mind by providing environmental stimulation to groups of people. By reaffirming these stimulations through narcotic visions they produce neurally inbuilt images which have become socially agreed signs representing objects and ideas.

When discussing the concept of *gunyáro*, as located in the left hemisphere, and the process of *gunyári*, 'to remember', as operating in the right hemisphere, a commentator said: "*It is not necessary to remember, because an inspiration is a presence, it is a traditional moral value. That does not need a memory. A memory is something personal, but that is something different. A shaman knows what kind of feeling he must activate. So why should one remember? Why trace a big trail where there are so many small ones? He who truly sees, does not need a personal memory.*" The commentator was speaking here of the idea/icon/action sequence, and of the total cultural – and not individual – moral values imbedded in the left hemisphere. He pointed out that the conscious process in the right hemisphere consisted of the identification of phosphenes ("*those shapes, tracings, outlines*", as he called them) and added that this act of identification was possible only if there existed artifacts or natural phenomena which repeated these phosphenes. This, he stated, was truly a process of remembering what the phosphenes stood for. Neurally inbuilt phosphenes were thus being used as a kind of artificial memory.

Psychotherapy

Brain lateralization and the relationship between the two halves provide the basis for shamanistic theories of psychotherapy. The underlying processes were described in the following manner.

When a person commits a fault, that is to say, when he acts contrary to traditional rules, this misbehaviour is bound to express itself in a material way through the right hemisphere; the culprit will develop physical symptoms of illness, will become prone to accidents, or will find himself otherwise beset by ill luck. All this will affect the left hemisphere; not that it will create a disorder out of nothing, but it will refer back to a *kaë* ventricle, the sensibility of which mirrors the corresponding *kaë*'s of the right hemisphere. This referred disorder or hurt is far more serious to a person's physical and mental health than the one experienced on the right side, and shamans must immediately minister to the left side and try to cure its particular condition. The precise *kaë* can be located in the course of diagnosis, during which the shaman questions the patient and asks him to describe his hallucinations. The next step consists in pronouncing spells accompanied by lengthy songs and rapid sound vibrations produced with the gourd rattle. Characteristically, the words of the spells refer to breast milk, to seminal colours and energizing temperatures, to the birth-giving image of the river, to cardinal directions, and to *bogá* energies. To pronounce these spells is called bayiri, from *bári*, 'to eat', and *yíri*, 'to do, to make'; in fact, the casting of these spells means 'to make eat'. The patient is taken back to an infantile condition in which disorders and discontents are appeased by the soothing environment of maternal care associated with warmth, nourishment, and the hugging rhythmic motions and sounds of monotonous songs and whirring rattles. The patient/infant is thus being 'nursed back to health', as we would say.

The concept of curing demands further comment. Any illness is thought to be caused by a 'germ', a pollen or semen-like grain which enters a cavity (*kaë*) and there develops like a pathogenic and pathological embryo. The act of *bayíri*, 'to make eat', was glossed on several occasions as '*to nourish so it won't produce more cavities*'; bayiri was also translated as 'to level, to smooth, to replenish'. A commentator said: "*In the spell the cavity is filled with milk, with seminal sap, with colours*". It is obvious, then, that this restorative nourishment is the symbolic equivalent of a fertilizing act.

The same mechanisms are used in many other curing practices, in rituals of the life cycle, or in conflict situations when people come to ask for advice. On the individual level the person is expected to learn to work back, from the image to the idea, to become able to interpret his inner imagery or incoming sensory information in terms of their respective abstract meanings.

I should emphasize here that many people are quite aware of the power shamans acquire in the course of these ministrations. But all agree that a shaman will rarely use his influence for material gain; what he may be striving for is intellectual prestige, but such an incentive is not resented, and in this manner shamans are believed to be conscientious guides and counsellors. The Desana would also emphatically deny the suggestion that their neurological theories of behaviour and illness might be interpreted as reductionist, indeed, as a kind of social engineering by applied biochemistry. On the contrary, they are convinced that they participate actively in a moral universe, and that they are linked to cosmic forces which, by their very timelessness, are true guiding principles.

Summary

The wider cosmic image is this: the isomorphic chain formed by the human brain, the longhouse, and the hills continues in the celestial vault. This, too, is an immense brain; the Milky Way is the great fissure which separates the two hemispheres and is called the Trail of the Master of Animals, because the constellations and all other stars are the animals and people, the butterflies and flowers which occupy the brain compartments. In another image the Milky Way and its swaying motion represent the same two intertwined serpents: the female anaconda and the male rainbow boa.

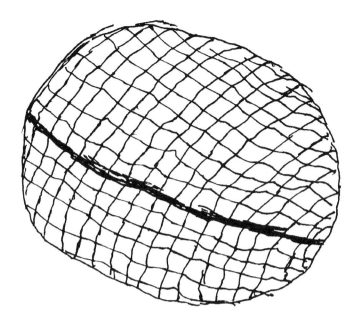

Figure 7. The human brain. Drawing made by a Matapi Indian (Arawak, Miriti-paraná)

Beyond the Milky Way lies space, and cosmic space is said to be a womb; it is called *ëmësée paa toré*, an expression that can be glossed as 'time-seat-abdominal-cavity'. This cosmic womb is a limitless hexagonal rock crystal. The entire chain, from the cosmic crystal to the human brain, is linked together by a steady flow of solar energy (*bogá*) which forms a line of conduction that pulsates in synchronization with the human heartbeat. In this way, the material and the immaterial world come to constitute a single whole.

In this essay I have explored a higher level of shamanistic learning and conceptualization – the level of brain structure and function. If we seriously consider shamanic affirmations that it is the human brain which provides the model for social behaviour, we might indeed catch a glimpse of a new dimension of shamanistic thought. Desana shamans believe that the two cerebral hemispheres constitute, in form and function, the model for the dualistic patterns which underlie not only social organization, but most other aspects of their sociocultural behaviour. In other words, they believe that the basic foundations of the great organizational principles of social behaviour are largely neurally based and that the hierarchical structure of Desana society (elder brother/younger brother) is a reflection of brain lateralization.

The ethnographic information I have presented in this essay shows that Professor Claude Lévi-Strauss and other theorists are not alone in suggesting that conceptual structures are epiphenomena of brain structures. In fact, they are in good shamanic company. It remains to evaluate their speculations.

I should add here that similar neurological concepts seem to be current among the Kogi Indians of northern Colombia and among the Matapí, an Arawakan group of the upper Amazon (fig. 6). In any case, if the shamans of a simple rainforest tribe like the Desana have been able to formulate theories as complex as those I have described here, we may well suppose that the intellectual leaders of the ancient Andean and Mesoamerican societies had an even better understanding of these matters (fig. 7).

It is clear that we cannot dismiss these native ideas as mere shamanistic imagery; we must seriously consider their formulations and try to learn more about their intellectual achievements. And it is also clear that we should so so while we can obtain the living testimony of shamans and other native thinkers. For tomorrow will be too late.

Notes

1. For a concise account of how these control mechanisms operate, see Reichel-Dolmatoff 1976a (essay I in this book).
2. On petroglyphs and pictographs, see Reichel-Dolmatoff 1967b, 1971 *passim*, 1978b; 2, 3, 139ff, 158.
3. On the concept of the Master of Animals, see Reichel-Dolmatoff 1971 and 1975, indexed under "Master of Game Animals".
4. 'Hill houses', *ëhtëngë vii*, 'water houses', *dia vii*.
5. Monkeys are immediately decapitated by the hunter, and their brains must not be brought into a longhouse.
6 On the use of hallucinogenic drugs among the Desana, see Reichel-Dolmatoff 1969, 1975, 1978a.
7. On longhouse construction, see Reichel-Dolmatoff 1971, indexed under 'maloca'.
8. On the symbolism of rock crystals, see Reichel-Dolmatoff 1978a, 1979a (essay 6 in this book).
9. On the Desana concept of the *Doppelgänger*, see Reichel-Dolmatoff 1975:84, 191.
10. The root *ka* has several interrelated meanings: (*a*) undifferentiated origins, legitimate or illegitimate descent, good or evil habits of a people; (*b*) fence, in the sense of a set or a body of norms; for example: *yahu ka*, 'one circle, one party, one association'; *iri ka*, 'that group, that party'; *gahi ka*, 'other group, other people'. The element *ka* is often found in combination with the term *sëriri*, which refers to 'body odour, sympathy, personality', in connection with attractive or repellent pheromonal characteristics. For example, *ka sërigë* means 'descendance of the same pheromonal aspects'; *kaa sëriri*, 'crude, contrary, toxic'; *kaa sëriro*, 'abstract evil, aggressive egoism'. The verb *kaanyári* expresses the interference or dissonance of people with incompatible pheromonal characteristics. The term *ka'i* implies a coherent, organized matter.
11. When a person commits a serious fault, without being conscious of it at the time, but later realizes his offence, one says: *mahsare kaia yuhpë*, 'person him-aware-he', meaning 'he became aware of it, he became conscious of what he had done'. The

term *ka'í* implies the existence of moral awareness.

12. "Like the people of the Summer Institute of Linguistics", said one informant.

13. See Reichel-Dolmatoff 1978b, essay 2 in this book.

14. Other images of the brain are, for example, a pineapple cut in half; the central axis, *sera-goá*, 'pineapple-bone', is the fissure. Another image is that of the fruit of a palm (*Jessenia policarpa*), called *nyumúye*, '*Jessenia*-thing'. The capsule is said to be of hexagonal shape. Similar comparisons are made with peach palm fruits, and some informants said that they represented a *kaë* ventricle, while a cluster of fruits formed a single brain. A 'hill-house' can also be seen as a tourmaline crystal, the intensity of the colours varying from lighter on the top to darker at the bottom. A commentator pointed out that the energy (*bogá*) contained in these prisms produced perceptible sound waves. 'The sounds want to activate something, but we don't know what it is,' he said, and added that this image reminded him of a volcanic eruption he had heard of.

15. The fish in question is called *varí*, *Cichliasoma* spp., called 'Juan Viejo' in the Spanish vernacular. The stork is *Jabiru mycteria*.

16. Column one (left) contains concepts the names of which end in *-ro*, a suffix indicating an abstract sense, while column two (right) terminates in *-ngë*, referring to a two-person relationship. One might say, for example, when referring to side one: *iropëre nomé*, 'after this-woman', which, on side two, corresponds to *gahí turí nomé*, 'other-dimension-woman'. In the same sense one might refer to *iropëre birari*, 'after this (then)-to play'; *gahi turí birarí*, *iropëre bari*, 'after this-to eat', *gahí turí bari*, *iropëre doári*, 'after this-sit'; *gahí turí doári*, etc. The difference between the two 'columns' is of great importance in everyday life because it constitutes a control mechanism of socially and naturally caused illnesses. The key word is *doahári*, derived from *doári*, 'to sit down, to settle down, to establish oneself', and *ariri*, 'to be'. This can be glossed as 'it sits down and establishes itself' and refers to any illness, ill feeling, or malaise caused, for example, by dietary infractions. The pathogenic process is called *doré birari*, from *dore-këri*, 'illness-to have', *doréri*, 'to send, to transmit', *birari*, 'to play, to take a chance'. Illness, *doréri*, is a 'gift'; it is something that has been sent, an the person has become a victim of it because 'he chanced' to fall ill. On the other hand, a woman's periods of 'illness', such as menstruation, morning sickness, pregnancy, childbirth, post-partum malaise, etc., are also designated as *nomé birari*, 'woman-plaything', meaning that she has become a chance victim of her female condition.

17. *Peeri*, 'to hear (physically)'; *peóri*, 'to hear (with the inner ear);' from *peerí*, 'to hear', *oóri*, 'to send a message, to carry a message'. This refers to a kind of extrasensorial communication said to exist between shamans, or between a shaman and his patient or another person; this is called *peeró dohpá*, 'to hear abstract-similar to', that is to say, 'as if one was hearing a voice'. These messages are said to be transmitted by means of mental concentration.

18. During rituals a shaman will constantly encourage people to 'hear' and will call out: *peké*, 'listen', or *pepike*, 'understand and be stirred!' Should a person show no understanding, the shaman might say: *yeerú ariri pepibigë*, '[like] a penis you are-listening feeling not', an expression which means that the person is not really spiritually motivated, but reacts only sensorially. It is understood that there exist several ritual bodily postures in which the participants find it easier to assimilate the shaman's words; for example, *inya doári*, 'to visualise-to sit', *pe doári*, 'to listen-to sit'.

19. The etymology of *gunyáro* is unclear. The following comparisons were suggested by several informants: *gëyaró* is a term referring to a dangerous, conflicting situation; from *gë*, a suffix indicating an abstract sense and found in expressions referring to danger, violence, and death. The term *gëyaró* was translated as 'danger-from-abstract', and was glossed as 'pertaining to an abstract danger'. I venture to say that by this the subconscious is being referred to. Consciousness is *pe mahsíro*; the unconscious (or subconscious) is *inyamahsibéro* or, in shamanic terminology, *gunyáro*.

20. This expression was also glossed as 'to make something visible'.

21. *Gurunyá*, the name of a red pigment prepared from the shrub *Ginonia chica*. In the Amazonian vernacular it is called *carayurú*.

22. On phosphenes and their significance, see, among others, Reichel-Dolmatoff 1978a:43-47.

23. *Mahsari*, 'to become strong, to become conscious of oneself, to realize oneself'; related to *mahsiri*, 'to know', *mahsiro*, 'wisdom'.

24. A commentary adds: '*To be able to fertilize, one must let oneself be fertilized first.*'

25. See Reichel-Dolmatoff 1969, 1978a: 43-47.

26. For illustrations of labyrinthic designs, see Reichel-Dolmatoff 1978a:31, plates X, XIV, XX. The term *penyari*, meaning 'to synthesize, to achieve cohesion', expresses the concept of closed, mandala-like forms.

27. See the mandala comparison in note 26.

28. *Amakuriró*, 'quest, search'; from *amári*, 'to search', *kúriri*, 'to walk, to wander about'.

29. The idea of life as a journey at the end of which one returns to one's beginnings is expressed by the term *bohkahári*, translated here in the sense of *rencontre*. One commentator said: "*To return, after a long while, to the cause of a conflict, is a pleasurable experience.*"

30. One commentary runs: "One uses *gunyári* to reach *gurunyá* which is matter. Hence one returns to *gunyáro*."

31. *Pe mahsiri yiri*, 'to hear-to know-to act', glossed as 'free will'. The contrary would be *inya mahsibiri*, 'to see-to know not'.

32. A commentary runs: "*One can listen without paying attention; one can look without seeing a light. If I find an obstacle on my way – say, a snake – I illuminate it and know that I must not pass. This looking and knowing is what is mean by pesíri, 'to assimilate'. One must have pesiro, from péri, 'to hear', and siári, 'to illuminate'. If you concentrate on your gunyáro, its abstract thoughts will guide you; you need no drugs to do that; drugs increment, but do not create. In the gunyáro, a beautiful sensation is not an illusion.*"

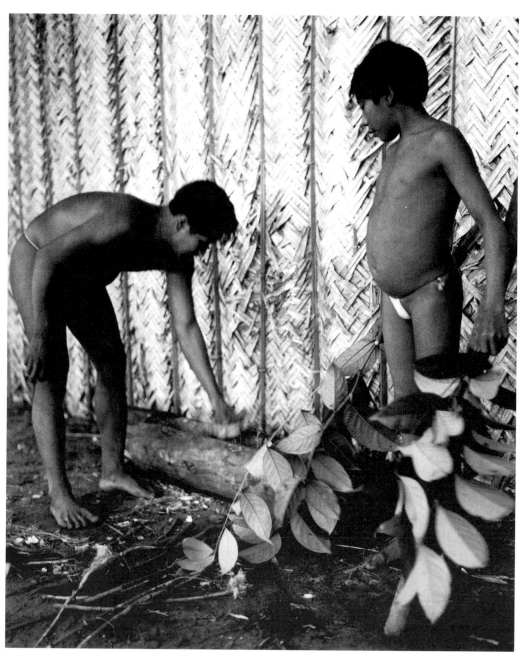

Barasana shaman and a boy clean a wooden trough for *Banisteriopsis* preparation. Ohkoya creek, Pira-paraná

IX

Drug-induced Optical Sensations and their Relationship to Applied Art among some Colombian Indians

The use of narcotic substances, the ingestion of which produces a wide range of altered states of consciousness on the perception-hallucination continuum, is a common feature in many native societies of Colombia. There is archaeological evidence for drug-use in the prehistorical past and the early Spanish sources contain abundant references to the use of narcotics, especially in connection with shamanistic practices. The principal plant sources were – and still are – tobacco (*Nicotiana* spp.), coca (*Erthroxylon coca*), yopo (*Anadenanthera peregrina*), vihó (*Virola* sp.), several species of *Datura*, and the jungle vines of the genus *Banisteriopis*, a malpighiaceous plant with certain photic sensations produced by the chemical components contained in *Banisteriopsis* and with their possible influence upon the origin and significance of certain native art styles.

Banisteriopsis was discovered by the British explorer Richard Spruce, in 1852, when travelling among the Tukano Indians of the Northwest Amazon (Spruce, 1908). The geographic distribution of hallucinogens prepared from *Banisteriopsis* in South America has been traced by Friedberg (1965). In Colombia, these drugs are used by many native groups of the humid tropics where they play an important role in religious rituals, medical practices, or in divination. The vine (and the drug prepared from it) is known under a number of vernacular names: in Colombia, *yajé*, in Peru and Ecuador, *ayahuasca* and in Brazil, *caapi*. The botanical species used by Colombian Indians are mainly *B. caapi*, *B. inebrians*, and *B. rusbyana*. For actual use these drugs are prepared from the bark of the vine, mainly in the form of a beverage or, occasionally, of a finely powdered snuff.

Phytochemical and pharmacological research on the psychotropic substances derived from the Colombian Malpighiacea began over fifty years ago when Fischer (1923) first isolated a crystalline alkaloid from *Banisteriopsis*. In 1928,

Elger showed that this alkaloid was identical to the harmine isolated years earlier from a shrub found in the Near East, *Peganum harmala*, the narcotic properties of which had been known since antiquity. As valid botanic identification became more precise, it was possible to detect the presence of harmine in *B. caapi* (Chen and Chen, 1939) and in *B. inebrians* (O'Connell and Lynn, 1953). Furthermore, Hochstein and Paradies (1957) found other derivatives of the beta-carbolines in stems of *B. caapi* – for example, harmaline and d-tetrahydroharmine (Bristol, 1966, 115-16; Naranjo, 1967, 394; Schultes, 1969, 250). *Banisteriopsis rusbyana* was found to contain large amounts of the hallucinogen N, N-dimethyltryptamine (Agurell, Holmstedt and Lindgren, 1968: Poisson, 1965).

The anthropological, botanical, and pharmacological literature contains descriptions by several authors of the psychotropic effects of the components of *B. caapi* and other species of Malpighiacea (see, among others, Harner 1968, Naranjo, 1965, 1967; Reichel-Dolmatoff, 1972). From these descriptions we learn that the ingestion of an infusion prepared from *Banisteriopsis* causes vertigo, nausea and vomiting, followed by states of euphoria. After a while, colourful images will appear, which may be of sublime beauty but which may also involve great anxiety. Animals – usually felines and reptiles – appear in these visions, sometimes turning into threatening monsters, or one may behold shouting crowds, men brandishing their weapons and other scenes of violence. Sometimes the individual finds himself flying on the winds, visiting far-off places, or communicating with divine beings, dead relatives, or shamans of neighbouring groups.

In the following I shall refer mainly to the Tukano Indians, who use a number of different narcotic substances in order to produce altered states of consciousness on certain occasions. *Banisteriopsis* infusions play an important part in many of their collective rituals, during which the participants claim to have visions of spirit-beings and mythological scenes. However, *Banisteriopsis* is also used by them for purposes of divination and in medical practices. In any case, drug-induced trances and hallucinatory experiences are at the core of many – if not most – native beliefs and are of great consequence in myth and rituals and in many practical affairs of everyday life.

According to the Indians, there exist essentially three stages of *Banisteriopsis* intoxication. Shortly after the ingestion of the drug, after an initial tremor and the sensation of rushing winds, harmaline produces a state of drowsiness during which the person concentrates with half-closed eyes upon the luminous flashes and streaks which appear before him. This first stage is characterised by the appearance of small, star-shaped or flower-shaped elements which flicker and float brilliantly against a dark background, in repetitive kaleidoscopic patterns. There is a marked bilateral symmetry to these luminous perceptions which sometimes appear as clusters of fruits or feathery leaves. Grid patterns, zigzag lines and undulating lines alternate with eye-shaped motifs, many-coloured concen-

An Indian and his son playing pan-pipes in front of stems of *yajé* (*Banisteriopsis*) vines

Above left. A Barasana shaman washes a gourd bowl before a ritual. Ohkoya creek, Pira-paraná Above right. Indians sifting a *Banisteriopsis* infusion through a large basketry sieve

Ritual vessel for *Banisteriopsis* preparation and gourd cups to drink it

A Barasana shaman drawing his visions in the sand

tric circles or endless chains of brilliant dots. The Indians interpret this stage as one of pleasant reveries during which the person watches passively these innumerable scintillating patterns which seem to approach or to retreat, or to change and recombine into a multitude of colourful panels. After a while the symmetry and the overall geometrical aspect of these perceptions disappears and the second stage sets in. Now figurative, pictorial images take shape; large blots of colour will be seen moving like thunderclouds and from them will emerge diffuse shapes looking like people or animals, or unknown creatures. The Indians interpret these images as mythological scenes peopled by spirit-beings, visions which to them bear witness to the essential truth of their religious beliefs. In a third stage, all these images disappear. There will be soft music and wandering clouds, a state of blissful serenity.

While the second stage obviously marks the onset of hallucinations, the first stage is a trance-like state during which the person, while not divorced from reality, visualises elements that appear in external objective space as geometrical patterns, clearly outlined and brilliantly coloured, but which cannot be designated as true hallucinations. The Indians themselves recognise quite clearly that this is not an inner subjective dimension; they call these luminous sensations 'sprigs', 'little flowers', or 'clusters' and consider their sight as a pleasant experience, quite different form the emotion-charged images of the second-stage.

The literature on native hallucinatory content abounds with descriptions of the weird imagery produced by advanced harmaline intoxication. It should be kept in mind here that the sphere of hallucinations is one of subjective interpretations in which the person projects a set of pre-established, stored material upon the wavering screen of shapes and colours. Understandably, the mythical scenes seen by the Tukano during the second stage of the drug experience, can be seen only by members of *their* society. But the repetitive luminous patterns perceived during the first stage of the toxic condition represent neurophysiologically an entirely different aspect of the experience and it is this dimension that is of interest to our inquiry.

While engaged in ethnographic field work among the Tukano Indians, I had asked the men to depict the visual images they perceived while under the influence of *Banisteriopsis*. I offered the men a choice of twelve coloured pencils and some sheets of white paper 28 cm. x 28 cm., mounted on a wooden tablet. They were all adult males who frequently took *Banisteriopsis*; further, all were non-acculturated Indians who did not live in contact with civilisation, none of whom spoke Spanish. The men showed great interest in this task and spent from one to two hours finishing each drawing. For our drawings, they first traced a rectangular frame and then divided the space into convenient quadrants. The colours they selected spontaneously were exclusively red, yellow and blue, on very few occasions adding a shade of hazel brown. There were comments that there was not a good choice of the various tones of the basic colours, since the Tukano dis-

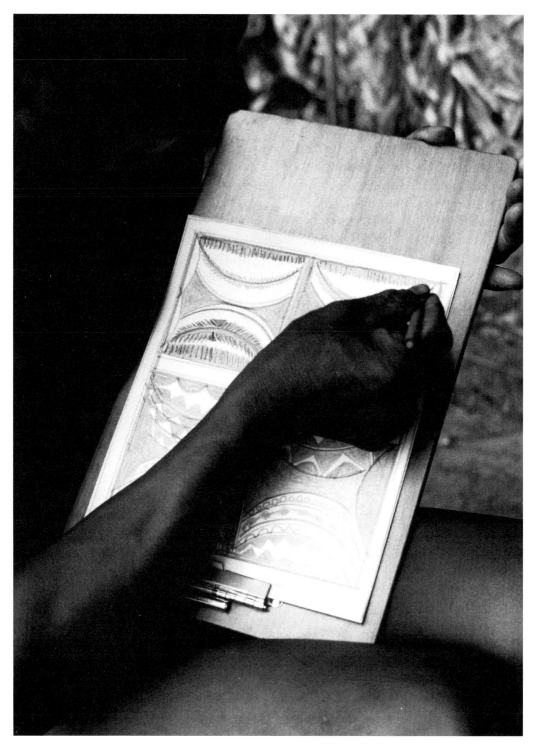

A Barasana Indian drawing his visions

criminate carefully between a number of shades of the same pigment, such as clear yellow, orange yellow, reddish yellow, etc. and evidently would have preferred to execute the drawings in a wider range than allowed by each of the basic colours. When each drawing was completed, I recorded on tape the explanation the artist gave for his work. Sometimes these comments were extremely concise: others were long and detailed explanations.

Once I had obtained a short series of drawings it became clear that some of them represented the stage of repetitive geometrical patterns, while others depicted the stage of figurative imagery seen during hallucination. The Indians themselves readily pointed out this difference. But, more important still, I noticed that the drawings – mainly those of the first category – consistently repeated certain design motifs. The elements were rarely exactly the same, but each motif had in common a certain basic shape: a zigzag line, a triangle, a circle, a U-shaped element, and others. There were variations in size, colour, or elaboration, but the essential outline was the same within each motif and could easily be recognised. They could be drawn in a single, a double, or a triple line; in one, two, or three colours, with little appendages or other secondary additions; but the basic shape was the same.

I now proceeded to isolate these design motifs by drawing each of them on a numbered card and showing these around, soliciting comments. It soon became clear that the drawings contained individual variations of some twenty well-defined design motifs. As a matter of fact, it seemed that different people, men belonging to different age-groups, occupying different social positions, and representing different personality types, all perceived basically the same geometrical patterns during the first stage of *Banisteriopsis* intoxication. This observation brought to mind the possibility of an underlying biological basis, that is, of the question whether similar brain stimuli would produce similar optical sensations in different people.

The fleeting perception by the human eye, of specks, stars, or irregular patterns, is a common phenomenon known by the name of *phosphenes*. Phosphenes are subjective images, independent of an external light source, and are the result of the self-illumination of the visual sense (Oster, 1970). As they originate within the eye and the brain, they are common to all people. Occasionally, phosphenes can appear quite spontaneously, especially when the person has been deprived for a certain time of visual stimuli, such as would be the case in prolonged darkness or when exposed to extremely unvaried sights such as a cloudless sky, the sea, or rain in open country. They can also be produced by external stimuli: pressure on the eyeballs, a sudden shock, or by looking into the darkness when waking up at night. In all these cases the eye may perceive photic sensations which vary from tiny dots to intricate moiré patterns, and from fan-shaped rays to glowing circles, all in different shades, generally blue, green, orange, and yellow.

Moreover, phosphenes can be induced by a number of chemical agents.

Hallucinogenic drugs such as LSD, psilocybin, mescaline, bufotein and harmaline are known to produce phosphenes of abstract design motifs, and frequently the after-images can be observed for several months after the initial experience.

Laboratory experiments carried out by Max Knoll (Oster, 1970), who induced phosphenes in more than 1,000 people, gave the following results: when applying low voltage square-wave pulses to the temples, pulses in the same frequency as brain waves produced luminous sensations in the visual field of the subjects and about half of them perceived geometric design motifs. The patterns of these designs changed whenever the frequency of the pulses varied and it became possible to group these motifs into fifteen categories.

A cursory comparison between Knoll's categories of fifteen universal phosphenes and the twenty design motifs isolated from the Tukano drawings shows the following correspondences:

TABLE 1

TUKANO NO.	KNOLL NO.
1	13
2	9
6	3
7	9
8-9	12
10	10
11	15
13	7
14	1
15	2
17	3
18	4

Moreover, Knoll's numbers 5, 8, 11 and 14 are found in numerous drawings. These correspondences are too close to be mere coincidences; they seem to demonstrate that the geometrical patterns perceived by the Indians under the influence of *Banisteriopsis* are phosphenes comparable to those isolated by Max Knoll (Fig. 1).

I have mentioned before that I had asked the men for comments on the complete drawings and especially on the individual design elements. In the majority of cases their interpretations coincided and I was led to conclude that these phosphene-based motifs were codified, each having the fixed value of an ideographic sign. At the same time I observed that the interpretation of these signs often made reference to aspects of sexual physiology and, in direct relation to this, to the tribal laws of exogamy.

Taken one by one, the native interpretation of the Tukano design elements appears as follows:

KNOLL

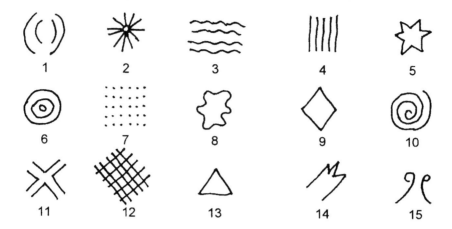

TUKANO

Figure 1. Phosphene patterns

1. Male organ	8. Group of phratries	15. Sun
2. Female organ	9. Line of descent	16. Plant growth
3. Fertilised uterus	10. Incest	17. Thought
4. Uterus as 'passage'	11. Exogamy	18. Stool
5. Drops of semen	12. Ritual box	19. Rattle
6. Mythical canoe	13. Milky Way	20. Cigar holder
7. Exogamic phratry	14. Rainbow	

This is not the place to go into the details of Tukano symbolism. Suffice it to say that the sun, the Milky Way, the rainbow, etc. are all connected with native concepts of procreation and fertility, and with the details of marriage rules.

The interpretation given to the design motifs revolves almost entirely around the problem of incest, a problem which is all-pervading in the native culture, and the message transmitted by the code insists on the observance of the laws of exogamy. The important point, however is that the code is extended beyond the narrow confines of individual trance and is applied to the wider physical environment of everyday life. In fact, the designs and patterns perceived under the influence of *Banisteriopsis* are transplanted to the concrete objects of material culture where they come to constitute an art form. Practically all decorative elements that adorn the objects manufactured by the Tukano are said by them to be derived from the photic sensations perceived under the influence of the drug; that is, are based on phosphenes. A closer look at the applied art of the Tukano is most revealing.

The most outstanding examples are the paintings executed on the front part of the longhouses. The walls, made of large pieces of flattened bark, are covered wholly or in part with bold designs painted with mineral colours – occasionally with the admixture of vegetable dyes – and represent the same geometric motifs I have discussed above. Sometimes they are combined with figurative designs of people and animals. When asked about these paintings the Indians simply reply, 'This is what we see when we drink *Banisteriopsis*'.

Further examples are numerous. The bark-cloth aprons used during ritual occasions are painted with phosphene patterns and among some Tukano groups that manufacture bark-cloth masks these, too, exhibit the same designs. One apron shows the sign for exogamy painted prominently over the genital region while others are adorned with the sun, the rainbow, or other designs. The large stamping tubes which the Tukano use to accompany their dances are covered with similar designs showing zigzag lines, rhombs and rows of dots. The gourd rattles are sometimes covered with phosphene patterns. The large drums that were formerly in use were painted with these designs and occasionally a modern beer trough will be adorned with similar patterns. At present the Tukano have almost abandoned the manufacture of pottery, at least of small vessels that are likely to be decorated. The older people assured me that formerly many pottery

A longhouse (*maloca*) with its walls painted with designs based on hallucinations under the influence of *yajé* (*Banisteriopsis*). Pira-paraná river

vessels were decorated with phosphene patterns and even now one can occasionally find a small vessel adorned with these design motifs. The ritual vessel in which the narcotic beverage is prepared is always adorned with painted designs, generally in red, yellow and white, showing wavy lines, rows of dots, or a series of rainbow-shaped patterns. On some of these ritual vessels the U-shaped design of the uterine 'passage' is painted on the foot of the container.

It is important to point out here that the after-images of phosphenes can repeat themselves for up to six months. Within this time span it is very probable in our case that the person will have taken part in one or more Banisteriopsis sessions, or that he has consumed another narcotic drug, so that the after-images are likely to persist in a latent, chronic state, appearing in the visual field at any instant when they are triggered off by a change in body chemistry or an external stimulus. As these after images might appear superimposed on the normal vision of the individual and in plain daylight, the particular spectrum of phosphenes, together with their cultural interpretations, can be said to accompany the person in a permanent manner. That phosphenes and their after-images are occasionally being reinforced, brought into focus or, perhaps, triggered off by normal visual

Detail of a longhouse wall painted with designs based on hallucinations under the influence of *yagé* (*Banisteriopsis*)

perception, is also quite possible. It has been proved experimentally (Oster, 1970) that, when flickering, shapeless phosphenes are combined with normal visual perception, the phosphenes begin to take a more definite form.

The physical environment during a *Banisteriopsis* session provides many models or stimuli which are almost permanently before the eyes of the individual as, for example, the very symmetrically interwoven leaves of the thatched roof and of the walls of the long-house, basketry trays, feather head-dresses and other ornaments. There are probably other stimuli present, many of which seem to be well recognised as such by the Indians. The intense red light of a torch used during *Banisteriopsis* rituals seems to be an important factor in the production of phosphenes and, eventually, of true hallucinations. Obviously, the Indians practise various non-drug techniques in order to produce endogenously certain altered states of consciousness.

In summarising, with the exception of a few more or less realistic designs of animals or houses, the entire art style of the Tukano can be said to be based on drug-induced phosphenes. Most of the elements that compose this art style carry a message: exogamy, and everywhere, especially on ritual occasions, the individ-

Bark loincloth with red paint patterns

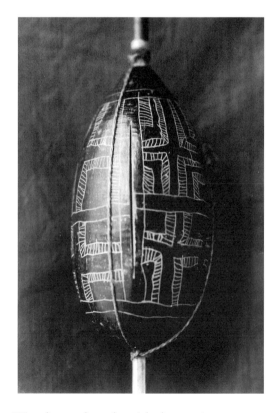

Ritual gourd rattle with decorative patterns

Shamanic wooden stools with painted seats

Basketry tray

ual is reminded of the law of exogamy, expressed by these visual metaphors which adorn utensils, or which are ever-present in the spectrum of his phosphenes.

Motifs such as rainbows, stars, circles or bright dots, undulating lines or multicoloured stripes, all figure in a wide range of sensations perceived during the initial or advanced stages of intoxication by *Banisteriopsis* and other drugs as well. Paintings and drawings executed by individuals of our culture under the influence of LSD, mescaline, peyote and other drugs, or when attempting to fix the visions after the primary effect has worn off, frequently have common characteristics. It would be difficult to attribute this commonality solely to the cultural experience shared by these artists. On the one hand it is true that when the Indians interpret their visions, certain projective and feedback processes are at work, as well as earlier cultural experiences; they are therefore influenced by their visual and circumstantial memory and by the models that appear in their physical environment. But on the other hand, there exists an element of rhythm, of pulsation in the imagery of *Banisteriopsis* intoxication, that seems more likely to be organically based than determined *only* by a visual and culturally moulded memory.

More than a thousand kilometres to the north-west of the Tukano territory, in the Pacific lowlands of Colombia, the Choco Indians have developed an art style which, in many ways, is similar to the one associated with the Tukano. Although both groups are inhabitants of the humid tropical forests, they vary widely in their cultural characteristics. In the case of the Choco, colourful geometrical designs are painted on all ritual objects, most of which are manufactured of wood. Again, the designs have a distinct phosphene character and it is hardly a coincidence that the Choco Indians, too, use *Banisteriopsis* infusions for their religious purposes (Reichel-Dolmatoff, 1960). It may be added here that those Colombian Indians who apparently do not use *Banisteriopsis*, cannot be said to have a readily recognisable art style.

It would not be difficult to find parallels to phosphene-derived design motifs in prehistoric artifacts, such as the decoration of ceramics, or petroglyphs and pictographs. The pottery of a prehistoric burial cave in northern Colombia, associated with snuff tablets and bone containers suggesting the use of narcotic snuff, is decorated with designs clearly comparable to the Knoll-Tukano series (Reichel-Dolmatoff, 1949).

Could archaeology lead us then to a zoning of these symbolic systems? If we suppose that the use of hallucinogens by the American aborigines is a very ancient practice, and that in general it is related to the religious sphere, we may also assume that ceremonial objects were manufactured and decorated by specialists, or at least by persons who were thoroughly immersed in the religious symbolism of their culture. But can we then speak of 'decoration' in an aesthetic sense? And would this not put into doubt the value of many cross-cultural similarities?

The assessment of the possible relationship between drug-induced phosphenes and applied art in native societies is far beyond the competence of the field ethnologist. Only interdisciplinary research, with the participation of specialists in the neurosciences, of biochemists, pharmacologists, botanists and psychologists, can show us the way through this borderline area, and help us avoid its pitfalls, or provide us with new insights.

Addendum

Between the writing of this article and its appearance in print the topic here treated has been discussed in various publications. The author wishes to draw special attention to the following book: Joseph Eichmeier and Oskar Höfer, *Endogene Bildmuster*, Munich-Berlin-Vienna, 1974. This work contains a detailed study of neurophysiological phenomena and discusses the relationship of phosphenes to primitive and modern art.

Petroglyphs on a boulder near some rapids

X

ASTRONOMICAL MODELS OF SOCIAL BEHAVIOUR AMONG SOME INDIANS OF COLOMBIA

Among many native tribes of Colombia, the tropical night sky and the cyclic motions of celestial bodies constitute models for certain forms of human behaviour. The sky is seen as an enormous blueprint of everything that did, does, or will happen on the earth; an enormous map replete with information on every aspect of biological and cultural behaviour, time, space, evolution, and psychological phenomena; in sum, an encyclopedic body of what one might call 'survival information', the knowledge of which alone can give Man a measure of security.

The most obvious aspect is time, cyclic time. In Colombia, the yearly seasonal round is divided into four ninety-day periods that coincide with the beginnings and the ends of the two rainy and two dry seasons. Observation of the sun therefore becomes important for the management of natural resources. By this I refer not only to agriculture, but also to seasonal events, such as fish runs, bird migrations, the rutting and breeding seasons of different game animals, the various fruiting seasons of trees, and the cyclic availability of edible insects or molluscs, of honey, and of many other food resources. The precise prediction of the onset, progress, and end of each season is important not only to the horticulturalists, but also to the hunter and gatherer, to the prospective traveller, to the canoe builder, and to any group of people who intend to build a house.[1] Cyclic time, then, is observed by the natives on a scale that extends from hourly changes of phsyiological and psychological functioning and environmental changes in light, temperature, humidity, and so on, to changes in circadian rhythms, to monthly, seasonal, and yearly cycles, and, beyond that, even to the observation of equinoctical precession. Upon these cyclic phenomena of the heavens and of nature, the Indians project cycles of specific cultural relevance, such as the menstruation cycle, the cycle of embryonic development, the human life cycle, psychological developments, plant growth, and any number of other recurring events, as recognized by the natives.

Another aspect is space. Those facets of heavenly space that are of immediate importance to the Indians refer either to stable relationships, such as the outlines of certain constellations or to dynamic relationships, such as those that exist between celestial bodies.[2] This refers mainly to the changing relationships between the sun, the moon, and the larger planets and to the changing position of the Milky Way. These fixed spaces and fixed orbits are very important to the Indians, who see in them a set of principles of order, of organization. For the same reason, any dissonance in this heavenly harmony is thought to be harmful. Eclipses, comets, meteorites, shooting stars, tektites, and planetary conjunctions are greatly feared, because they are thought to mirror calamitous conditions that exist somewhere on this earth. Dissonances do not predict coming events; instead, they point to malfunctionings that are actually taking place in human society or in nature. The observation of these celestial dysfunctions is thus a diagnostic procedure, not a prognostic one. Native astronomy is not much concerned with astrological prediction, but with learning to read the sky, which mirrors this world; the sky must be scrutinized in every detail because it is a map and a mirror of nature. What counts is the correct reading, because the sky is not only an ecological blueprint for Man's tenancy of this earth, but also a guide to spiritual development and moral integration.

* * * *

In the following I shall refer to three aboriginal cultures of Colombia: first, the Desana, from the Vaupés Territory;[3] second, the Kogi Indians of the Sierra Nevada de Santa Marta, in northern Colombia, at about 11° north;[4] and, third, the Muiska Indians of the Andean Highlands.[5] The Desana and Kogi still number several thousands; the Muiska have disappeared and have become assimilated into the rural mestizo population, so that information on them is derived from archaeological remains and from the accounts of the early Spanish chroniclers.

I shall speak mainly of the equatorial Desana and their neighbours, and only briefly refer to the other tribes, to point out some similarities or differences. In Desana origin myths a frequent motif is the 'search for the centre', the 'Centre of the Day', as the Indians call it. In brief, the story is this: A supernatural hero who carries a staff goes in search of a spot where his staff, when standing upright, will not cast a shadow. He eventually locates this spot on the equatorial line, and it is there where he subsequently establishes his people. In one of many shamanic images, the staff is said to be a shaft of sunlight, which, falling vertically into a womb-like lake, fertilizes the earth. This idea of the 'central point' is all-important to the Indians; it is, in essence, a spot where a cosmic sexual contact takes place, a meeting between Sky and Earth, and life on this earth subsequently develops in a bounded space that extends around this centre.

The model for this bounded space is perceived in the sky. It consists of the huge hexagon formed by the stars Pollux, Procyon, Canopus, Achernar, T3 Eridani, and Capella. The centre of this hexagon is said to be Epsilon Orionis, that is, the central star in Orion's belt.

Now, among the Desana and other Colombian Indians, hexagonal shapes and outlines constitute fundamental ordering principles.[6] These recurring shapes are observed, for example, in the hexagonal structure of rock crystals, which are common shamanistic power objects; they can be seen in honeycombs and wasp's nests, and in the hexagonal plates on the back of a tortoise shell. In the shamanist world-view, all these hexagonal shapes are said to be imbued with transformative energies, and in this manner, all places, spots, and objects where a transformation is said to take place are imagined as hexagons, or as hexagonal containers. Thus, in shamanist imagery, the female womb is seen as a hexagonal body; the human brain is seen as a hexagon divided into innumerable hexagonal ventricles; and the structure of a house is imagined as a hexagon. All these hexagonal shapes symbolize continuity by transformation; they symbolize an eternally recurrent natural model that, by its unchanging persistence, expresses a sense of world order.

I have said that the model of bounded terrestrial space is seen in the sky, in the great hexagon of a number of bright stars centred upon Epsilon Orionis. Now, this celestial hexagon is projected upon the earth, where it delimits the tribal territories of the Tukanoan Indians. The image is that of an enormous transparent rock crystal standing upright, the six corners of which are the six stars I have mentioned, while, on earth, the corners are formed by six major waterfalls located on certain rivers (Figure 1). The centre, the axis of this crystal tower, is a vertical line between Epsilon Orionis and a large boulder covered with petroglyphs, located approximately at the spot where the equatorial line crosses a north-to-south flowing river.[7] In other words, the crystal axis is the phallic staff that joins the male sky to the female earth. Within this terrestrial hexagon all major celestial phenomena have their counterparts and mirror images. For example, the Vaupés river corresponds to the Milky Way; certain landmarks, such as isolated hills, lakes, or large rocks, are associated with stars or constellations, and Orion's belt is centred upon the equator, in an east-west direction.

According to the Desana and their neighbours, the twenty or so Tukanoan tribes are, ideally, grouped into six phratries, each one consisting of three exogamous tribes. Since each tribe consists of males and their virilocal by residing spouses, a phratry can be said to consist of six units. This phratric, tribal, and sexual division is imaged as a series of interrelated, adjoining hexagons. The great celestial hexagon that is projected upon the land is divided into six hexagons representing phratries; each phratry is divided into six triangles, that is, three so-called "male" and three "female" ones (Figure 2). Although, at present, this territorial division does not correspond to a social and geographical reality,

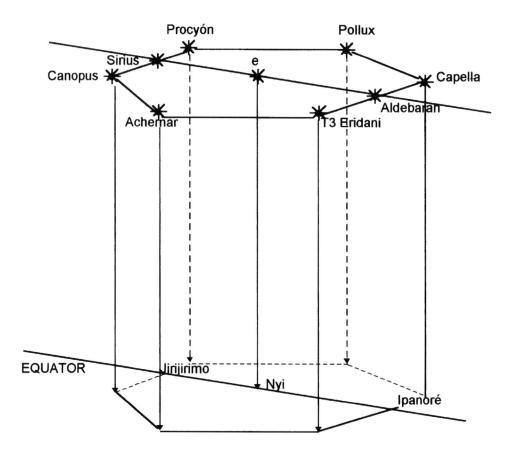

Figure 1. The hexagonal prism between sky and earth. The falls of Ipanoré are the point of origin of the tribe; the Jirijirimo falls are the largest in the entire territory; the other points correspond to minor falls. The centre is the rock of Nyi, a large boulder covered with petroglyphs, located at the spot where the Pira-paraná crosses the equatorial line.

it continues to be an important shamanistic model, the true origin of which is seen in the sky, and the dynamics of which constitute a body of complex esoteric lore.

A basic principle of Tukanoan social organization is exogamy. Incest laws are very strict and their origins are elaborated in many myths and shamanistic texts. As is often the case in these tribal societies, there is some overlapping of different situations, such as father/daughter incest, mother/son incest, sibling incest, or plain adultery. The human actors in these dramatic situations are personified in the sky, where Sun is either Moon's husband, father, or brother, while Venus is a daughter of Sun or a son of Moon. The precise identification may vary from tribe to tribe, but the essential interpretation is the same: The incestuous (or adulter-

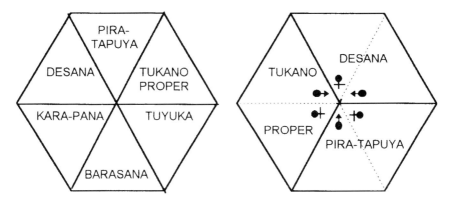

Figure 2. The hexagon as territorial unit and social model. Left: The Vaupés territory and the ideal distribution of the six original Tukanoan tribes. Right: The ideal distribution of a phratry of three intermarrying tribes.

ous) male is castrated and his penis is thrown up into the sky where it turns into Orion's belt. Sometimes the castrated man is a father figure, at other times he is the son who is being punished by the father; in any case, the victim acquires the proportions of a hero.[8]

In Desana shamanist imagery, Orion is the Master of Animals, a supernatural gamekeeper. He is a mighty hunter who can be seen walking over the sky, over the Milky Way, which is his trail, carrying a game animal, a string of fish, or a basket of fruits, thus announcing the different harvesting seasons.

* * * *

In what I have said so far, I have referred to a number of symbolic equivalences, and before I can continue I must clarify some of these concepts. In Tukanoan ideology, a symbolic or metaphorical relationship is never limited to a one-to-one comparison; symbolic images are always seen as chains of analogies. For example, the Milky Way can be conceptualized as a river, as a trail in the forest, as an immense cortège of people, a cast-off snake skin, a fertilizing stream of semen, and so on. In the same way, the celestial hexagon can be seen as a rock crystal, a tortoise shell, a honeycomb, a womb, a brain, a ritual enclosure, a tribal territory, a fish trap, and so forth. The entire concept of transformation is thus based upon likeness, not identity. Astronomical interpretations are thus always based on multiple chains of analogies, never on one single image.

To continue—I have spoken here of the astronomical models of tribal territories and social organization and I have touched upon the problem of marriage rules. I now must add some observations on native concepts of fertility and growth in relation to astronomy.

According to the Indians, the energy of the universe is generated by the sun.

The sun, too, is imagined as a rock crystal that is said to contain an unlimited amount of what the Indians call 'colour energies'. The principal colour energies have a male fertilizing power. The moon, on the other hand, contains a female principle of colour energies related to plant growth and the human menstrual cycle. Now, solstices and equinoxes are of relatively little importance on the equatorial line, so the Sun's cycle is not measured through them, but is taken to be a continuous, perennial force. However, lunar phases and positions in relation to earth and sun are closely observed and are thought to be correlated with female fertility and, in general, with the growth cycles of animals and plants. Most interestingly, the different lunar phases constitute a calendar for birth control, for game protection, and for the restriction of the production of many materials. In fact, every month, during the sixteen or so days between the first and third quarters, sexual intercourse is prohibited, as are hunting, fishing, and the gathering of raw materials for such things as basketry, wood carving, and pottery making. Shamans recommend instead agricultural labour and gathering activities, mainly of insects and larvae. Of course, these prohibitions are not too severe but, since they are reinforced by shamanist threats of impending illness, they do constitute an effective mechanism of control. The lunar calendar, then, is essentially a guide to the protection of natural resources and a means of population control.

In order to explain the reasons why the first and third quarters of the moon's phases occupy this important position, I must refer to another cyclic phenomenon. The Milky Way is imagined as two huge snakes; the starry, luminous part is a rainbow boa, a male principle, and the dark part an anaconda, a female principle. The cycle of fertilizing forces emanating from the sky is punctuated by the shifting of the Milky Way, which is seen as a swinging motion made by the snakes. Now, in ordinary nature, anacondas and boas are said to copulate at two periods of the year, approximately at the vernal and autumnal equinoxes. Late in March and again in September anacondas swim upriver at night and, now and then, lift about one-third of their bodies out of the water and then slap down with a loud splashing sound. This is part of their mating behaviour, but the Indians say that, when the snakes rise out of the water, they watch the stars in order to ascertain the proper time. At these times of the year, and during the nightly shifting of the Milky Way, the Indians transfer the image of the two snakes to that of the intersecting of the ecliptic and the celestial equator, and to the intersections of the path of the moon and the path of the earth, at the first and third quarters. In everyday nature the two equinoctial dates are associated with periods of fertility; by the end of March and the end of September the spawning seasons of fish are beginning and these fish runs provide the model for sib distribution along the rivers, for patterns of reciprocal food exchanges, and for ritual dances in which spawning behaviour is equated with human procreation. This, too, is the harvesting season for many wild fruits, and it is the proper

Güio (snake)

time for male initiation rituals.

The image of the intertwining snakes, that is, of two bent, snake-like bodies that intersect at two points – ◊ – is an important shamanistic icon.[9] It is thought that two snakes lie in the fissure between the two hemispheres of the human brain, and that their rhythmically shifting motion determines the relationship between the unconscious and the conscious in what concerns sex, food, and aggression. Now, this image of the human brain is patterned after the shamanist image of the entire celestial vault as one gigantic brain divided by the great fissure of the Milky Way. The Desana believe that both brains, the cosmic and the human, pulsate in synchrony with the rhythm of the human heartbeat, linking Man inextricably to the Cosmos.

* * * *

I must return once more to the hexagonal pattern. The great hexagon in the sky is also an architectural model, and traditional longhouses are built according to this celestial plan. The houses are large structures contained within six points of reference marked by strong houseposts that are identified with stars (Figure 3). The middle section of the roof is supported by another set of six strong vertical posts that delimit a hexagonal central part that has ritual functions.[10] An imaginary line drawn at a right angle to the longitudinal axis of the house divides both the outer and the inner hexagon into two halves and represents the equatorial line. At the same time, it represents the Orion's belt, Zeta and Delta being the middle houseposts, while Epsilon is not visibly marked but coincides with the true centre of the hexagon and the house. But this is not all: The basic outline of the structure delimited by the inner hexagon can be perceived, in a very schematic way, as a longitudinal ridgepole and three parallel cross-beams.[11] The Desana see in this the constellation of Orion and, in one shamanistic image, it is a rack upon which the hero is crucified. In this outline, Betelgeuse and Bellatrix are the summer solstice points, Saiph and Rigel are the winter solstice points, and the belt is called the "Path of the Sun". It is at the centre, on Epsilon Orionis,

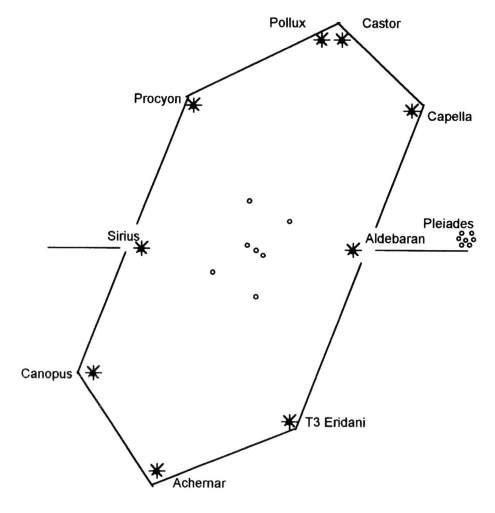

Figure 3. The longhouses as an astronomical model; Achernar marks the men's door and Gemini (Castor & Pollux) mark the women's door.

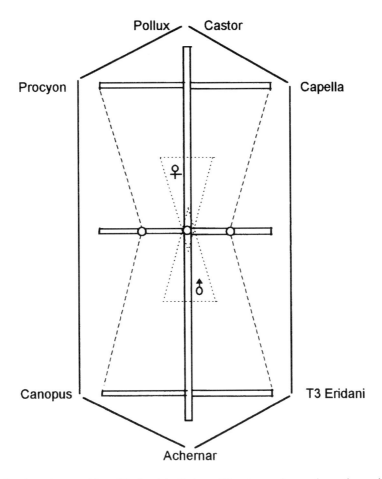

Figure 4. The longhouse identified with Orion. The inner hourglass-shaped outline marks the overlapping male/female dance pattern. The diamond centred upon Epsilon Orionis represents a vagina.

where, on ritual occasions – at the two equinoctial dates – heaps of palm fruits are deposited. In this case, the clusters of fruits are identified with the Pleiades, which rise after sunset in the east late in September and set before sunrise late in March, in both cases announcing the onset of the principal fruiting seasons, the fish runs, and the proper time for initiation rituals.

Within the inner hexagon of a longhouse the Indians perform ritual dances related to the multiple symbolism of Orion. Men and women dance in the centre, between the six main posts. They dance back and forth, each group representing a 'triangle' and this interpenetration of male and female triangles will trace the hourglass-shaped outline of Orion (Figure 4). The dancers move back and forth over the dividing line, which is Orion's belt. Now, the front part of a longhouse represents an abstract dimension where shamans and chiefs have their seats, while the back part represents ordinary reality, the domain of women, children, servants, and food preparation. The pattern of Orion thus forms an area of articulation between male and female, light and darkness, fertility and restraint.

Obviously, the most important constellation is Orion. Orion is Man: Man the Progenitor, the Hero, the Hunter, the Sinner and, finally, the Victim. But every year he rises anew and, when people see him resurrected in the sky, shamans remind them of everything this constellation stands for. In some images, Orion is a rack upon which the adulterer has been put; in other images, Orion is a tapir hide stretched out to dry between six stakes; or a potstand, or a fish trap. Orion's belt is the severed penis of the incestuous youth, or the castrated father; in another image, the belt is the adze used to extracting starch from split palm trunks, a phallic instrument that is the main attribute of the Master of Animals. In still another image, the constellation is seen as an evil shaman turned jaguar who had his penis (or tongue) cut off and was hung from a tree and burned; he disappeared in a cloud of smoke and then reappeared in the sky as Orion. Some shamans see in Orion a jaguar copulating with his sister, a huge snake. And, according to the imagery involved, the Great Orion Nebula becomes a stream of semen, a heap of palm starch, or a cluster of fruits.[12]

What really matters is that this ambivalence of Orion does not offer a simplistic, polarized choice between conventional concepts of Good and Evil, but that it presents the intelligent and searching beholder with a guide to self-knowledge and subsequent adaptive behaviour. I shall attempt to reduce a large body of related shamanist concepts to its basic propositions in order to elaborate upon this point.

Among the Desana, all mental and psychological processes are believed to arise in the left cerebral hemisphere, which is said to harbour the unconscious, and where latent ideas must be activated by shamanistic procedures; the induction of altered states of consciousness is essential in this case. Once identified and isolated, an idea must be transformed into an image, an icon. This process of increasing awareness is achieved in the right cerebral hemisphere, while the act of transformation takes place in the great fissure, which, as I mentioned before, contains the two rhythmically twisting snakes. Once the idea has become transformed into an icon, that is, into a culturally coded sign, it can be expressed by action. Now, the three steps of this mental process are represented by Orion: The left cerebral hemisphere is Zeta Orionis, the point of transformation is Epsilon, and the right hemisphere is Delta Orionis.

I have gone into these shamanistic details because I want to make this point: It would be very mistaken to think that the astronomical thinking of these Amazonian Indians refers only to practical affairs of resource management and to the modelling of social organization. Far from it. Shamans are quite explicit about the importance of the philosophical dimensions that capture the mind when contemplating the sky, and will insist that the celestial vault is the one and only model for Man's material and spiritual well-being. Let me give you one more example: The six straight lines of the celestial hexagon that encompass sacred space, both in the sky and on the earth, represent an important metaphysical model, a moral proposition called 'the Path, the Way', which the individual must travel in his or her life. In Desana theology the idea of the Quest is very elaborate; it corresponds to a process of individuation, under shamanistic guidance. The starting point for the Quest, for both sexes, is Aldebaran (and, by extension, the Pleiades); this is the place of birth. Thence, men proceed in a counterclockwise direction to Capella, which marks the ritual of naming; from Capella he proceeds to Pollux, where initiation takes place; from there he goes on to Sirius the star of marriage, and then he turns sharply toward the east and arrives at the centre. This is Epsilon Orionis, the star of procreation, of multiplication, of fatherhood. The last stretch continues toward the east and ends at Aldebaran, now designated as the point of death, of rebirth, and of return. Women travel first in the opposite direction and then, after their marriage at Sirius, they proceed jointly with their husbands. The entire trajectory, a spiritual pilgrimage, divides the human life span into three periods: youth, from Aldebaran to Sirius; maturity, from Sirius to Epsilon Orionis, and old age, from there back to Aldebaran. In shamanistic imagery these three parts of the life span are marked off by the two intersections of the snakes.

Before turning briefly to other tribal cultures of Colombia, I should like to add one more point. In Northwest Amazonian shamanistic thinking there exists a close relationship between astronomical observations, cosmological speculations, and drug-induced trance states. This gives a very peculiar stamp to native astronomy. Under the influence of a narcotic drug an Indian would imagine himself to be flying through space, ever deeper into unknown dimensions. He would believe himself to be moving among dazzling stars, turning sun wheels, and flashing beams of many-coloured lights. At the same time, shamans will point out that the narcotic experience is not as one-directional ecstasy, but an inner voyage that also leads into the many layered dimensions of the human mind. The human brain, shamans say, is modelled after the celestial vault and the human mind functions according to the stars, which are the ventricles and sensoria of the cosmic brain. Drug-induced trance states develop in a dimension where ordinary concepts of space and time are cancelled out; in fact, narcotic drugs are expressly said to constitute a mechanism for modifying space and time and to be a means for exploring other cosmic dimensions where hitherto unknown models for human faculties might be discovered. In using drug experiences, together with the behavioural models encoded in them, as a key to interpret celestial phenomena, shamans can operate with a very convincing mechanism, because all Indians who consume drugs under shamanistic guidance are likely to have similar sensations and experiences.

* * * *

I shall briefly refer to the Kogi Indians of the Sierra Nevada. Kogi culture is very different from that of the Amazonian rainforest Indians, and Kogi religion, philosophy, and historical traditions are of a complexity that can be compared only to that of the High Cultures of Mesoamerica. Although, at present, the Kogi form a scattered peasant population, there still exist lordly and priestly lineages with a strong sense of privilege and rank. The Kogi are agriculturalists; hunting and fishing are practically non-existent.

Kogi astronomical knowledge is based upon the observation of rising and setting points on the horizon and on zenithal observation. A small hole in the conical temple roof admits a ray of sun or moonlight that, in the case of the sun, traces the outline of solstices and equinoxes in the dark interior. Stone alignments, horizon markers, fixed observation points in the form of priestly stone seats, stone circles, gnomons, and similar stone settings, can be found over much of the Sierra Nevada. Kogi villages, ceremonial centres, isolated temples, shrines, and other structures, are always sited according to astronomical principles.

The entire Sierra Nevada is imagined to have a hexagonal plan and to constitute one huge rock crystal, very much like the Desana image of their world. The corners of this crystal correspond to six sacred sites, while, in the sky, they correspond to six first-magnitude stars; the celestial centre, again, is Epsilon Orionis.[13] In fact, Orion's belt corresponds to the three principal ceremonial centres, which lie in a line, although many kilometres apart, the middle one of which is designated 'the only one'.

Since the Sierra Nevada has an approximately conical shape, with rivers radiating in all directions and valleys opening toward the lowlands and the sea, the entire mountain massif constitutes one huge sundial with which the priest-shamans watch the horizons of their particular valleys. All constructions – shrines, roads, and bridges – conform to celestial sightlines; there is not a single spot of any importance in the Sierra Nevada of which the native priests will not say that it has some astronomical implication.

The sky over the Sierra Nevada is, again, conceived as a map of the land with all its topographical details and its mythical geography, being peopled by divine personifications, animals, artifacts, and all kinds of personified forces of nature. In one very telling image, a Kogi priest is described as sitting in the centre of a dark temple, holding in his hand a mirror facing upward. A vertical ray of sunlight penetrates the roof and falls upon the mirror surface; but this ray of light proceeds from the disk that is the sun's face, and this disk, too, is a mirror. The reflection is, thus, endless, and expresses the Kogi concept of eternity and the dimension of cosmic space.

The astronomical division of the Sierra Nevada implies a division into clan territories and into a number of lineages that are associated with particular celestial phenomena. The most important priestly lineage is the one called the 'Keepers of the Rock Crystal' and the sacred number six is repeated in many contexts. Once again, Sun, Moon, and Venus represent a triangle that holds the potential for drama. Incest and adultery on earth can be seen in the sky in eclipses, conjunctions, or in the unusually close proximity between two or more celestial bodies. Since all these phenomena are models of behaviour on earth that must be followed in detail, ritual incest is practised on certain occasions.

The scheduling of ceremonies is entirely geared to astronomical happenings; the main ritual dances take place at the solstices and equinoxes, each in a different village. The rituals of the life cycle have their specific shrines and temple mountains, identified with constellations or individual stars. Marriages are celebrated at equinoxes, while death rituals take place on solstices. Temple architecture conforms to cosmological and astronomical principles. Although, when seen from the outside, a temple has a circular shape, the interior structure shows a combination of circle, square, and hexagon, which corresponds to sacred spaces that are occupied by particular individuals during ceremonies.

* * * *

Let me finally turn to the highland Muiska, the most advanced culture of prehistoric Colombia. In the early sixteenth century the Muiska formed two incipient states; the ceremonial centre of one was the Temple of the Sun, while the centre of the other was the Temple of the Moon. Both temples were associated with the principal priestly and lordly lineages. The heart-land of the Muiska was formed by a chain of old Pleistocene lake beds that provided fertile soil.[14] It so happens that this chain of flat valley bottoms extends for more than 200 kilometres in a southwest-northeast direction; that is, in the direction of summer solstice sunrise. In other words, by chance of nature, the entire Muiska territory is oriented in this manner, the chiefdom of the Moon Temple being located in the southwestern section, the chiefdom of the Sun Temple occupying the northeast.

Two highland valleys in this territory are known to present a clear, dark, cloudless sky during most of the year.[15] In both valleys one still can observe huge stone columns, alignments, and other stone settings. As observed from one of these structures, the sun rises on summer solstice exactly over a sacred lagoon whence, according to tradition, the Creator Goddess (Bachué) of the Muiska emerged in mythological times.[16] From the same observer's position an alignment of large cylindrical columns runs in an east-west direction.

A constellation of six sacred lakes[17] is located in the central area and is combined with many mountain-tops that constitute astronomical sightlines. In the same region, a pattern of Catholic shrines and pilgrimages continues ancient aboriginal models described by the early chroniclers.

Rock crystals have been found in many shamans' graves, and emeralds, also of hexagonal structure, were important as offerings and in other ritual contexts. The overall similarity of these symbolic interpretations is best illustrated by a Muiska myth recorded at the time of the Spanish conquest. The myth tells that the daughter of a local chieftain was impregnated by the rays of the divine sun at a certain date. She eventually gave birth to a huge emerald. The stone burst open and from it emerged a child who grew up to become a great chief.[18]

* * * *

Among the equatorial Tukanoans there is little interest in a horizon calendar. Zenithal observation is limited to the mythic motif of locating the 'centre', and all other practical astronomical knowledge refers to cyclic seasonal phenomena, the interpretation of constellations, the nature and motions of the Milky Way, and some aspects of astral proxemics. The great model is the hexagonal rock crystal. All these aspects of calendrics and astronomy exist among the Kogi who, in addition, have the following elaborations: a very detailed horizon calendar, zenithal observations, temples as astronomical observatories, associations between astronomy and weaving, record keeping with notched sticks, and pilgrimages and dances according to astronomical patterns. In both cultures, the sky is a map. Among the Kogi there is less emphasis on the relationship between astronomy and hallucinogenic drugs, and more weight is given to precise observation, to sight lines, record keeping, and the details of ritual structures. Many of these features seem to have been present among the ancient Muiska Indians, among whom we find astronomically-oriented architecture, a division into sun- and moon-associated states, a pattern of pilgrimages, the Sun/Moon incest theme, the hexagonal symbolism of mineral structures, and other details.

All three cultures have, thus, a truly fundamental astronomical substructure. This substructure consists not only of a body of practical knowledge used in timekeeping, but contains complex intellectual elaborations conceding time/space relationships, the importance of biological cycles, and many philosophical formulations. In trying to explain forms of cultural behaviour through native astronomy, it is obvious that we must go beyond the utilitarian level of calendars, architecture, astrology, and so forth, and take into account the intellectual and spiritual aspects as conceived by the Indians, which can be found in, e.g., their concepts of cosmogony and the time/space continuum, and their notion of a participatory universe.

Notes

1. I would suggest that certain ring-shaped shell mounds or midden sites of early prehistoric cultures might have been used as horizon calenders.

2. In the shamanistic world-view, the universe is layered. The Desana refer to a sublunary dimension, followed by the spheres of Sun, Moon, and Venus; then comes the Milky Way and beyond that, another, deeper dimension.

3. On the Desana, see the following works by G. Reichel-Dolmatoff: 1971, 1975, 1978a, 1978b, 1979a.

4. On the Kogi, see the following works by G. Reichel-Dolmatoff: 1950-51, 1967a, 1977, 1978c.

5. On the Muiska see, among others, José Pérez de Barradas 1950/51.

6. See G. Reichel-Dolmatoff, 1978b, pp.265-71 (essay 2 in this book), and 1979a (essay 6).

7. The spot is said to be the rock of Nyi on the Pira-paraná river. See G. Reichel-Dolmatoff 1975 pp.155-56, and 1978a pp.138-41.

8. On this particular motif, see R. Lehmann-Nitsche, 1921.

9. Mesoamericanists might recognize in it the Ollin motif.

10. In reality, the six posts form a rectangle, but the space enclosed by them is said to be 'like a hexagon'. There are some indications that, in former times, houses had a circular ground plan that included six main posts forming a hexagon.

11. The three crossbeams are designated 'jaguars'. See G. Reichel-Dolmatoff, 1971 pp.104-10.

12. Obviously, Orion symbolism is closely related to the *yuruparí* initiation ritual, but that is beyond the scope of this paper. On the *yuruparí*, see Stephen Hugh-Jones 1979. Also, G. Reichel-Dolmatoff, 1989 (essay 11 in this book).

13. On the earth, the centre is located at the highest snow peak. This world axis is imagined as a spindle; see G. Reichel-Dolmatoff 1978c.

14. Most of these lakes dried up some 30,000 years ago, but the ancient lake bed and the surrounding land provided the best agricultural soils for the Muiska.

15. These are the valleys of Villa de Leyva and of Ramiriquí, both in the Boyacá district.

16. This observation was made at Saquenzipa, near Villa de Leyva. According to myth, the goddess Bachué rose from the Laguna de Iguaque.

17. These lakes are still in existence.

18. Reference is made to the myth of Goranchacha, the Son of the Sun, as recorded by the Spanish chronicler Fray Pedro Simon in 1882-1892 (see bibliography).

Peach palm (Bactris gasipaes). Vaupés river, near Pacú

XI

BIOLOGICAL AND SOCIAL ASPECTS OF THE YURUPARÍ COMPLEX OF THE COLOMBIAN VAUPÉS TERRITORY

Few themes in South American Indian oral tradition and ethnology have lent themselves to more confusion and misconceptions than the so-called *Yurupari* legend. This widespread body of myths and narratives, said to refer to motifs as extravagant as immaculate maidens, devil worship, and wise lawgivers, has occupied many authors, some of whom have seen in it a lofty contribution to Amerindian oral literature. It seems, however, that much of what has been written on this subject is poorly documented, poorly understood, uncritical, and often pervaded by romantic fancy.

This essay suggests, in the form of an introductory study to a larger treatise, a new approach to the *yurupari* theme as it appears among the Indians of the Colombian Vaupés territory, a region which, according to some, is the point of origin of this cycle. The argument of this essay is concerned with some of the biological and social bases, mechanisms, and objectives of what, so far, has appeared to be mainly a product of aboriginal fantasy.

Author's Note: I want to express my sincere appreciation to the people and institutions who generously gave of their time in discussing and documenting this essay. In Belem do Pará, the Museu Paraense Emilio Goeldi opened its research library to me, and Dr. Anthony Anderson of the Departmento de Botánica kindly helped me with bibliographical sources. In Manaus, Dr. Charles Clement, of the Instituto Nacional de Pesquisas da Amazonia, took me on a guided tour of the palms of the Botanical Garden and provided me with reprints of his palm studies. Dr. Andrew Henderson and Dr. Michael Balick of the New York Botanical Garden patiently answered my queries and sent me their research articles on palms and palm pollination. I also wish to express my sincere gratitude to Dr. Vera Penteado Coelho, of the Museu Paulista, Sao Paulo, for her unfailing help in providing me with Brazilian sources. As always, special thanks to my Indian friends of the Vaupés. Antonio Guzman, of Desana/Pira-Tapuya parentage, and his family and friends were a constant source of valuable information and were especially helpful in the translation and discussion of my recordings.

Preliminary Definitions

The term *yurupari* appears in the early literature on the Amazon basin and has been associated by various authors with the southern Tupi, as well as with the tribes of the general Vaupés-Rio Negro region. This double association has led to some inconsistencies based mainly upon the oversimplifications of contemporary missionaries and travellers who believed they were confronted with a metaphysical principle of evil which, in the southern regions, was named *anhanga* while in the Northwest Amazon its name was *yurupari*. This matter of a supposed Tupi-Vaupés devil kinship has been clarified by some nineteenth-century authors and, lately, by several others.[1] Therefore I shall not concern myself with this discussion which has ceased to be used, not only by missionaries but also in the literature, as if it had a somewhat mysterious, supernatural meaning. The words 'Jurupari et anhanga significant simpliciter diabolum', written in 1648, still echo in the minds of many 'civilized' people one can meet in the Amazon lowlands.

I shall first of all give a concise definition of what I shall refer to in this essay as the Yurupari Complex of the Colombian Vaupés. The Yurupari Complex is, in essence, a patriarchal foundation myth containing a social code which explains and exhorts exogamy. The code is transmitted orally by shamans and elders in a metaphoric, polysemic language, both on formal and informal occasions. It constitutes the basis of male physiological and social puberty initiation rituals during which the novices are taught the historical origins of exogamy, the inconveniences of endogamy, and the basic facts of human reproductive behaviour. These rituals take the form of social isolation followed by the display of certain musical instruments, and the strict observance of the rules of reciprocity accompanied by specific regulations and admonitions referring to hunting, fishing, gathering, food preparation and consumption, sexual activities, and other biological or social functions.

Once the novices have undergone the escalated tests and trials inherent in this initiatory period, they are allowed to partake in the collective exchange rituals which formalize exogamy. The Yurupari Complex centres upon three well-defined parts: (1) an all-male puberty ritual which, in part, is kept secret from women; (2) a fruit-gathering and exchange ritual, usually of palm fruits, during the initial part of which woman are excluded; (3) periodic social/ritual gatherings of two or more exogamic units, the purpose of which is the reaffirmation of alliances and the symbolic or factual exchange of marriage partners. By Colombian Vaupés I refer mainly to the middle course of the Vaupés river, to the Papurí river, and to the Pira-paraná, concentrating chiefly upon the Desana, Pira-Tapuya, Tukano proper,[2] and Barasana. I shall not include in this presentation the Cubeo habitat.

From this definition and the discussion that follows, it will become clear that, at least as far as the Colombian Vaupés territory is concerned, *yurupari* is neither a 'cult' nor a 'religion'; it does not represent a 'culture hero' nor a 'law-giver'; in fact, it is not a personalized concept at all. *Yurupari* is not a 'secret society' nor does it use 'sacred' paraphernalia. *Yurupari* is not a 'legend' except in the fantasy of some romanticists; it is not an 'epic poem' nor can it be compared, by any stretch of the imagination, with the Mayan Popol Vuh, the Germanic Nibelungen Lied, or the Finnish Kalevala.[3]

The ideological foundations of the Yurupari Complex range from myths and tales to teachings transmitted to an all-male audience, and to simple behavioural rules observed at social/ritual gatherings, which are common knowledge and are shared by the majority. The entire body of knowledge, esoteric or profane, includes aspects of a biological, social and psychological nature which constitute cognitive systems in which our Western logic does not operate too well. The interdependence and interpenetration of these and other fields of knowledge constitute, from the Indians' point of view, a coherent whole, indeed, a coherent worldview. The Yurupari Complex is thus an all-embracing cognitive system, a communication system operating through, what we would call, symbols, signs, and metaphors forming clusters and strata of meanings.

The fact that this world-view, like that of many other societies, is composed of widely different experiences, ideas, and wordless messages which, in Western terms, appear to combine, rather arbitrarily, reality with the sphere of imagination makes it necessary to use an eclectic approach in trying to explain and analyze it. In fact, we shall have to consider the relationships between social and biological phenomena apparently as different as exogamy and plant pollination, ritual paraphernalia and limnology, sex and hallucinations. In the course of this analysis I shall not attempt to follow our linear 'logic'; I shall not draw a dividing line between the real and the ideal. I shall use words like metaphor, symbol, transformation, soul, energy, and others simply because I do not find other terms that provide a more satisfactory translation of Indian concepts. All I can do is try to *explain*, on the basis of my knowledge of aboriginal texts and my discussions of them with Indian informants. There will be some moot points, some passages or trains of thought in the elucidation of which I must admit my ignorance, my incapacity to recognize relationships or the relevance of specific details. Moreover, in the course of writing down my thoughts I shall have to follow the categorizations of my own culture and shall speak of myth and ritual, social organization and agriculture, botany and astronomy while warning the reader that these fields of study and knowledge may have a much more inclusive or exclusive meaning to the Indians than they have in Western ratiocination.

Recent Research

In the last decades the *yuruparí* theme, in its aspects of oral tradition, in the Colombian Vaupés, has been the subject of several studies. The first one is Ute Bödiger's (1965) analysis of what she calls 'Tukano religion' while the second study is Jacqueline Bolens's (1967) brief analysis of Bödiger's work. These studies are based exclusively upon published sources. The lack of firsthand field experience and linguistic competence is noticeable and presents severe limitations. A third study, based upon long-term fieldwork and taking into account the ethnological context, is Stephen Hugh-Jones's (1979) structural analysis of ritual and cosmology among the Barasana, a Tukano tribe of the southern part of the Colombian Vaupés; it is altogether a different kind of study the nature and scope of which go far beyond the attempts of Bödiger and Bolens. There does exist a common ground of underlying ideology but the predominant impression, at the present stage of research, is that of a large number of local elaborations, of shifting emphasis, but not of a truly fundamental variability in focalization. It is clear that *yuruparí* research is still in its initial stage; much of it is still unpublished and much more remains to be done, in the field and in the library.[4]

My present study of the Yuruparí Complex is based upon the minutiae of fieldwork and a fair knowledge of the linguistic background. My descriptions and interpretations may differ from those given in the aforementioned studies but in no way diminish the scholarly efforts of my predecessors. A detailed critical reading of recent publications is beyond the scope of the present essay, the sole purpose of which is to offer a concise description of some biological and ethnographic facts not mentioned before, paired with a broader, multidisciplinary vision which I find lacking in the work of my predecessors in the particular field of *yuruparí* research; I am referring here to my use of textual materials, semantic analysis, and ethnobotany.

The Ethnohistorical Background

From the analysis of more than a hundred origin myths I have recorded in the field in their original language, it is possible to reconstruct, in part, the demographic succession in the Colombian Vaupés territory, and to suggest a more or less clearly defined sequence of correlated phases.

Phase 1

Until several centuries ago the Colombian Vaupés territory was inhabited by various aboriginal groups: Arawakan-speaking, sedentary agriculturalists, vaguely referred to as 'Tapir People' by the present-day Desana and many of their neigh-bours; pre-agricultural or incipient agricultural Tukanoans; and a scattered, but not really nomadic, population of Makú-speaking groups of interfluvial hunters and foragers, some of which might have been occasional cultivators. The ques-tion of who were the 'first', autochthonous inhabitants of any given territory is a controversial one in most origin myths. As far as I can judge at present (and I have had to revise my ideas several times) the 'first' people of the Colombian Vaupés were those designated as *yebá mahsá* in many myths. *Yebá* is an Arawakan word meaning 'land', 'earth', and seems to refer to forest-dwelling hunters and foragers. The linguistic relationships are: *kepe* (Guarekena), *jipai* (Kuripáko), *jasipe* (Baniwa) (de Civrieux and Lichy 1950:41). The term for tapir, in Arawakan languages, is *ema* (Baniwa, Guarekena), *emma* (Kuripáko), *tema* (Baré) (ibid.:23), from which the Desana seem to have derived the term *ëmë-kori mahsá*, to designate their ancestors while tapir's name was changed, in Tukanoan languages, to *vehkë*, *behkë*, meaning 'father-in-law' (Reichel-Dolmatoff 1985:111 ff, essay 3 in this book). It would seem, then, that the term *yebá* stands for tapir, pre-agricultural or agricultural, but in any case represent-ing the forest and many of its wild-growing fruits while the so-called Anaconda people, the Pira-Tapuya,[5] represent the river and its fishes and, possibly, manioc cultivation on a more or less advanced scale. In fact, according to some Pira-Tapuya texts the Tukano proper were already established above the confluence of the Rio Negro and the Vaupés but had no agriculture; this was introduced by Pira-Tapuya groups which travelling up the Rio Negro, began to establish exchange relationships with Tapir People or others.

Phase 2

In time, other groups of Tukanoan-speaking hunters and fishermen arrived from the east, ascending the Rio Negro and the Vaupés. At Ipanoré, near the spot where the equatorial line crosses the Rio Negro, many people 'emerged' and it was there where the first *yurupari* rituals were performed. Tukanoan bands were small and were in need of women; their material culture was rather limited but they possessed two items that proved to be of great value to the local population: they had tobacco and a knowledge of hallucinogenic plants. During a *yajé* (*Banisteriopsis* sp.) ritual they tried to establish a formal exchange of women but failed because the local inhabitants insisted upon practising endogamy. According to this particular tradition the mythical name of Ipanoré was *ohpé-duri* or *ohpéniduri*, from *ohpé*/'female breast', ~ *ohpeni*/'breasts', *duri*/'breast-shaped rock formations'; *ohpéni* is also the term for a decorated basketry tray. According to these myths it was at Ipanoré where these trays, symbolizing man-ioc/women/exogamy, were given for the first time by Tapir People to the newly arrived Tukano (Tukano proper, Pira-Tapuya, Desana). Ipanoré is thus designated as 'place of breasts, of exogamy'. In some myths it is said that the Tukano proper were already established at Yavareté where, after having made contact with the Tariana, an Arawakan group, they adopted manioc and, as part of that complex, received decorated basketry trays.

Phase 3

This Tukano penetration which arrived in several successive waves led to conflict with Arawakan Tapir People whose women were being abducted by Tukano raiders. The Makú, however, established friendly contacts with the Tukanoans and locally intermarried with them, both groups sharing in a common hunting/fishing/foraging subsistence economy.

Phase 4

After a period of initial hostilities the Arawak accepted Tukanoan husbands for their daughters but imposed upon them the rules of matriliny, uxorilocal residence, and humiliatingly hard work in their manioc fields. Having lived in small bands during their migratory period, the Tukano had developed a strong aversion to endogamy, in reaction to what is referred to as a 'time of incest'; now they were eager to gain access to 'other women'/*gahí nomea*. The Arawakan Tapir People, divided into local descent groups, were endogamous and their women occupied a high status in their social structure.

Phase 5

Eventually, Arawak and Tukano (not all groups, nor all at the same time) agreed upon patrilocal, patrilineal exogamic relationships, and developed a set of elaborate exchange rituals in which Tukano-owned tobacco and other narcotics played an important mediatory role. At the same time, manioc cultivation was developed by Tapir women in those Tukanoan groups that still lacked it. However, Arawak women who had been given in marriage to Tukanoan men frequently abandoned their husbands and returned to their families of origin, complaining of ill-treatment, unaccustomed food, and toilsome work in the manioc gardens.

Phase 6

With the passing of time, some formerly large Arawakan groups, notably the Cubeo and Tariana, became strongly Tukanoized while other Arawak preferred to migrate away from the Tukano. At present, the main Arawak habitat lies to the north of the Tukano, in the Guainía territory, on the Isana river and its tributaries. There tensions persist between Arawak and Tukano, expressed mainly in mutual accusations of magical aggression. In any case, it would seem that the mythologies and oral traditions of all concerned can be understood only in terms of the successive Tukano penetration, the periods of intertribal hostilities, and the establishment of exogamic marriage rules accompanied by a change from matriliny to patriliny.

Palms and Marriage Rules

The diversity and abundance of palms that grow in the Vaupés territory constitute for the Indians a very important food resource. Next to the common staple food derived from the cultivation of bitter manioc (*Manihot esculenta*), palm fruits are the most basic vegetable food item.

The principal fruit-bearing palm species are shown in Table 1, in order of their relative importance as food.

The *buhu-nyu* palm (*Socratea exorrhiza*), paxiúba in LG[6] and macána in other vernaculars, is of great importance in myth and ritual and in the manufacture of mainly ritual objects; its fruits, however, are not eaten, being few, small, and very acid. The fruits of *gohá-nyu* (*Mauritiella cataractarum*), cúcura in LG, were eaten in former, apparently pre-agricultural, times while the *muhí-nyu* palm (*Mauritia carana*) is the main source for roof thatch but has hardly any other uses; it seems to be unknown in the Pira-paraná region, where roofs are thatched with leaves of a palm called *ubí* (*Manicaria atricha*).

TABLE 1

DESANA	LINNEAN TERMS	LENGUA GERAL	OTHER VERNACULAR
nee-nyu	*Mauritia flexuosa*	miriti	moriche
nyumu-nyu	*Jessenia bataua*	patabá	seje
ëri-nyu	*Bactris gasipaes*	pupunha	pejibaye
mihí-nyu	*Euterpe oleracea*	uassai	manacá
ënga-nyu	*Orbignya* sp.	babassú	temiche

Given the great importance of palms in food procurement, material culture and ideology, it is only natural that the Indians should have accumulated a large body of ethnobotanical knowledge with reference to floral biology mechanisms. As a matter of fact, these palms have come to constitute a focal point of tradition and ritual, of symbolism and metaphor.

Many palm species are characterized by sexual dimorphism, that is, the same individual palm produces male and female organs. Pollination takes place periodically, dehiscence being an abrupt event during which large masses of pollen are scattered in bursts over the female flowers, the powdery substance covering

Uassai (L.G.) palms, Pira-paraná river

in the process parts of the adjacent trunk, leaves, and the forest floor.

The entire process of pollination is accompanied by an interrelated complex of sensorial phenomena which form part of the sexual physiology of these plants. In the first place, one can observe certain changes in form; while the female buds begin to swell and open, the male stamens rapidly elongate and become erect. As soon as the pollen has been discharged, however, detumescence sets in, and the rod-shaped stems assume a pendulous position and begin to wither. The female flowers of the local palms are generally of a whitish or yellowish colour but at pollination the efflorescences take on a rosaceous or brownish hue. The pollen itself varies in colour from whitish to an almost orange-hued yellow, depending upon the palm species. Another notable change is a marked rise in temperature of the sexual organs of the plant; in fact, a temperature elevation of more than 10°C has been observed in pollen and flowers, in relation to the surrounding air temperature. Finally, when the buds open, and during the process of pollination, a strong and peculiar odour can be perceived near the palms.[7]

All these phenomena have been observed by the Indians, and have come to constitute a complex field of knowledge in which sensorial experiences and mental elaborations have combined into a paradigmatic model. For obvious reasons the Indians compare the reproductive process of palms and certain other plants with human sexual physiology and have singled out some species of sexually dimorphic palms or other trees as models for human conduct.

It seems that the principal pollinators of palms growing in the Vaupés territory are Coleoptera (*Rhynochophorus* ssp. and others) although smaller insects or even squirrels may be incidental pollinators. When the flowering season approaches and the intense fragrance of the efflorescences begins to attract beetles, the Indians will fell a few nearby palms to serve as breeding places for Coleoptera larvae. The palms that are felled are preferably ënga-nyu (*Orbignya* sp.) and nyumu-nyu (*Jessenia bataua*) because, according to the Indians, their pith is more plentiful and the palm-grubs, which are a highly appreciated food item, are said to grow fatter and become well flavoured; it was emphasized that buhu-nyu (*Socratea exorrhiza*) and ëri-nyu (*Bactris gasipaes*) were not felled for this purpose because their bark was too thick and hard. At distances of about one or two metres small notches are cut into the bark with an axe, and a bit of pith (*dii/*'flesh') is extracted from the incision, so that its scent will attract female Coleoptera for oviposition. The thick, whitish grubs are ready to be collected in about three to four months when, upon knocking on the log, one can hear a humming noise coming from its interior.

I shall discuss first the pollinators. The large black beetles which are attracted by the scent of the just opening buds penetrate them in search of nectar, and sometimes copulate inside the flowers. When, a day later, the anthers have dehisced, the beetles become covered with pollen which sticks to them because of the insects' contact with nectar. The female beetles now fly off in search of a place for oviposition while the male beetles, after having fed on the nectar of the now rapidly withering efflorescences which had been fertilized by the pollen that fell down from the anthers above them, fly off, covered with pollen, and now visit the first-day efflorescences of other palms, fertilizing them with the pollen that adheres to their bodies.

What I have described so far refers only to the most elementary mechanisms of pollination as observed in nature. The biological and cultural text, however, goes greatly beyond these simple botanical facts. The central truth of their palm knowledge lies in the Indians' observation that palms and their ethnobotanical interpretation provide an interrelated set of paradigmatic models for social structure. Palm pollination, as observed and interpreted by the Indians, is equated with human reproductive behaviour and from this comparison a large and intricate body of social norms, ritual practices, and mental processes is derived. I shall try to explain these thought processes and their social consequences in greater detail.

Apart from the observation of such obvious phenomena as tumescence and detumescence of the male stamens, the swelling and heating up of the flowers, and the abrupt dehiscence of pollen, the Indians put great emphasis upon olfactory sensations. Human body odours are classified into several categories which ideally at least determine mate selection and recognition (Reichel-Dolmatoff 1985:124-126, essay 3 in this book). Spouses should belong to the same odour category and body odour determines to a large degree whether a person belongs to 'other people'/*gahí mahsá*, or to 'our people'/*mári mahsá*. Animal odours and pheromonal communication among animals are well understood, and since social segments are often associated with certain animals, odour categories acquire importance in hunting practices and food habits. Emphasis is placed upon the difference between male and female odours, between sexually attractive or repulsive odours. Some of these odour qualities are said to be hereditary; others are said to depend upon (real or supposed) food habits: hunter's odour, fisherman's odour, agriculturalist's odour, and so on; another odour category depends upon a person's or an animal's age. Plant odours refer to flowers, pollen, fruits, leaves, barks, saps, wood, pith, roots, and other details of plant anatomy and physiology. To these categories are added soil odours, honey odours, wax odours, the particular odours of smoke produced by the burning of certain materials, and the odours of running or stagnant waters. All odours are said to be conditioned by the particular ecosystem in which they can be perceived.

Similar categories are established with reference to colours (Reichel-Dolmatoff 1978b, essay 2 in this book). The Indians distinguish an ample spectrum of, to them, highly significant colours in which a yellowish-white hue symbolizes male seminal fertility, a red hue female fecundity, and purple to darkish hues are associated with illness and putrefaction. If we add to this the no less complex categories of sounds, thermal effects, and kinesic communication systems, and correlate them with palm pollination, an extremely complex but quite coherent picture begins to emerge, in which the key idea is exogamy, an institution that constitutes the most important social norm in the entire Colombian Vaupés territory.

This brings us back to the problem of palms. To the Desana and their neighbours all palms incorporate an essentially female element expressed by sexually attractive odours, the flavour of their fruits, and a number of other aspects which are evocative of the female sex. From these associations to the formulation of rules about what is forbidden and what is prescribed is but a short step. In fact, palms and palm pollination provide models for marriage rules in several ways.

In the first place, self-fertilization (self-pollination) is interpreted by the Indians as an example of endogamy, if not of incest. It is designated as *gamé inyarí*, lit. 'to look after each other', with the implicit connotation of sexual intent; *inyarí* is 'to look' but *ga'me* is related to the verb *gaméri/*'to love', 'to desire sexually', an expression used when referring to forbidden, endogamous, or incestuous relationships. Metapohorically endogamy, or incest are termed as 'to eat one's own flesh'.[8]

Women are strictly forbidden to take note of this botanical fact and are discouraged from looking at buhu-nyu (*Socratea exorrhiza*) palms or other monoecious species, at least during staminate anthesis and dehiscence. The entire pollination syndrome, associated with morphological, olfactory, chromatic, kinesic, thermal, and fertilizing phenomena, is compared to human sexual physiology. The odour of pollen has been compared to that of human semen, not only by the Indians but by botanists as well (Barbosa Rodrigues 1903:7-8). One cannot speak here of symbolism; the analogies are too obvious.

The withering and 'sickly' discolouring of the male and female organs shortly after anthesis are taken by the Indians to be sure signs of the perils of endogamy and/or incest. In fact, the image of a male being inseminating, in a culturally forbidden manner, a female being which occupies, spatially, a lower position is a recurrent myth motif which refers to the danger of endogamy. For example, in one myth a man insists upon putting up his hammock *above* that of a woman when tying their hammocks for the night to the branches of a monoecious tree; in another myth, a man who is eating a 'male' fruit while lying in his hammock, in a culturally disapproved sleeping arrangement in a maloca, drops bits of the fruit upon a woman occupying a hammock just below him. Thus, self-fertilization is evil, and this cultural truth must be taught insistently to all male members of society.

The culturally approved form of conjugal union is exogamy and, here again, it is the palm which provides the analogue model in nature. As a matter of fact, there are two models, one provided by the male beetle and another by the female one. The male beetle, proceeding from a buhu-nyu (*Socratea exorrhiza*) palm, has given an example of exogamy; covered with pollen it has gone off to insem-inate another palm and thus exemplifies that most important cultural norm. And so does the female beetle, though in a more involved way. In the minds of the Indians oviposition is an act of impregnation, of insemination. The notches the indians cut into the fallen logs that serve as breeding places for the palm-grubs are intentionally vagina-shaped taking the forms of a V or a ◊, and the act of oviposition is called *pingusári*/'to inseminate' (a woman, a log). The log itself is compared to a womb and the grubs that eventually develop inside it are desig-nated as 'children'.[9] Grubs are eaten raw, boiled, or toasted, and are said to be aphrodisiac. When toasted they can be conserved for some time and are an appreciated item of symbolic food exchange between two or more exogamic units. The logs which were 'inseminated' by the beetles were trunks of ënga-nyu (*Orbignya* sp.) and nyumu-nyu (*Jessenia bataua*), palms which, because of their markedly 'female' odour and flavour characteristics, are associated with the wombs of women pertaining to a complementary exogamic unit. In other words, the beetle proceeding from the buhu-nyu (*Socratea exorrhiza*) palm has given an example of exogamy by impregnating the 'womb' of another palm species. The fact that it was a female beetle that oviposited does not affect its phallic sym-bolism;[10] palm beetles represent, in essence, a male principle. The entire process is interpreted by the Indians as one of impregnation and embryological develop-ment. The felled trunk has become a womb; the beetle, although female, has impregnated the womb, and the larvae are 'young males' to be offered in the highly formalized sister exchange rituals.

The semantics of palm nomenclature provide additional data on the relation-ship between these trees and marriage rules. I shall enumerate here some of the principal palms.

In discussing neé-nyu (*Mauritia flexuosa*) the first observation made by the Indians referred to a Tukano sib that intermarries with the Desana and which is called *neé-porá*/'neé-sons' or Mirití-Tapuya, mirití being the LG name of the neé palm. Attempts at explaining the root *neé* were countered with a cryptic metaphor; it was said that "whenever a cooking vessel overflows due to a woman's negligence, a shaman-macaw will drop, screeching, vertically into a lagoon", an act that was designated as *maha-pu neé-ro*/'macaw-leaf ncé-ro,' the last word said to be related to the verb ~ *neréri*/'to lick'. The image of the 'over-flowing vessel' was said to refer to forbidden sex but was not further elaborated. However, the following commentaries were added: the fruit of the neé palm is the preferred food of tapir and is important in alliance ritual when the Desana offer umarí (*Poraqueiba sericea*) while Tapir offers neé-nyu (*Mauritia flexuosa*). The expression *maha-pu neé-ro* was said to suggest the idea of sucking or suck-ling, of depriving someone of 'energies' (*bogári*), of nourishing oneself with the life 'energy' of others, in an imagery that, apart from its exogamic exchange implications, led to the further suggestion that the root neé was related to *ne-*

du/'tongue', a 'tongue-shaped protuberance', and that this referred to the clitoris of the women of Tapir People. The symbolism of the 'overflowing cooking vessel', sometimes combined with the actions of singeing, or burning hair, or of urinating into the fire, seems to be related somehow to exogamy but the connections are far from clear. There is said to exist a close relationship between neé palms and the Tukano proper but this point was not elaborated.

The fruit of nyumu-nyu (*Jessenia bataua*) is said to taste and smell of something essentially feminine, in fact, 'maternal'. "There is a kin relation with this palm", it was said. In analyzing the name of the palm it was pointed out that the word for father-in-law was *nyëmë* (T, PT, U), ~ *nëmë* (D), alluding to Tapir, the owner of women (Reichel-Dolmatoff 1985, essay 3 in this book). Some informants suggested the following linguistic/semantic relationships: in Tukano proper, *Jessenia bataua* is frequently referred to as *ti nyo*, lit. 'that-palm', *nyo* having the same meaning as *nyu* in Desana. In Tukano proper a complementary exogamic group can be referred to as *mahsá nuasé/*'people-to copulate with,' *nyu* (*nyo*) standing for 'palm' and for 'sexual partner'. A related Tukano expression is *mahsá~nyosé/*'people-to form'. It may be of interest to botanists to add here that on several occasions it was said that nyumu-nyu palms had been cultivated in the past and that there were two varieties: one with large fruits and another with smaller fruits; the first variety was suggested to have been the formerly cultivated one. Again, it should be remembered that nyumu-nyu fruits are a preferred food of tapir.

The name of the peach palm, ëri-nyu (*Bactris gasipaes*), was said to be derived from or related to the verg *óri/*'to give', 'to reciprocate', and thus to refer to the ritual exchange of these fruits. Since old habitation sites of the ancient Tapir People can readily be recognized by clusters or stands of ëri palms and of umarí trees, both growing in secondary growth ('rastrojos', 'terra preta'), both being monoecious and having been cultivated, the root *ëri-óri* might refer to reciprocal Arawak/Tukano relationships. To this was added that the semantic range included the term *urá*, which means 'relative', 'kin', as in *mári úra/*'our-relatives'. If nasalized and pronounced ~ *u'rá*, the word means Howler monkey, an animal that is sometimes designated as a 'relative', a reference to the close relationship between the Makú, a Howler monkey-associated group, and the newly arrived Tukano, especially the Desana. In a Desana myth on the yuruparí theme, it was Howler monkey who cut off and used a short tubular segment of a nyumu-nyu palm as a flute and thereby 'made the leaves fall down', a clear indication that he took part in the segmentation of the nyumu-nyu-derived offspring. However, the myth goes on, the sound was very 'painful' to those who heard it, an expression which was interpreted as a rejection of Makú progenitors. A small parrot then made a similar instrument but it only produced a feeble sound: pe-pe-pe, and parrot, too, was rejected. This scene is followed by an episode in which the competitors of Tapir, the owner of ërí and umari, use a blowgun shaft made of a nyumu-nyu stem as a channel, a duct, to steal a fruit (that is, a woman) from Tapir's umarí tree. In this myth Howler monkey is not an ally of Tapir but occupies a subservient or intermediate position. In fact, in several conversations it was suggested that Howler monkey represented the forest-dwelling, band-organized Makú Indians who, as mentioned before, have established conjugal unions with the first Tukanoan invaders, notably with the Desana. Howler Monkey People were, after all, among the true 'ancients'/*mëra*, preceding Tapir People in the Colombian Vaupés, it was suggested in discussing this point. A Desana sib, considered to be one of the earliest ones, is called *ëri-porá*/'Bactris-sons'.

The etymology of mihi-nyu (*Euterpe oleracea*) was explained in the following terms. The root *mihí* is related to the verb *mihiri*/'to concentrate'; *mihiri bogá* means 'to concentrate an energy'. The same verb is related to the verb *bihiri*/'to squeeze out something', 'to tickle', which belongs to the same semantic field. For example, the expression *nomé bihiri*/'woman-squeeze' is used to describe the process by which a woman squeezes out the poisonous juice from the mass of freshly grated manioc tubers, with the help of a tripod that sustains a large circular sieve. The juice is being 'filtered' through the sieve, an image that, to the Indians, suggests transformation and impregnation. This female symbolism was confirmed by the observation that mihí fruits are 'like blood'/*diá nyiri*/'red-dark', alluding, according to some, to menstrual blood, according to others, to the colour of female fecundity. The extracted juice contains *bogá*/'energy', and it was said that mihí palms contained concentrated male and female procreative energies.

The radicals *bu*, *mu* of buhu-nyu (*Socratea exorrhiza*) are said to have a feminine connotation which is also present in nyumu-nyu (*Jessenia bataua*) and muhí (*Mauritiella carana*). The term *mu* conveys the image of a mass of fertilizing elements; *iri mu*/'that-school' (of fish), *vera mu*/'starch-heap,' *ímika mu*/'(rain) clouds-mass'; the last term, if pronounced with the stress on the second *í*, means 'small fish-school'. The expression *diári-mu*/'red mass' refers to 'redness' as a visual impression or as a fecundity concept. To this is added the Indians' observation that buhu-nyu fruits have a very repulsive odour, 'similar to putrid meat', 'like menstrual blood', as the Desana put it. The muhí palm (*Mauritiella carana*), the leaves of which are used preferentially for roof thatch, also is a 'relative', its name being related to *buhi*/'son-in-law' (D, T, PT, U). A son-in-law should be, above all, a protector, just like the thatch that protects a large number of people. Although the sun is usually designated as *abé*/'father', an alternative designation is *muhí-pu*/'sun-leaf', meaning that the essential function of the sun consists in protecting mankind and nature. Muhí-pu can also be used as a personal name.

The *ëngá* (*Orbignya* sp.) palm seems to derive its name from *ë'kësíri*/'to establish kinship ties', a verb related to *ëhsëríro*/'something delightful', referring to an odour. In Desana the expression *ë'kësíri mahsá* refers to a complementary group

Howler monkey

of people who have a pleasant masculine odour; *ë'hkaro* means 'reasonable', 'profound' (D, T, PT, U), while *ëhëro* means 'hot', in the same languages. In T, D, PT, UA, the ëngá palm is called *ihkí*, which is essentially the same root. The main characteristics of ëngá palms were verbalized thus: "The fruit is yellowish, whitish. The palm represents kinship, warmth, favour, and sound thinking. It is a male concept; *ë'sëriro* is a pleasant male odour."

The gohá (*Mauritiella cataractarum*) is called *kohsá*, in T, PT, U; the element *-go* is a feminine suffix but the radical *goá* means 'bone' and, in a transferred sense, can stand for penis or phallus. In T, PT, G, *kohsóro* means 'leg' or 'thigh'.

From Endogamy to Exogamy

So far, the botanical phenomena of palm pollination have provided a set of models for two alternative marriage rules: endogamy and exogamy. The question arises why endogamy, in botanical terms self-fertilization, should have become a focus of strong anxieties among the Tukano Indians of the Vaupés. Indeed, marriage rules among these Indians never are a simple matter of prescribed or preferential exogamy but contain an element of passionate rejection of endogamy, matrilocal residence, and matriliny, apparently quite out of proportion with the everyday reality of customary reciprocity behaviour.

In order to approach the problem posed by this strong and all-pervading reaction, it is necessary to resume the discussion of yet another aspect of palm pollination, and to relate it to certain mythical/historical developments which refer to the time-dimension of demographic succession, culture contacts, and shifts in social structure and organization.

With reference to palm pollination, the following observations are of special relevance. From field data and textual analyses it appears that the Vaupés Indians, and also some of those dwelling beyond the limits of that territory, have discovered that pollination can be culturally manipulated, that it can be induced by the booming noise made by large trumpets (Reichel-Dolmatoff 1981a-1983:89). Many data refer to rituals performed near stands of palms, involving the blowing of trumpets or flutes, chanting, or shamans addressing trees in a loud voice. That sound waves produced by these acts might precipitate or stimulate dehiscence has been suggested by botanists (Huxley 1978:136-138).

In order to put these aspects into their proper perspective, we must sort out a number of minor or major biological and ethnographic elements.

Let us return once more to the mythical/historical time when the Arawak dominated the Colombian Vaupés scene, and the Tukano were their subservient in-laws. At that time, so oral tradition tells us, Tapir personified the Arawak. Tapir was the owner of women, a powerful chief and potential father-in-law, but difficult to please because in exchange for his daughters he demanded hard agricultural toil. What was more, Tapir had a loud, droning voice, so strong that its roaring sound 'made the leaves fall down'. Howler monkey, associated with the endogamous Makú, was subservient to Tapir and with their joint voices they dominated everything, especially the womenfolk and, in a wider sense, fertility in general. But the Tukano, too, had their allies and finally outwitted Tapir: They stole Tapir's loud and commanding voice; they simply took it away and left Tapir, that huge, powerful brute, with the feeble whistling voice it still has to this day.

From texts recorded in Desana, Pira-Tapuya, Uanano, Tukano proper, and other languages of the Colombian Vaupés territory, the meaning of the episodes which together describe this intertribal situation becomes clear as soon as a number of different versions are discussed. The circumstances, then, are described as follows. Tapir, whose voice 'made the leaves fall down', was the owner of the yuruparí trumpets, the droning voice, and thus was able to manipulate pollination. Representing at the same time the ownership of women, Tapir was a powerful force of fertility; he was the dominating father-in-law, a father figure; he was Thunder (*buhpu*); he was the owner of the most important palms and also of umarí (*Poraqueiba sericea*).

But eventually the Desana and other Tukanoans who had become Tapir's sons-in-law found out about plant dimorphism, pollen manipulation, and cross-fertilization. After a few generations of matrilocal residence and servitude in Tapir's manioc gardens, they had produced numerous offspring and so found themselves in a bargaining position. After lengthy negotiations, squabbles, and infights, they demanded and imposed patrilocal residence rules and had their Tapir women look after most agricultural tasks while they themselves continued, to a large degree, their traditional ways of hunting and fishing. This development, marked by the introduction of manioc agriculture, language exogamy, and a modified Yuruparí Complex, is described in many texts which, although they refer to different local situations and developmental stages, all fall into the same pattern.

The women, it seems, never quite assented to this development. Their new subservient status was accompanied by many physical hardships, food restrictions, and sexual frustrations, the latter owing to the fact that the men had to observe frequent sexual abstinence, not only before and during ritual occasions but also in connection with everyday hunting, fishing, and manufacturing activities.

The insistence upon exogamy and on a male-dominant society was accompanied by a change in the function of the yuruparí trumpets; while formerly they were said to symbolize palm pollination and fertility, they now became the stentorian voice of warning, and their use during male initiation and palm fruit rituals gave expression to the ominous memory of the 'ancients' who had practiced endogamy and allowed their women to occupy a high status in their society.

present, Tukano women must hide at the first sound of a trumpet, and popular Indian lore has it that a woman who sees or touches a trumpet must die immediately.[11]

The exogamous message, on the other hand, is being transmitted by trumpets and flutes during male initiation rituals when adolescent boys are taught the traditional background and the present-day use of the instruments. The palm fruit distribution ritual also emphasizes this theme and during its initial part, when the trumpet and flute players make their ostentatious entrance into the festive maloca, all women and children must go into hiding. In many cases this is followed by an interlude during which the men whip the legs and backs of the adolescent boys with their fishing rods. Once the fruits have been deposited on a certain spot inside the maloca and the instruments have been put away, the men return and now, in a tumultuous scene, the men chase after the women, trying to touch their backs with certain foods that carry a marked seminal connotation. The palm fruit distribution is clearly an increase festival during which hallucinogenic potions (*Banisteriopsis* sp.) and tobacco play an important mediatory role. In all palm fruit rituals at least two complementary exogamic groups are represented while frequent minor exchange rituals can be organized at most any convenient time when some exchange items become available. On all these occasions exogamy is being extolled in the recital of genealogies, although the Tapir heritage and former matriliny are alluded to in songs and declamations.

In summary, the Arawak-Tukano contact, which presumably developed during many generations before the Tukano achieved their dominant position in the Vaupés territory, had far-reaching consequences. The Arawak were manioc cultivators and fairly stable sedentary maloca-dwellers. Their marriage relationship with the Tukanoans was far from being a friendly alliance, as far as one can judge from oral tradition, but was marked by tensions in which open warfare, matrilocally based in-law servitude, and traditional cultural differences constituted major obstacles to social integration. Arawakan women propagated agriculture and the manioc complex among the Tukanoans, establishing thus a new role for women as food-producers, while Arawakan men propagated the endogamous *yuruparí* ritual, with its emphasis on matrilocal residence rules which obliged young Tukano males to renounce their hunting tradition and to dedicate themselves to the tiresome tasks of rainforest agriculture, the cleaning of fields, and the monotonous starchy diet. Women occupied a strong position among the Arawak and, in a matrilocal society, their Tukanoan husbands often felt at the mercy of censorious foreigners. This generalized account may sound like an oversimplification but these situations are well documented in many recorded narratives.

The same texts describe how eventually these conditions began to change. Tukano men began to take control, and with this a major shift in social structure and ideological orientation took place. Patrilocal residence and patrilineal descent become the rule; the Tukanoans adopted manioc agriculture and the multifamiliar maloca, but the male worldview continued to be forest- and river-oriented, and the men paid but scant attention to agriculture which continued to be a female domain. This change in social structure led to a change in the interpretation of the Yuruparí Complex. Among the endogamous Arawak, it seems that self-fertilization of monoecious trees had been the focus of palm lore and, more than that, of a religious complex in which Kaoi, Yaperikuli, and others played a major role as creators of fruit-bearing palms. Among the Tukano of the Colombian Vaupés, these mythical beings lost their importance and were, at best, transformed into marginal figures. In fact, the Vaupés river became a major ideological divisory line; while on its left and eastern banks Kaoi and Yaperikuli continued to be mentioned prominently in oral tradition, because of the vicinity of Arawakan groups to the south in the Colombian Vaupés, the emphasis of the Yuruparí Complex was placed upon exogamy; the endogamous customs of the 'ancients', the Arawakan Tapir people, were condemned and the entire complex became a social code, with hardly any religious overtones.

The Oral Traditions of *Yuruparí*

The yuruparí theme, as documented in the published literature on the general Vaupés-Rio Negro area, has been summarized by Bolens (1967). She, however, has used for her analysis many different sources which contain Arawakan versions as well as Tukanoan versions. The episodic richness, literary style, and ethnographic depth of these published narratives vary greatly. The principal version Bolens dissects into separate episodes is that of the Baniwa of the Issana river, north of the Tukano area. To this she adds a lengthy Tariana version, another Arawakan group from the general Yavareté region, recorded seventy years before the Baniwa text. The longest (and most confusing) Tukano version comes from the headwaters of the Papurí river. The Cubeo version she quotes belongs to the Arawak cluster. This, then, is a palimpsest in which different time levels, geographical areas, and culture contacts have produced a series of themes and motifs, the connecting thread of which is difficult to follow.

The main theme refers to a 'divine' creator, the miraculous birth of a 'culture hero', his sacrifical death and ascension, and his legacy consisting in some moral admonitions, and a fruit-bearing palm that rises from his earthly remains. To commemorate his wordly existence he institutionalizes the ritual of the 'sacred' trumpets. There can be no doubt that many of these episodes contain Christian elements, especially the Baniwa versions. Bolens's short article cannot serve as an introduction to the yuruparí theme; those interested in more complete and detailed versions available in the literature, must turn to the Brazilian sources, especially to Barbosa Rodrigues (1890), Brandao de Amorim (1928), and the

French traveller Coudreau (1887). Hugh-Jones's book on the Barasana is a rich source on *yurupari* myths and rituals as practised in the southern part of the Colombian Vaupés; it also contains two appendixes with bibliographical lists of references to *yurupari* rites and mythology (Hugh-Jones 1979:309-310).

In the following section I shall condense the essence of several clusters of oral traditions referring to the Yurupari Complex, which I have recorded in the field, in the Colombian Vaupés territory. It is obvious that there can be no basic, original rendering of the *yurupari* theme; there is no Ur-*yurupari*. All texts that have been collected are, more or less, extensive variants of a similar theme (or themes) but in the telling and retelling of this tradition the narratives and their episodes have become garbled or contaminated, condensed or elaborated, and, in any case, have been adapted and readapted to an ever-changing variety of different physical, social, and psychological conditions. Stradelli's text, as we shall see, is one example of what can happen to an ancient oral tradition; my texts, recording the same themes but in the native languages and in the voices of shamans and elders, constitute, I hope, an anthropologically more valid example.

I have numbered the principal scenes and put in parentheses some of the major variants I have recorded so far.

SCENE 1. A man (old man, founding ancestor, lineage head, shaman) has an adolescent son (or sons) and several adolescent daughters or other female kin. They all live in a house near a river but have no close neighbours.

SCENE 2. While the young women are a vivacious lot the son (or sons) are 'lazy'; each morning, while the women busy themselves at the hearth, the young men oversleep.

SCENE 3. When the old man notices that his son has reached puberty, he admonishes him to rise early and to go before dawn to the port for ritual cleansing. As an incentive the old man tells the boy in great secrecy that at the landing place he will find a 'thing' (a 'red thing', the mouthpiece of a musical instrument, a 'thunder-producing' thing, a foam-producing sap to be used as a shampoo, etc.) the old man has hidden in a tree that stands near the port.

SCENE 4. The tree is described as a paxiuba (*Socratea exorrhiza*) palm, with reddish stilt roots, occasionally as a mirití palm (*Mauritia flexuosa*), or as a tall forest tree with buttress roots, or a tree with a very irregular stem marked with oval depressions and staff-shaped ridges. Stilt roots and crevices are emphasized and the tree, whatever its species, is described in terms that leave no doubt about its essentially anthropomorphized bisexual nature. In spite of the old man's insistence, the boy pays no attention and goes on sleeping.

SCENE 5. Pretending to be asleep, the women have overheard the old man's admonitions and have become curious. In the dark before dawn they stealthily go down to the landing place and with a lighted torch search for the 'thing' which, from what they have heard, is an object that symbolizes male dominance. In fact, the thing is *'yurupari'* (a trumpet, the mouthpiece of a trumpet, etc.).

SCENE 6. The women find the 'thing' which turns out to be a short rod-shaped or tubular object of wood with tassels on both ends. They 'capture' the 'thing', an episode which in the literature has become known as 'The Theft of Yurupari'. Puzzled by its shape and 'brilliance' they 'play' with it, 'blow' upon it, and finally introduce it into their vaginas. There follows an episode with lesbian overtones, in which the women experiment with sex but soon become disappointed by what they have found out about it.

SCENE 7. Having discovered the men's 'secret' but being disappointed, the women decide to abandon their menfolk. They (their number varies) embark in one or various canoes and paddle downstream until they reach a maloca inhabited by 'other people' where they become the willing concubines of the local males. In some versions the women travel on and finally establish themselves at an isolated spot (an island, the mouth of a river, etc.) where from now on they receive male visitors only for the purpose of procreation. This episode has led some authors to elaborate on the Amazon motif.

SCENE 8. The old man and his companions have become aware that the women have 'stolen' their secret and start out in pursuit of them.

SCENE 9. In the meantime some of the fugitive women have gone on to other malocas owned by 'other people'; by that time all of them have become pregnant.

SCENE 10. At long last the men of their original home catch up with them and, after lengthy dealings with the men of the 'other people', arrive at a compromise and make a solemn pledge; they agree upon an exchange ritual by which the two groups formalize an exogamous patrilocal alliance, thereby recovering their male dominance over the young women of the 'others', as well as over their own daughters they have to give in exchange.

The 'thing' hinted at in the different versions of these myths is the botanical phenomenon of dehiscence and self-fertilization of monoecious trees; no matter how the texts describe the nature of 'it', there can be no doubt about this fact. Some narratives emphasize its phallic shape, while others refer to it as a vagina or a womb; still others describe it as a lingam/yoni-like combination. It is this natural phenomenon and its human analogue the women have become aware of. I certainly do not pretend to say that this is what the whole yuruparí theme is all about but this is what appears to be its fundamental meaning in the context of Vaupés Indian societies.

The women experiment with the 'thing' but find it unsatisfactory; they try it out on their own bodies and on those of their sisters but 'self-fertilization' (masturbation, homosexuality) does not gratify them. Having discovered the men's 'secret' they do not 'steal' any object; rather, they reject an institution which imposes upon them male dominance. The institution is endogamy which is reified in the form of a phallus-shaped 'tube', a flute, a stamen and this reification of a social/sexual convention, described in the metaphoric language of myth, has helped to create the misleading story of 'The Theft of Yurupari'.

In several oral versions the 'thing' is described as a tubular piece of wood with a ruff or fringe of colourful extensions that radiate from both extremes. This image is said to symbolize exogamy and is reified in a long flute which is played at initiation or palm fruit rituals. The flute is called *buí*, a term I shall analyze later, and is adorned at its lower end with a circular frill of white heron feathers. These herons, being migratory birds that come from *gahí tabú*/'another-section', are called *yahí*, a word related to *gahí*/'other' and referring to the women of 'other' people. The fact that the actual flute consists only of one half of the 'thing' indicates the two complementary elements of exogamy.[12]

There exist long discussions about the possible etymology of the name yuruparí (see, for example, Camara Cascudo 1962:408-409). In most of these etymological interpretations it is taken for granted that yuruparí is a word taken from the lingua geral, the Amazonian vernacular of Tupi origin.

The most obvious shortcomings of all these speculations lie in the fact that they treat both the word and its eventual meaning out of context. Most authors rely on tales collected by missionaries or occasional travellers who, as the case may be, have embellished, impoverished, expurgated, condensed, or simply misunderstood this body of oral tradition, hardly ever taking into account the wider cultural framework, and still less the subtleties of language and the patterns of symbolic structures.

I have attempted to analyze this term with the help of Indians conversant in seven or eight languages spoken in the Vaupés territory and they all agreed that yuruparí was a word taken from the Tukano proper language, and that its correct pronunciation was *yërëparí*. In many Tukanoan languages the vowels *u* and *ë* are closely related; for example, *uhúri* (D) means 'to speak' while *ëhëri* (D) means 'to smoke'; *nuganyoma* (D) means 'to begin with' while *nëgë* (D) means 'he started'.

Now in Tukano proper the word yërëparí is said to be derived from the verb *yërësé*/'to pass', 'to transit', 'to overcome an obstacle', 'to pass from one state of being to another'; and from the Desana verbs *paríri*/'to dehisce', 'to burst open' (seed vessel), *~paríri*/'to open', 'to gape' (a door, a vagina). For example, *~ pari ma sahara* means 'to open-penetrate' and describes the act of defloration. The verb *bári* (D) means 'to eat', an act which is symbolically equivalent to male sexual activity; the same word, *bári* (D), is the name of a fruit (*Erisma japura*) called *japurá* in LG, which, according to the Indians, has a pronounced sexual odour. In fact, this fruit is of considerable symbolic importance to the Indians; after boiling it a paste is made from it which is wrapped in leaves which are buried for several days. The paste is then consumed with fish or is used as a seasoning with boiled manioc and the green leaves of *Phytolacca rivinoides*. For several days before, people who prepare this paste must observe sexual abstinence.

The Tukano verb *yurusé* (cf. supra *yërësé*) means 'to swing from a vine', for example when crossing a creek or when trying to avoid stinging ants; it also means 'to get rid of something', 'to free oneself from something'.

Taking into account this cluster of meanings, my informants simply translated the term yuruparí as 'passage-to open-inseminate' or 'passage-to dehisce-to open', derived from *yëre* (T), *yuru* (T), + *paríri* (D), ~ *pariri* (D). In other words, *yuruparí* means puberty ritual and, in a wider sense, refers to a complex of biological facts, traditional beliefs, and a number of ritual objects or practices connected with this rite de passage or 'passing from one state of being to another'.

The Indians themselves use the term yuruparí almost exclusively in conversation (in Spanish, Portuguese, or lingua geral) with non-Indian outsiders, that is, with missionaries, government agents, colonos, anthropologists, or other occasional visitors. Among themselves, when speaking of the *yuruparí* as an initiation ritual the Indians use various descriptive terms the most common of which is *miriá-porá* (D, T) or *minía-pona* (PT, G). This term can be glossed as 'the overwhelmed-sons', from *mirituári*/'to drown'. The semantics of *miroári* and cognate terms and of *porá* (*poná*) are very involved and I shall discuss them more fully on another occasion. The expressions refer to the initiates (*gamá-mahsa*) as being in a state of transformation brought about by shamanic admonitions and the 'voices of the ancestors' who communicate the exogamic code by means of musical instruments and the dances, chants, and spells that accompany them. At the same time, the instruments represent each individual or group of initiates according to his respective phratry and sib. In being initiated (*ga'mári*) they now become important links, articulations, with other exogamous units. They now are the 'sons of saturation', of social and sexual continuity.

Initiation is called *poorí nël*/'to scatter-day', with the explicit meaning of 'fertilization', 'pollination', 'impregnation'. Upon reaching sexual and social maturity the initiates are said to receive an impact comparable to the shock suffered from contact with an electric eel, a sensation compared with ejaculation. In fact, initiation was designated as *saá biúri nël*/'electric eel-to confer-day'. The eel's name was said to be related to the concept of 'impregnation', 'fertilization', 'to take possession of' a new privilege. It was repeatedly stated that the *yuruparí* initiation ritual belonged to 'this world' (*turi*), in contrast to rituals in which drug-induced hallucinations allowed a glimpse into 'another world'.

Yurupari Instruments and Their Associations

The principal material objects used during the initiation ritual and part of the palm-fruit distribution ritual are large trumpets and long tubular flutes; indeed, the entire Yurupari Complex can be identified by these instruments. The usual term to designate these instruments is *mahsá bëgë*/'people-ancestors' (D) but often the term *mahsá mëra* (plural of *bëgë*) is employed. The root term is *bë*, *më*/'being', followed by the singular -*gë* or the plural -*ra*. This root term includes the semantic range of *mohó*/'power' (in an abstract sense), *momé*/'semen', 'honey', and, most importantly, *muríu*/'tobacco', in the sense of an abstract 'breath' or 'effluvium'. [13] Whether this root is also related to the root of *nomé*/'woman', as some informants suggested, is a questionable point which eventually must be clarified by linguists. At major rituals there is always a large trumpet called *diámë*/'red-thing', which is blown by a high-ranking shaman or elder; the same term is used to designate the queen of an ant or termite colony. The root *bë*, *më* was described as a vital essence, a legacy the true origin of which was Tapir. (The comparison of tapir names shown in Table 2 is revealing.) The term bëgë does not distinguish clearly between man and animal but, although in vernacular Spanish the Indians are likely to translate this term as '*bicho*', that does not mean that that bëgë is 'beastly.' On the contrary, bëgë always carries the meaning of something venerable, time-honoured; mëra are not marginal beings but are very much present in nature and in imagination because in its threatening, negative aspects bëgë refers to the endogamous Tapir while in its mandatory, preceptive aspects it refers to the historical ancestors who established the exogamous, male-dominant tradition.

TABLE 2

TAPIR NAME	MEANING
Desana	
mahsá bëgë	'people-one-ancestor'
mahsa mëra	'people-old-beings'
Pira-tapuya	
mahsá bëhkëro	'people-father-in-law'
mahsa këná	'people-complementary'
Tukano Proper	
mahsa bëhkëro	'people-complementary'
mahsá bëhkerá	'people-tapirs'

Uanano
mahsa bëhkëro   'people-tapirs'
mahsa bëkëna   'people-complementary'

The trumpet consists of an elongated cone-shaped body, the total length of which is about 1 to 1.5m. The diameter of the widest part of the instrument may be as large as 18 cm or as small as 6 cm. The sound of the instruments varies according to the diameter and the overall size of the trumpet. Most of these trumpets are made by spirally twisting a broad strip of bark into a drawn-out cone or bell, sometimes strengthening it with two or more long, straight rods that are tied parallel to the body of the trumpet. Since these rods extend for about 5 to 8 cm beyond the end of the trumpet where it is widest and heaviest, they also serve to stick the instrument into the ground when at rest. The body of the trumpet is made from the bark of the *puikarogë* tree, a material which is said to have a strong 'female' odour and which shamans invoke according to different 'colour energies' of the bark; occasionally the trumpets can be made from any tree that has a strong, pliable bark (*gahsi-rogë*, from *gahsíro*/'bark', 'shell', 'womb').

The most important part of the trumpet is the mouthpiece, a short, well-polished tube of dark palm wood (*Socratea exorrhiza*) about 30 cm long; in fact, it is above all this mouthpiece to which the term *mahsá bëgë* is applied; otherwise it is simply referred to as *buhurú dëhká*/'*Socratea exorrhiza*-piece'. It might be added here that *buhurú* also means 'blowgun' and that both objects, the mouthpiece and the blowgun, have phallic connotations. The suffix *-ru* indicates a tubular object. The mouthpiece is also the part that may not be seen by women whereas the conical bark body of the trumpet is not hidden and can be seen and touched by them. In spite of its being taboo, the mouthpiece cannot be called 'sacred', an expression that cannot be applied to the yuruparí implements. As material objects, they do not have a sacred character; it is the message they transmit that is of a hallowed, venerable quality and not the material form, even if the latter is kept hidden from women and uninitiated youths.

The symbolic interpretation of these large trumpets which, as mentioned, are of central significance to the entire Yuruparí Complex, is the following: the elongated tubular part is called *poré*/'vulva', while the mouthpiece is called *bári sero*/'to eat-clitoris'. It is, of course obvious that the *yurupari* are symbolically equivalent to the large leaf-covered cigars Tukano Indians smoke and pass from hand to hand during exchange rituals.

Occasionally another type of trumpet is used, known under the name of *bari bëgë*. This trumpet is similar to those previously described but consists of an almost funnel-shaped body in which the spirally twisted bark has been compressed so that the lower end is much wider than that of the other trumpets. This type, too, is combined with a tubular palmwood mouthpiece.

Another musical instrument of importance in the ritual context is a long tubular flute made of a single polished piece of *Socratea exorrhiza* wood. These are so-called duct flutes provided with deflectors (Izikowitz 1935). As I have mentioned already, these flutes are adorned at their lower extremes with a circular frill of white heron feathers symbolizing the women of 'other people'. According to some myths the 'thing' the women found on the tree at the port consisted of a hardwood tube with frills on *each* end. Some informants compared this with a paxiúba palm, with stilt roots on one end and swaying leaves on the other. Occasionally the flutes are decorated with incised geometric design motifs, most of which seem to be derived from phosphene patterns (Reichel-Dolmatoff 1978a, 1978d, essay 9 in this book).

During all rituals of the *yuruparí* initiation or palm fruit distribution a number of trumpets should be used. The exact number varies according to local tradition and elaboration but occasionally up to twelve instruments may be displayed, the usual number being eight. It is said that of some instruments there should be pairs while of others there should be three of each type, representing three intermarrying phratries.

The mouthpiece of the trumpets and the long flutes of palm wood have to be kept under water when not in use, and are carefully hidden by the men at some distance from the maloca and the port. Since the hiding place must be chosen according to certain qualities of the water, the safekeeping of these instruments becomes a matter of a specific set of concepts. The rivers and creeks of the Amazon basin have been classified by limnologists who recognize two principal classes: blackwater rivers which account for most of the drainage of the so-called senile soils of the Brazilian shield, and nutrient-rich whitewater rivers, the main sources of which are their Andean tributaries; some authors mention a third class, the clearwater rivers (Junk and Furch 1985). The Vaupés Indians, however, make other distinctions. The Desana, for example, distinguish the following categories of river waters (*dehkó*): *boréri*/'white', *diári*/'reddish to cloudy yellowish', *nyíri*/'black', *yahsári*/'greenish blue', and others. These waters have different 'temperatures' and 'flavours' recognized on a scale that extends from 'bad' (white, yellowish) to 'good' (greenish blue to black), depending in each case on different lunar phases. These various aspects are thought to be correlated with cosmic 'energies' (*bogári*). The *yuruparí* trumpets and flutes are said to be imbued with these cosmic energies which refer, above all, to procreative forces in nature and society. For this reason the instruments must be submerged at certain spots and depths, in quiet waters where they can regain their energy after this has been spent during a ritual. The act of submerging the instruments should always be accompanied by lengthy ritual chants in which different intangible essences are invoked: colours, odours, temperatures, shapes, all of them symbolized by animals, plants, or minerals.

Each of the *yuruparí* instruments is associated with a certain animal species which, in turn, represents a sib from the complementary phratry of the local residence group. All these animals are said to be frequent visitors to buhu-nyu (*Socratea exorrhiza*) palms, to which they are attracted by the specific odour of efflorescence and pollen, or by the palm fruits. These animal species are the following:

1. *dëtë*, a small squirrel of a reddish-brown colour. Like other species of squirrels, these are often found in stands of palms where they feed on the flesh and/or kernels of the fruits and, by their staccato movements, may contribute to pollination. In fact, in September-October, at staminate dehiscence, squirrels are known to visit palms and by their jumpy movements 'make the pollen visible', as the Indians put it. The dëtë squirrel often feeds on the kernels of the nyu (*Astrocaryum vulgare*) palm, the stones of which are very hard, but its frequent presence near buhu-nyu (*Socratea exorrhiza*) is attributed to the attraction of the palm's fragrance. All dëtë squirrels are classified into colour categories: *borégë*/'white', *diágë*/'red', *ebol*/'yellow', and *nyígë*/'black'. These colour qualities correspond to 'cosmic energies' and are important in shamanic spells when these animals are invoked to assist the shaman in ritual practices. The term *dëtë* is Pira-Tapuya and is related to the verb *dë'teyel*/'to unite', 'to bind together', alluding to exogamous alliance. The tune played by *dëtë* flutes, which usually are of two slightly different sizes, is very characteristic and marks the rhythm of the women's dance, once the taboo instruments have been put away.

2. *mihsóka*, a large reddish squirrel that feeds on the flesh of palm fruits. These, too, are classified into four colour categories: white, red, yellow, and black. The term *mihsóka* is said to be a Desana word related to *mihpí*, the name of a palm (*Euterpe oleracea*) and of the coati (*Nasua rufa*), an animal which because of its banded tail is associated with the concept of social segmentation, while its *baculum* symbolizes its phallic character.

The symbolic associations within the Yuruparí Complex and beyond it are the following: squirrels represent virility; all species of squirrel have a penis bone, a conspicuous bushy tail of phallic connotation, and powerful incisors which, in shamanic practice, may be called upon in curing spells to help destroy pathogenic matters or to gnaw and tear apart the placenta-like covering from which a sick person must be freed to be 'reborn' again to a state of health (Reichel-Dolmatoff 1976b, essay 7 in this book). In describing squirrels and squirrel behaviour most informants took pains to point out that the females had eight mammae, this being the ideal number of a *yuruparí* trumpet unit. The movements of the animals were described as 'graceful', 'jumpy', 'like dancers'. On several occasions it was mentioned that squirrels were attracted by the pollen of palms and that they sometimes 'licked' the pollen that covered the ground around the palm trees. Squirrels were said to exude a pleasant odour. In summary, they were described as fertility and virility symbols, and their identification with certain *yuruparí* trumpets was quite definitely attributed to their phallic, seminal connotation. The large red squirrel was said to be directly associated with *Pamurí mahsë*, the progenitor, a mythical personage figuring prominently in the Creation Myth cycle (Reichel-Dolmatoff 1971:286).

Next to squirrels, three larger, ground-dwelling rodents are associated with three *yuruparí* trumpets or flutes: (a) *sëmé* (*Coelogynis paca*), (2) *buí* (*Dasyprocta fuliginosa*), and (3) *bohsó* (*Myoprocta*).

All rodents are designated as *masá tëori maháral*'people-nearby-belonging', because they are frequently found near Indian settlements or clearings, and thus constitute the principal game in garden hunting. Bohsó is the smallest of the three and is a favourite pet in many Indian houses; it is a lively little animal which often hides in the tubular cassava squeezers that lie about on the floor of the cooking section of a house. Agoutis are somewhat larger and paca is the largest; these two are rarely kept as pets but are eagerly hunted for their tasty meat.

Symbolically these rodents are closely associated with the female human element, partly because of their horticultural feeding strategies and food patterns, and partly because of their 'pleasant' body odour. Their territoriality, too, is considered to be a female characteristic. What is more, their names – bohsó, buí, sëmé – are related to kinship terms that refer to Pira-Tapuya and Tukano proper sibs (Reichel-Dolmatoff 1985, essay 3 in this book). In other words, these animals represent potential marriage partners of complementary exogamous groups. According to the Indians these rodents 'smell of semen, of sex', and so do certain fruits these animals feed on preferentially, such as the fruits of *mëë/Poraqueiba sericea* and *semé/Eperna purpurea*.

One aspect of animal behaviour which closely parallels that of women is the habit of rodents to scatter hoard, that is, to bury seeds along fallen logs or branches. The seeds 'planted' in this way are mainly palm fruits, the fruits of *mëë* (*Poraqueiba sericea*), *ukuki* (*Pouteria ukuqui Schultes*), and *vahsú* (*Hevea pauciflora* var. *coriacea*). Women are seed planters and occasionally they prepare a mass of grated manioc (*boo*), wrap it in Heliconia leaves, and bury these lumps along the side of a maloca for about eight to ten days. This is called *kíi-bo-yaríl*'manioc-mass-to bury'; with this processing the slightly fermented mass becomes very palatable and can be preserved in leaf-lined baskets on long canoe trips or overland excursions. Because of this similar behaviour the rodents associated with the musical instruments are referred to as *bohsóa nomél*'cavi-women', *buhía nomél*'agouti-women', *sëméa nomél*'*Pouteria ukuqui* Schultes-women', and *vahsú nomél*'*Hevea pauciflora*-women'. Of course, not all men play squirrel, agouti, or cavi instruments; their use and that of other trumpets or flutes always depends on the man's membership in certain descent groups and relative age. Because of their vegetarian food habits, these rodents are said to be 'pure' and their meat can be eaten without harmful consequences. Since food and sex are equated, the behaviour of these animals implies rules of human sexuality. When the flutes representing these rodents are brought into a maloca, the men who play them occupy certain spots or spaces in the room, or walk along certain lines while playing these instruments.

Several birds are associated with *yuruparí* trumpets. Among them are ~ *angá*, a large tinamou (*Tinamus* sp.), and ~ *angá diamë*, a smaller species of a reddish colour. The name ~ angá was said to be related to *ohkó*/'water', and this to *ohká*/'of the same flavour', meaning a kinperson or, rather, a female member of a complementary exogamous unit. The reddish bird is also called *diámë petó-ëno*, a Pira-Tapuya term used to designate an ancestral group the name of which was said to be derived from *pehtá*/'landing place' (PT) and *ëno*/'people', 'beings' (PT), referring to the mythical 'landing place' of origins at Ipanoré. Another, smaller species of tinamou, associated with a third trumpet, is called ~ *nairó*, a term that means 'cooked', 'transformed'. During the great mythical World Fire this bird is said to have survived by hiding under a clump of bunch-grass, thereby conserving for future generations the cosmic 'colour energies' contained in its brightly hued eggs. It was pointed out that the trumpet is associated not so much with the bird image as with the concept of transformation, of being 'cooked' and reborn, this being the essential objective of male initiation. Additionally it was said that all three tinamous are phallic birds because of their yellowish 'semen-coloured' plumage and that in one version of the World Fire myth tinamou was hiding in the vagina of the Daughter of the Sun. The meat of tinamou is considered to be 'pure' and is eaten as a ritual diet. Occasionally one of the trumpets represents a small species of toucan which visits a certain (unidentified) palm; its name is *vehe-pu-bero*/'palm-leaf-arc', the last word referring to the shape of the bird's curved beak.

Two insects are closely associated with *yuruparí* trumpets; one is the Praying Mantis, designated as ~ *poreró* or *bári ~ sero* (*bári bëgë*); the other is an unidentified tree cricket, also referred to as *bári ~ sero*. The latter's appearance in large numbers near palms or malocas is said to be correlated with certain lunar phases, and during the waning of the moon these insects are collected and eaten toasted. The term ~ *poreró* is related to *po'óri*/'to scatter', 'to dehisce'; when pronounced *poóri*, it means 'to inseminate', 'to prepare a seed bed'. If stressed on the last syllable – *poorí* – it means 'to provide (fruits) to be transformed into a beverage', an expression that carries the implicit meaning of providing marriage partners for a drug ritual, that is, for exogamous sex. The term *póri* means 'to liquate', 'that which is liquid', 'something that gives pleasure'. The root term *poo* (*poosé* in T; *poóye* in PT) refers to a semantic field that includes insemination, pollination, germination, hallucination, transformation, sex, genital organs, the mating call of deer, the sound of *yuruparí* trumpets, and a number of other associations. These semantic contents are, of course, related to the palm fruit ritual and to the common exchange rituals called *dabucurí* in LG. The element ~ *sero* in the term *bári ~ sero* signifies a cone-shaped object and is said to represent a clitoris or vagina. Since *bári* means 'to eat', 'to copulate', the alternative name of the insect is 'clitoris-eater' or 'old-copulator'. In a variant interpretation it was suggested that *barí* was the Desana name of a tall jungle tree called japurá in LG, the fruit of which is shaped like a groundnut and is similar to a cashew nut but smaller. As mentioned already, the odour of that fruit has a marked sexual connotation. Ground into a paste and boiled, it can be stored in leaf-lined baskets for up to three months and is sometimes used in ceremonial exchanges between exogamic units. As is usual in the processing of these kinds of food, they are boiled together with manioc leaves and leaves of *Phytolacca rivinoides*. The gathering and processing of this fruit should always be accompanied by sexual abstinence because otherwise the fruit's particular odour would make it unfit for ritual exchange.

These two groups of animals, the rodents and the insects, are said to have been eyewitnesses to the 'first incest' episode, that is, they had observed the self-pollination of palms and thus had been witnesses to a time period when endogamy was practised. From their hiding places in the underbush and the leaves they had observed people and plants, and now, temporarily transformed into musical instruments, their voices remind society of chaos and disorder in the past and the need for order and exogamy.

Wilhelm Saake (1958:275), when speaking of the *yurupari* trumpets of the Arawakan Baniwa, mentions the following flute names: Jacamin, Jauarete, Aracu, Paca, Uari, Suassu, Uairi, Cotia, Tucano. Saake does not attempt to analyze these names, which obviously are those of exogamic groups the Baniwa consider as complementary. My identification is as follows: Jacamin is the LG name of the trumpeter bird (*Psophia crepitans*), which figures in some Desana myths as the representative of 'other people' who speak an incomprehensible language. Jauarete is Yavareté, meaning 'true jaguar' in LG, and is the place name of a settlement, Salesian Mission, rapids, and general region on the middle Vaupés, in front of the mouth of the Colombian Papurí river. According to various travel reports of the later part of the nineteenth century, the Yavareté region was inhabited at that time by Arawakan groups. Aracu is the LG name of a fish (*Leporinus copelandi*), called *boréka* in Desana, who consider this fish to be an important sib ancestor at a time before exogamy and patrilineality were introduced. Paca is the LG name of *Coelogynis paca* while Uari is a fish called *uarí* in D, PT, T, G, and 'Juan Viejo' in the local Spanish vernacular. It has yellow, red, and black annular marks, said to have been made in mythical times with the mouthpiece of a *yurupari* trumpet. Uaripë is a place name on the Vaupés river, situated between the Desana, Pira-Tapuya, and other groups, and *uari-pora*/'uari-sons' is another sib name of the Desana (or Pira-Tapuya?). The Indians living there are designated as *uari-pë mahara*/'uari-place-belonging'. Cotia is the self-name of the Uanana; Tucano might refer to any Tukanoan-speaking group but in this case probably refers to the Tukano proper, that is, to the first wave of newcomers to the Vaupés who established contact with the Arawak between Ipanoré and Yavareté.

Until recently the use of certain masks was an important aspect of initiation rituals, especially in the region of the Papurí river. In the literature these masks, which should not be confused with the well-known Cubeo masks of bark-cloth, are referred to by the term macacaraua, a word derived from the Brazilian Portuguese macaco/'monkey' (Coudreau 1887: 157, 163, 187; Koch-Grünberg 1909:II, 252-253, 254, fig. 174). These are head-masks made of palm fibre strings interwoven with monkey hair and the hair (head and pubic) cut off at a girl's first menstruation rituals. In describing these materials the Indians emphasize their different odour qualities. These *yurupari* masks are associated with three species of noctural monkeys: *ahëkamë*, *ukuámë*, and *muhúu*. The name of the first monkey is derived from *ahëári*/'soft', *ahëaye*/'softness', 'to soften'; and *kamóye*/'to rut', 'to be in heat'. While the first monkey's name is thus of Desana origin, the name of the second monkey – *ukuámë* – is derived from *ukusé*/'to speak', 'to converse', a Tukano proper term referring to ritual conversations during an exchange ceremonial. The third name – *muhúu* – is derived from *muhúri*/'to guide', ~ *muhúri*/'to begin', 'to introduce someone'; ~ *mohotó* is 'hand' in Desana and the idea is that the third monkey is the guiding hand, the one who introduces the initiate into his new status and to his prescribed marriage partners. The term *gahkí* (D) refers to monkeys in general and is a common metaphor for penis. The three monkey masks represent three intermarrying phratries: the Desana, the Pira-Tapuya, and the Tukano proper. This again is a telling example of the close relationship between the Yurupari Complex and social structure.

Stradelli's 'Yurupari Legend'

During the decade from 1881 to 1891 the Italian poet, lawyer, and traveller Count Ermanno Stradelli visited the Rio Negro-Vaupés area on several occasions. In 1881 he spent some time on the Tiquié river not far from Ipanoré; in 1882 he travelled up to Yavareté whence he ascended the Papurí up to Piracuara. A third excursion (1890-1891) took him once more to the Vaupés but little is known about his itinerary on this occasion.

In 1890 Stradelli published his 67-page *Leggenda dell' Jurupary*. According to Stradelli the story had been written in *nheengatú* by an acculturated caboclo by the name of Maximiniano José Roberto, who had given it to Stradelli who translated it into Italian. A recent Brazilian author describes Maximiniano as 'filho de indios Manáos e Tarianas, tuixáua, espiritual de Taruma-miri, principe amazonico, recolhedor apaixonado de centenas de lendas, maravilhosas e seguras como documentaçao etnológica da divinidades selvagem de Jurupary...' (Camara Cascudo 1967). Ever since its first publication, Stradelli's *yurupari* 'legend' has been discussed, here and there, in the enthnological and folkloric literature but, above all, it has stirred the imagination of certain *littérateurs* who have seen in it an outstanding example of Amerindian oral literature of great aesthetic value and profound meanings.

I have read Stradelli's 'legend' in Italian, Portuguese, and Spanish, and have formed my own conclusions about it. In my opinion, Amazonian Indians do not talk like that; they do not use florid images of immaculate maidens, wise law-givers, and purified spirits rising heavenward.[14] It is not the purpose of this essay to discuss Stradelli's version of the *yurupari* theme but there can be no doubt that a detailed analysis of it might be very revealing if based on the insights gained from our semantic readings of original Tukanoan texts. As an example of the kind of work that might be done, I shall comment on a few incidental events described at the very beginning of Stradelli's 'legend'. Stradelli describes the miraculous birth of *Yurupary* in the following episode which I have despoiled of its poetic garb.

Once upon a time, the Indians of the Serra de Tenui[15] were in serious danger of dying out because in their settlement only old, impotent men were left. To discuss this situation the women secretly gathered at the shore of a lake called *muypa*/'Pleiades', access to which at night had been strictly forbidden to women by the Sun himself. One of the women's suggestions was "di tentare se donna potesse fecondar donna" (Stradelli 1890: 659 ff.). An old shaman who had over-heard this talk angrily declared the lake to be polluted by the women's disobedience and warned that the Pleiades, who used to bathe there, would not return to the lake. However, he ordered the women to bathe in it now. The shaman himself climbed to the top of a hill and threw himself down into the lake whereupon the surface of the lake 'restò tutta coperta di una polvere bianca. Era la polvere con cui il paie, che non era vecchio como pareva, aveva nascosta la sua giovinezza.' When the women emerged from the lake they all were pregnant and soon gave birth to numerous offspring. Among these children was a girl who, because of her beauty, was called Seucy. One day Seucy avidly wanted to eat the fruit called *pihycan*, forbidden to pubescent girls. She found these fruits at a place where some monkeys had dropped them from a tree.[16] While gorging herself on the fruits, the juice trickled down between her breasts until the liquid reached her vagina. Seucy became pregnant and gave birth to a male child. His name was *Yurupari*.

In this episode, mentioned in the first three pages of Stradelli's 'leggenda', we recognize a series of motifs from our Tukanoan texts and their commentaries. Divested of their embellished language and decoding the metaphors of Tukanoan languages, the biological and social bases appear here in their own logic.

The initial setting is that our Scene 1, which shows the 'old men' and the disconcerted young women. When the women gather at the 'forbidden shore' they 'pollute' the waters and indulge in sexual experimentations, as described in our Scene 6. The 'bathing' of the women suggests their spatially subjacent position (during staminate anthesis) with respect to the shaman who, 'rejuvenated' (tumescent), scatters his semen (pollen) over them, fertilizing the women (efflorescences). Now the Pleiades are reborn and with them the fruiting season arrives, accompanied by the Yuruparí Complex.[17] The nature of the 'forbidden fruit' *pihycan* has been investigated by some authors. Camara Cascudo writes: "Entre os indios do rio Uaupés a fruta foi o pihycan, na cucura no rio Negro e a puruma no Solimoes. (*Pourouma cecropiae folia* (*sic*), Aublet). Barbosa Rodrigues colheo duas versoes também no rio Uaupés (Ukairy) e diz que a fruta era chamada fruta de Uacu, *uacu-iua*." (Camara Cascudo 1967:55) I am afraid that these statements require some corrections. In the first place, Ukairy seems to be quite an unusual Arawakan name of the river, unknown in the Colombian Vaupés territory. The LG name of *Pouteria ucuqui* Schultes, a large jungle tree with ovoid edible fruits, should not be confused with *Eperna purpurea*, a tree with edible lentil-shaped fruits, which is called *uakú* in Tukano proper, *sëmé* in Desana, and *hímio* in Tatuyo. The LG term *simió*, obviously derived from the Tukanoan words, is occasionally used to designate an old-fashioned fifty-centavo coin of silver, alluding to the fruit's shape. Boys and girls who have not yet reached puberty are strictly forbidden from eating this fruit, especially if it is roasted. It has an astringent flavour and culturally 'improper' sexual connotations. Lemos Barbos (1967:155) mentions the Tupi word *uá* with the meaning of *fundo*, *assento*, which might suggest a procreative connotation. In the second place, cucura is not *Pourouma cecropiaefolia* but is a palm (*Mauritiella cataractarum*), the fruits of which are not eaten because, as mentioned, they are small and very acid; no symbolic importance whatsoever is attached to it in the Colombian Vaupés, as far as I know.

Next to *Pouteria ucuqui* Schultes, it seems to be *Pourouma cecropiaefolia* that has the fertilizing qualities which seduced Seucy. Called *uvilla de monte* in the Spanish vernacular and *imbaúba do vinho* in LG, its Desana name is *igí moho*. In Desana, *mohó* means 'hand' and might refer to the shape of the leaves, but some informants glossed it as *igë*/'he', 'male', combined with the root term *muhúri*/'to begin to copulate', 'to set up', 'to establish the foundations of something'. The texture of the juice of this small (2 cm diameter) spherical fruit is said to be 'just like human semen' while its flavour is compared to that of *Pouteria ucuqui* Schultes. The fruit puruma, mentioned by Camara Cascudo for the rio Solimoes, is indeed *Pourouma cecropiaefolio* and is monoecious. None of my Vaupés informants claimed to have heard of a fruit called pihycan.

Some Marginal Myth Cycles

Marginal to the Yuruparí Complex of the Colombian Vaupés we find two other myth cycles: the Goa cycle and the Bisíu cycle. Both are superficially related to the Yuruparí Complex, the goa tradition referring to culture contact and

exogamy and the bisíu tradition to the male initiation ritual. Based on recordings, of the field data, and published sources, it seems that both cycles have a
rather northern and northeastern distribution where they are known among the
Arawakan groups of the Guainía territory – Baníwa and Kuripáko – and the
Tariana of the Brazilian Yavareté-Sao Gabriel region.

I shall refer first to the *goá-më* (D) cycle of myths. According to the Desana,
Pira-Tapuya, and others, the term goá-më is derived from *goa*/'bone', and *më*, a
word that stands for 'being'; goá-më is 'bone-being', with the implicit meaning
of a phallic being. The basic concept is called *go'a* (D), *o'á* (T), *ko'á* (PT, U), the
root term referring to a semantic field that includes the following concepts: phallus, bone, skeleton, substructure, basis. Among the Vaupés Tukanoans this concept is not personified; it is not a distinct supernatural being but rather refers to
a remote ancestry, an original procreative energy. But individual interpretations
vary; some people said that the 'bone' aspect referred to the now extinct
Arawakan custom of mixing the burned and pulverized bones of fore-fathers
with a ritually consumed beverage (chicha); others mentioned the possibility that
goa or *koa* was, in essence, a female concept. The Desana expression *goá-
mahára*/'bone-belonging to' was glossed as 'descendant of an exogamic union'.
Practically all informants agreed that the *goa/koa* concept was not of Tukanoan
but of Arawakan origin, and that among the latter a personalized 'creator god'
was being designated by these or similar names.[18]

The other cycle refers to Bisíu, a spirit-being which is said to personify the
appointed custodian and teacher of a group of novices who must spend part of
their training period in isolation, living in the forest under the guardianship of
an older person, usually a shaman. The narratives about Bisíu I have recorded
mention a sequence of situations and episodes which can be summarized as follows:

1. A small group of initiates lives in the forest under the tutelage of Bisíu, in
whom the boys' parents and relatives have put their trust.

2. At a given moment Bisíu warns the boys not to eat a roasted wild-growing
fruit which has a marked sexual connotation. The boys, however, disobey these
orders.

3. Presumably in punishment, Bisíu causes a great thunderstorm and offers
the boys protection in a cave, a hollow tree, or his wide-open anus. All but one
of the boys accept Bisíu's offer.

4. When told about this matter the boys' parents become infuriated and
threaten Bisíu, who refuses to leave his hiding place in a tree.

5. The parents entice him to come to a drinking bout by offering him a beverage made from *umarí* (*Poraqueiba sericea*).

6. Bisíu cannot resist the temptation; when he is inebriated the men seize him
and burn him in a huge fire. After mocking his captors, whose sons he admits to
have abused sexually, Bisíu rises heavenward.

In commenting upon various versions of this narrative, the informants explained at the outset that during the initiatory period in the forest homosexual practices between the boys and their custodians were fairly common; indeed they almost formed part of ritual sexual initiation. All informants agreed that the 'caves' and 'hollows' were metaphors and that Bisíu was a fiendish seducer and rapist.

There appear to exist some parallels between these Vaupés narratives and the *yurupari*-koaí cycles of the Arawak, wherein *yuruparí*, the miraculously born 'culture hero', is being burned in punishment for 'cannibalism' or other misdeeds but rises heavenward. The motif of the 'forbidden fruit', especially of the dangerous, sexually arousing odour produced by the 'toasting' of it, is another element these myth variants have in common. The fact that Bisíu 'descends' from a tree, that is, from a spatially higher position, because he is being offered umarí beer, suggests the self-pollination/forbidden sex theme of the Vaupés Yuruparí Complex.

Bisíu is said to produce strange humming noises, a kind of polyphonous music which is very beguiling and which seems to imitate the voices of all kinds of forest creatures. In some largely unexplained ways, he is a forest spirit that personifies the forest's fertility potential, the sexual 'energy' of forest animals which the initiates are required to share in order to foment it through rituals. According to some informants the name bisíu is derived from *bihsíri*, a sonorous 'impact' which is sexually arousing.

A widely known forest spirit that is marginally, or perhaps quite fundamentally, related to the Yuruparí Complex is the Kurupíra (LG), or *boráro* as the Desana call him. The term *borá* means 'stake', 'house-post', 'pillar'; the element -*ro* is an augmentative suffix. In the sense of 'big post' the boráro is unequivocally designated as a phallic being, at times almost akin to the Master of Animals.[19] The interesting point is that the boráro is closely associated with palms; in fact, he is the guardian and kinsman of palms, and since he occasionally will attack lonely hunters or foragers, solitary stands of palms, especially of *Mauritia flexuosa*, might be dangerous places to visit. The hidden presence of the boráro can be recognized by the sudden sound of a falling, dry palm leaf.

The boráro is said to carry a characteristic 'weapon' (*yohóka*) in the shape of a short hooked stick, an elbow-hafted adze provided with a sharp blade of palm wood or turtle shell. He carries this hoe over his shoulder and uses it to 'grasp' or 'hook' lonely forest travellers, especially foraging women. In many mythical and conversational contexts a phallic connotation was given to the boráro's adze. Until recent times these adze-shaped instruments formed part of the ritual attire of dancers, and Koch-Grünberg (1909:I, 350, fig. 225) describes a *yurupari* initiation ceremony among the Desana and Tukano, during which the principal dancers carried these hoes over their left shoulders. While discussing these instruments the use of which has practically disappeared, it was stated that in the old days these hoes were used for palm starch extraction. The palms, mainly *Mauritia flexuosa*, were felled at certain times of the year, their trunks were split open, and the pithy starch was carved out to be used in sago production. From what I was given to understand, palm stem starch was formerly an important food resource in much of the Vaupés-Guainía area, and its extraction and processing took place in an elaborate ritual context in which the boráro played a major role. He was *nyehkë mahsë*/'ancestor', it was said; 'he was the original Procreator/*pamuri mahsë*, the true Master of Animals/*vai-mahsë*'. Palm starch is no longer consumed today; the adze has become an almost forgotten ritual object; and the boráro has little or no importance in myth and shamanism, his role being reduced to that of a lonely roaming forest monster.

Summary

I have suggested some guidelines for a new approach to the study of the *yurupari* theme, one of the major myth cycles of tropical South America. Shorn of its romantic trappings and examined under the light of its biological components, the *yurupari* 'legend', 'cult', or whatever one chooses to call it is likely to provide valuable insights into the dynamics of social structure, of shifts in marriage rules and subsistence strategies and, in general, of the social and cultural history of the Colombian Northwest Amazon.[20]

Notes

1. See, among others, Orico (1975:61) and Schaden (1959).
2. Tukano is the name of a linguistic family consisting of some twenty tribes speaking different languages. One of these tribes is called Tukano and I use the designation 'Tukano proper' when I refer to the tribe, while Tukano or Tukanoan refers to the collective aspect.
3. Orjuela (1983:174-175) compares the *yurupari* theme with the Popol Vuh; Saake (1958:271) compares it with the Nibelungen and the Kalevala.
4. Other sources on recent research in the Colombian Vaupés, referring to the Tukano, are Arhem (1981), Bidou (1976), Fulop (1954, 1955, 1956), Goldman (1963), Jackson (1983), Langdon (1975), Torres (1969), Trupp (1974). Apart from their dissertations and monographs, most of these authors have published a number of shorter research articles. For a fairly complete bibliography, see Reichel-Dolmatoff (1987:vii-xi).
5. The Pira-Tapuya have sometimes been designated as Fish-People because *pira* means fish in LG. This, however, is an error; the Pira-Tapuya often change their pronunciation of *r* to *n* and refer to themselves as Pino-Tapuya, 'Anaconda People'.
6. The following abbreviations have been employed: LG = lengua geral, the Amazonian vernacular; lit. = literally. Most Indian words are italicized only at their first mention. Tukanoan languages are indicated thus: (D) for Desana, (PT) for

Pira-Tapuya, (T) for Tukano proper, (U) for Uanano. If an Indian term is not followed by an abbreviation, it is understood that it is in the Desana language, which was the author's main vehicle of communication.

7.   On palms I have consulted mainly Anderson and Balick (1988), Barbosa Rodrigues (1903), Clement (1987, 1988), Dugand (1976a, 1976b), Henderson (1985, 1986).

8.   The expression 'to eat one's own flesh' reads in Desana: *yëë poréru baa górovereka*, lit. 'I-hinder parts-eat-intoxicated'.

9.   Pora (D). The isomorphic chain of tree trunk/womb/homunculi/shamanic flight of beetle/pollinator, etc, has not escaped the attention of the Indians.

10. This type of inversion is fairly common in connection with shifts in social structure.

11. I have heard rumours of some cases of poisoning. Judging from some myth contexts it seems more probable that in the past disobedient women were gang-raped.

12. A good photograph is in Allen (1947:Fig. 7).

13. The OED gives, as one definition of 'breath', the following: 'An exhalation or vapour from heated objects, etc., steam, smoke, reek…'

14. Tastevin bitingly observes that Stradelli's 'legends' might have been of more interest had he published them in their original Indian language (quoted in Camara Cascudo 1967:91).

15. The Serra di Tenui, where Stradelli locates the origin of Yurupari, the hero, should not be confused with the Sierra de Tunahi of the headwaters of the Vaupés river, just north of Miraflores. It is rather Tunuhy, on the middle Isana river.

16. The motif of monkeys dropping fruits from trees upon the petition of some female ground-dwelling animal is frequent in Tukanoan myths. In a Desana myth, when tortoise asks some *wau* (*Callicebus*) monkeys sitting on a palm to drop some fruit, she (tortoise is a 'female' being) addresses them as 'cousins'. The monkeys say: '*nyégo terí buro arimó*'/'ugly-lazy-old one-is coming'.

17. Seucy is a misreading of Siusi, the name of the Pleiades in Baniwa; there is a sib by that name. On the Pleiades and their relationship with palm fruiting seasons see Hugh-Jones (1979), and for a detailed astronomical/mythical discussion see Magana (1988).

18. On *kaoi* see Wright (1981).19. On the Master of Animals among the Tukano Indians of the Vaupés see Reichel-Dolmatoff (1971, index, p. 289, under *Vaimahsë*).

20. Ruddle et al. (1974) contains a chapter titled 'Sago Myth and Ritual' which summarizes various accounts from Indonesia and of the Pacific regions. Some of these beliefs and rituals show striking parallels with Tukanoan and Arawakan myth motifs, such as: the origin of palms from the body of a slain culture hero, incestuous relationships, or from the 'scattering' of some substance; the close relationship between the fertility of palms and that of women; the cutting up of a palm stem into a sequence of named social segments; and the use of 'sacred' flutes which women are not allowed to see. In the absence of proof of culture contact, I think it is reasonable to suggest that many of these similarities are based upon the observation of palm pollination. Quoting a Warao (Venezuelan) myth on the origin of Mauritia flexuosa, Wilbert (1976:221, 363-364) writes: 'Indians discover strange people in a distant place who do not answer when spoken to. The Indians notice that the man has blossoms and the woman has fruit. They cut the people down, and as they fall they become real moriche palms.' Although in this case culture contact is quite possible, I am inclined to believe that the underlying idea is based upon a knowledge of pollination of monoecious palms.

BIBLIOGRAPHY

AGURELL, S.; HOLMSTEDT, B.; LINDGREN, J. E.: "Alkaloid content of *Banisteriopsis rusbyana*". In *American Journal of Pharmacy*, 140, 5, 1968, pp. 148-151.

ALLEN, PAUL H.: "Indians of Southeastern Colombia". In *Geographical Review*, New York, 35(4), 1947, pp. 567-582.

ANDERSON, ANTHONY B.: "The Names and Uses of Palms among a Tribe of Yanomama Indians". In *Principes. Journal of the Palm Society*, New York, 22(1), 1978, pp. 30-41.

ANDERSON, ANTHONY B.; BALICK, MICHAEL J.: "Taxonomy of the Babassú Complex (*Orbignya* spp.: Palmae)". In *Systematic Botany*, 13(1), 1988, pp. 32-50.

ÅRHEM, KAJ: "Fishing and Hunting among the Makuna: Economy, Ideology and Ecological Adaptation in the Northwest Amazon". In Goteborgs Etnografiska Museum, *Årstryck*, 1976., pp. 27-44.

Makuna Social organization: A Study in Descent, Alliance and the Formation of Corporate Groups in Northwestern Amazonas. Acta Universitatis Upsaliensis, Estocolmo, 1981.

BALDUS, HERBERT: *Lendas dos Indios do Brasil.* Sao Paulo, Editora Brasiliense Limitada, 1946.

BARBOSA RODRIGUES, JOAO: "Poranbuda Amazonense ou Kochyma-Uara Porandub". In *Annaes da Biblioteca Nacional do Rio de Janeiro*, 14(2), Rio de Janeiro, 1890.

Les noces des palmiers. Remarques préliminaires sur la fécondation. Bruselas, Imprimerie Ad. Mertens, 1903.

BENDER, BARBARA: *Farming in Prehistory: From Hunter-Gatherer to Food-Producer.* London, John Baker, 1975.

BERLIN, BRENT; KAY, PAUL: *Basic Color Terms: Their Universality and Evolution.* Los Angeles, University of California Press, 1969.

BIDOU, PATRICE: *Les fils de l'Anaconda Céleste (Les Tatuyo): Etude de la structure socio-politique.* Thèse de Doctoral de troisième Cycle, Université de Paris, 1976.

BIOCCA, ETTORE: *Viaggi tra gli Indi: Alto Rio Negro, alto Orinoco. Appunti di un biologo.* Milán, 1967, 4 Vol.

BÖDIGER, UTE: *Die Religion der Tukano im nordwestlichen Amazonas.* Kölner Ethnologische Mitteilungen, Universitäts-Verlag, Colonia, 1965.

BOLENS, JACQUELINE: "Mythe de Jurupari: introduction à une analyse". In *L'Homme*, 7(1), Paris, 1967, pp. 50-66.

BRANDAO DE AMORIM, ANTONIO: "Lendas em Nheengatú e em Portuguez". In *Revista do Instituto Histórico e Geografico Brasileiro*, 100(154), Río de Janeiro, 1928, pp. 3-475.

BRISTOL, MELVIN L.: "The psychotropic *Banisteriopsis* among the Sibundoy of Colombia". In *Botanical Museum Leaflets*, xxi, Harvard University, Cambridge, Mass, 1966, pp. 229-248.

CAMARA CASCUDO, LUIS DA: *Dicionàrio do folclore brasileiro.* Segunda Edición, Río de Janeiro, Instituto Nacional do Livro, Ministério da Educaçao e Cultura, 1962.

Antologia do folclore brasileiro. Tercera Edición, Sao Paulo, Martins, 1965.

In memoria de Stradelli. Biografia. Jornadas geográficas. Livraria Clássica, 1936. Segunda edición, Manaos, Ediçao do Governo do Amazonas, 1967.

Geografia dos mitos brasileiros. Segunda edición, Brasilia, Instituto Nacional do Livro, 1976.

CHEN, A. L.; CHEN, K. K.: "Harmine, the Alkaloid of caapi". In *Quarterly Journal of Pharmacy and Pharmacology*, xii, 1939, pp. 30-38.

CLEMENT, CHARLES R.: "Pupunha: Uma árvore domesticada". In *Ciencia Hoje*, 6(20), 1987, pp.42-48.

"Domestication of the Pejibaye Palm (*Bactris gasipaes*)". In *Advances in Economic Botany*, 6, The New York Botanical Garden, 1988, pp. 155-174.

COLE, SONIA: *The Neolitic Revolution.* 5th ed., London, British Museum, 1970.

COUDREAU, HENRI A.: *La France équinoxiale: Voyage à travers des Guyanes et l'Amazonie.* Paris, Challamel, 1887.

CROCKER, WILLIAM H.: "The Canela (Brazil) Taboo System: A Preliminary Exploration of an Anxiety Reducing Device". In *Verhandlungen des XXXVIII Internationalen Amerikanistenkongresses, Stuttgart-München, 1968.* Munich, 1971, Vol. 2, pp. 323-331.

DE CIVRIEUX, MARC: "Clasificación zoológica y botánica entre los Makiritare y los Kariña". In *Antropologica*, 36, Caracas, 1973, pp. 3-82.

DE CIVRIEUX, MARC; LICHY, RENÉ: "Vocabularios de cuatro dialectos arawak del río Guainía". In *Boletín de la Sociedad Venezolana de Ciencias Naturales*, 8, Caracas, 1950, pp. 121-159.

DER MARDEROSIAN, A. H.; PINKLEY, H. V.; DOBBINS, M. F.: "Native use and occurrence of N, N-Dimethyltryptamine in the leaves of *Banisteriopsis rusbyana*". In *American Journal of Pharmacy*, 140, 1968, pp. 137-47.

DETIENNE, MARC: *Les jardins d'Adonis: la mythologie des aromates in Grèce.* Paris, Gallimard, 1972.

DOUGLAS, MARY: *Purity and Danger: An Analysis of Concepts of Pollution and Taboo.* London, Routledge & Kegan Paul, 1966.

DUGAND GNECCO, ARMANDO: "Palmas de Colombia". In *Cespedesia*, 5(19-20), Cali, 1976a, pp. 207-255.

"Palmarum Colombiensium Elenchus". In *Cespedesia*, 5(19-20), Cali, 1976b, pp. 257-330.

DURKHEIM, EMILE; MAUSS, MARCEL: "De quelques formes primitives de classification: contribution à l'étude des représentations collectives". In *Année Sociologique, 1901-1902*: 6. Paris, 1903, pp. 1-72.

EFRON, DANIEL, ed.: "Ethnofarmacologic search for psychoactive drugs". In *U. S. Public Health Service Publication*, No. 1645, 1967.

EICHMEIER, JOSEPH; HÖFER, OSCAR: *Endogene Bildmuster.* Urban & Schwarzenberg, Munich/Berlín, Vienna, 1974.

ELGER, F.: "Über das Vorkommen von Harmin in einer südamerikanischen Liane (Yagé)". In *Helv. Chim. Acta*, xi, 1928, pp. 162-166.

EWER, R. F.: *The Carnivores.* Ithaca, New York, Cornell University Press, 1973.

ELIADE, MIRCEA: "Spirit, Light, and Seed". In *History of Religions*, 11 (1), 1971, pp. 1-30.

FISCHER, CARDENAS: Estudio sobre el principio activo del Yagé. Doctoral thesis, Universidad Nacional, Facultad de Medicina, Casa Editorial de `La Cruzada', Bogotá, 1923.

FREUD, SIGMUND: *Totem and Taboo.* Trad. A. A. Brill, New York, Moffat, Yard, 1918.

FRIEDBERG, CLAUDINE: "Des Banisteriopsis utilisés comme drogue in Amérique su Sud". In *Journal d'agriculture tropicale et botanique appliquée*, xii, 1965, pp. 403-437, 550-590, 729-780.

FULOP, MARCOS: "Aspectos de la cultura Tukana: Cosmogonía". In *Revista Colombiana de Antropología*, 3, Bogotá, 1954, pp. 97-137.

"Notas sobre términos de parentesco de los Tukano". In *Revista Colombiana de Antropología*, 4, Bogotá, 1955, pp. 121-164.

"Aspectos de la cultura Tukana: Mitología, Parte I". In *Revista Colombiana de Antropología*, 5, Bogotá, 1956, pp. 335-383.

FURST, P. T., ed.: *Flesh of the Gods: The Ritual Use of Hallucinogens.* New York, 1972.

GALVAO, EDUARDO: "Aculturaçao indígena no Rio Negro". In *Boletim do Museo Paraense Emilio Goeldi*, Nova serie, No. 7, Belén, 1959.

GIACONE, ANTONIO: *Pequeño catecismo portugués-tucano.* Belém, Tipografia da "A Palavra", 1949a.

Os Tucanos e as outras tribos do Uaupés. Sao Paulo, Imprensa Oficial, 1949b.

Gramática, dicionários e fraseologia da lingua dahceié ou Tucano. Cantribuiçao da Universidade do Pará para o Cinquentenário das Missoes Salesianas do Amazonas. Belén, Imprensa Universitária do Pará, 1965.

GILL, SAM D.: "The Color of Navajo Ritual Symbolism: An Evaluation of Method". In *Journal of Anthropological Research*, 31(4), 1975, pp. 350-363.
GOLDMAN, IRVING: *The Cubeo: Indians of the Northwest Amazon*. Illinois Studies in Anthropology, 2, Urbana, University of Illinois Press, 1963.
    "Perceptions of Nature and the Structure of Society: The Question of Cubeo Descent". In *Dialectical Anthropology*, 1(3), 1976, pp. 287-292.
    "Time, Space, and Descent: The Cubeo Example". In *Actes du XLIIe Congrès International des Américanistes*, 2, Paris, 1977, pp. 175-183.
GOLLEY, FRANK B.; MEDINA, ERNESTO, eds.: *Tropical Ecological Systems: Trends in Terrestrial and Aquatic Research*. Berlin/Heidelberg, Springer, 1975.
GOSSEN, GARY H.: "Animal Souls and Human Destiny in Chamula". In *Man*, 10(3), 1975, pp. 448-461.
GRATTAN, J. H, G.; SINGER, CHARLES: *Anglo-Saxon Magic and Medicine*. London, New York, Toronto, Oxford University Press, 1952.
HALVERSON, JOHN: "Animal Categories and Terms of Abuse". In *Man*, 11(4), 1976, pp. 505-516.
HAMES, RAYMOND B.; VICKERS, WILLIAM T., eds.: *Adaptive Responses of Native Amazonians*. New York, Academic Press, 1983.
HARNER, M. J., "The sound of rushing water". In *Natural History*, ixxvi, 1968, pp. 28-33, 60-61.
    ed.: *Hallucinogens and Shamanism*. Oxford, 1973.
HEINEN, H.D.; RUDDLE, K.: "Ecology, Ritual and Economic Organization in the Distribution of Palm Starch among the Warao of the Orinoco Delta". In *Journal of Anthropological Research*, 30, 1974, pp. 116-138.
HENDERSON, ANDREW: "Pollination of *Socratea exhorriza* and *Iriartea ventricosa*". In *Principes, Journal of the International Palm Society*, 29(2), New York, 1985, pp. 64-71.
    "A Review of Pollination Studies in the Palmae". In *The Botanical Review*, 52(3), New York, 1986, pp. 221-259.
HOCHSTEIN, F. A.; PARADIES, A. M.: "Alkaloids of *Banisteriopsis caapi* and *Prestonia amazonicum*". In *Journal of the Am. Chem. Soc.*, 79, 1957, pp. 5735-5736.
HUGH-JONES, CHRISTINE: "Skin and Soul: The Round and the Straight: Social Time and Social Space in Pira-Paraná Society". In *Actes du XLIIe Congrès International des Américanistes, Paris, 1976*, Paris, 1977a, Vol. 2, pp. 185-204.
    "Social Classification among the South American Indians of the Vaupés Region of Colombia". Doctoral thesis, University of Cambridge, 1977b.
    From the Milk River: Spacial and Temporal Processes in Northwest Amazonia. Cambridge, Cambridge University Press, 1979.
HUGH-JONES, STEPHEN: "Male Initiation and Cosmology among the Barasana Indians of the Vaupés Region of Colombia". Doctoral thesis, University of Cambridge, 1974.
    The Palm and the Pleiades: Initiation and Cosmology in Northwest Amazonia. Cambridge, Cambridge University Press, 1979.
HUXLEY, A.: *Plant and Planet*. Harmondsworth, Penguin Books, 1978.
IZIKOWITZ, KARL GUSTAV: *Musical and Other Sound Instruments of the South American Indians*. Göteborgs Kungl. Vetenskaps-och Vitterhets Samhälles, Handlinger, Femte Följden, ser. A. Band 5, No. 1, Gotemburgo, 1935.
JACKSON, JEAN: "Vaupés Marriage: A network system in the northwest Amazon". In *Regional Analysis*, 2, 1976, pp. 65-93.
    The Fish People: Linguistic Exogamy and Tukanoan Identity in Northwest Amazonia. Cambridge University Press, Cambridge, 1983.
JUNK, WOLFGANG J.; FURCH, KARIN: "The Physical and Chemical Properties of Amazonian Waters and Their Relationship with the Biota". In *Amazonia*. Ghillean T. Prance and Thomas E. Lovejoy, eds., pp. 3-17. Oxford, Pergamon Press, 1985.

KNOLL, M.: "Anregung geometrischer Figuren und anderer subjektiver Lichtmuster in elektrischen Feldern". In *Zeitschrift für Psychologie*, xvii, 1958, pp. 110-126.

KNOLL, M.; KUGLER, J.: "Subjective light pattern spectroscopy in the encephalographic frequency range". In *Nature*, 184, 1959, pp. 1823-1824.

KNOLL, M.; HÖFER, O.; LAWDER, S.D.; LAWDER, U.M.: "Die Reproduzierbarkeit von elektrisch angeregten Lichterscheinungen (Phosphenen) bei zwei Versuchspersonen innerhalb 6 Monaten". In *Elektromedizin*, vii, 4, 1962, pp. 235-242.

KNOLL, M.; KUGLER, J.; LAWDER, S.D.: "Effects of chemical stimulation of electrically-induced phosphenes on their bandwith, shape, number and intensity". In *Confinia neurologica*, xxiii, 1963, pp. 201-226.

KOCH-GRÜNBERG, THEODOR: *Zwei Jahre unter den Indianern: Reisen in Nordwest-Brasilien*, 1903/1905. Berlin, Wasmuth Verlag, 1909, 2 vols.
  "Die Völkergrupierung zwischen Río Blanco, Orinoco, Río Negro und Yapurá". In *Festschrift Eduard Seeler*, ed. Walter Lehmann, Stuttgart, 1922, pp. 205-266.

LANGDON, THOMAS A.: "Food Restrictions in the Medical System of the Barasana and the Taiwano Indians of the Colombian Northwest Amazon". Doctoral thesis, Tulane University, New Orleans, 1975.

LATHRAP, DONALD W.: "The `Hunting' Economies of the Tropical Forest Zone of South America. An Attempt at Historical Perspective". In Richard B. Lee and Irven Deyore, eds. *Man the Hunter*, Chicago, Aldine, 1968, pp. 23-29.

LEHMANN-NITSCHE, R.: "Las Constelaciones de Orión y de las Híadas". In *Revista del Museo de la Plata*, Vol. 26, 1921, pp. 17-69.

LEMOS BARBOSA, A.: *Pequeño vocabulario Tupi-Portugues*. Rio de Janeiro, Livraria Sao José, 1967-70, 2 Vol.

LEVI-STRAUSS, CLAUDE: *La pensée sauvage*. Paris, 1962.
  Le cru et le cuit: Mythologiques I. Paris, Plon, 1964.
  "Le triangle culinaire". In *L'Arc*, 26, 1965, pp. 19-29.
  Du miel aux cendres: Mythologiques II. Paris, Plon, 1966.
  L'origine des manières de table: Mythologiques III. Paris, Plon, 1968.

MAGAÑA, EDMUNDO: *Orión y la mujer Pléyade: Simbolismo astronómico de los indios Kaliña de Surinam*. Centre for Latin American Research and Documentation, Dordrecht, 1988.

MAGAÑA, EDMUNDO; MASON, PETER, eds.: *Myth and the Imaginary in the New World*. Centre for Latin American Research and Documentation, Dordrecht, 1986.

MARCH, KATHRYN S.: "Deer, bears and blood: A Note on Nonhuman Response to Menstrual Odor". In *American Anthropologist*, 82, 1980, pp. 125-126.

MAY, PETER H.; ANDERSON, ANTHONY B.; BALICK, MICHAEL J.; FRAZAO, JOSE MARIO F.: "Subsistence Benefits from the Babassu Palm (*Orbygnya martiana*)". In *Economic Botany*, 39(2), The New York Botanical Garden, 1985, pp. 113-129.

MAY, P.H.; ANDERSON, A.B.; FRAZAO, J. M. F.; BALICK, M. J.: "Babassu Palm in the Agroforestry Systems in Brazil's Mid-North Region". In *Agroforestry Systems*, 3, Dordrecht, 1985, pp. 275-295.

McKNIGHT, DAVID: "Sexual Symbolism of Food among the Wik-Mungkan". In *Man*, 8:2, 1973, pp. 194-209.

MEGGERS, BETTY J.; AYENSU, EDWARD S.; DUCKWORTH, DONALD, eds.: *Tropical Forest Ecosystems in Africa and South America: A Comparative Review*. Washington D. C., Smithsonian Institution Press, 1973.

MEYER DE SCHAUENSEE, R.: *The Birds of Colombia and Adjacent Areas of South and Central America*. Narberth, Pennsylvania, Livingston Publishing Company, 1964.

MONBERG, TORBEN: "Tikopia Color Classification". In *Ethnology*, 10(3), 1971, pp. 349-358.

MURPHY, ROBERT M.: "Mammalia Americae Australe: A Table of Taxonomic and Vernacular Names". In *Ciencia Interamericana*, 17(1), pp. 16-32; 17(2), pp. 18-30; 17(3-4), pp. 26-35. 1976.

NARANJO, C.: "Psychological aspects of *yagé* experience in an experimental setting". Paper presented at the 64th annual meeting of the American Anthropological Association, Denver, 1965.

"Psychotropic properties of the Harmala alkaloids". In D. Efron (ed.), *Ethnopharmacologic Search for Psychoactive Drugs*, 1967, pp. 389-391.

NIMUENDAJU, CURT: "Reconhecimento dos Rios Içána e Uaupés". In *Journal de la Société des Américanistes*, N. S., 39, Paris, 1950, pp. 125-182.

O'CONNELL, F.D.; LYNN, E. V.: "The alkaloids of *Banisteriopsis inebrians* Morton". In *Journal of the American Pharmaceutical Association*, xlii, 1953, p. 753.

OLIVARES, ANTONIO; HERNANDEZ C., JORGE: "Aves de la Comisaría del Vaupés (Colombia)". In *Revista de Biología Tropical*, 10(1), 1962, pp. 61-90.

OLIVEIRA, ADELIA ENGRACIA; GALVAO, EDUARDO: *A situaçao actual dos Baniwa (Alto rio Negro), 1971*. Publicaçoes avulsas, Museu Paraense Emilio Goeldi, Belén, 1973.

ORICO, OSVALDO: *Mitos Amerindios. Sobrevivencias na tradiçao e na literatura brasileira*. Sao Paulo, Sao Paulo Editora Lit., 1930.

Mitos Amerindios e crendices Amazonicos. Civilizaçao Brasileira, Coleçao Retratos do Brasil, Vol. 93, Sao Paulo, 1975.

ORJUELA, HECTOR H.: *Yurupary: Mito, leyenda y epopeya del Vaupés*. Publicaciones del Instituto Caro y Cuervo, Bogotá, Vol. 64, 1983.

OSTER, G.: "Phosphenes". In *Scientific American*, ccxxii, 2, 1970, pp. 83-87.

PEREZ DE BARRADAS, JOSE: *Los Muiscas antes de la Conquista*. Madrid, Consejo Superior de Investigaciones, 1950-1951, 2 Vol.

POISSON, J.: "Note sur le `Natem', boisson toxique peruvienne et ses alcaloides". In *Annal. Pharm. Françaises*, 23, 1963, pp. 242-244.

PRANCE, GHILLEAN T.: "The pollination of Amazonian Plants". In *Amazonia*. Ghillian T. Prance & Thomas E. Lovejoy, eds., Oxford, Pergamon Press, 1985.

PRANCE, GHILLEAN T.; LOVEJOY, THOMAS E., eds.: *Amazonia*. Oxford, Pergamon Press, 1985.

REICHARD, GLADYS A.: *Navajo Religion: A Study of Symbolism*. Bollingen Series, Vol. 18, Princeton y London, Princeton University Press, 1950.

REICHEL-DOLMATOFF, G.: "La cueva funeraria de La Paz". In *Boletín de Arqueología*, ii, 5-6, 1949, pp. 403-412.

Los Kogi: Una tribu indígena de la Sierra Nevada de Santa Marta, Colombia. Bogotá, 1950-51, 2 Vol.

"Notas etnográficas sobre los indios del Chocó". In *Revista Colombiana de Antropología*, ix, 1960, pp. 75-158.

"Notas sobre el simbolismo religioso de los Indios de la Sierra Nevada de Santa Marta". In *Razón y Fábula*, No. 1, Bogotá, Revista de la Universidad de los Andes, 1967a, pp. 55-72.

"Rock-Paintings of the Vaupés: An Essay of Interpretation". In *Folklore Americas*, 26(2), 1967b, pp. 107-133.

"El contexto cultural de un alucinógeno aborigen: *Banisteriopsis caapi*. In *Revista de la Academia Colombiana de Ciencias Exactas, Físicas y Naturales*, XIII (51), Bogotá, 1969, pp. 327-345.

Amazonian Cosmos: The Sexual and Religious Symbolism of the Tukano Indians. Chicago & London, University of Chicago Press, 1971.

"The cultural context of an aboriginal hallucinogen: *Banisteriopsis caapi*". In P. T. Furst (ed.), *The Flesh of the Gods*, 1972, pp. 84-113.

The Shaman and the Jaguar: A Study of Narcotic Drugs among the Indians of Colombia. Filadelfia, Temple University Press, 1975.

"Cosmology as Ecological Analysis: A View from the Rain Forest". In *Man*, II, 1976a, pp. 307-318.

"Desana Curing Spells: An Analysis of Some Shamanistic Metaphors". In *Journal of Latin American Lore*, Los Angeles, UCLA Latin American Center, 2(2), 1976b, pp. 157-219.

"Templos Kogi: Introducción al simbolismo y a la astronomía del espacio sagrado". In *Revista Colombiana de Antropología*, Bogotá, 19, 1977, pp. 199-246.

Beyond the Milky Way: Hallucinatory Imagery of the Tukano Indians. Los Angeles, UCLA Latin American Center, University of California, Latin American Studies, Vol. 42, 1978a.

"Desana Animal Categories, Food Restrictions, and the Concept of Color Energies". In *Journal of Latin American Lore*, Los Angeles, UCLA Latin American Center, 4(2), 1978b, pp.243-292.

"The Loom of Life: A Kogi Principle of Integration". In *Journal of Latin American Lore*, 4(2), 1978c, pp. 5-27.

"Drug-Induced Optical Sensations and their Relationship to Applied Art among Some Colombian Indians". In *Art in Society*, Michael Greenhalgh and Vincent Megaw, eds., London, Duckworth, 1978d, pp. 289-304.

"Desana Shaman's Rock Crystals and the Hexagonal Universe". In *Journal of Latin American Lore*, Los Angeles, UCLA Latin American Center, 5:1, 1979a, pp. 117-128.

"Some Source Materials on Desana Shamanistic Initiation". In *Antropológica*, Caracas, Fundación La Salle, Instituto Caribe de Antropología y Sociología, 51, 1979b, pp. 27-61.

"Algunos conceptos de geografía chamanística de los Indios Desana de Colombia". In *Contribuiçoes a antropologia em homenagem ao Professor Egon Schaden*, Universidade de Sao Paulo: Fondo de Pesquisas de Museo Paulista, 1981a, pp. 255-270. También publicado in: *Myth and the Imaginary in the New World* (Edmundo Magaña y Peter Mason eds.), Dordrecht, Centre for Latin American Research and Documentation, 1983, pp. 75-92.

"Brain and Mind in Desana Shamanism". In *Journal of Latin American Lore*, Los Angeles, UCLA Latin American Center, 7(1), 1981b, pp. 73-98.

"Astronomical Models of Social Behaviour among Some Indians of Colombia". In *Ethnoastronomy and Archaeastronomy in the Amazon Tropics*, Vol. 385, ed. Anthony F. Aveni and Gary Urton, *Annals of the New York Academy of Sciences*, 1982, pp 165-181.

"Tapir avoidance in the Colombian Northwest Amazon". In *Animal Myths and Metaphors in South America*. Gary Urton, Ed. Salt Lake City, University of Utah Press, 1985, pp.107-143.

"A Hunter's Tale from the Colombian Northwest Amazon". In *Journal of Latin American Lore*, Los Angeles, UCLA Latin American Center, 12:1, 1986, 65-74.

Shamanism and Art of the Eastern Tukanoan Indians. In Iconography of Religions, 9:1. Institute of Religious Iconography, State University of Groningen, Brill, Leiden, 1987.

"Biological and Social Aspects of the Yuruparí Complex of the Colombian Vaupés Territory". In *Journal of Latin American Lore*, 15:1, 1989, pp. 95-135.

RENARD-CASEVITZ; FRANCE, MARIE: "Su-acu: Essai sur les cervidés de l'Amazonie et sur leur signification dans les cultures indiennes actuelles". In *Travaux de l'Institut Français d'Études Andines*, Paris-Lima, 1979, Vol. 20.

RIVIER, L.; LINDGREN, J. E.: "`Ayahuasca', The South American Hallucinogenic Drink: An Ethnobotanical and chemical investigation". In *Economic Botany*, 26, 2, 1972, pp. 101-129.

ROSS, ERIC BARRY: "Food Taboos, Diet, and Hunting Strategy: The Adaptation to Animals in Amazon Cultural Ecology". In *Current Anthropology*, 19(1), 1978, pp. 1-36.

RUDDLE, KENNETH; JOHNSON, DENNIS; TOWNSEND, PATRICIA K.; REES, JOHN D.: *Palm Sago: A Tropical Starch from Marginal Lands*. Honolulu, East-West Technology and Development Institute, University of Hawaii, 1978.

RUDOLPH, EBERMUT: "Indianische Tierherrenvorstellungen: Ein Beitrag zur Frage der Entstehung von Wildgeist-und Eignerwesen". In *Zeitschrift für Ethnologie*, Braunschweig, 99(1-2), 1974, pp. 81-119.

SAAKE, WILHELM: "Die Jurupari Legende bei den Baniwa des Rio Issana". In *Proceedings of the XXXIIth International Congress of Americanists*, Copenhague, 1958, pp. 271-279.
"Mythen über Inapirikuli, den Kulturheros der Baniwa". In *Zeitschrift für Ethnologie*, 93, Berlín, 1968, pp. 260-273.

SCHADEN, EGON: *A mitologia heróica de tribos indígenas do Brasil*. Río de Janeiro, Impresa Nal., 1959.

SCHLEIFFER, H.: *Sacred Narcotic Plants of the New World Indians: An Anthology of Texts from the 16th Century to Date*. New York, 1973.

SCHULTES, RICHARD EVANS: "A New Narcotic Snuff from the Northwest Amazon". In *Botanical Museum Leaflets*, Harvard University, Cambridge, Mass. 16:9, 1954, pp. 241-260.
"The identity of the malpighiaceous narcotics of South America". In *Botanical Museum Leaflets*, Harvard University, Cambridge, Mass, xviii, 1957, pp. 1-56.
"Hallucinogens of plant origin". In *Science*, clxiii, 1969, pp. 245-254.
"`De plantis toxicariis e mundo novo tropicale commentationes X'. New data on the malpighiaceous narcotics of South America". In *Botanical Museum Leaflets*, xxxiii, Harvard University, Cambridge, Mass, 1972, pp. 137-147.
"Palms and Religion". In *Principes, Journal of the Palm Society*, 18(1), New York, 1974, pp. 3-21.

SCHULTES, R. E.; HOFMAN, A.: *The Botany and Chemistry of Hallucinogens*. Springfield, 1973.

SEITZ, GEORG: "Epéna, the Intoxicating Snuff Powder of the Waika Indians and the Tucano Medicine Man, Agostino". In *Ethnofarmacologic Search for Psychoactive Drugs* (Daniel H. Efron, editor), Public Health Service Publication, No. 1645, Washington D. C., 1967, pp. 315-338.

SIEGEL, RONALD H.; WEST, LOUIS JOLYON: *Hallucinations: Behaviour, Experience, and Theory*. New York, John Wiley & Sons, 1975.

SIMON, FRAY PEDRO: *Noticias Historiales de las Conquistas de Tierra Firme en las Indias Occidentales* (1623). Bogotá, 1882-1892, 5 Vol.

SOLDI, HARALD: "Tropical Rivers as Expression of Their Terrestrial Environment". In *Tropical Ecological Systems* (Frank B. Golley y Ernesto Medina, eds.), Berlín/Heidelberg, Springer Verlag, 1975, pp. 275-288.

SORENSEN, ARTHUR P.: "Multilingualism in the Northwest Amazon". In *American Anthropologist*, 69(6), 1967, pp. 670-684.

SPRUCE, RICHARD: *Notes of a Botanist on the Amazon and Andes*. A. R. Wallace, ed. London, 1908.

STRADELLI, ERMANNO: "Leggenda dell'Jurupary". In *Bolletino Società Geográfica Italiana*, Serie III, 3, Roma, 1890, pp. 659-689 y 798-835.

SUAREZ, M.: "Les utilisations du palmier `Moriche' (*Mauritua flexuosa*) chez les Warao du Delta de l'Orénoque, Territoire Delta Amacuro, Vénézuela". In *Journal d'Agriculture Tropicale et Botanique Appliquée*, 13, Paris, 1966, pp. 33-38.

TART C., ed.: *Altered States of Consciousness: A book of Readings*. New York, 1969.

TAYLOR, KENNETH I.: *Sanumá Fauna: Prohibitions and Classifications*. Caracas, Fundación La Salle de Ciencias Naturales, Instituto Caribe de Antropología y Sociología, 1974.

TORRES LABORDE, ALFONSO: *Mito y cultura entre los Barasana, un grupo indígena del Vaupés*. Bogotá, Universidad de los Andes, 1969.

TRUPP, FRITZ: *Mythen der Makuna*. Acta Ethnologica et Linguistica, No. 40, Series Americana, 8, Vienna, 1977.

TURNER, VICTOR W.: "Colour Classification in Ndembu Ritual: A Problem in Primitive Classification". In Michael Banton, ed., *Anthropological Approaches to the Study of Religion*, London, Tavistock, 1966.

BIBLIOGRAPHY

UCKO, PETER J.; DIMBLEBY, G. W., eds.: *The Domestication and Exploitation of Plants and Animals*. Chicago, New York, Aldine-Atherton Inc., 1969.

USCATEGUI M., NESTOR: "The Present Distribution of Narcotics and Stimulants amongst the Indian Tribes of Colombia". In *Botanical Museum Leaflets*, Harvard University, Cambridge, Mass, xviii, 6, 1959, pp. 273-304.

USENER, H.: "Milch und Honig". Rheinisches Museum, LVII 17ff. *Kleine Schriften*, IV, 398ff, Leipzig, 1913.

WALLACE, ALFRED RUSSEL: *A Narrative of Travel on the Amazon and Río Negro*. Segunda edición de 1889, Dover Publications, New York, 1972.

WILBERT, JOHANNES: "The Calabash of the Ruffled Feathers". In: Stones, Bones and Skin: Ritual and Shamanic Art. *Artscanada*, XXX (184-187), Toronto, 1974, pp. 90-93.

"*Manicaria saccifera* and Its Cultural Significance among the Warao Indians of Venezuela". In *Botanical Museum Leaflets*, 24, Harvard University, Cambridge, Mass, 1976, pp. 275-335.

WRIGHT, ROBIN M.: "The history and Religion of the Baniwa People of the Upper Rio Negro Valley". Doctoral thesis, Stanford University, 1981.

WYSS, KARL: "Die Milch im Kultus der Griechen und Römer". In *Religionsgeschichtliche Versuche und Vorarbeiten*, XV, Band 2, Heft, Gressen, 1914.

INDEX

NOTES: Page numbers in **bold** refer to a photograph. After a page number, "fig." indicates a figure.

abstinence 13, 116, 123, 141
acculturation 2, 3, 99, 248, 307
Achernar 263, 264 fig., 268 fig., 269 fig.
adaptive behaviour 7, 8, 16, 18, 163, 214, 230, 270
adze 270, 311, 312
  see also phallic symbolism
aggression 13, 118, 119, 152, 267
  and the Master of Animals 60, 202
  control 7, 15
  magical 180, 283
agouti 13, 26, 27, 30, 31, 36, 69, 79, 102, 104, 107, 133, 304
  symbolic image 71
  see also Agouti People, Agouti-Women
Agouti People 102
Agouti-Women 71, 146, 304
agriculture 209, 261, 266, 279, 293
  gardens 9, 15, 79, 91, 100, 117, 143, 213, 230, 282, 293
  firing of fields 102
  soils 9, 15, 24, 273
  see also fields, harvesting, manioc
ahki fish 186, 187
Aldebaran 264, 268 fig., 271
Amazon river and basin 1, 3, 5, 8, 77, 107, 159, 164, 179, 235, 278, 297, 312
  limnology 302
amphisbaena snake 36
anaconda 27, 30, 32, 35, 36, 67, 98, 214, 225, 266
  and geographical divisions 24, 124, 153, 154
  and the ancestral canoes 23, 70, 152, 216, **218**
  and the images of the brain 220, 221 fig., 225, 226 fig., 235
  and the myth of creation 46
  and the supernatural longhouse 217
  as central axis of the longhouse 217, 218
  as a personification of the Master of Animals 175
  as shaman's avatar 128
  in astronomical symbolism 264

see also Anaconda People, Anaconda-Woman
Anaconda People 98, 281, 312
Anaconda-Woman 72
ancestors *see* anaconda, canoes, dancers, deer, fish, food, game animals, Makú, singers, tapir, Tukano
Andes cordillera 1, 160
anhinga darter 27, 36
animal behaviour 12, 35, 36, 57, 111, 112, 163, 172, 192, 194, 196, 202, 266, 303, 304
  as a model for dances 190
  in spells 202
  pathogenic effect 166, 168
  when wounded 215
animals
  and the constellations 14, 49, 56
  as metaphors 12, 81, 89, 111, 116, 163, 195, 222, 308
  as models of/for human behaviour 111-12
  associations with the Yuruparí instruments 300-5
  butchering 60, 118, 215
  colour 89
  Desana classifications 25-38
  domesticated 35, 104, 208, 209
    pets 196, 304
  in the Desana theory of disease 164
  odour 49, 91
  scavengers 178, 181, 189, 203, 204, 209
  talking (in myth) 71
  see also animal behaviour, anteater, armadillo, aurochs, bat, birds, bush dog, coati, constellations, crab, deer, earthworm, feline animals, fish, fresh water dolphins, frog, game animals, hill houses, hills, hunting, insects, jaguar, kinkajou, leopard, marten, Master of Animals, monkeys, opossum, otter, peccary, reptiles, ripeness, rodents, sheep, sloth, snail, squirrel, snakes, spirit essence, spirits, tapir, tayra, toad, worms
ant 26, 35, 36, 183, 184, 185, 222, 233, 299, 300
  as pathogenic agent 166

as food 190
seminal connotations 222
in spells 175
odour 59, 64, 112
anteater 25, 26, 30, 36, 59
Apaporis river 1, 67, 79, 153
aphrodisiacs 80, 135, 190, 288
aracú fish 37, 60, 83, **84**, 131, 138
Arawak (language family) 4, 80, 82, 98,
104, 149, 235, 237 fig., 282, 294, 306-12
passim
Arawak/Tukano relationships 90, 99-107
passim, 280, 281, 287, 291-93 *passim*
as Tapir People 80, 84, 91, 98, 117, 281,
282, 293, 295
women 85, 98, 281, 293
archaeology 20, 258
armadillo 30, 35, 36, 69, 71, 79, 102, 104
see also Armadillo People, Armadillo
Women
Armadillo People 72, 104
Armadillo Women 104
arrows 130, 166, 167, 168, 171, 196, 201
art 243-259
decorative 233
see also Banisteriopsis, basketry, body
paint, facial paint, mural painting,
dancers, dances, music, pottery, singers,
songs, Tukano, yajé
astronomy 75, 159, 261-75
and narcotic drugs 271, 273
and fertility 265-67
and social organization 261-75
see also anaconda, constellations,
Desana, equinoxes, horizon calendar,
Kogi, longhouse, Muiska, solstices,
stars, Tukano
aurochs 208

Bachué 273, 275
see also Muiska
Baniwa people 295, 306, 310
flutes 306
Bará people 1, 85, 107, 113
Barasana people 1, **40**, 85, 107, 113, **212**,
242, **246**, **247**, **249**, 265 fig., 278, 280,
296
territory **51**, **103**
Barbosa Rodrigues, João 295, 309
bark-cloth aprons, ritual 253
Banisteriopsis 130, 136, 143, 145, 168,
242, 243-48, 251

and the decoration of objects 251-57
chemical composition 244
phytochemical and pharmacological
research 241-42
psychotropic effects 242
stages of *Banisteriopsis* intoxication 244-
48
use by the Chocó Indians 258
use in rituals 57, 98, 241-56 *passim*, 279
vernacular names 241
visions 98, 242
visual images under its effect 246-57
Banisteriopsis caapi 130, 207, 243, 244
Banisteriopsis inebrians 243, 244
Banisteriopsis rusbyana 130, 243, 244
basketry 94, **97**, 255, 266, 281
basketry sieves **246**, 255, **257**, 281
exchange of 281
bat 35, 38, 135
bayapia 140
leaves 131-33 *passim*, 146
Bateson, Gregory 20
bee 35, 142, 151, 261, 263
odour 59
see also hexagonal forms
beer 63, 65, 66, 85, 86, 113, 114, 117,
171, 181, 253, 309, 310
beetle 75, 202, 313
as a model for exogamy 285
see also phallic symbolism
Behkára people 79, 80, 83
see also Kuripáko
Bellatrix 268
Bering strait 210
beta-carbolines 244
Betelgeuse 268
Beyond, the 178
birds 12, 35, 89, 111, 112, 114, 221
as food 15, 64
associations with the Yuruparí
instruments 303
colour 25
in spells 125, 130, 176, 195, 200
migrating 98, 259
odour 112
of prey 198
songbirds 166
waterfowl 33
see also anhinga darter, bluebird, cacique
bird, cock of the rock, curassow, duck,
guan, harpy eagle, heron, humming
bird, ibis, King Vulture, macaw,

oropendola bird, parrot, pheasant, pigeon, swallow, swallow-tailed kite, tinamou, toucan, trumpeter bird, turkey vulture, vulture, woodpecker, yabiru stork
birth control 7, 13, 53, 66, 112, 266
    see also population control
Bisíu (myth cycle, Yuruparí Complex) 309-11
blowgun 72, 201, 289
    phallic connotations 301
bluebird 30
boa constrictor 36
Bödiger, Ute 280
body paint 5, **40, 41**, 59, 68, 146
Bolens, Jacqueline 280, 295
bow tree 180, 201
brain 4, 136, 213-40, 221 fig., 226 fig., 227 fig., 237 fig.
    and phosphenes 250
    as a model for social behaviour 235
    colour 220
    consciousness 222-33
    fissure 220, 221 fig., 224, 226 fig. 236, 239, 264, 267, 270
    hemispheres 220, 223 fig., 220-35 passim, 267, 270
    lateralization 223-24, 235, 237
    psychotherapy 235-37
    sources of Desana knowledge 213-14
    structure 218-21
    symbolic imagery 89, 216-19, 222, 237, 239, 263, 267, 271
    workings of the mind 223-24
    see also anaconda, hexagonal forms, longhouse, odour, rainbow boa, rock crystals
Brandão de Amorim, Antonio 295
Brazil 1, 79, 243
bufotenine 123, 251
burials 159, 169, 204, 209
bush dog 25, 36
butterfly 89, 222, 236
    in spells 175

cacique bird 48, 166
caiman 27, **28**, 31, 35, 36, 64
Camara Cascudo, Luis 307, 309
Canopus 263, 264 fig., 268 fig., 269 fig.
caimo, tree and fruit 26, 125, 129, 179, 181, 197, 198, 201
Caquetá river 67

canoes 17, 116, 136, 171, 191, 253, 261, 297, 304
    ancestral 23, 70, 152-53, 216
    funerary 158
    see also anaconda
cannibalism 99, 118, 311
Capella 263, 264 fig., 268 fig., 269 fig., 271
capybara 27, 36
carrying capacity 7, 15, 205
Carurú 74
cassava bread 65, 157
Castor 268 fig., 269 fig.
catfish 60, 64, 190, 197, 198, 202
Çatal Hüyük (Anatolia) 209
cattle 207, 208
cavi 30, 36, 69, 71, 102, 104
Cavi-Women 71, 304
cecropia (tree, fruit) 31, 107, 128, 135, 172, 309
ceremony 10, 19
    ceremonial cigars 104
    ceremonial costume 181
    ceremonial dialogues 15
    ceremonial exchange 306, 307
    ceremonial masks 181
    ceremonial objects 252
    Kogi ceremonial centres 272
    Kogi scheduling of ceremonies 273
    Muiska ceremonial centres 273
    Yuruparí initiation 311
    see also ritual, skull
chicha see beer
childbirth 15, 19, 61, 62, 63, 102, 142, 158, 172, 175, 207, 215, 234, 236, 239, 271
    and transformation 34, 145
children 53, 60-63 passim, 90, 144, 145, 157, 159, 217, 269
    care 67, 232
    food restrictions 80
    and the Yuruparí trumpets 294
Chocó Indians 258
cicada 35
cigars 104, 253, 301
    in spells 183
    see also tobacco
chromatic energy see energy, colour
classification systems 33-35
    animals 25-38
    colours 41-46, 166
    ecological environments 25-33, 69

fish 35, 37, 49
flavours 61
food 23, 35, 38
game animals 35, 70
odours 58-60, 70, 92, 286
river waters 302
clay 15, 67, 68, 90, 133, 136, 145, 147, 222
in spells 131, 132, 184, 186
coati 26, 30, 35, 36, 303
see also phallic symbolism
coca 45, 86, 107, 128, 207, 243
cock of the rock 26, 36, 48, 47, 196
Cole, Sonia 209
colonos (settlers) 9, 299
colour 4, 23
classification 41-46, 166
hues 17, 34, 42, 44-46, 199
colour spectrum 38, 45, 52, 53, 151, 156, 159
colour symbolism 41, 201
importance in reestablishing health 54
see also hexagonal forms
conception 61-64, 135, 215
constellations 14, 49, 56, 236, 262, 263, 269-74 passim
and animals 14, 49, 56
see also Orion
contamination see pollution
contraceptives 13
cooking
rules 65
symbolism 62, 66-68, 124, 137
cooking (as transformation) 61, 67, 69, 137, 140, 141, 145, 304-5
cooking vessels, symbolism 67-68, 145, 157, 288
Coudreau, Henri A. 296
couvade 15
crab 36, 64, 67, 133, 202, 219
in spells 131
crab-clay 67, 133, 137, 184
Creation, la 10, 19, 52, 169, 202, 214, 302
see also anaconda, Desana, myths, Tukano
Crete 207
cricket 305
crocodyliae 202
Cubeo people 2, 104, 181, 278, 282, 305
Cuduyarí river 74
culture contacts 1, 74, 292, 295, 309, 313
curassow 26, 27, 31, 36, 64, 69, 80, 196

in myth 71
in spells 195-96
feeding habits 196
see also Curassow Sons
Curassow Sons 104
cyclic time 5, 261

d-tetrahydroharmine 244
dairy farming 207
dancers 127, 174, 226, 230, 269, 303, 311
ancestral 153, 217
costume 48, 127, 174, 178, 181, 189, 202, 226, 311
dances 82, 173, 253, 269, 274
fertility associations 190, 202
ritual 15, 266, 269, 273, 299
see also dancers, dances, fertility
Daughter of the Sun 66, 150, 169, 172, 305
Day People 85, 97
death 62, 178, 181, 186, 205, 208, 223, 238, 270
and energy flow 49, 88, 111
and lunar energy 39
and the shaman 90, 115
symbolic 142
deer 13, 108, 111, 112, 114, 129, 171, 173, 208, 214, 215, 306
as ancestor 73, 98
as food 64, 74, 80, 96, 100
as game animal 79, 118
as pathogenic agent 166
brocket deer 25, 26, 30, 31, 36, 65, 90, 91, 92, 93, 94, 97, 100, 139, 173, 192, 200
categories 93
in myth 70, 88, 99, 106
in spells 172, 190
odour 59, 87, 91, 92, 93, 96
pheromonal communication 91, 102
restrictions 69, 94
symbolic image 88-101 passim
territoriality 93
whitetailed deer 91-97 passim, 102
zoological image 91
see also Deer Sons, Hombre Deer, women, Deer Women
Deer Man 98
Deer Sons 98, 104
Deer Women 97, 98, 102
Delta Orionis 270
Desana people 1-8 passim, 68, 72, 77, 78,

80, 96, 101, 213, **228**, 278, 282, 307, 310
as Wind People 108
astronomical concepts 262-71
classifications of animals 25-38
classifications of colours 41-46
classifications of flavours 61
classifications of odours 58-60
colour energy concepts 38-57
cosmological concepts 46-49, 199, 202
Desana/Pira-Tapuya exchange 105
Desana/Makú relationships 73
evolution of descent rules 83-85
food restrictions 69-75
hexagonal forms 261
hexagonal patterns in material culture 157-59
limnology 303
musical instruments 232
myth of creation 23-24
odour 91, 92
origin myths 102, 178, 218, 262
origin of curing spells 169
pottery decoration 145
river symbolism 124
sibs 71, 72, 83, 137, 104-5, 146, 290, 307
symbolic relationship with tapir 81
territory concepts 153
theories of conception and fetal development 61-64
theories of disease 163-68, 177-78, 180-82, 203, 204
universe concepts 38, 39 fig., 46-49, 198-99, 202, 274
use of narcotic drugs 214, 232
see also brain, exogamy, menstruation, shaman, tapir
descent, matrilineal 83, 101, 280, 282, 292
descent, patrilineal 5, 10, 24, 83, 101, 282, 295
descent, uterine 83
disease 4, 7, 10, 12, 63, 95, 112, 115, 140, 163, 215, 223, 224, 239, 266, 287
abdominal pain 72
amebiasis 165
as punishment 18, 53, 118, 164, 165
transmission as sexual impregnation 198-201
bronchitis 165
categories 165
causes 14, 16, 18, 197, 236

curing spells 4, 53, 163-208, 304
fever 117, 132, 145, 164, 165, 168, 176, 186
garment symbolism 179-82 *passim*, 195, 196, 201, 202
headaches 165, 192
indigestion 81
malaria 164
nausea 164
numbness 186-92 *passim*
pains 164, 165, 167, 176
pathogenic agents 198-202
psychotherapy 235-236
smallpox 165
toothache 175, 176, 199
unconsciousness 196
see also animals, ant, deer, Desana, dreams, feathers, fish, game animals, insects, jaguar, lightning, Master of Animals, monkey hair, pathogenic splinters, rock crystals, shaman, termite, wasp, worm
dreams 72, 87, 111, 116, 118, 123, 182, 206, 210, 223, 224
and disease 202
and hunting 118, 168
erotic 14, 60, 136, 202, 205
symbolism 107
drugs 3, 19, 62, 63, 72, 87, 98, 111, 115, 123, 136, 146, 152, 216, 219, 230, 232, 233, 234, 240, 243, 244, 258, 259, 271, 299, 305
psychotropic 123, 230, 243
see also astronomy, *Banisteriopsis*, coca, Desana, hallucinations, hallucinogenics, narcotic snuffs, narcotics, ritual, shamanistic initiation, vihó, yajé, yopo
duck 35, 36
in spells 195
Duck Women 83

ear-pendants 177, 186, 200
in spells 183-86
earthworm 193
in spells 191
Eastern Tukanoan people *see* Tukano
ecological adaptation 7-21 *passim*, 23, 24, 74, 104, 206
ecological balance 12, 15, 16, 18, 19, 90, 206
ecological environments 25
forest environment 25-27, 30, 33, 59, 69,

73, 93, 106, 137, 171
lakes environment 30, 33
low open forest environment 27, 33, 69, 89, 91, 93, 94, 135
riverine environment 30, 31, 33, 85, 100
secondary growth environment 30, 33, 90, 91, 93, 100, 102, 289
swamp forest environment 27, 33, 94
windfalls environment 31
see also ecological adaptation, ecological balance, ecology, ecosystem, environment
ccology 4, 11, 23, 38, 90, 118, 262
and ritual 9
see also ecological adaptation, ecological environments, ecological balance, environment, ritual, Tukano
ecosystem 11, 15, 17, 93, 105, 286
and the longhouse 93
see also ecological environments
Ecuador 243
Egypt 207
electric eel 27, 165, 299
in spells 182
Elger, F. 244
emeralds 159, 273
see also hexagonal forms
endogamy 4, 278, 281, 282, 287, 298, 306
and exogamy 292-94
energy 23, 24, 38-57, 66, 138, 150, 177, 185, 279, 311
and ripeness 64
balance 4, 11, 55
bogá 39, 42, 48, 53, 56, 61, 63, 90, 130, 135, 136, 151, 220, 221, 226-39 *passim*, 289, 290, 303
cosmic 4, 42, 111, 199, 220, 223, 230, 303
colour energies 38-57, 61-69 *passim*, 81, 87, 90, 142, 144, 151, 152, 156, 159, 222, 223, 265, 301, 306
flow 4, 10, 11, 16, 17, 39 fig., 46, 49, 57, 73, 112, 115, 202
in spells 132, 133
kinetic 53
lunar 39, 41, 49, 263
replenishment 14, 115
solar 10, 11, 17, 39, 49, 88, 143, 151, 199, 220, 237
see also death, Desana, fertility, hexagonal forms, lakes, plants, rock crystals, seminal symbolism, sex,

shaman, spells, Tukano, women
environment 4, 9, 11-17 *passim*, 24, 38, 69, 72, 90, 93, 94, 118, 136, 164, 207, 230, 255, 258
see also ecological adaptation, ecological environments, ecology, ecosystem, ecological balance
Epsilon Orionis 263, 268, 269 fig., 271, 272
and the celestial hexagon 263
equinoxes 261, 263, 266, 269, 272, 273
ethnography 100, 108, 147
exchange *see* basketry sieves, ceremony, Desana, fish, food, Pira-Tapuya, ritual, women, worms
exogamy 4, 5, 79, 108, 115, 178, 251, 258, 278, 279, 281-89 *passim*, 306, 310
and Desana territorial division 56
and endogamy 292-95
and exophagy 94
and flavours 61
and hexagonal forms 145, 154-55
and odours 59
and pottery 133
and the Master of Animals 60
and the Yuruparí Complex 278, 293, 295
as a mechanism for social control 15
as a mechanism for social organization 13, 77, 264
graphic representation 253
in Tukanoan imagery 68, 298
rules 154, 155, 198, 251
see also beetle, palms, ritual
exophagy 13
and exogamy 94

facial paint **41**, 232
family, extended 9
family, nuclear 150, 213, 216
fasting 125, 136, 175
Fátima 74
fauna 10, 15, 18, 30, 33, 79, 167
feathers 128, 155, 166, 173, 177, 186, 197, 202, 255, 298, 302
as pathogenic agents 166
seminal connotations 202
in spells 173, 197-98
feline animals 92, 202, 244
fertility 57, 92, 128, 143, 158, 159, 199, 207, 208, 236, 290, 292, 294, 303, 311, 313
and astronomy 265-68

and colour energies 87, 186, 266, 286
and dances 190, 202
and fruits 56, 81
and hexagonal forms 151, 153
and lunar phases 266
and rapids and pools 102
and solar energy 10
and starch 130
and the jaguar 177
and the Vai-mahsë 46, 48
and the Yuruparí trumpets 83
ritual 49, 207, 208
symbolism
    tail-feathers of oropendola bird 128
    celestial bodies 253
    fruits 199
    macaw feathers 140
    down feathers 178, 190
see also dances, manioc starch, palms,
    self-fertilisation
fields, agricultural 30, 57, 60, 64, 69, 71,
    79, 80, 83, 86, 92, 94, 100, 102, 113,
    163, 172, 176, 196, 282, 293, 294
fire 52, 53, 68, 106, 129, 134-36 passim,
    143, 146, 157, 289
    in spells 142, 143, 183, 310
firewood 67, 135, 138, 157 fig., 158, 171
in spells 131
First People 55, 78, 99, 152
Fischer, Cardenas 243
fish 7, 34, 24, 27, 33, 35, 48, 58, 60-68
    passim, 74, 89, 92, 94, 101, 158, 168,
    171, 175, 176, 202-6 passim, 222, 223,
    265, 269, 280, 290, 299
    ahki 186, 190
    aracú 37, 60, 83, 84, 131, 138
    catfish 60, 64, 190, 197, 198, 202
    cachama 37
    cascudo 37
    classification 36, 37, 49
    colour 36, 37
    as pathogenic agents 166-67
    as ancestors 306
    as food 65, 111
    cuyucuyú 37
    exchange 105
    in spells 175, 186-88, 189, 192, 193
    guavina 37
    symbolic image 116
    migration 12, 14, 90, 232, 261, 262, 268
    moharra fish 27, 33, 37
    abodes of fish 54, 56, 57, 144, 167, 189,

    219
    nyandiá 37
    odour 58, 59, 112
    pacú 37
    payala 37
    pez espada 37
    pirahiba 37
    restrictions 16, 17
    stingray 33, 37, 165
    sardine 37
    surubim 37
    tarira 37
    electric eel 37
    tucunaré 37
    uarí 306
    fish poison 17, 63, 133, 157, 211
    yacundá 37
    and the Vai-mahsë 46, 49
    see also fish, fish-system, fishing, food,
        Gente Pez, Master of Animals, piranha,
        pools, ripeness, smoking (food), water
        houses
Fish People 312
fish-system 49
Fish Woman 105
Fish Women 83
fish-yajé 125, 130, 132
fishing 9, 14-18 passim, 24, 33, 36, 53, 57,
    60, 65, 70, 73, 79, 91, 105, 153, 163,
    164, 213, 266, 272, 278, 282, 293, 294
    abundance 85
    nets 155
    time of catch 37
    see also ritual
flame 157, 186
    in spells 132, 135, 142, 143, 144
Flannery, Kent 20
flavour 4, 23, 35, 46, 48, 81, 105, 108
    classifications 61
    of people 61
    origin 61
flora 10, 30, 33
Flood, the (myth) 66
flutes 107, 210, **229**, 232, **245**, 289, 292,
    294, 298, 300, 302-6 passim, 313
    decoration 302
    duct flutes 302
    of the Baniwa people 306
    of Yuruparí 300, 302, 303
    panpipes 144, **231**
food and food resources 9, 15, 46, 49, 75
    and people's odour 92

and the ancestors 73
and the ecological environments 33
cassava bread 65
control 7, 11, 15, 74
classifications 23, 35, 38
depletion of 18
exchange 15, 18, 59, 105, 154, 266
fish 34, 65
food/sex associations 13, 57, 63, 65, 80,
    81, 118, 142, 186, 279, 304
in myth 304
necessary boiling of 65
necessary smoking of meat 64, 65
restrictions 4, 13-15 *passim*, 23, 63, 65,
    69-74 *passim*, 96, 142, 199, 204, 230,
    293
roasting 65
starch 312
vegetables 15, 17, 25, 53, 102, 105
see also ant, game animals, cassava
    bread, children, deer, Desana, fertility,
    fish, fishing, fruits, hunting, insects,
    larvae, manioc, manioc starch,
    menstruation, monkeys, odour, paca,
    palm starch, palms, peccary, peppers,
    piranha, pollution, pregnancy,
    resources, ritual, smoking (food), tapir,
    tinamou, tortoise, women
forest gap **32**
freshwater dolphins 38
Friedberg, Claudine 243
frog 27, 33, 35, 36, 64, 222
    in spells 183, 185
fruits 7, 9, 16, 79, 105, 205
    and the Vai-mahsë 46, 49
    as food of game animals 71, 80-81
    avocado 31, 65
    cashew nut 26, 306
    fertility connotations 56, 80, 198
    gathering 15, 17, 79, 117, 278, 306
    guamo 26, 31
    guaraná 26
    in spells 56
    japurá 299
    odour 59
    of forest environment 25-26
    of lakes environment 31
    of low open forest environment 26-27
    of riverine environment 31
    of secondary growth environment 30-31
    of swamp forest environment 27
    palm fruits 80, 105, 113, 143, 239, 269,

278, 283, 287-304 *passim*
    distribution ritual 294, 298, 300, 302,
        305
    poisonous 196
    Pouteria ucuqui Schultes (ukuki) 26, 56,
        59, 105, 304, 309
    restrictions 15
    rubber tree 26
    sëmé 26, 59, 65, 71, 80, 104, 105, 143,
        304
        uterine connotations 129
        in myth 102
    sexual connotations 181
    soursop 31
    star apple 26
    uvilla 31
    vahsú 59, 65, 71, 81, 105 143, 304
    vivapichuna 31, 65, 105
    "warm" and "cold" 65
    see also pineapple, ripeness, umarí,
        women
Fulop, Marcos 3

game animals 7, 9, 13-18 *passim*, 24, 34,
    48, 53, 58, 60-66 *passim*, 69-74 *passim*,
    79, 80, 88-94 *passim*, 102, 106, 107,
    115, 119, 131, 158, 168, 172, 173, 175,
    204, 207, 261, 266
    abodes of game animals 54, 56, 60, 86,
        87, 115, 118, 144, 171, 214, 218
    abundance 85
    as ancestors 71, 72, 85, 91, 98, 99, 117,
        138
    as pathogenic agents 165-66 *passim*, 198,
        200, 201, 203
    classifications 36, 70
    of forest environment 25-26
    of lakes environment 31
    of low open forest environment 26-27
    of riverine environment 31
    of secondary growth environment 30-31
    of swamp forest environment 27
    traps **28**
    see also animals, constellations, deer,
        dreams, fruits, government, hill houses,
        hills, hunting, Makú, Master of
        Animals, peccary, pollution, resources,
        ritual, rodents, shaman, tapir, women
gathering 9, 16, 17, 18, 57, 105, 266, 278,
    280
    of insects 266
    of fruits 15, 17, 79, 117, 278, 306

of medicinal herbs 15
genealogical recitals 70, 99, 154
geodes 54, 219, 222
gestation 11, 57, 61, 63, 69, 87, 137, 141, 156, 214, 229
Goá-më (myth cycle, Yuruparí Complex) 310
Goldman, Irving 2
Goranchacha 159, 275
    see also Muiska
gourd 66, 129, 252
gourd rattles 123, 213, 235, 253, **256**
    in spells 125
    phallic symbolism 129
    shaman's 128, 129, 177, 235
    structure and decoration 125, 128-29, 253
    see also seminal symbolism, uterine symbolism
gourd vessels 67, 125, 133, 175, 183-85 *passim*, **212, 246**
government 2, 299
    and depletion of game 74
Greece 207, 208, 209
groundnut 61, 108
    in spells 183-84
    symbolism 56
Guainía river 149, 312
Guainía territory 282, 310
guamo tree and fruit 26, 30, 31, 145, 181
guan **29**, 30, 31, 36, 79
Guiana Shield 25, 214
güío snake **267**

hallucinations 19, 62, 63, 87, 98, 110, 111, 168, 177, 193, 223, 230, 235, 243, 248, 250, **254, 255**, 255, 279, 299, 305
    see also Banisteriopsis, hallucinatory visions, hallucinogenics, drugs, narcotic snuffs, narcotics, ritual, sex, shaman, visual perception, vihó, yajé
hallucinatory visions 7, 19, 54, 98, 216, 223, 230, 244, **249**
    see also Banisteriopsis, coca, Desana, drugs, hallucinations, hallucinogenics, plants, narcotic snuffs, shamanistic initiation, vihó, yajé, yopo
hallucinogenics 3, 5, 86, 87, 107, 115, 136, 143, 160, 168, 177, 233, 238, 243, 244, 251, 258, 274, 281, 294
see also Banisteriopsis, coca, drugs, hallucinations, narcotic snuffs, narcotics, plants,

vihó, yajé, yopo
harmaline 244, 248, 251
harmine 123, 244
harpy eagle 30, 36, **126, 127**, 128, 129, 154, 155, 177, 190
    as shaman's avatar 128
    in spells 124, 125, 176, 196
harvesting 10, 13, 265
head-dress **127**, 128, 178, 181, 200, 255
health 11, 42, 54, 118, 186
    see also sanitary conditions
hearths 157, **158**, 296
    see also hexagonal forms
Heine-Geldern, Robert von 3
heron 130 298, 302
hexagonal forms 155, 158, 275
    hearths 157 fig.
    among the Kogi 159, 272
    among the Muiska 159, 273
    and energy 263
    and exogamy 144, 154-55
    and fertility 151, 153
    as conceptual models 144, 150
    as metaphysical models 270-71
    as models for architecture 267-68
    as models of order 159-60, 263
    as models of regenerative powers 151
    as social models 154, 156, 157 fig., 263, 264 fig.
    between the sky and the earth 264 fig.
    emeralds 159, 273
    in pottery 67
    honeycomb 142, 151, 261, 265
    on pineapples 142, 151
    on the earth 263, 264 fig.
    on the sky 262-63, 264 fig., 267
    in rivers 142, 144
    rock crystals 54, 141, 150, 263, 265, 274
    sacred space 152
    spider webs 151
    symbolism 144, 154-55, 157, 274
    the earth 48
    the human brain 222-23, 263, 265
    the layout of the hearth for firing cooking vessels 68
    the pelvic region of the human body 157
    the plan of the Sierra Nevada de Santa Marta 272
    the territory 56, 141-42, 152-54, 265
    the universe 38, 237
    the uterus 159, 263, 265
    tortoise shells 142, 150 fig., 263, 265

wasp's nests 142, 151, 263
  see also uterine symbolism
hill houses 54, 56-57, 60, 73, 87-90
  passim, 106, 108, 171, 191, 210, 214,
  218, 238, 239
hills 9, 25, 55 fig., 57, 152, 213, 263
  as animal abodes 14, 54, 56, 73, 86-90
    passim, 115, 144, 167, 214
  symbolism 54, 72, 213-15, 216, 217
  see also hill houses
Hochstein, F.A. 244
Höfer, Oskar 259
homosexuality 298, 309
honey 15, 63, 108, 173, 178, 190, 196,
  198, 203, 207, 208, 222, 261, 286, 300
horizon calendar 274
House of Thunder 107, 176, 177
  see also myths, Thunder-People, Thunder-
  Jaguar, thunder
Howler Monkey People 289
Hugh Jones, Stephen 280, 296
hummingbird 26
hunting 9, 24, 33, 66, 79, 100, 106, 152,
  163, 213, 215, 266, 272, 278, 281, 293-
  94 *passim*
  control 7, 14, 16, 17, 118, 203, 213
  depletion of game 74
  overhunting 16, 17, 18, 53, 57, 87, 115,
    205
    and the missionaries 74, 116
  restriction 94, 113
  ritual preparation 14, **41**, 60, 204
  scarcity 14, 74
  women as bait 60
  see also dreams, game animals,
    government, Master of Animals,
    pollution, resources, ritual, rubber
    gatherers, shaman, tapir, women

ibis 27
Iguaque, laguna de 275
illness *see* disease
incantations 49, 53, 57
incest 19, 65, 78, 79, 106, 112, 115, 219,
  253, 282, 306
  as self-fertilisation 286
  celestial models 273
  in myth 72, 98, 150, 165
  laws 264
infant mortality 90
Inírida river 149
insects 164, 178, 222, 285, 305

as food 15, 111, 266
as pathogenic agents 166
associations with the Yuruparí
  instruments 305
colour 25
edible 9, 75, 186, 261
gathering of 266
odour 58
social 12, 33, 36, 111
see also ant, bee, beetle, butterfly, cicada,
  cricket, spider, termite, wasp
invisible world 24, 46, 72
Ipanoré, falls 70, 71, 264 fig., 281, 304,
  306, 307
Isana river 80, 149, 282, 295, 313

jaguar 25, 27, 31, 36, **43**, **45**, 100, 112,
  115, 143, **148**, 165, 175, 177, 181, 190,
  218, 270, 306
  and rock crystals 52
  and transformation 140
  as a manifestation of the Master of
    Animals 48
  as pathogenic agent 166
  as shaman's avatar 128
  in myth 72
  see also fertility
japurá tree and fruit 299, 306
Jirijirimo, falls 264 fig.

Karapana people 72
  sibs 104
King Vulture 177
kinkajou 27, 36
Koch-Grünberg, Theodor 1, 2
Knoll, Max 251, 252 fig., 258
Kogi people 5, 159, 236, 262, 272, 274
  astronomical concepts 272-74
  ceremonial centres 272
  scheduling of ceremonies 272
  see also hexagonal forms
Kuripáko people 80, 83, 89, 106, 281, 310
  Kuripáko/Tukano relationships 106
  see also Behkára
Kurupíra 311
  see also Master of Animals

La Pedrera 67
Lake of Milk 144, 178, 179, 204
lakes and lagoons 49
  as "filters" 179, 203
  colour energies 144

in myth 178, 203
in spells 179-80, 187, 188
sacred (Muiska) 273, 275
symbolism 262, 263
landing place 114, 117, 183, 296, 300, 301, 305
Land of Milk 203-204
larvae 75
as food 65, 75, 111, 266, 285, 288
symbolic image 288
Lemos Barbosa, A. 309
leopard 209
Lévi-Strauss, Claude 237
lightning
as pathogenic agent 177
in myth 177
symbolism 48, 202
liver 60, 61, 63, 64, 167
lizard 26, 35, 36, 48, 198
in spells 175, 176
loincloth **256**
longhouse 4, 9, 14, 15, 17, 48, 55, 57, 67, 68, 75, 78, 79, 84, 93, 104, 117, 139, 152-56 *passim*, 159, 160, 166, 169, 205, 213, 214, 238, 283, 288, 292-98 *passim*, 302-5 *passim*
and rock crystals 54, 216
and the human brain 236
as a social unit 89, 156 fig.
as an astronomical model 265, 268 fig., 269 fig.
mural painting 253, **254**, **255**
structure and form 214-15, 217 fig., 218, 220, 255, 267, 269
supernatural 87, 115, 116, 118, 218, 220
symbolism 216
Tapir's 81, 82, 86
see also anaconda, ecosystem, Orion, ritual
love potions 15
LSD 251, 258

macaw 33, 36, 131, 140, 197, 288
Makú-paraná river 70, 74, 99
Makú people 70, 74, 281, 293
as ancestors 24, 70, 289
as hunters 99-100
Makú/Desana relationships 73
Makú/Tukano relationships 101-2, 117, 282
Makú/peccary associations 100-1
ritual services to the Desana and Tukano

104-5
sibs 101
tapir avoidance 99
maloca *see* longhouse
man-tapir 87, 88
manioc 9, 24, 63, 71, 75, 79, 86, 92, 100, 101, 104, 113, 114, 117, 125, 149, 157, 163, 176, 213, 281, 282, 283, 293, 294, 295, 299, 304, 306
colour 52
in spells 171, 175, 183-85
preparation 65, 94, **95**, 290, 304
see also manioc starch, ripeness
marriage 67, 97, 104, 150, 153, 272, 278
and the palms model 283-92
and transformation 61
intermarriage 10, 24, 56, 97, 117, 153, 156, 282, 288, 300
rules 56, 58, 201, 233, 253, 265, 283
marten 173, 174, 202
in spells 173
see also Marten-People, tayra
Marten-People 180, 181
masks, ritual 181, 253
of Yuruparí 306-7
Master of Animals 56, 57, 64, 73, 86, 87, 89, 107, 115, 118, 168, 192, 194, 197, 270
appeasement of 175-76, 182-86
disease as punishment by 53, 167
as Master of Fish 49, 167, 214, 220
as the Boráro 33, 48, 175, 176, 311, 312
in the origin myths 24
manifestations 48, 220
abodes 14, 56, 210, 220
personifications 13, 46, 167, 214
in the Old World 210
celestial trail 46, 48, 49, 237, 265
and aggression 60, 200
and hunting 14, 46, 54
and the distribution of resources 49
and disease 16
and sexual activity 175, 185
and the shaman 14, 16, 87, 88, 115, 182-86, 219
see also aggression, anaconda, exogamy, jaguar, Kurupíra, Orion spells, spider
Matapí people 237, 238 fig.
meditation 230, 234
mëë river 177, 179, 196, 203
menstruation 14, 15, 59-60, 61-64, 72, 73, 84, 95, 175, 215, 239, 261, 266

and food restrictions 69, 73
meaning to the Desana 62
menstruation enclosure 84, 158
odour 58, 59, 64, 91, 92, 135, 290
ritual 307, 159
mescaline 251, 258
Mesopotamia 209
Meyú rapids **103**
mice 102, 198
migration 4, 18, 70, 82, 214, 282
recitals 70, 99, 106
milk 134, 137, 138, 176, 178, 181, 206-10
in spells 131-33 *passim*, 176-96 *passim*,
203, 235
sexual connotations 178, 207
symbolism 139, 178, 203
milk and honey ritual 209
milk and honey symbolism 178, 207-9 *passim*
Milky Way 48, 49, 72, 129, 178, 199, 253,
262, 263, 266, 274
symbolism 46, 235, 253, 265, 266, 267
see also trails
miratavá, tree and fruit 131, 133, 136, 145,
188, 190, 201
missionaries 2, 74, 116, 218, 278, 298, 305
see also hunting
Mitú 2, 74, 84, 220, **228**
moharra fish 27, 33, 37
monkey hair 179, 181
sexual connotations 201
as pathogenic agent 166
Monkey-People 193, 194
monkeys 13, 33, 35, 59, 179, 181, 194,
215, 238, 308, 313
as food 14, 64
cacajao monkey 25
capuchin monkey 30, 31
howler monkey 25, 31, 36, 69, **291**
in myth 71, 289, 292
symbolic image 289, 290
in myth 70
in spells 172, 191-94
night monkey 26
nocturnal 172, 173, 174, 180, 307-8
odour 59, 95
sexual connotations 196, 202
spider monkey 25, 36, 139
titi 26, 30, 31, 36
woolly monkey 25, 36, 69
in myth 70
see also Howler Monkey People, monkey

hair, Monkey-People
Montfort 74
moon 38, 39 fig., 44-48 *passim*, 98, 114,
262, 273
in myth 72, 165, 264, 272
lunar calendar 266
lunar energy 39, 41, 49, 263
phases 65-66, 266, 302, 305
symbolism 63, 165
see also fertility, Temple of the Moon
Muiska 159, 262, 273-74, 275
astronomical concepts 273-74
ceremonial centres 273
see also Bachué, Goranchacha, hexagonal
forms, Iguaque, lakes, myths,
Saquenzipá
mural painting 209, 253, **254**, **255**
music 216, 223, 230, 232, 248, 311
drums 252
musical instruments 136, 172, **229**, 230,
233, 304, 306
ritual instruments 278, 299-306
stamping tubes 253
submersion of musical instruments 128
whistles 232
see also flutes, trumpets
mythology 12, 23, 121, 128, 206, 283, 296
Greek 208
Roman 208
myths
and *Banisteriopsis* 145
as a guide for survival 20
Bachué (Muiska) 273, 275
cosmological 14, 20
Daughter of the Sun 170
Fish Woman 105
Goranchacha (Muiska) 159, 273, 275
of creation 303
of Yuruparí 277-313
on migration 101
on narcotic snuff as semen of the Sun 138
on origin 4, 77, 83, 152, 280, 281, 282
Thunder 81
women and the sacred trumpets 83
World Fire 66, 305

N-dimethyltriptamine 244
narcotic snuffs 81, **120**, 123-41 *passim*,
177, 243, 258
seminal connotations 128, 138
see also Banisteriopsis, coca, drugs,
hallucinations, narcotics, plants, vihó,

yajé, yopo
narcotics 5, 7, 14, 19, 24, 52, 57, 86, 100,
    106, 123, 134, 144, 155, 168, 193, 196,
    201, 216, 230, 243, 244, 254, 271, 282
    and astronomy 271, 274
narcotic trances 14, 53, 57, 87, 90, 116,
    136, 146, 152, 168, 169, 177, 216
    optical sensations 243-259
    see also Banisteriopsis, coca, Desana,
        drugs, hallucinations, hallucinogenics,
        narcotic snuffs, plants, shamanistic
        initiation, vihó, yajé, yopo
Netherworld, the 176, 177, 178, 197, 198,
    203
nettles
    in curing spells 94
    see also fertility
New Archaeology 20
Night-People 85, 181
night-women 85, 97
nuts 9, 15, 80, 81
Nyi, rock of 264 fig., 274

odour 4, 23, 38, 81, 91-95, 96, 108
    and heat 58
    and the brain 221
    classifications 58-60, 70, 92, 286
    of animals 48, 92
    of menstrual blood 58, 59, 64, 91, 92,
        135, 290
    of people 59, 91-92, 286
    of plants 285
    of pollen 287
    in spells 58-59
Ohkoya creek 40, 51, 242, 246
opossum 30, 36
oral tradition 4, 78, 100, 276, 280, 283,
    292-98 passim
Orinoco river 1, 8, 149
Orion 90
    Orion's belt 98, 263, 265-72 passim
    as Master of Animals 265
    identification with the longhouse 268,
        269 fig.
    imagery 270
    symbolism 269
    and Yuruparí 275
oropendola bird 26, 30, 36, 125, 128, 166,
    188, 197, 198
"other house", the 219, 224
Otherworld, the 123, 167, 203-4, 210,
    224, 299

otter 33, 35

paca 13, 27, 31, 36, 104, 108, 304, 306
    as food 69, 71, 79, 102
    in myth 102, 104
    odour 102
    symbolic image 71
    see also Paca Woman, Paca-Women
Paca Woman 101
Paca-Women 71
Pacú (place) 276
palms 5, 27, 30, 33, 75, 82, 98, 187, 277,
    283-92, 312
    and marriage rules 283-92
    and women fertility 314
    as a model of exogamy 288
    as a social model 286
    as food resource 283
    Astrocaryum (cumare) 198, 199, 200,
        202
    Astrocaryum vulgare 303
    Bactris gasipaes (peach palm) 31, 239,
        276, 283, 285, 289
    caraná 27
    Euterpe oleracea 65, 75, 290, 304
    Euterpe precatoria (uassay) 27, 142, 195,
        283, 284
    fruit distribution ritual 294, 300, 302,
        306
    fruit palms (table) 283
    fruits 80, 105, 113, 142, 239, 268, 278,
        283, 289-306 passim
    in longhouse building 15, 55, 215, 255,
        283, 292
    Jessenia bataua (seje) 26, 105, 283-90
        passim
    Jessenia polycarpa 65, 239
    Manicaria atricha (ubí) 283
    Mauritia flexuosa (mirití, moriche) 27,
        33, 65, 75, 80, 94, 283, 288, 289, 297,
        312, 314
    Mauritiella caraná 290, 292
    Mauritiella cataractarum 283, 292, 310
    nomenclature 288-92
    Oenocarpus bataua (milpesos) 31, 56,
        75, 142
    Orbygnia sp. (babassú) 31, 56, 65, 105,
        283, 285, 288, 292
    palm fruit beer 113
    pollination 285, 286, 287, 292, 293, 294,
        303, 307, 314
    Socratea exorrhiza (paxiúba) 283-90

passim, 297, 302, 303
see also gathering, palm starch, seminal symbolism, uterine symbolism, Yuruparí
palo de sangre 129
Papurí river 3, 70, 74, 77, 92, 99, 100, 278, 295, 306, 307
Paradies, A.M. 244
parrot 33, 115, 173, 195, 289
Path of the Sun 268
pathogenic splinters 89, 130, 166, 167, 172, 177, 178, 197, 201
    in spells 125, 171, 176-77 *passim*, 179-80 *passim*
    see also phallic symbolism
peccary 13, 17, 25, 31, 33, 36, 70, 71, 98, 100-2, 116, 210, 214, 215
    as food 14, 64, 74, 80, 100
    as game animal 79, 100, 118
    collared 25, 30, 31, 36, 100, 138
    feeding habits 100
    identification with women 101
    in myth 71, 106
    odour 59, 87, 92, 100, 101
    peccary/Makú associations 100
    restrictions 69, 74, 80
    symbolic image 90, 101, 102
    see also Peccary-People, Peccary-Women, women
Peccary-People 71
Peccary-Women 70, 101
peppers 60, 195, 205
    in spells 175, 194-96 *passim*, 197
    see also smoking (food), ritual
Peru 243
petroglyphs 214, 238, 258, **260**, 263, 264 fig.
phallic symbolism
    adze 270, 311
    beetles 288
    bones 128
    coati 303
    handle of a shaman's rattle 129
    pot stands 68, 157
    rattle stick 202, 155
    rock crystals 263
    splinters 199-201
    squirrel's tail 303
    tapir 81
    tinamou 66, 305
    toucan 196
    see also blowgun, cecropia, conception,

sex, vahsú
pheasant 30
pheromonal communication 96, 102, 104, 111, 286
    see also deer
phosphenes 136, 140, 232-35 *passim*, 250-55 *passim*, 252 fig., 258-59, 302
    categories 251
    closed form 233
    linear 233
    see also brain
phratries 1, 77, 82, 91-94 *passim*, 105, 152, 154, 253, 263, 265 fig., 299, 302, 307
pictographs 214, 238, 258
pigeon 26, 33, 36, 65, 115
pineapple 71, 142, 151, 173, 239
    see also hexagonal forms
Pira-coara 74
Pira-paraná river **29**, **32**, **50**, **51**, 74, 92, 100, **103**, 107, **127**, 153, **212**, **242**, **246**, **254**, 264 fig., 275, 278, 283, **284**
Pira-Tapuya people **2**, 24, 49, 54, 59, 61, 67, 68-80 *passim*, 85, 92, 96-104 *passim*, 122, 133, 141, 146, 152, 153, 156, 213, **228**, 277-78, 281, 303, 305, 306, 308, 312
    exchange with Desana 105
    odour 91, 92
    sibs 72, 98, 104, 146, 304
piranha fish 27, 33, 37, 179, 181, 201, 204, **205**
    as food 65
    in spells 179, 180, 184, 197, 198
plants 10, 12, 17, 19, 23, 24, 48, 49, 52, 60, 121, 123, 178, 204, 206, 223, 230, 285, 302, 306
    and colour variations 105
    Datura sp. 243
        dimorphism 293
        growth 137, 253, 261
            and colour energies 63, 266
            and colour of the moon 41
            and colour symbolism 42
            and lunar phases 266
            as transformation 124
            energies 136
            symbolism 147
    hallucinogenic 143, 214, 281
    narcotic 5, 19, 24, 72, 243
    odour 286
    paraphytic 59

see also fruits, tooka, trees
Pleiades 97, 269, 268 fig., 271, 308, 313
poison 15, 100, 196
　in spells 141
　fish poison 17, 63, 157, 213
pollen 82, 92, 236, 285, 286, 288, 293, 303,
　odour 286
　seminal symbolism 287, 309
　see also pollination
pollution 58, 64, 181, 197, 202, 203, 205
　and food 65, 66, 73
　and incompatibility of partners 58
　and odours 59-60
　by women 63, 308
　of hunting or fishing gear 14
　of women 60, 190, 202
Pollux 263, 264 fig., 268 fig., 269 fig., 271
pollination 82, 277, 279, 299, 301, 305, 313
　pollinators 285-86
　of palms 285-87 *passim*, 292-94 *passim*, 303, 305, 313
　see also pollen, soundwaves and pollination
Polynesia 153
population control 7, 13, 15, 17, 66, 90, 101, 205, 266
　see also birth control
pools 55 fig., 57, 104, 116, 129
　symbolism 213
　as fish abodes 14, 49, 54, 56, 167, 213
　in myth 213-14
　see also water houses, Master of Animals, fertility
pottery 15, 63, 90, **97**, 147, **158**, 188, **246**, 253, 258, 266
　and exogamic rules 133
　decoration 145, 155
　firing of 124
　sexual connotations 145
　symbolism 67-68
　see also clay, hexagonal forms, smoke
Pouteria ucuqui Schultes (ukuki) 26, 56, 59, 105, 304, 309
Poyá people 73, 79
pre-puberty 65, 69, 73
pregnancy 15, 62-64, 68, 69, 135, 140, 146, 158, 215, 239
　and food restrictions 73, 80
　and prohibition of sexual intercourse 141
Procyon 263, 264 fig., 268 fig., 269 fig.

psilocybin 251
puberty 63, 67, 112, 155, 278, 296, 299, 309

quartz 48, 166, 167, 177, 183
　crystals 125, 128, 135, 149, 202
　cylinders **148**
　in spells 183-85 *passim*, 187, 189
　seminal connotations 186, 190, 202
　see also rock crystals
Querarí river 181
Quest, the (spiritual pilgrimage) 269

rainbow 52, 253, 258
　seminal connotations 46, 53
　symbolic image 145, 253
rainbow boa 266
　in brain imagery 225, 226 fig., 236
Ramiriquí 275
rapids 1, 4, 9, 49, 77, **103**, 104, 124, 306
　in myth 55, 153
　see also fertility
rat 173
rattle stick **162**, 202
　shaman's 155, 156, 157
　in myth 23, 77, 208, 262
　see also phallic symbolism
rattles **174**
reciprocity 10, 83, 115, 154, 278, 292
religion 5, 11, 159, 165, 177, 216, 243, 248, 258, 272, 295
reptiles 9, 33, 100, 244
　colour 25
　see also anaconda, caiman, *crocodyliae*, güío, rainbow boa, boa constrictor, lizard, snakes, amphisbaena snake, tortoise
residence, matrilocal 292, 293, 294
residence, patrilocal 10, 293, 294
residence, uxorilocal 83, 101, 282
residence, virilocal 24, 98, 104, 263
resources
　management of 206, 261, 270
　depletion of 74, 213
　food 12, 14, 17, 33, 35, 53-57 *passim*, 90, 115, 118, 219, 261, 266
　hunting 14, 46, 74, 87
　protein 7, 15, 18, 70, 74, 78, 85, 164, 205
Río Negro river 1, 4, 70, 79, 153, 179, 278, 281, 295, 307, 309
ripeness (bogë) 64, 68, 72, 92, 133, 179

animal 64, 69, 73, 90, 94
colour 41
fruit 63
fish 65
manioc 65
ritual 19, 59, 62, 78, 106, 123, 154, 155,
 163, 164, 185, 204, 224, 225, 227, 230,
 236, 240, 246, 271, 274, 279, 280, 286,
 314
 abstinence 116, 294
 and body paint 68
 and ecological balance 18, 19
 and ecology 9
 and exogamy 258, 278, 298
 and musical instruments 107, 108, 232,
  245, 278, 293, 294-308 *passim*
 and rock crystals 140, 149, 273
 and social unity 19
 and the longhouse 217, 218, 267, 268
 beer consumption 117, 311
 curing 17, 18, 129, 170, 178, 202
 dances 15, 266, 269, 273, 230
 death 273
 exchange 13, 15, 59, 65, 105-107 *passim*,
  172, 278, 282, 289, 302, 306
 of women 56, 67, 79, 81, 282, 288, 298
 fertility 49, 207, 209
 fishing 60
 food restrictions 14, 15
 hallucinatory trances 53, 244-58
 hunting 60
 immersion 129
 increase 58
 ingestion of peppers 195
 initiation 206, 268, 230, 302, 307
 male initiation 82, 266, 278, 294, 310,
  311
 menstruation 159, 307
 milk and honey 208
 of life cycle 10, 15, 273
 palm fruit distribution 294, 300, 302,
  306
 preparation for hunting 203
 puberty 181
 purification 14
 ritual objects 128, 134, 155, 158, 177,
  217, **246**, 253, 254, **256**, 258, 279,
  283, 312, 313
 ritual vessels 254
 use of *Banisteriopsis* 57, 99, 243-58, 281
 use of drugs 19, 216, 232, 306
 Yuruparí 281, 295, 299

Yuruparí initiation 275, 299-300, 302
 see also bark-cloth aprons, ceremony,
  masks, music, shaman, shields,
  tinamou, universe
river lakes 30
River of Milk 178-82 *passim*, 198, 203
river systems of paradise 179
rivers 1, 9, 19, 24, 30, 42, 49
 in myth 153
 in shamanic metaphorical topography
  124, 141-42, 144, 153, 178
 in spells 177, 179, 182, 187, 196, 202
 limnology 279, 302
 symbolism 84, 124, 141-42, 144, 179,
  220, 263, 265
 see also Desana, hexagonal forms
Roberto, Maximiniano José 307
rock crystals 24, 52-54, **55**, 57, 142, 149-
 160, 273
 and brain imagery 222-223
 and energy 149-52, 218
 and human anatomy 157, 159
 and shamanic power 4, 52-54, 140, 149-
  69
 and the curing of illness 149
 and the diagnosis of illness 53, 69, 152
 and the image of order 159-160
 and the longhouse 218
 and transformation 52, 53, 68, 142, 156-
  59
 as a model for social organization 154
 as a model for time 274
 as a model of a longhouse 54
 as a model of the universe 54
 as pathogenic agents 166
 as a spatial model 141, 152-56, 237, 263,
  272
 divine 153, 216 fig., 220
 hues 151
 Keepers of the Rock Crystal 272
 see also hexagonal forms, jaguar, phallic
  symbolism, quartz, ritual, seminal
  symbolism, uterine symbolism, visual
  perception
rodents 214, 215, 306
 associations with the Yuruparí
  instruments 304
 as game animals 71, 73, 102
 feeding habits 102, 304
 habitat 33
 in myth 71, 104, 106
 odour 92, 304

symbolic image 116
see also agouti, capibara, cavi, mice,
    paca, rat
Rome 207
roofing 15, 27, 68, 216, 267, 272, 283,
    290
roots 49, 71, 92, 99, 102, 286, 296, 302
Royal Anthropological Institute 3, 7
rubber gatherers 2
    and depletion of game 74, 116
    see also rubber tree
rubber tree and fruit 26, 173, 196
    see also rubber gatherers

Saake, Wilhelm 306
sago 312
San Javier 74
San Miguel 74
sanctuaries 272, 273
    natural 115, 214
sanitary conditions 165-66
    see also health
Santa Cruz 74
São Gabriel 310
Saquenzipá 275
self-fertilisation 233, 287, 292, 295, 297
sëmë, tree and fruit 26, 59, 65, 71, 81, 104,
    105, 125, 134, 142, 180, 196, 200, 305,
    310
    uterine connotations 129
    in myth 102
seminal symbolism
    and quartz crystals 185, 189, 200
    and rock crystals 151
    cumare palm fibres 197
    feathers 200
    grains of maize 222
    grease 65
    in gourd rattles 129
    milk 178
    narcotic snuff 128, 138
    palm fibres 200
    pollen 287, 309
    rainbow 46, 53
    rock crystals 52
    solar energy 11
    the Milky Way, 46
    tooka milk 201
    tooka sap 178
    water 141
    see also ant, conception, sun, sex
Serra de Tenui 308, 313

settlement/s 7, 15, 100, 102, 117, 205, 304,
    306, 308
    pattern 9, 213
sex
    abstinence 13, 141, 168, 204, 232, 293,
        299, 306
    and hallucinatory experience 136
    and social control 57
    and the Master of Animals 175, 185
    continence 13, 14
    control 60, 112
    masturbation 140, 141, 298
    pollution through illicit intercourse 195,
        189
    prohibition of intercourse during
        pregnancy 141
    rape 83, 99, 106
    repressed sexual energy 11
    repression 13
    restrictions 13, 96, 142, 65
    seminal concepts 10, 61-63, 134, 135,
        197, 199, 200, 202, 204-5
    sex/food associations 13, 57, 63, 65, 80,
        81, 118, 142, 185, 281, 305
    sexual odours 96
    sexual symbolism
        sweet foods 174
        pottery decoration 145
        forked shapes 84
        palm pollination 82, 287-88
    transmission of illness as sexual
        impregnation 198-201
    uternine concepts
        female internal anatomy 213
        fetal development 213
    see also ant, aphrodisiacs, conception,
        contraceptives, fruits, homosexuality,
        incest, milk, phallic symbolism, pottery,
        pregnancy, quartz, rainbow,
        self-fertilisation, seminal symbolism,
        spells, spider, uterine symbolism
sexual abstinence 13, 141, 168, 204, 232,
    293, 299, 306
    see also ritual
shaman 4, 10, 215, 216 fig., **242, 246, 247,**
    286
    apprenticeship 123, 124
    paraphernalia box 150, 155, 253
    colour concepts 45, 46
    knowledge 12, 18, 270
    hunting and fishing control 17, 74, 115,
        118

INDEX

population control 90
curing of illness 17, 53, 54, 68, 69, 177, 232, 304
diagnostic practices 16, 17, 53, 116, 152, 216
hallucinatory contests 152
initiation 121-47
insignia **148**
interpretation of visions 19, 57
shamanic language 42, 44, 45, 66, 85, 111, 131, 133, 135, 137
ritual objects 155, 177
replenishment of energy 115
initiation ritual 124, 128, 146, 147
spell-reciting techniques 122, 169, 170
shamanic topography 142, 144, 153
trances 17, 18, 89
ecstatic flights 124, 129
and the Master of Animals 14, 16, 87, 88, 115, 182-86, 219
resource management 7, 18, 55
and the protection of animal and plant life 17, 18
and the classification systems 34
see also anaconda, death, gourd rattles, harpy eagle, jaguar, phallic symbolism, rattle stick, rock crystals, shamanistic initiation, spells, spirits, stools, transformation
shamanistic initiation 121-47
acquisition of pathogenic splinters 130
and river symbolism 124, 142, 144
as a narcotic trance 146
as transformation 124, 141
"cooling" of the initiate 136-37
"dizziness" of the initiate 137
effect of narcotic drugs 136
formal initiatory ritual 123-46
previous esoteric knowledge 123
spells 122-147
symbolic death 123-24, 144, 146
symbolic rebirth 123, 131, 132, 144, 146, 147
use of narcotic drugs 123-24, 128
Shanidar (Iraq) 208
sheep 208
shields, ritual 152, 158
shooting stars 53, 262
sibs 55 fig., 104, 145, 217, 266, 299, 313
and territorial division 55
Desana 71, 72, 83, 137, 104-5, 146, 290, 306

Karapana 104
Makú 100
Pira-Tapuya 71, 98, 104, 146, 304
symbolic animals 104-5, 138, 302, 306
Tukano 24
Tukano proper 71, 104-5, 288, 304
Sierra de Tunahí 313
Sierra Nevada de Santa Marta 5, 262, 271, 272
singers 230
ancestral 23, 78, 153
Sirius 271, 264 fig., 268 fig.
skull symbolism 214-15, 216
sloth 25, 35, 36, 59, 64, 69, 167
in myth 71
smoke
tobacco 81, 96, 106, 206, 215
and the manufacture of cooking vessels 68
to neutralize odours 96
smoking (food)
fish 60, 64, 65, 68
peppers 60
meat 59, 60, 64-65, 67, 68, 74, 85, 88, 96, 106, 158
tripod for smoking game meat/fish 95
as symbolic transformation 68
worms 59
see also food
snail 35, 219
snakes 35, 60, 64, 165, 203, 218, 265, 266
in myth 124, 153, 217
symbolic image 235, 266-71 *passim*
bushmaster snake 35, 36
see also amphisbaena snake, anaconda, boa constrictor, güío, rainbow boa, reptiles
soap 176
social control 13, 15
Solimoes river 309
solstices 264, 272, 273
summer 268, 273
winter 268
Son of the Sun Father 275
songs 15, 79, 82, 83, 152, 168, 215, 219, 223, 235, 293, 294, 300, 302
sound
classifications 232
colour 232
odour 232
soundwaves and pollination 82, 292-94
spells 17, 45, 79, 90, 215, 223, 235, 299,

303
curing spells 4, 53, 163-210, 303
  as "weapons" 169
  sexual connotations 198
  against dream-visitors 182
  metaphoric language 198
  origin of 169, 210
  to placate the Master of Animals 183-86
  for "numbness" 186-89, 191-93
  for "numbness", confusion and headaches 193-97
  for illness caused by splinters 176-79
  for unconsciousness 197-99
  to recover abducted souls 179-82
  reciting techniques 122, 169, 170
shamanistic initiation spells 122-147
and the Master of Animals 219
and animal energy 49
and energy flow 57
see also animal behaviour, ant, butterfly, cigars, clay, crab, curassow, deer, disease, duck, ear-pendants, earthworm, groundnut, electric eel, energy, feathers, fire, firewood, fish, flame, frog, fruits, gourd rattles, harpy eagle, lakes, lizard, marten, milk, monkeys, nettles, odour, pathogenic splinters, peppers, piranha, poison, quartz, rivers, spirits, swallow, termite, thunder, tinamou, toad, tobacco, toucan, vines, water, weapons, worms
spider 35, 75, 165
  as a personification of the Master of Animals 48
  vaginal symbolism 81
spiral symbolism 87, 96
spirit essence
  of people 115, 144
  of game animals 111, 115
spirit/s 16, 17, 148, 207
  animal-spirits 54
  Doppelgänger 219
  evil 18, 172, 173, 174, 219
  helpers of the shaman 181
  in spells 188-89
  of animals 7, 19, 85-88 passim, 167, 171, 214
  of the forest 60
  spirit-beings 174, 177, 179, 181, 199, 219, 244, 248

spirit-protectors 205
  vengeful 18
Spruce, Richard 243
squirrel 26, 30, 35, 36, 285
  associations with the Yuruparí instruments 303, 304
  feeding habits 303
  odour 303
  see also phallic symbolism
stalactite powder 128, 138, 139
starch, manioc 65, 95, 123, 125
  fertility associations 95, 157
starch, palm 70, 270, 312
stars 11, 236, 263, 266, 267, 271-72 passim
  see also Achernar, Aldebaran, astronomy, Bellatrix, Betelgeuse, Canopus, Capella, Castor, constellations, Delta Orionis, Epsilon Orionis, Milky Way, Pleiades, Pollux, Procyon, shooting stars, Sirius, T3 Eridani, Zeta Orionis
stools, shamanic 257
Stradelli, conde Ermanno 296, 307-8, 313
Sun 36, 38, 39 fig., 41, 48, 66, 85, 99, 128, 131, 136, 147, 151, 159, 222, 253, 261, 262, 265, 274, 291, 308
  in myth 271, 273
  energy 10, 11, 17, 39, 49, 88, 143, 151, 200, 219, 235
  seminal energy 10
  colour energies 87
  invisible 61
  seminal symbolism 63
  visible 46, 42, 52, 58
  visible and invisible 38
  see also fertility, Sun People, Daughter of the Sun, Son of the Sun Father, seminal symbolism, Sun Father, Path of the Sun, Temple of the Sun
Sun Father 10, 23, 24, 38, 39, 41, 46, 52, 138, 150, 151, 153, 177, 200, 204, 217, 223
Sun People 150
swallow
  in spells 176, 179
swallow-tailed kite 29, 30, 36
sweet potato 183, 186, 198, 207
  see also Sweet Potato Eagle
Sweet Potato Eagle 197, 198
symbolic rebirth 54, 68, 99, 124, 134, 142, 178, 200, 204, 207, 305

T3 Eridani 263, 264 fig., 268 fig., 269 fig.
tabú (limits) 142, 143, 144, 156
  territorial division 55 fig., 75, 141
  use of the word in Polynesia 153
  as division line 142, 153-55
tapir 4, 13, 25, 27, 31, 36, 71, 73, 75, **76**, 79, 80, **110**, 138, 166, 171, 196, 208, 215, 281, 301
  as ancestor 71, 84, 91, 98, 99, 117
  as food 64, 85
  categories 86, 87, 88, 117
  feeding habits 80, 81, 117, 289
  hunting 86, 88, 90, 111-19
  in myth 71, 81-82, 83, 98, 104, 106, 290, 293, 300
  odour 59, 87, 96
  phallic connotations 81
  restrictions 14, 69, 74, 80, 85, 113
  symbolic image 81-89 *passim*, 116, 117, 270, 294, 301
  tapir/women associations 71, 81-86 *pas sim*, 98, 102, 117, 282, 289, 293
  zoological image 80, 81, 82
  see also Arawak, longhouse, Makú, man-tapir, Tapir People, Tapir Women, trails
Tapir People 4, 71, 79-85 *passim*, 97, 104, 117, 281, 282, 289, 290, 295, 301
  see also Arawak
Tapir Women 85, 102
tayra 26, 30, 35, 36, 173
  symbolic image 173
  see also marten
Tayra-People 181
Taibano people **41**
Tariana people 104, 282, 295, 307, 310
Tatuyo people 1, **29**, **127**, **162**, **231**
Temple of the Moon 273
Temple of the Sun 273
temples 272, 273, 274
Teresita 74
termite 35, 221, 300
  as pathogenic agent 166
  in spells 175, 183, 184, 185
Thunder-Jaguar 177
  see also House of Thunder, Thunder-People, myths, thunder
Thunder-People 182
  see also myths, House of Thunder, Thunder-Jaguar, thunder
thunder
  associations with the Yuruparí

instruments 107
  in myth 81, 83, 177, 101-2, 292
  in spells 182
  see also House of Thunder, myths, Thunder-Jaguar, Thunder-People
Tí river 74
tinamou 31, 36, 79, 305
  and the Yuruparí trumpets 305
  as ritual food 305
  in myth 66
  in spells 195
  see also phallic symbolism
Tiquié river 70, 79, 104, 107, 153, 307
toad 35
  in spells 175, 198
tobacco 128, 243, 281, 282, 294, 300
  in spells 182
  smoke 81, 96, 106, 206, 215
  see also cigars
tooka (plant) 136, 145, 178, 207
  milk 176-84 *passim*
  symbolism 203
  sap 131-34 *passim*, 137, 139, 178, 181, 186-96 *passim*
  description 203
tortoise 26, 27, 33, 35, 36, 69, 142, 151 fig., 202, 263, 265, 313
  as food 80
  in myth 71, 150, 312
  feeding habits 150
  symbolic image 150, 156
  see also hexagonal forms, uterine symbolism
toucan **22**, 26, 31, 36, 195, 305
  in spells 196
  see also phallic symbolism, Tukano
trails 17, 73, 98, 111, 134, 155, 190
  Milky Way symbolism 46, 48, 49
  tapir's 90
transformation 61-69, 98, 104-8 *passim*, 123, 129, 133-36 *passim*, 141, 145, 153, 165, 202, 205, 230, 233, 263, 265, 270, 290, 300, 306
  agents of 96, 151
  and colour 61
  and flavour 61
  and heat 61
  and ritual objects 155
  and rock crystals 52, 53, 68, 142, 156-59 *passim*
  areas of 142, 144, 152
  of man and animals 34

places of 87
shaman imagery of 124
tools of 130, 140
see also cooking
trees 9, 17, 25, 31, 33, 35, 49, 59, 81, 82, 117, 166, 179
  bayapia 131-33 *passim*, 140, 146
  "bat" 131, 133
  bow tree 180, 201
  caimo 125, 179, 181, 197, 201
    seminal connotations 129
  cecropia 31, 107, 128, 172, 309
    phallic and seminal connotations 135
  Eperna purpurea 304, 309
  guamo 30, 145, 181
  japurá 299, 306
  miratavá 136, 190, 201
    in spells 131, 133, 145, 188
  rubber tree
    seminal connotations 173, 196
  sëmé 125, 135, 180, 197, 201, 309
  vahsú 56, 68
    phallic connotations 173
    seminal connotations 173
  virola 124, 128, 131, 133, 135-37 *passim*
tripods 68, 95, 96, 157, 290
trumpeter bird 26, 33, 36, 64, 80, 306
  in myth 71
  see also Trumpeter-bird Sons, Trumpeter-women
Trumpeter-bird Sons 104
Trumpeter-women 70
trumpets 107, 304
  of Yurupari 82-83, 107, 292-306 *passim*
  see also fertility
tubers 52, 65, 71, 92, 102, 105, 117
Tukano (language family) 1-3 *passim*, 75, 80-100 *passim*, 112, 122, 149, 154, 159, 160, 163, 189, 213, 244, 264 fig., 280, 296, 310, 313, 314
  ancestral animals 106
  and energy flow 10, 11, 17
  and the deterioration of the universe 19
  astronomical concepts 14, 263, 265, 274
  cosmological concepts 7-20
  cosmological myths 20
  creation myth 10
  decoration of objects 253, 258
  demographic succession in Vaupés 79, 2781, 282, 283, 290
  ecological concepts 11, 12, 13
  endogamy and exogamy 290

graphic representations 251, 253, 248-49
habitat 9
migration myths 4
origin myths 9, 55, 70-71, 77-79, 152
sibs 24
social organization 10, 15, 77, 94, 265, 295
territory 9
Tukano/Arawak relationships 90, 99, 101-107 *passim*, 282, 283, 289, 293-95 *passim*
Tukano/Kuripáko relationships 107
Tukano/Makú relationships 101-2, 117, 280
Tukano/toucan associations 194
Tukano proper people 1, 3, 24, 49, 54, 59, 61, 67-85 *passim*, 96-102 *passim*, 107, 122, 123, 133, 152, 154, 156, 159, 160, 213, 279, 281, 282, 289, 299, 307-13 *passim*
  sibs 72, 104-5, 288, 305
  odour 91, 92
  see also Makú
turkey vulture 27, 36
Tuyuka people 85, 113, 122, 213, 265 fig.

Uacari-coara 74
Uahti-maá 74
Uanano people 104, 122, 141, 156, 306
Uaripë, Vaupés river 306
umarí 31, 59, 74, 80, 90, 91, 99, 105, 108, 179, 288, 289, 293, 310, 311
uterine symbolism
  abodes of animals 54, 73, 87, 115, 144
  abodes of the Master of Animals 210
  cooking vessels 146
  cosmic space 237
  gourd rattles 129
  hexagons 157, 261
  palm logs 286
  rock crystals 159
  sëmé pods 129
  subaquatic houses 214
  tortoise 151
  see also conception, sex
universe 12, 33
  as a hexagon 39 fig., 149-60
  deterioration 19
  origin and structure 10
  ritual creation and re-creation 19
  visible and invisible world 46
  see also rock crystals, Desana, energy

Usener, H. 207

Vacuravá 74

vahsú, tree and fruit 56, 59, 65, 68, 71, 81, 105, 143, 173, 304

Vai-mahsë 46, 48, 49, 53, 57, 58, 60, 64, 72, 167, 176, 186, 199
  see also fertility, fish, fruits, Master of Animals

Vaupés, river 1, 3, 34, 70, 74, 77, 79, **84**, 92, 99, 153, 213, 263, **276**, 278, 281, 295, 306, 307, 310, 313

Vaupés territory 1-5 *passim*, 24, 67, 70, 71, 79, 80, 82, 85, 91, 95, 97-101 *passim*, 105-7 *passim*, 122, 124, 128, 133, 139, 142, 145, 149, 153, 154, 156, 213, 262, 264, 277-98 *passim*, 302-13 *passim*
  demographic succession 280-83

Venezuela 149

vihó (Virola sp.) **120**, 243
  see also Banisteriopsis, coca, drugs, hallucinations, narcotic snuffs, narcotics, plants, trees (virola), yajé, yopo

Villa de Leiva 275

vines 134, 141, 198
  in spells 132, 143, 194

visual memory 258

visual perception
  and rock crystals 52-53
  dobéri patterns 62, 67, 72, 140, 141
  in hallucinatory trances 53
  luminous spots 131-36 *passim*
  luminous spots during coitus 62
  marari patterns 135, 136, 141
  noméri dots 62, 67, 135-41 *passim*, 193
  stars and sparks 53
  under the effect of *Banisteriopsis* 248
  see also Banisteriopsis, drugs, hallucinations, hallucinatory visions, hallucinogenics, narcotics, Tukano

vulture 178, 181, 202, 209

Wainambí falls 70

Warao people, Venezuela 129, 313

warfare 10, 78, 215, 294

warriors 78, 153, 158, 217

Water
  colours 166
  in spells 186-87 *passim*, 192
  see also classification systems, lakes, pools, rapids, river lakes, rivers, seminal symbolism, waterfalls

water-system 49

water houses 54, 56, 108, 144, 214, 219, 238
  see also pools

waterfalls 1, 53, 77, 124, 167
  in myth 24, 70, 153, 213
  symbolism 263, 264 fig.

waters, primeval 144

waters, primordial 42

wasp 35, 164
  as pathogenic agent 166
  see also hexagonal forms

weapons 215, 244, 311
  in spells 171, 182

Wilbert, Johannes 129, 313

Wind People (Desana) 107

women 16, 34, 53-57 *passim*, 75, 78, 95, 111, 114, 117, 125, 134, 146, 171-75 *passim*, 182, 188, 203, 206, 216, 217, 224, 269, 271, 278, 312, 314
  Agouti-Women 72, 146, 305
  female anatomy 213
  Armadillo-Women 72
  associations with palms 287, 288
  Cavi-Women 72, 305
  colour 69
  as hunting bait 60
  as a disturbing element 135, 137, 138, 140
  pollution of 60, 189, 200
  pollution by 63, 307
  colour energies 41
  fertility 96
  Hevea pauciflora-women 305
  identification with game animals 71, 72, 100-107 *passim*, 116, 118, 168
  identification with forest fruits 71
  exchange 13, 15, 24, 56, 66, 67, 79, 81, 83, 101, 154, 156, 281, 282, 288, 298
  abduction of 4, 78, 79, 83, 106, 217, 282, 290
  and agriculture 293, 295, 305
  and food production 295
  and hunting 14, 15
  and the image of deer 102
  and the image of peccary 102
  and the image of tapir 71, 81-86 *passim*, 98, 102, 117, 282, 289, 293
  and the myth of Yuruparí 296-98, 302, 304, 309
  and the sacred trumpets 83, 294, 302, 304

body paint **40**, 68, 145
Fish Woman 105
flavour 61
night-women 85, 98
odour 58, 59, 60, 71, 92, 96, 134
Paca Woman 102
Paca-Women 72
Peccary-Women 71
pottery symbolism 67, 68
Trumpeter-Women 70
widows 219-20
see also Arawak, birth control,
   conception, childbirth, menstruation,
   palms, pregnancy, uterine symbolism
woodpecker 26, 36
World Fire (myth) 66, 305
worms 35, 36
   exchange of 59
   as pathogenic agents 176, 197
   in spells 175, 193, 197
   see also smoking (food)
Wyss, Karl 207

yabiru stork 27
yajé (*Banisteriopsis sp.*) 86, 107, 125, 128,
   132, 146, **212**, **242**, 243, **245**, 281, 292
   decoration of objects under its effect **254**,
   255

see also hallucinations, *Banisteriopsis*,
   coca, drugs, fish-yajé, narcotics, plants,
   narcotic snuffs, vihó, yopo
Yavareté 74, 220, 282, 295, 306, 307, 310
yopo 242
Yuruparí Complex 5, 83, 275, 277-312
   endogamy to exogamy 292-95
   ethnohistorical background 280-83
   flutes 300, 302, 303
   ideological foundations 279
   initiation ritual 275, 299-300, 302
   instruments and their associations 278,
      300-308
   marginal myth cycles 310-13
   masks 307-8
   oral tradition 295-300
   palms and marriage rules 283-92
   research 280
   Stradelli's legend 308-10
   Yuruparí etymology 298-300
   Yuruparí trumpets 82-83, 107, 293-307
      passim
   see also animals, Bisíu, birds, children,
      fertility, Goá-më, insects, myths, Orion,
      ritual, rodents, squirrel, thunder,
      tinamou, women

Zeta Orionis 270